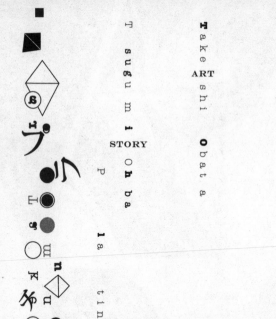

ART
Takeshi Obata

STORY
Tsugumi Ohba

Platinum End

PLATINVM END

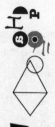

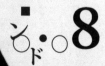

8

CHARACTERS

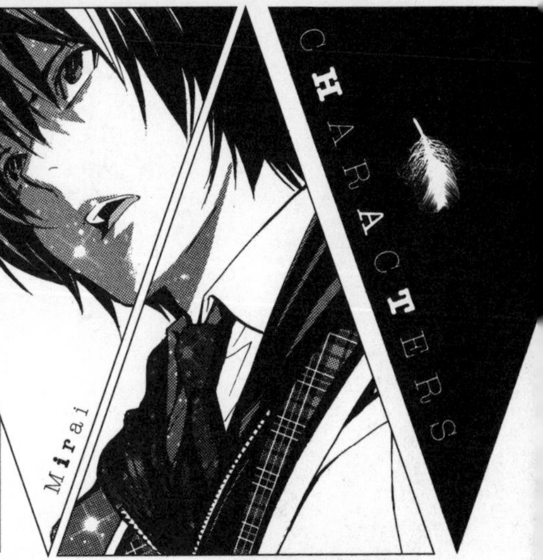
Mirai

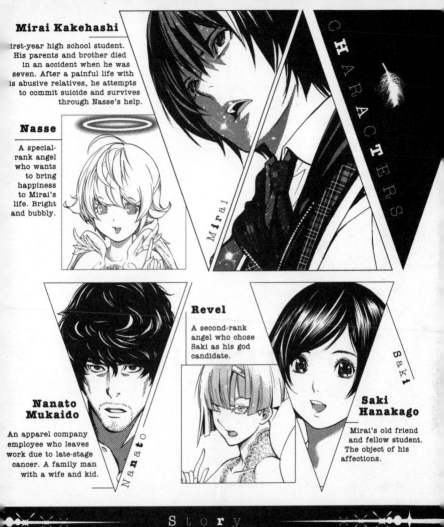

Mirai Kakehashi

irst-year high school student. His parents and brother died in an accident when he was seven. After a painful life with is abusive relatives, he attempts to commit suicide and survives through Nasse's help.

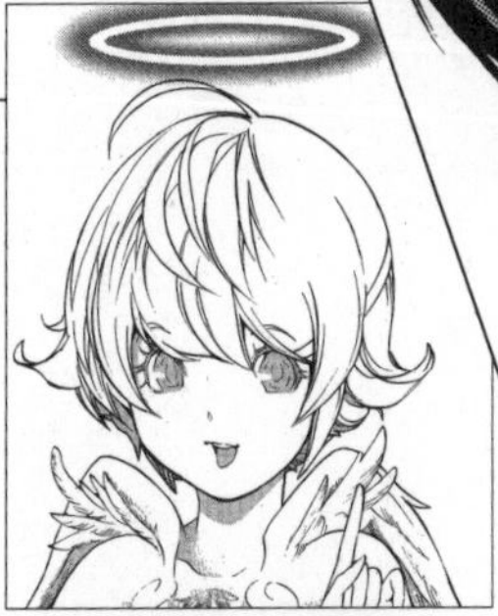

Nasse

A special-rank angel who wants to bring happiness to Mirai's life. Bright and bubbly.

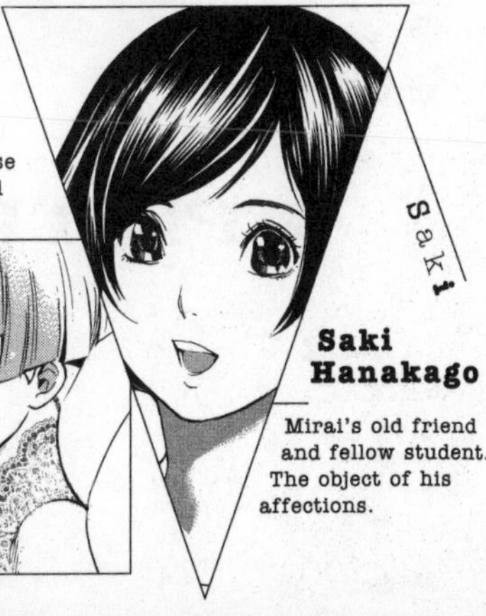
Saki

Saki Hanakago

Mirai's old friend and fellow student. The object of his affections.

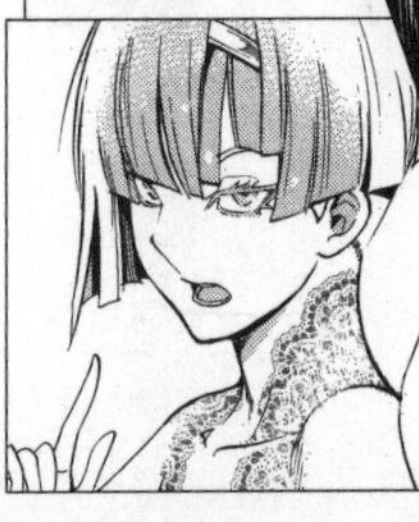

Revel

A second-rank angel who chose Saki as his god candidate.

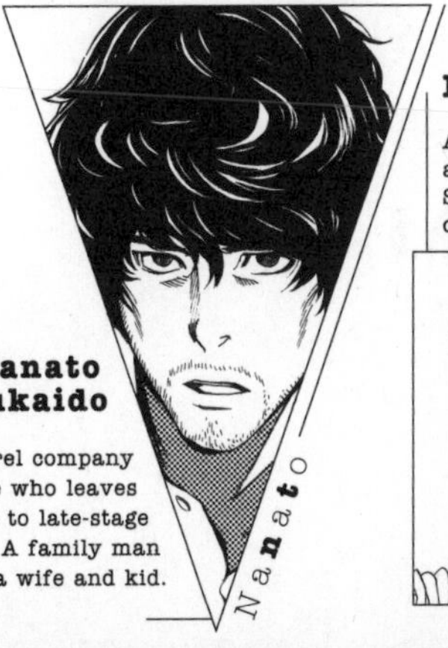
Nanato

Nanato Mukaido

An apparel company employee who leaves work due to late-stage cancer. A family man with a wife and kid.

Story

"My time has come. I leave the seat of god to the next human. To a younger, fresher power.

The next god shall be chosen from the 13 humans chosen by you 13 angels. When the chosen human is made the next god, your angelic duty is finished, and you may live beside that god in peace

CHARACTERS

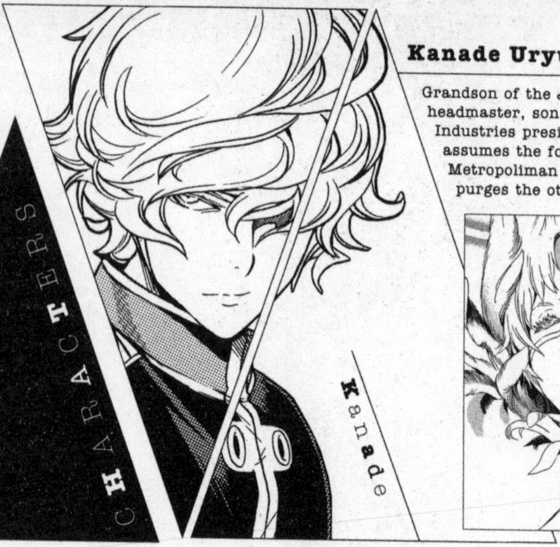

Kanade

Kanade Uryu

Grandson of the Joso Academy headmaster, son of the Joso Industries president. He assumes the form of the Metropoliman character and purges the other god candidates.

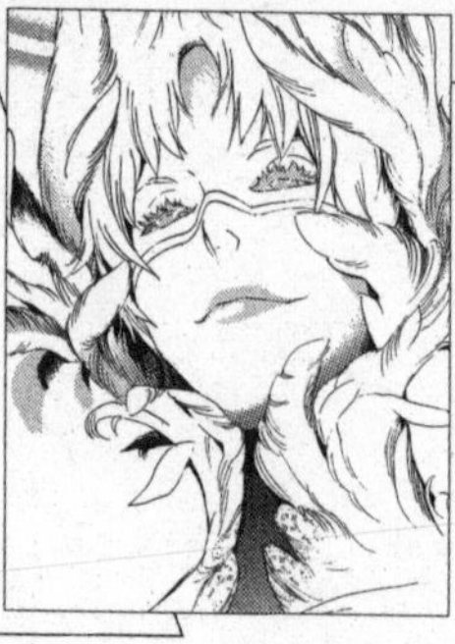

Meyza

The special-ran angel who chos Kanade. For unknown reaso she was elevate from rankless t the top special rank.

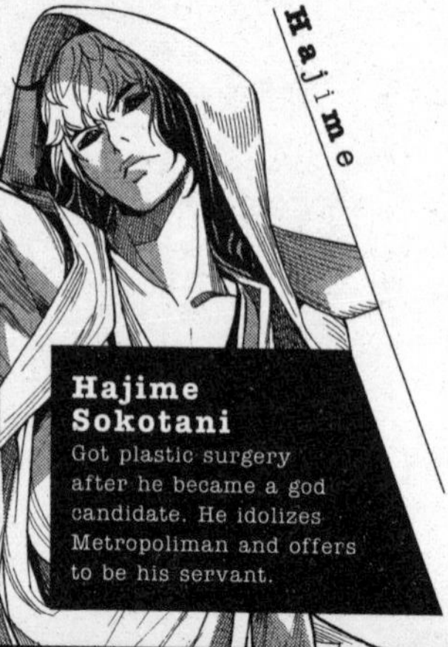

Hajime

Baret

The first-rank angel who chose Mukaido. Possesses great knowledge about the celestial world.

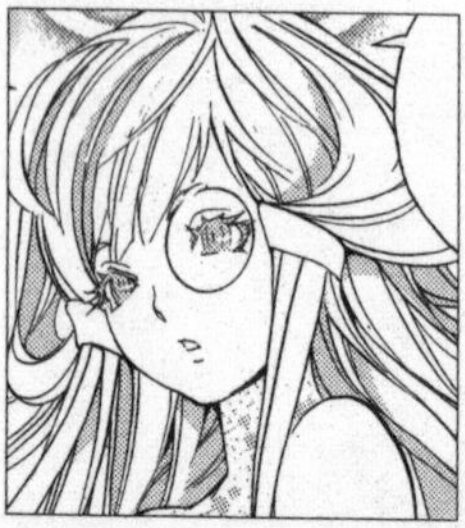

Balta

The first-rank angel who chose Hajime. The Angel of Intuition.

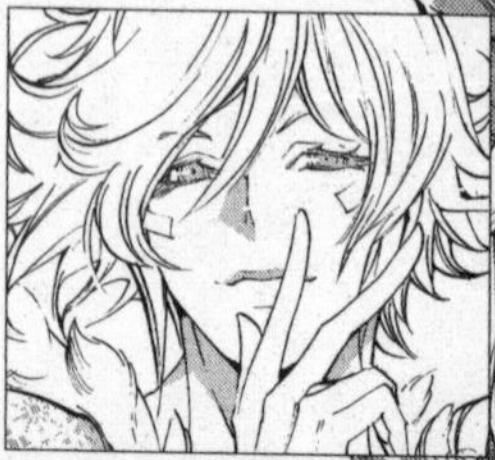

Hajime Sokotani

Got plastic surgery after he became a god candidate. He idolizes Metropoliman and offers to be his servant.

Story

DUEL

Mirai and Metropoliman engage in a one-on-one battle of arrows. They steadily approach one another.

THE LAST ONE

In his last moments, Hajime kills Fuyuko Kohinata. The strange masked boy escapes, leaving only Metropoliman behind.

HAPPINESS

Under the effects of Saki's red arrow, Hajime sacrifices himself to protect her from Fuyuko Kohinata's killer virus.

CONTENTS

8

#24 Absolute Confidence

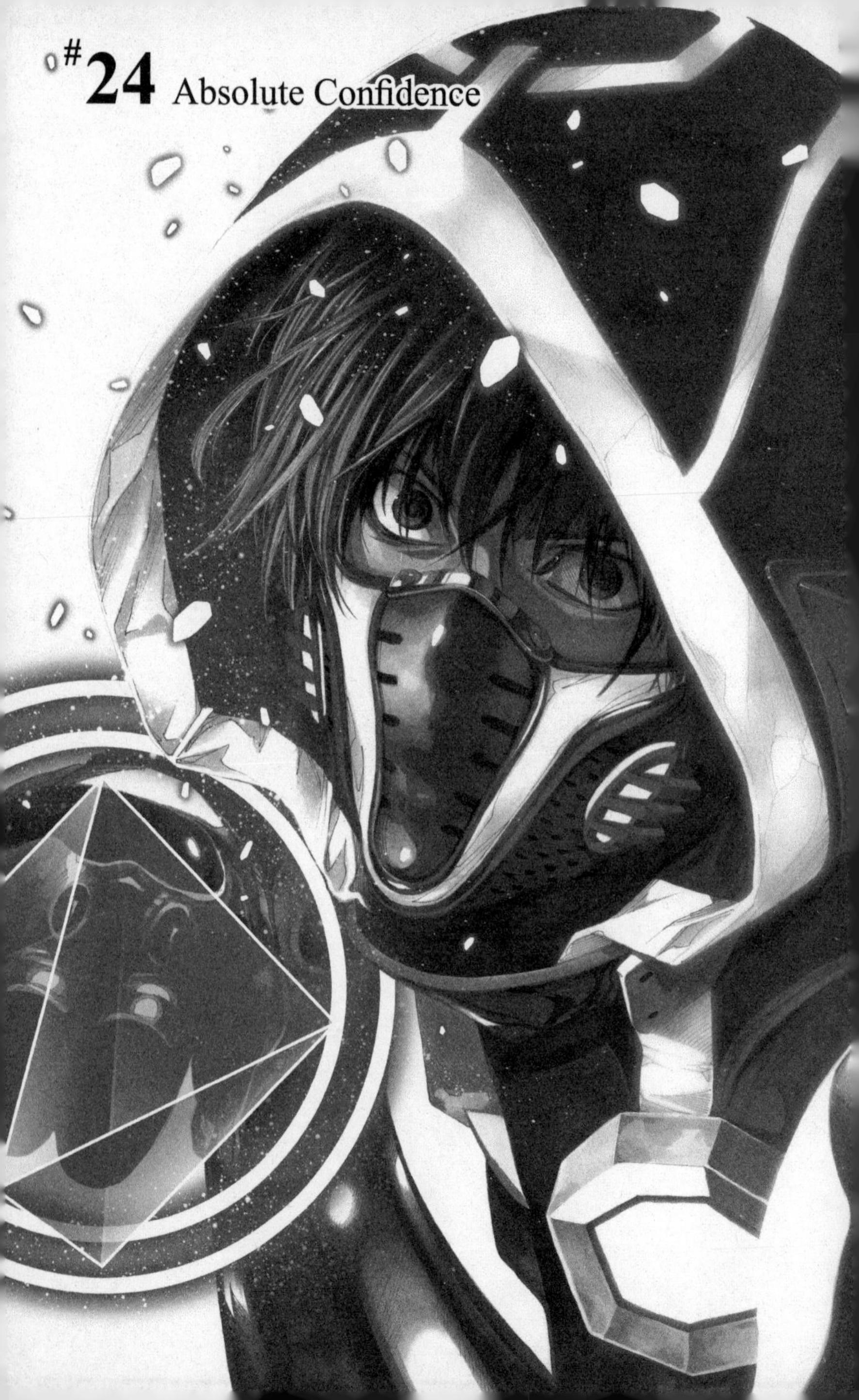

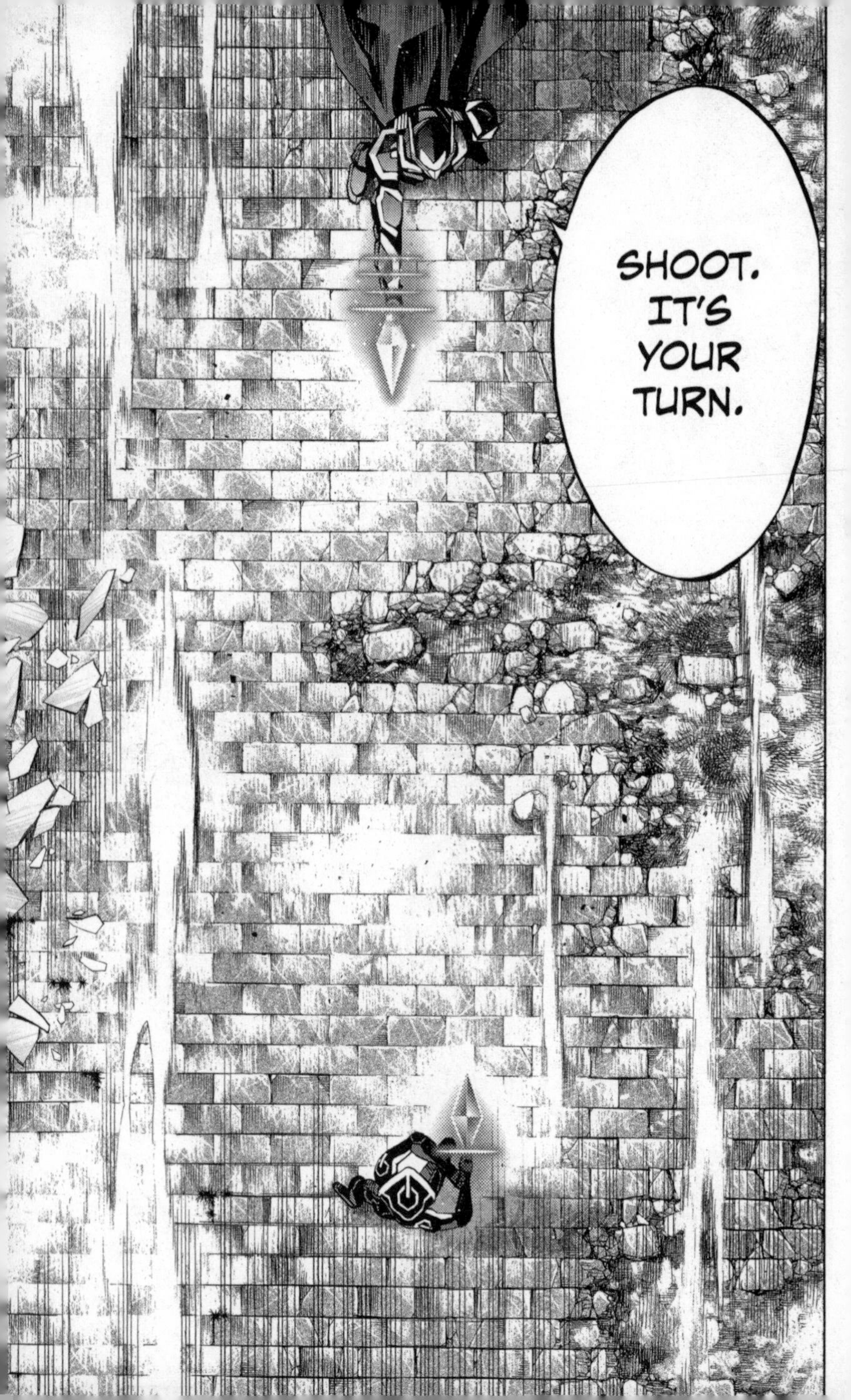
SHOOT. IT'S YOUR TURN.

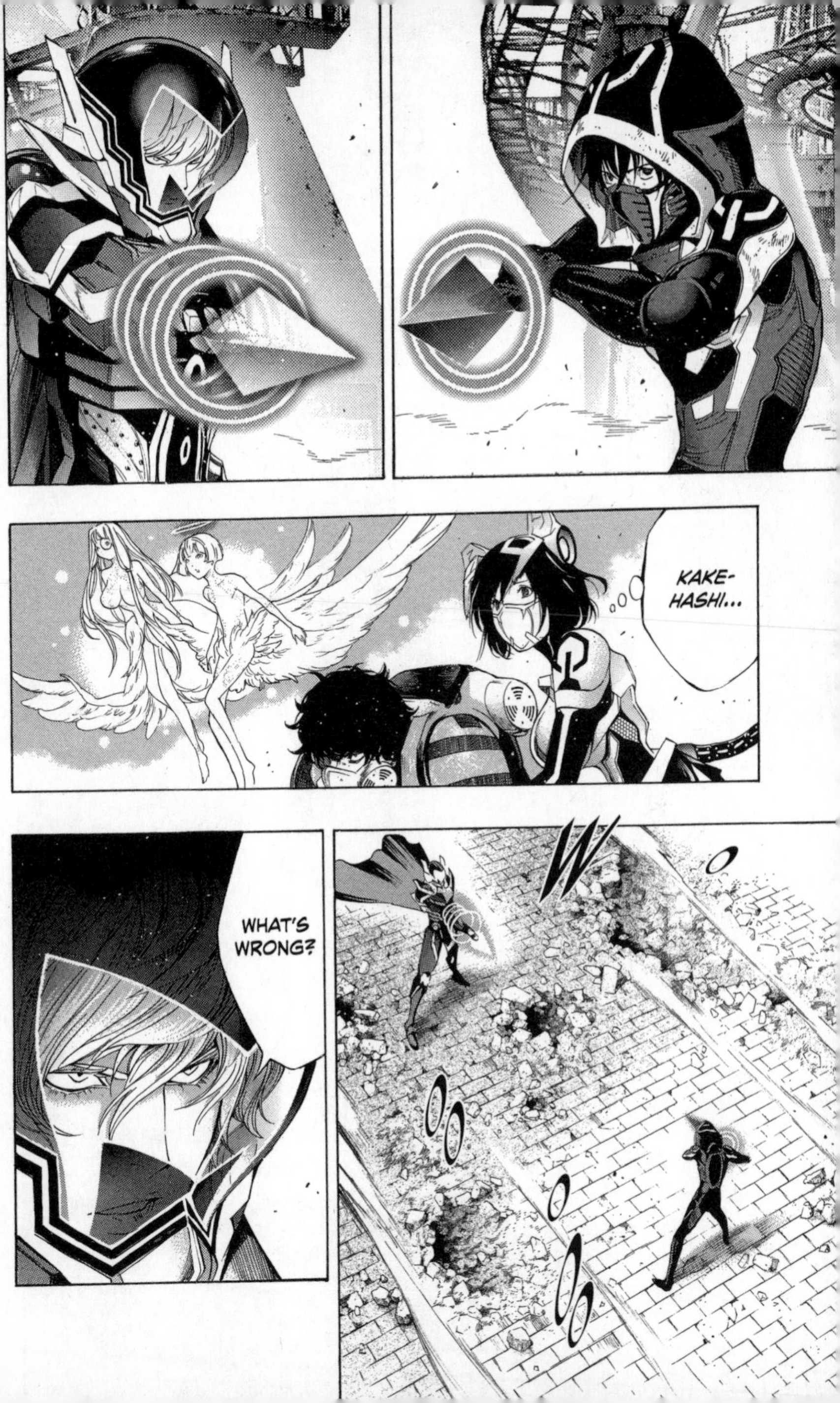
KAKE-
HASHI...
WHAT'S
WRONG?

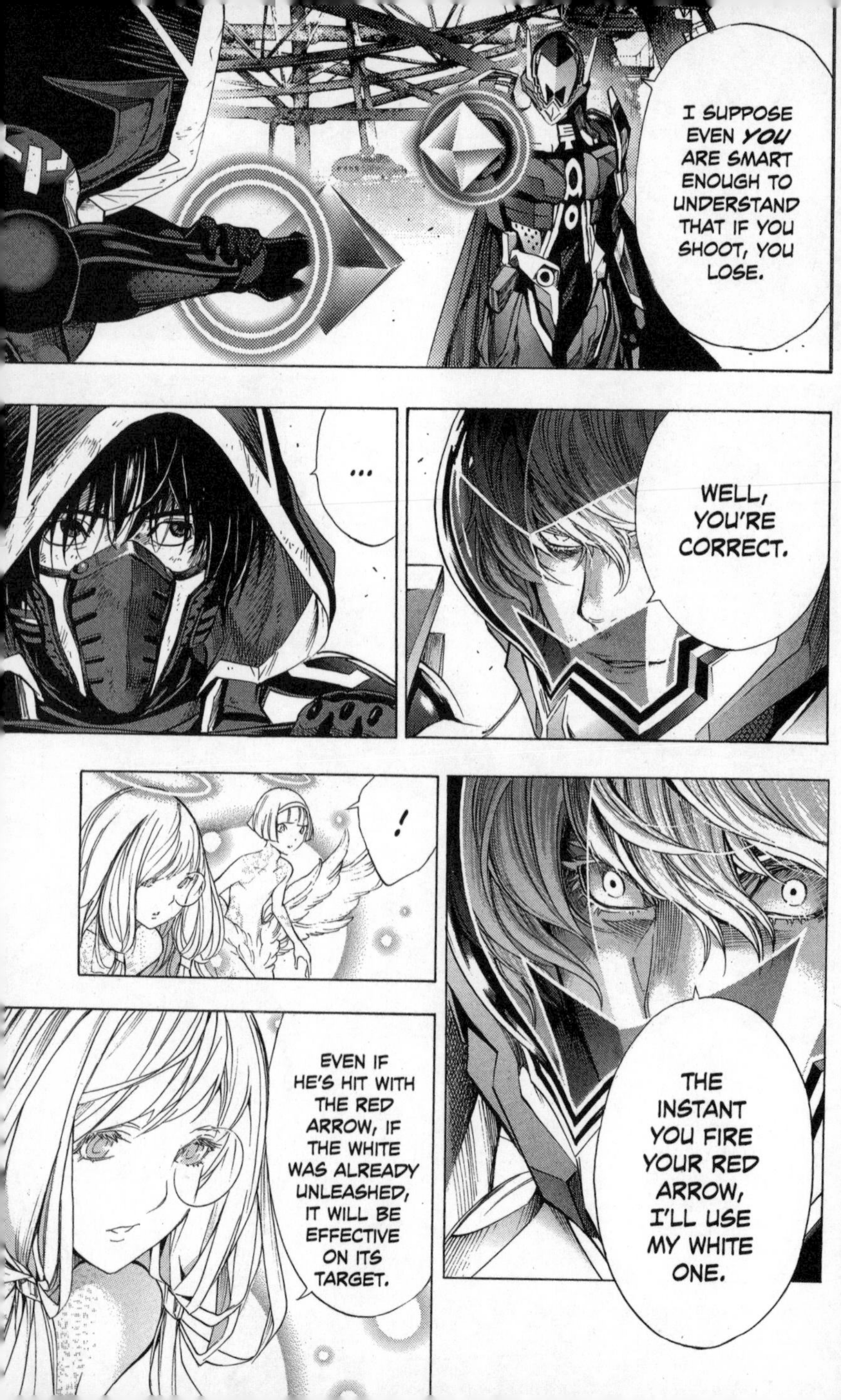
I SUPPOSE EVEN *YOU* ARE SMART ENOUGH TO UNDERSTAND THAT IF YOU SHOOT, YOU LOSE.
WELL, YOU'RE CORRECT.
...
THE INSTANT YOU FIRE YOUR RED ARROW, I'LL USE MY WHITE ONE.
!
EVEN IF HE'S HIT WITH THE RED ARROW, IF THE WHITE WAS ALREADY UNLEASHED, IT WILL BE EFFECTIVE ON ITS TARGET.

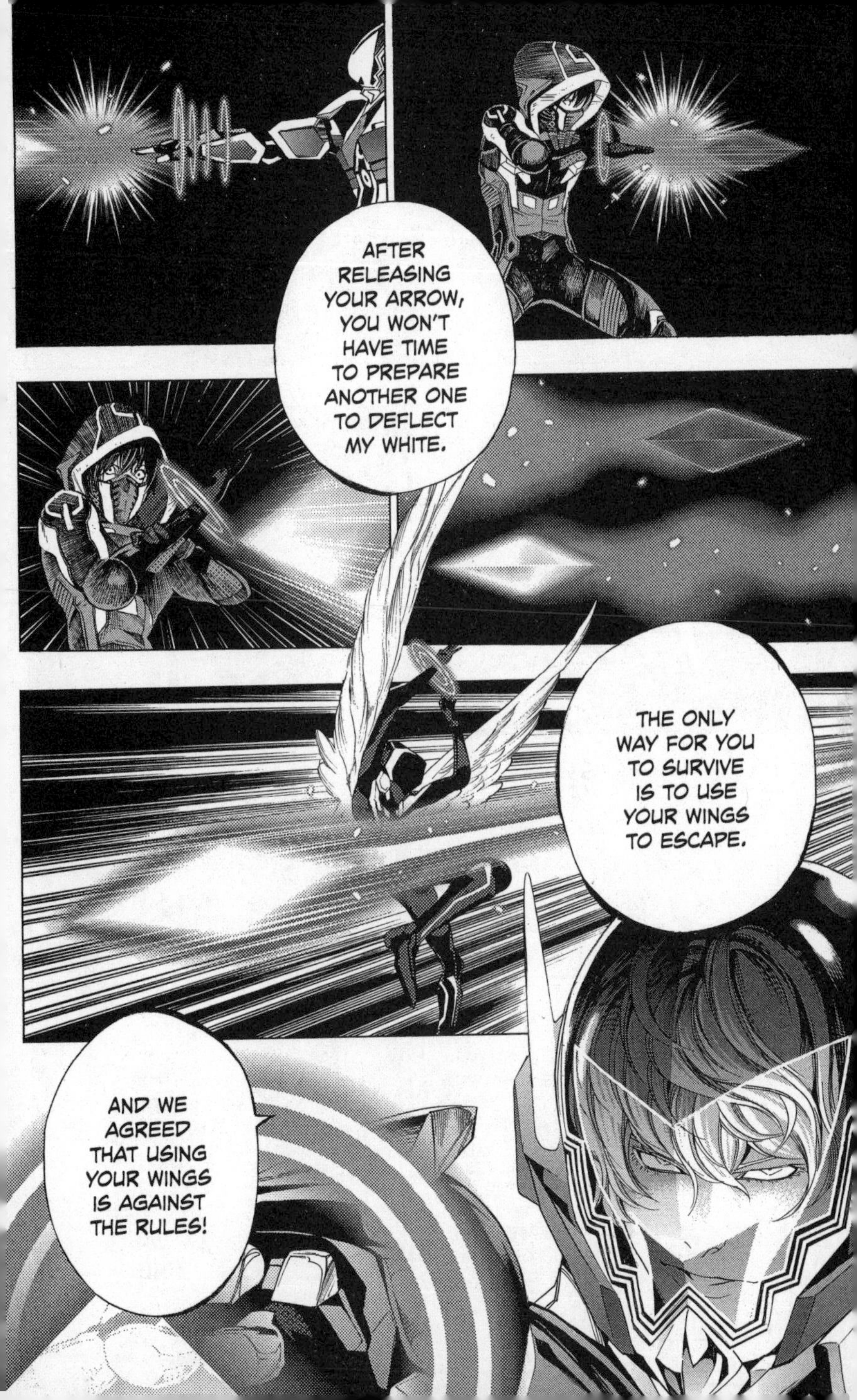
AFTER RELEASING YOUR ARROW, YOU WON'T HAVE TIME TO PREPARE ANOTHER ONE TO DEFLECT MY WHITE.
THE ONLY WAY FOR YOU TO SURVIVE IS TO USE YOUR WINGS TO ESCAPE.
AND WE AGREED THAT USING YOUR WINGS IS AGAINST THE RULES!

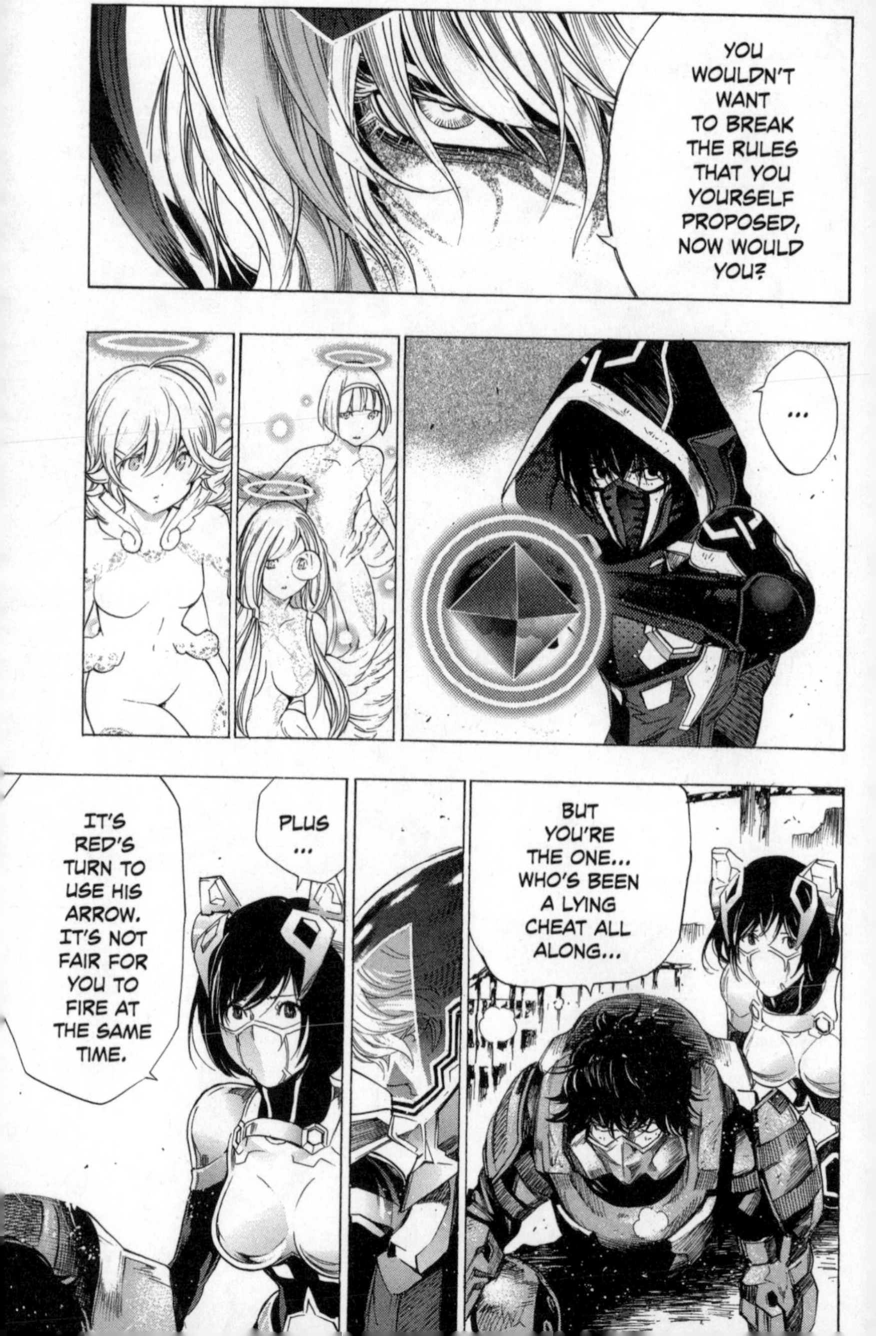
YOU WOULDN'T WANT TO BREAK THE RULES THAT YOU YOURSELF PROPOSED, NOW WOULD YOU?
...
BUT YOU'RE THE ONE... WHO'S BEEN A LYING CHEAT ALL ALONG...
PLUS ...
IT'S RED'S TURN TO USE HIS ARROW. IT'S NOT FAIR FOR YOU TO FIRE AT THE SAME TIME.

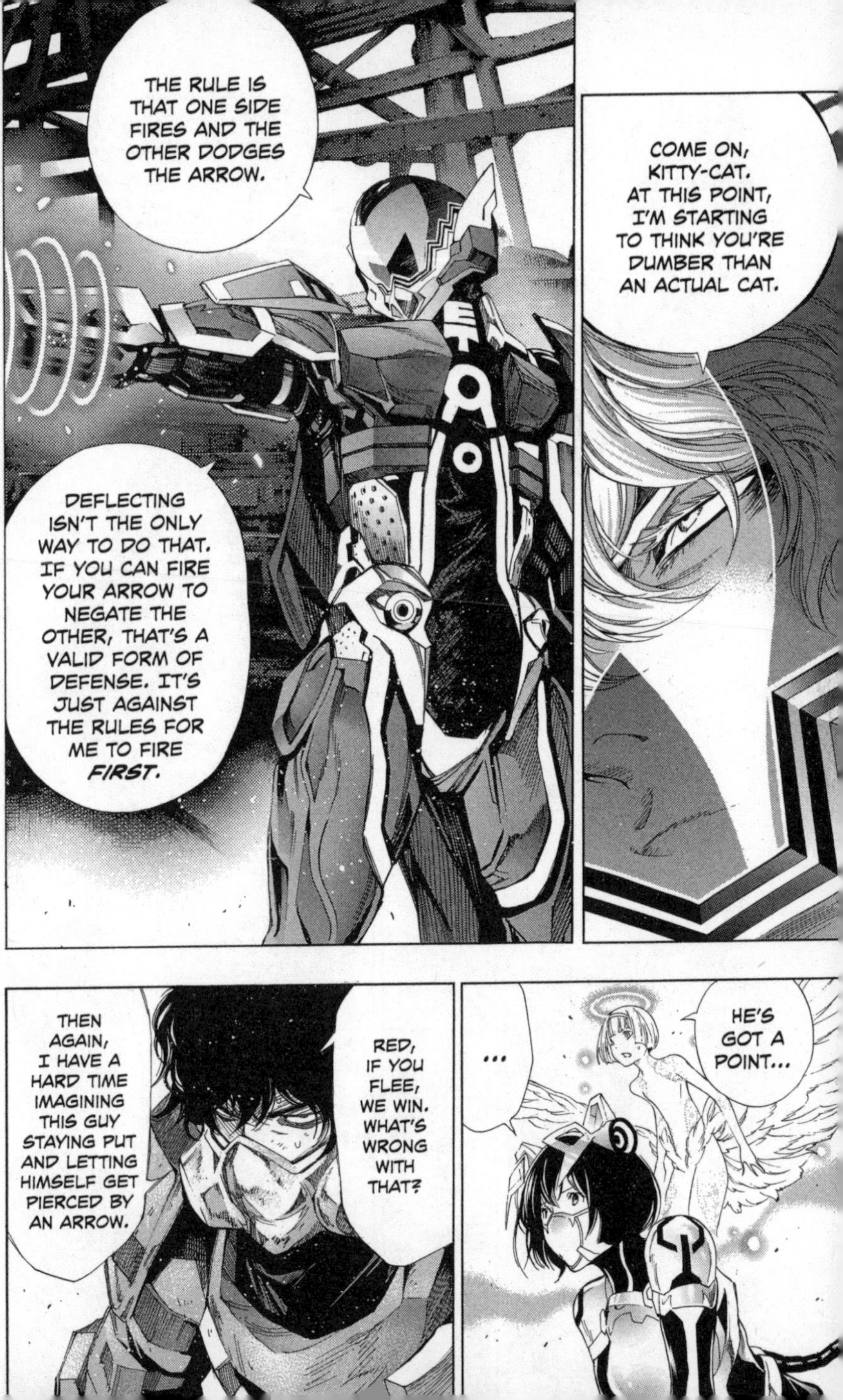
COME ON, KITTY-CAT. AT THIS POINT, I'M STARTING TO THINK YOU'RE DUMBER THAN AN ACTUAL CAT.
THE RULE IS THAT ONE SIDE FIRES AND THE OTHER DODGES THE ARROW.
DEFLECTING ISN'T THE ONLY WAY TO DO THAT. IF YOU CAN FIRE YOUR ARROW TO NEGATE THE OTHER, THAT'S A VALID FORM OF DEFENSE. IT'S JUST AGAINST THE RULES FOR ME TO FIRE *FIRST*.
HE'S GOT A POINT...
...
RED, IF YOU FLEE, WE WIN. WHAT'S WRONG WITH THAT?
THEN AGAIN, I HAVE A HARD TIME IMAGINING THIS GUY STAYING PUT AND LETTING HIMSELF GET PIERCED BY AN ARROW.

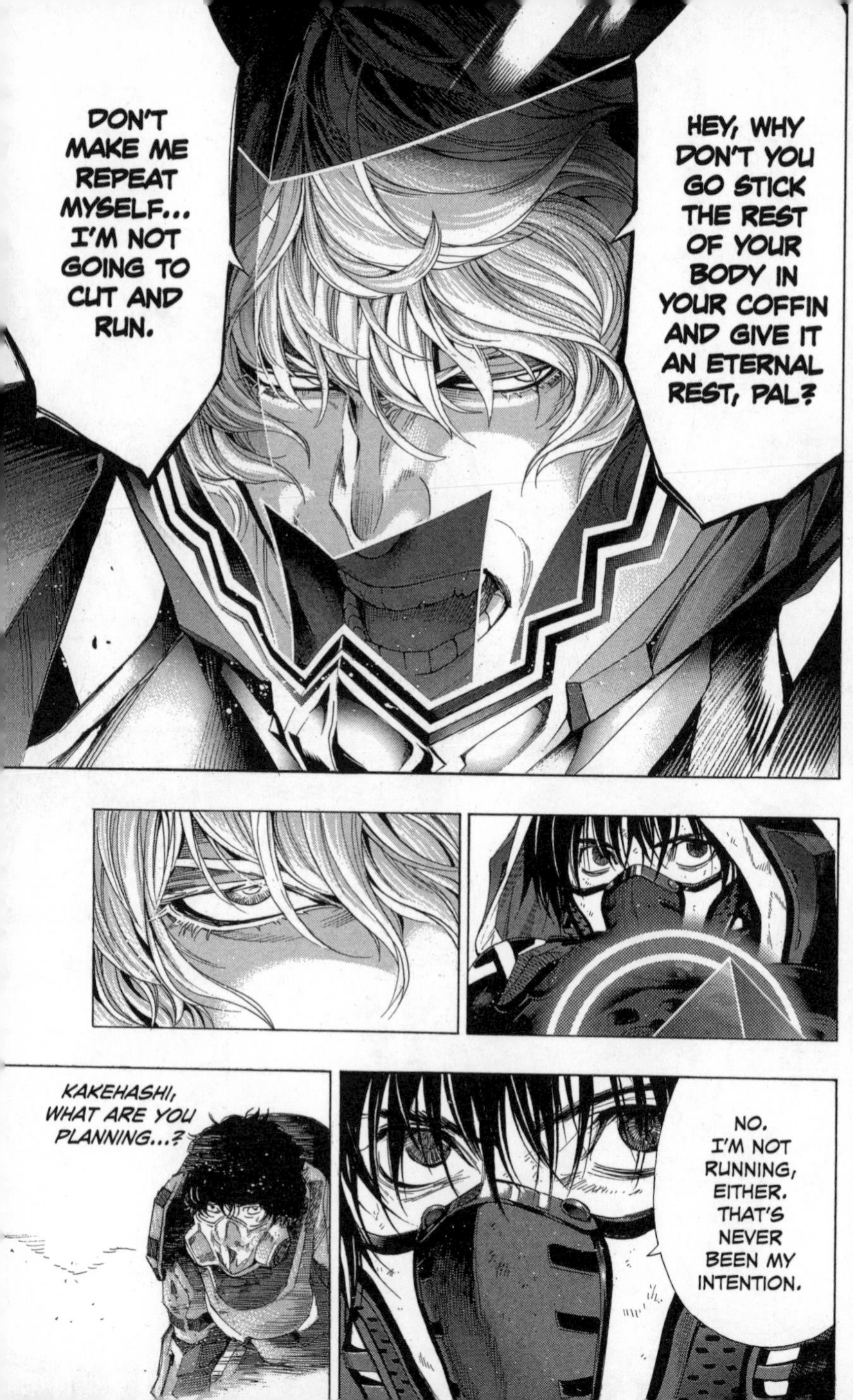
HEY, WHY DON'T YOU GO STICK THE REST OF YOUR BODY IN YOUR COFFIN AND GIVE IT AN ETERNAL REST, PAL?
DON'T MAKE ME REPEAT MYSELF... I'M NOT GOING TO CUT AND RUN.
NO. I'M NOT RUNNING, EITHER. THAT'S NEVER BEEN MY INTENTION.
KAKEHASHI, WHAT ARE YOU PLANNING...?

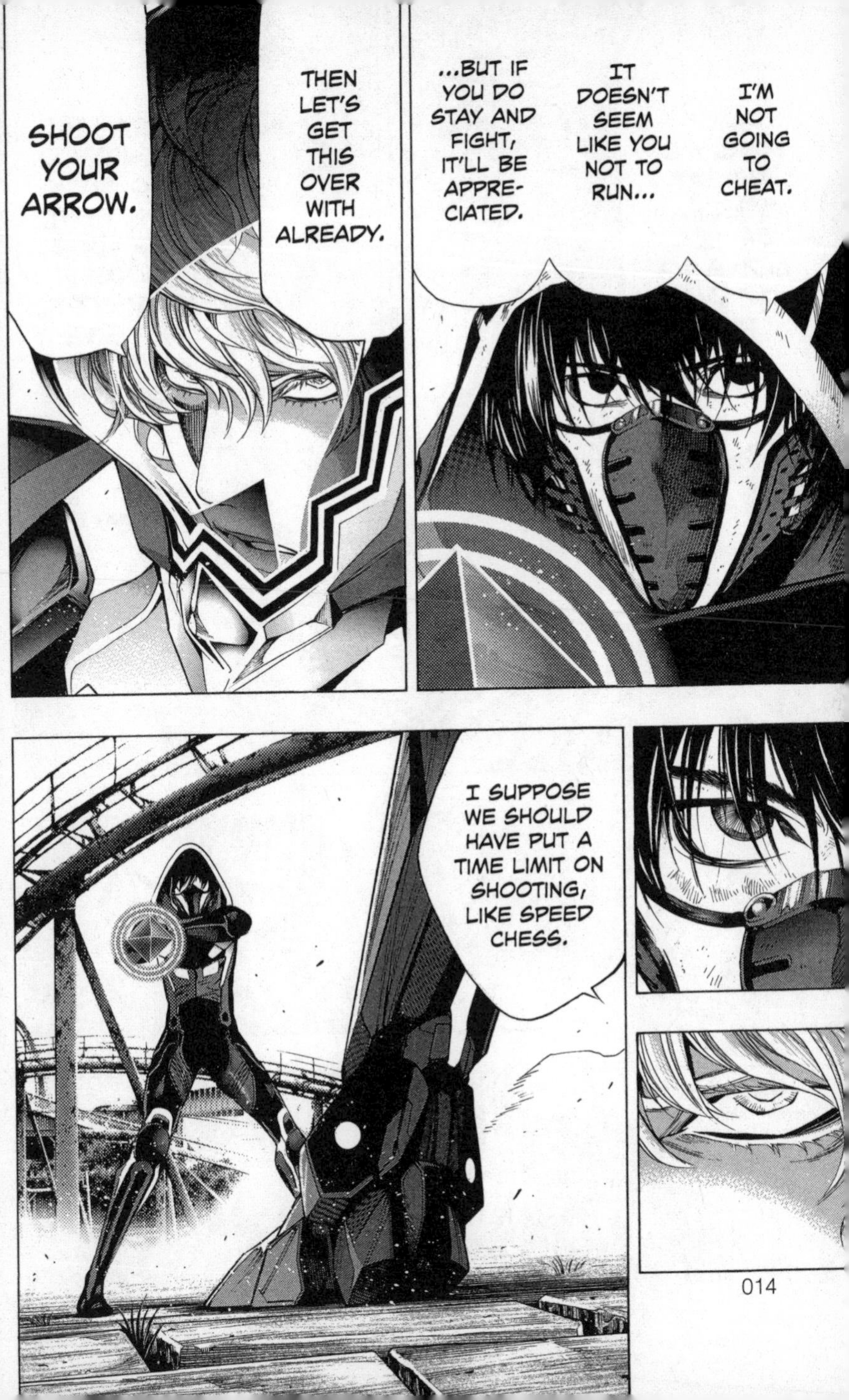
I'M NOT GOING TO CHEAT.
IT DOESN'T SEEM LIKE YOU NOT TO RUN...
...BUT IF YOU DO STAY AND FIGHT, IT'LL BE APPRE-CIATED.
THEN LET'S GET THIS OVER WITH ALREADY.
SHOOT YOUR ARROW.
I SUPPOSE WE SHOULD HAVE PUT A TIME LIMIT ON SHOOTING, LIKE SPEED CHESS.

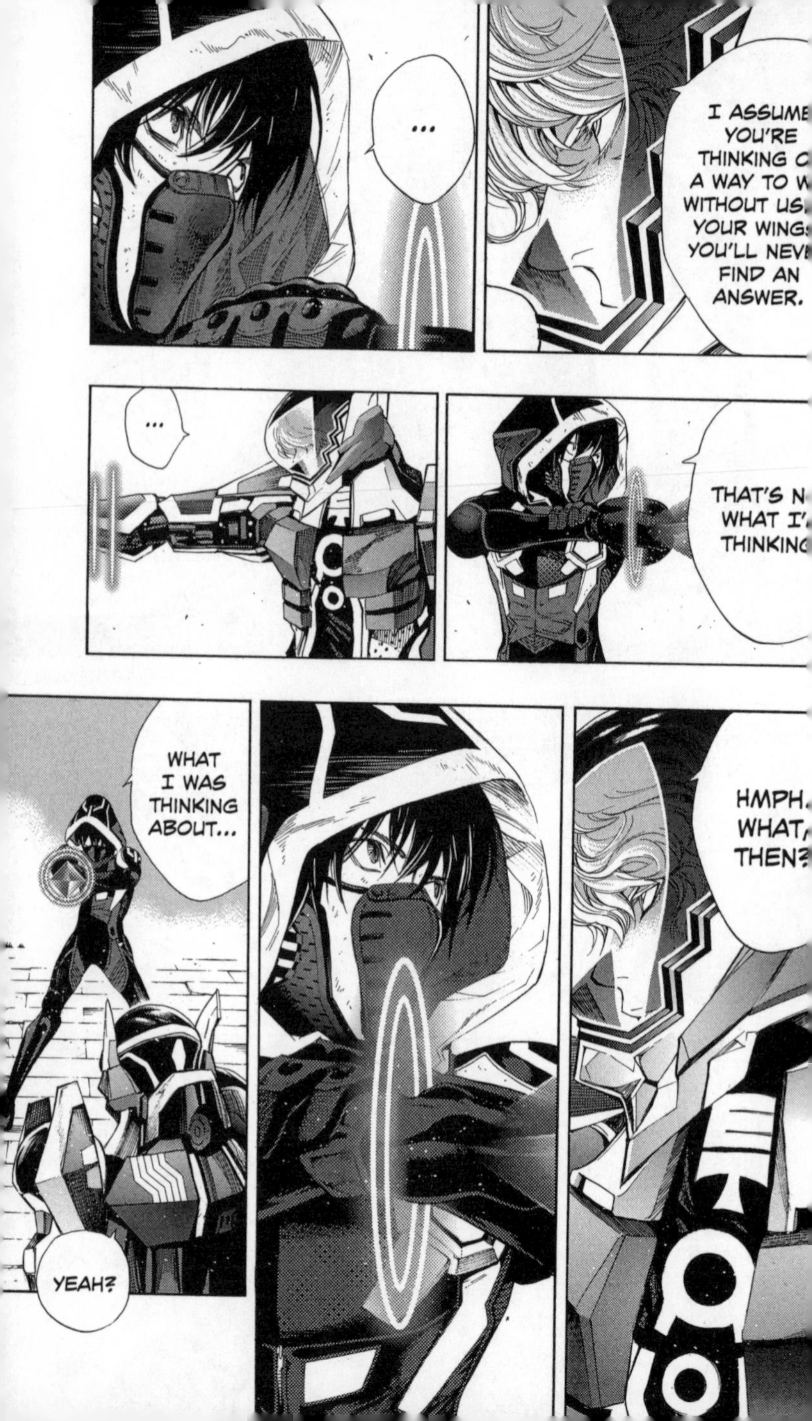
I ASSUME YOU'RE THINKING O A WAY TO W WITHOUT US. YOUR WINGS YOU'LL NEVE FIND AN ANSWER.
...
THAT'S N WHAT I' THINKING
...
HMPH. WHAT, THEN?
WHAT I WAS THINKING ABOUT...
YEAH?

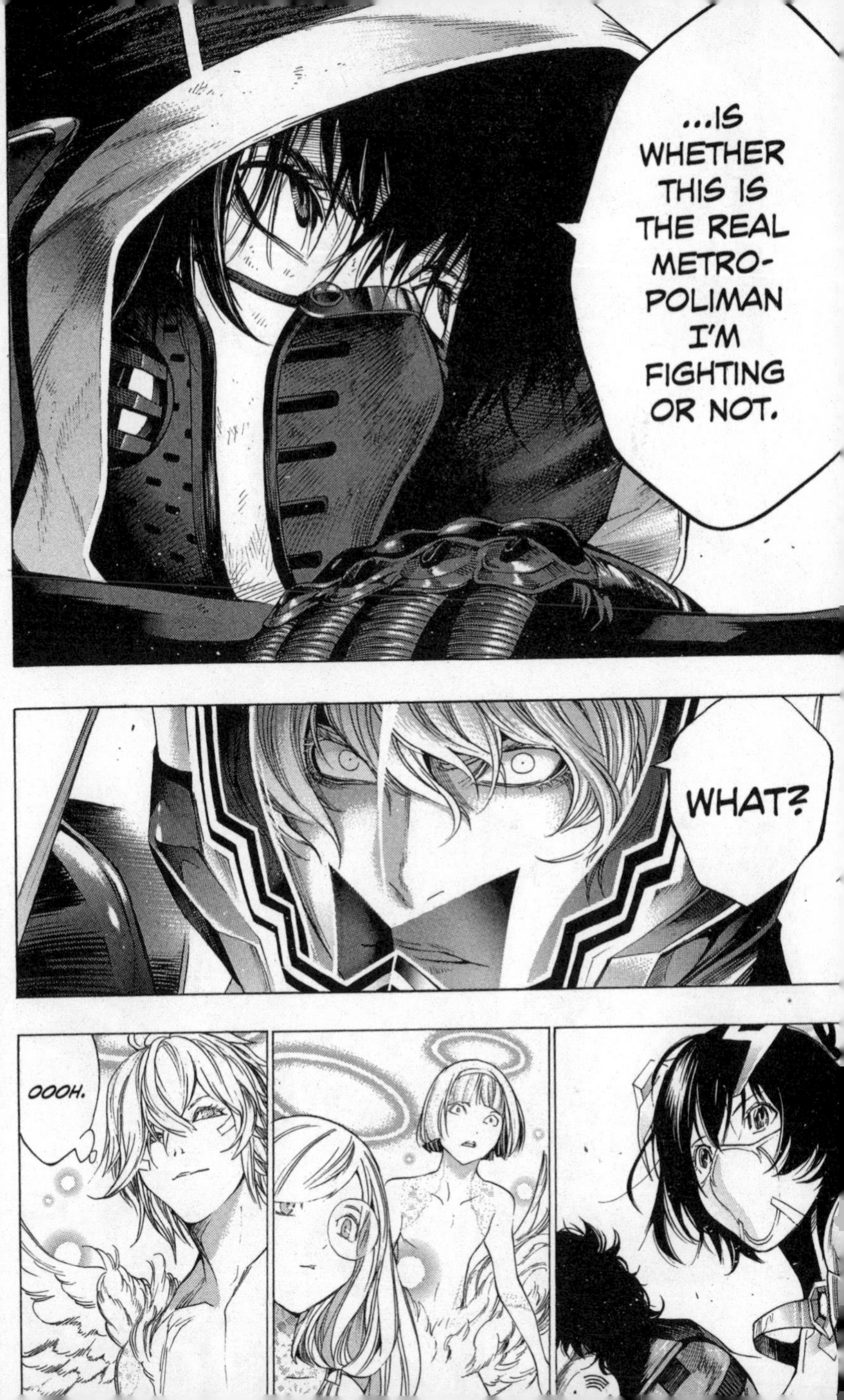
...IS WHETHER THIS IS THE REAL METRO-POLIMAN I'M FIGHTING OR NOT.
WHAT?
OOOH.

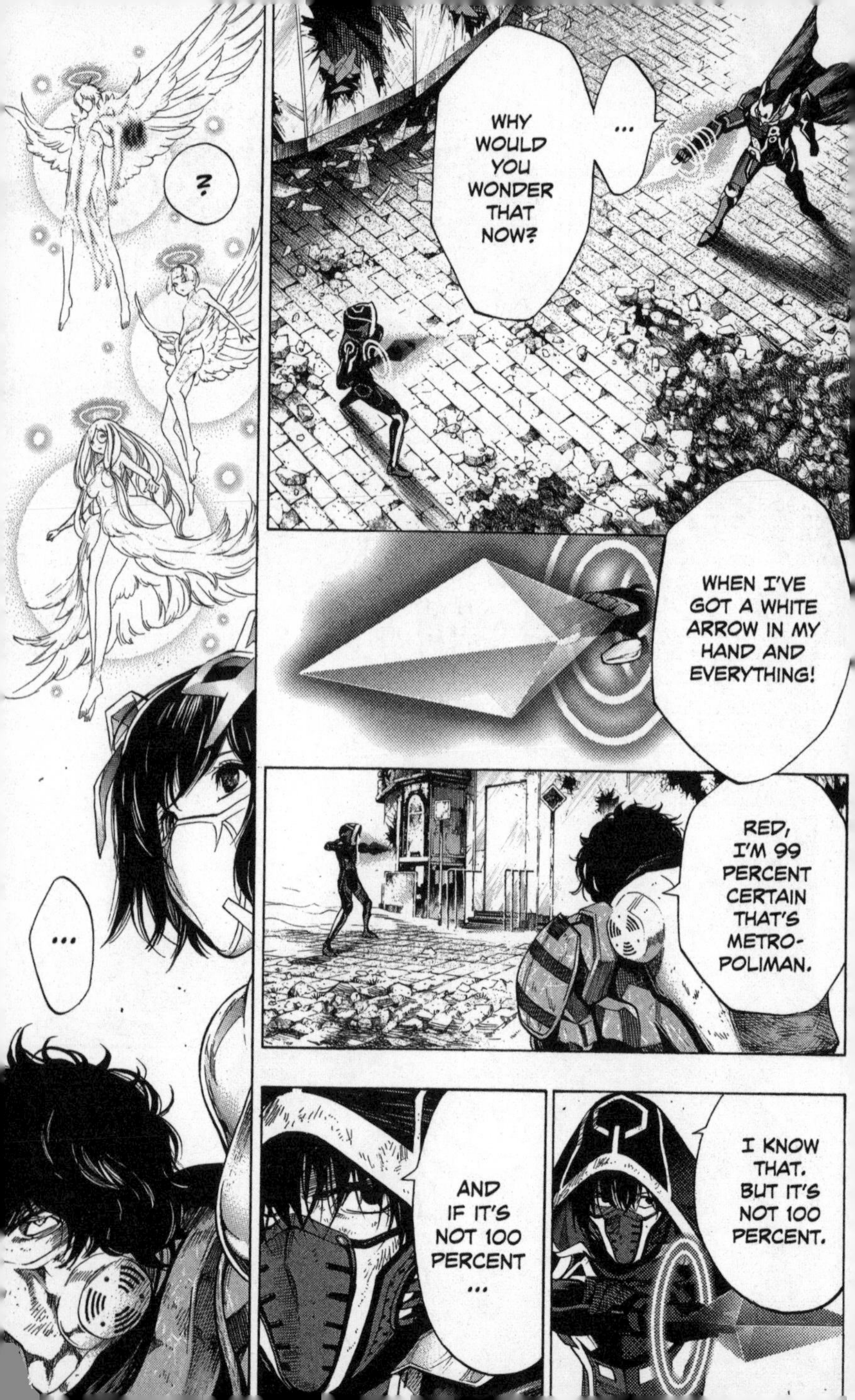
...
WHY WOULD YOU WONDER THAT NOW?
WHEN I'VE GOT A WHITE ARROW IN MY HAND AND EVERYTHING!
RED, I'M 99 PERCENT CERTAIN THAT'S METRO-POLIMAN.
I KNOW THAT. BUT IT'S NOT 100 PERCENT.
AND IF IT'S NOT 100 PERCENT...
?
...

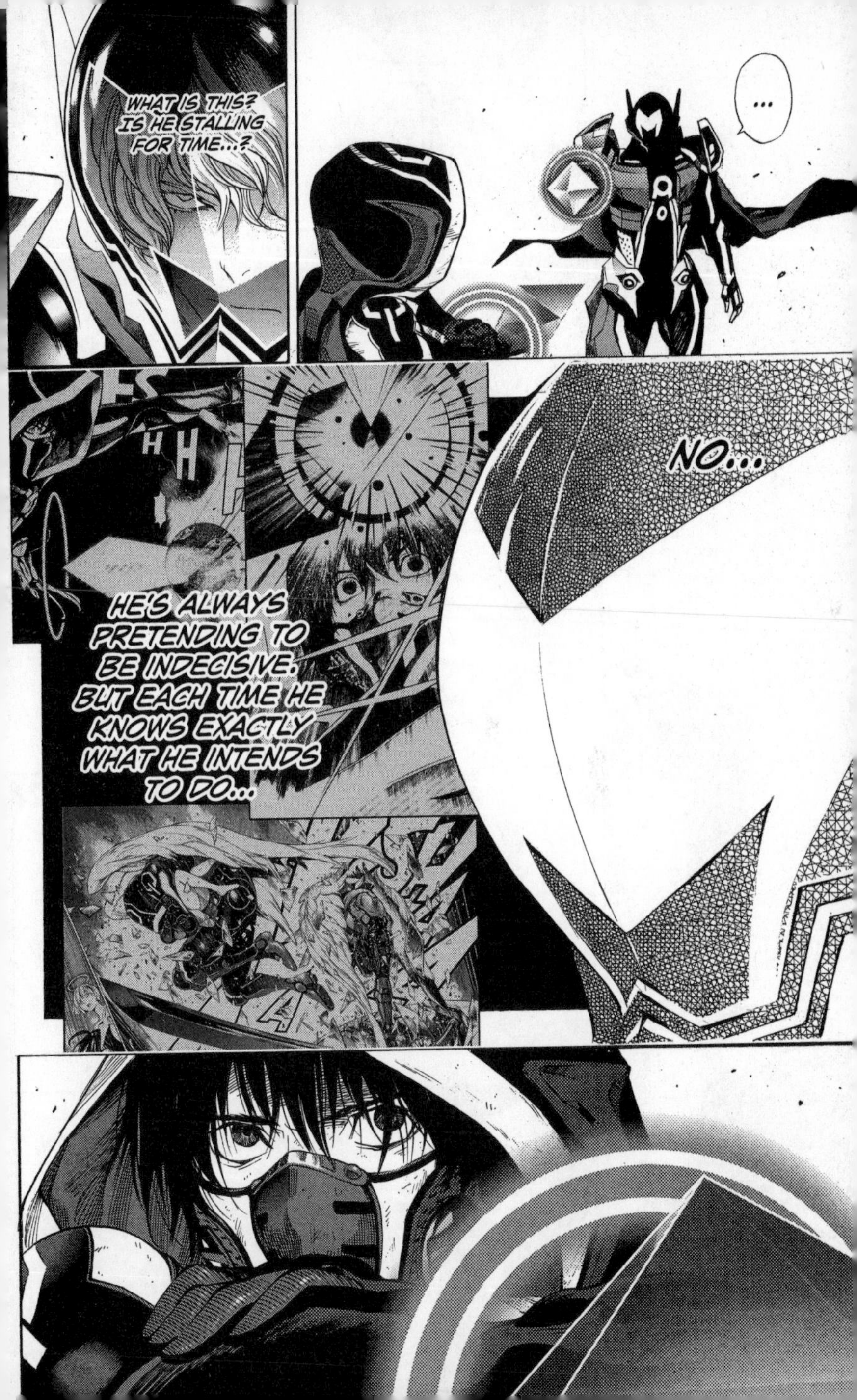
...
WHAT IS THIS? IS HE STALLING FOR TIME...?
NO...
HE'S ALWAYS PRETENDING TO BE INDECISIVE. BUT EACH TIME HE KNOWS EXACTLY WHAT HE INTENDS TO DO...

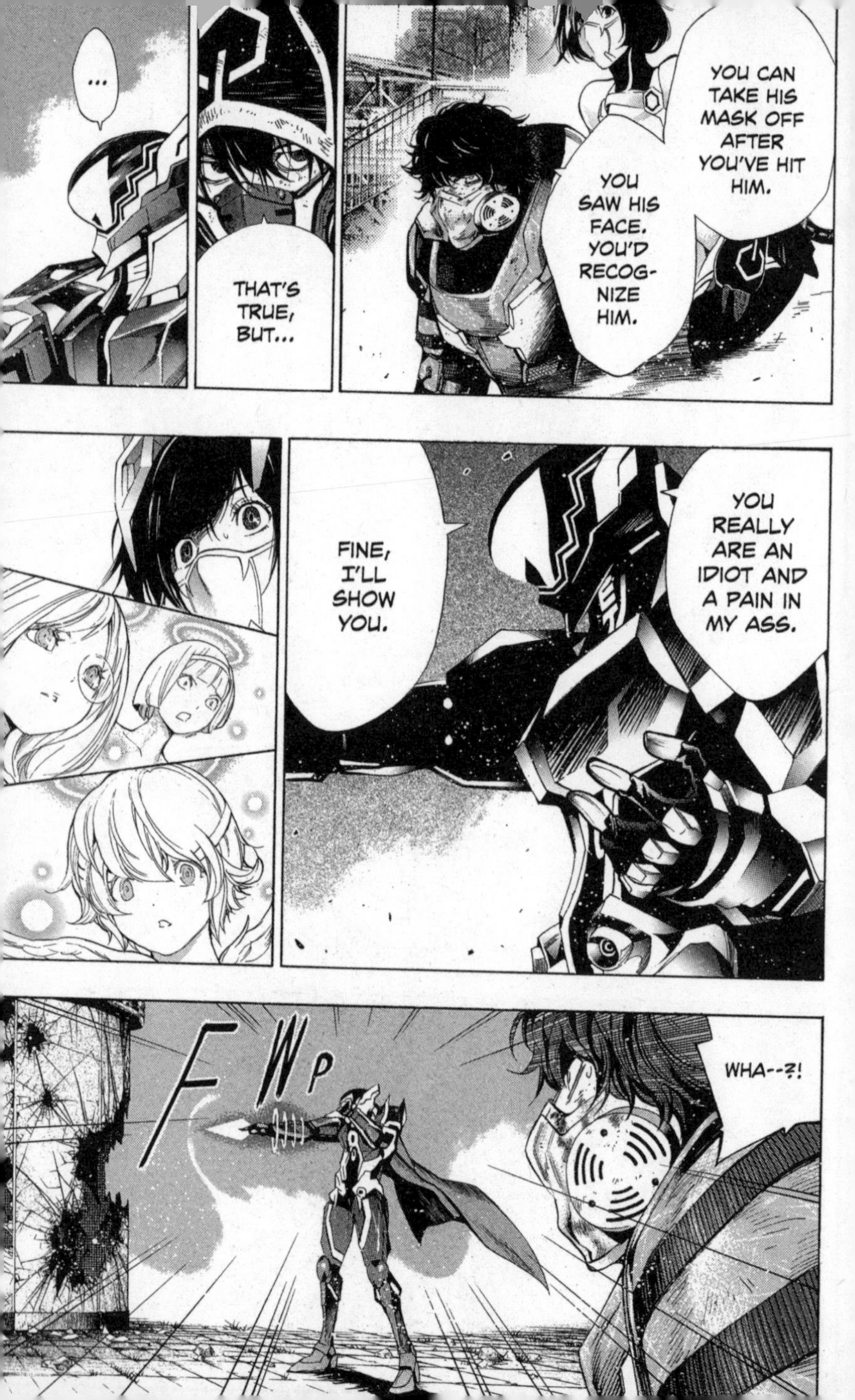
YOU CAN TAKE HIS MASK OFF AFTER YOU'VE HIT HIM.
YOU SAW HIS FACE. YOU'D RECOG-NIZE HIM.
THAT'S TRUE, BUT...
...
YOU REALLY ARE AN IDIOT AND A PAIN IN MY ASS.
FINE, I'LL SHOW YOU.
WHA--?!
FWP

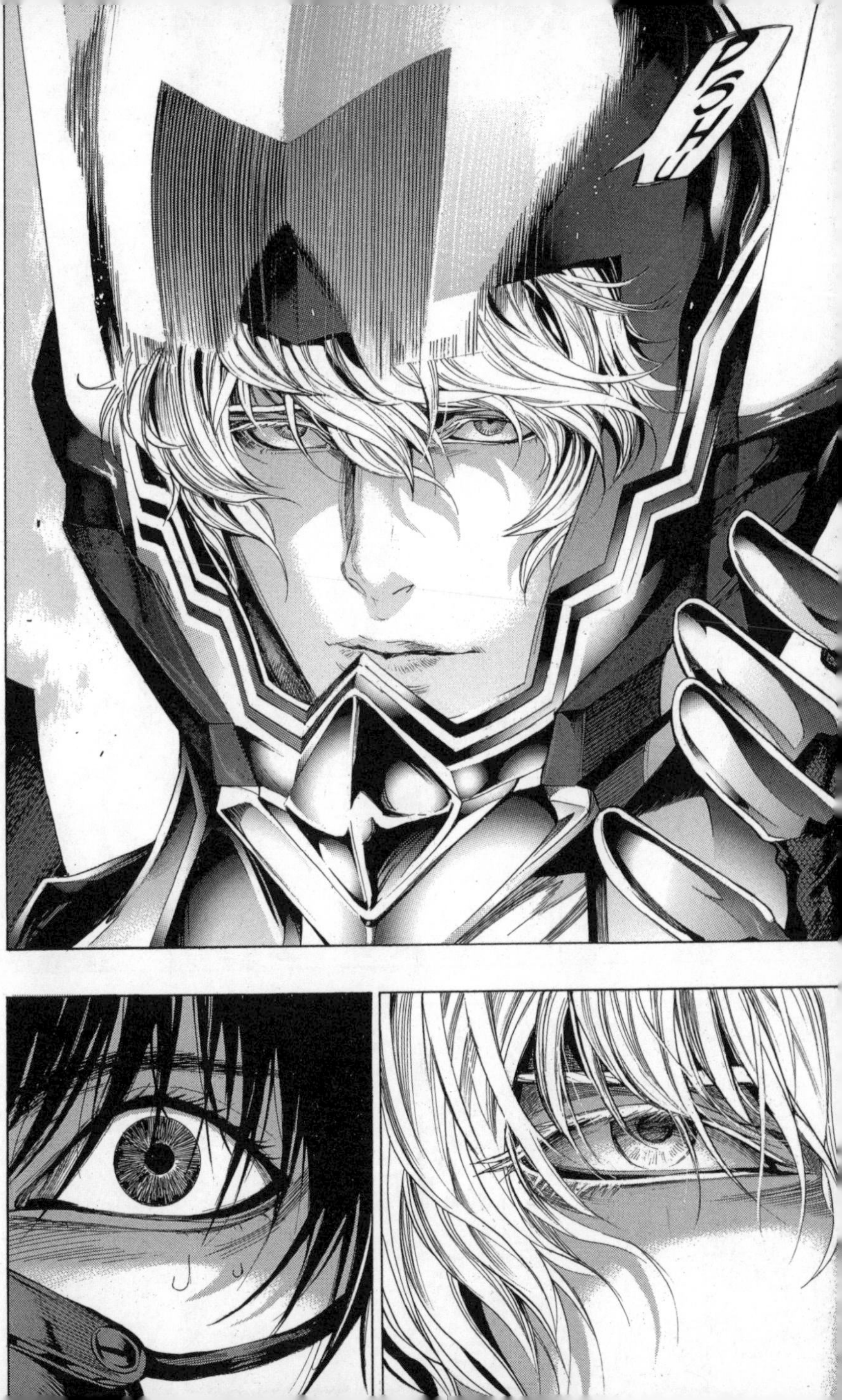

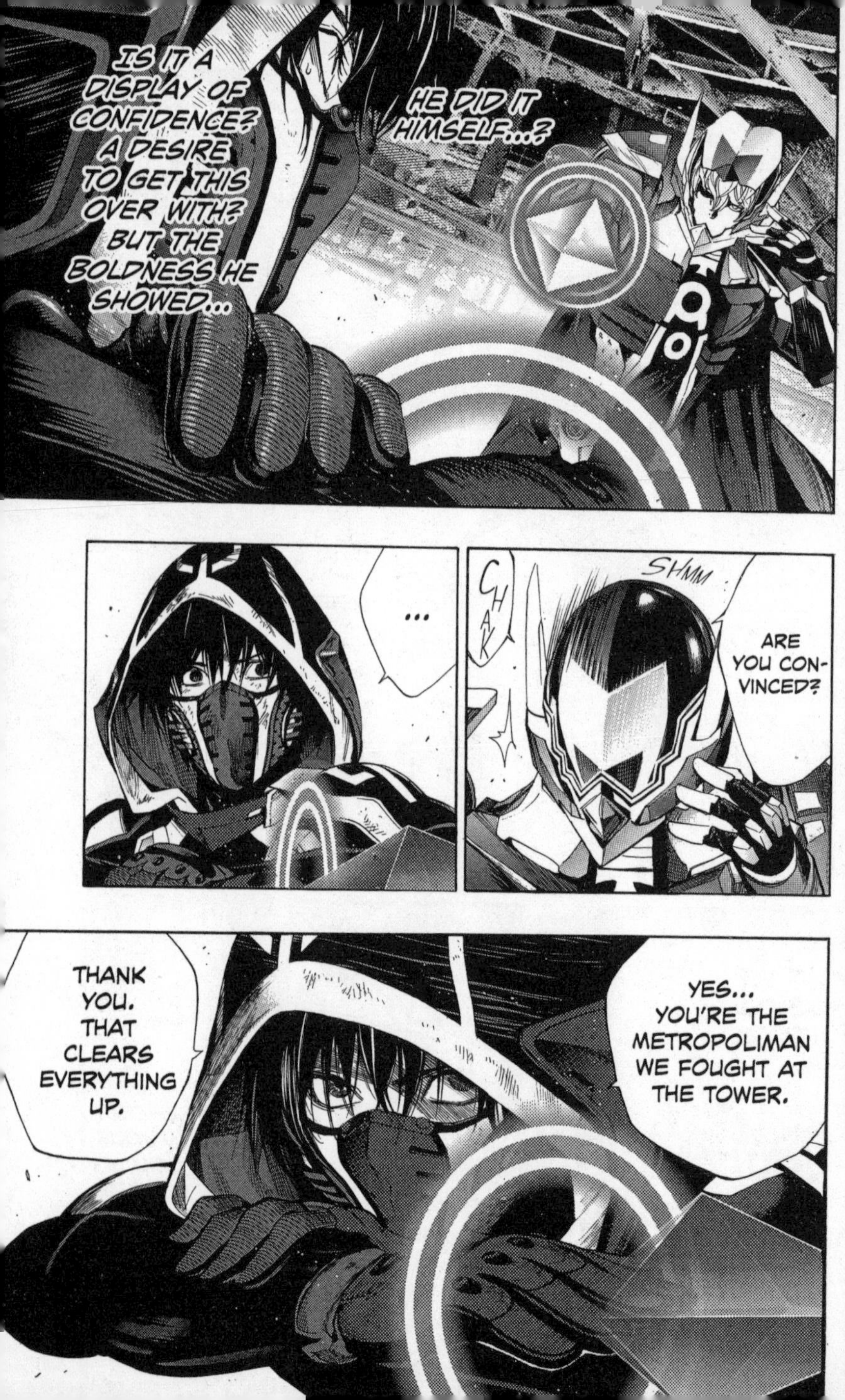
HE DID IT HIMSELF...?
IS IT A DISPLAY OF CONFIDENCE? A DESIRE TO GET THIS OVER WITH? BUT THE BOLDNESS HE SHOWED...
SHMM
CHAK
ARE YOU CON-VINCED?
...
YES... YOU'RE THE METROPOLIMAN WE FOUGHT AT THE TOWER.
THANK YOU. THAT CLEARS EVERYTHING UP.

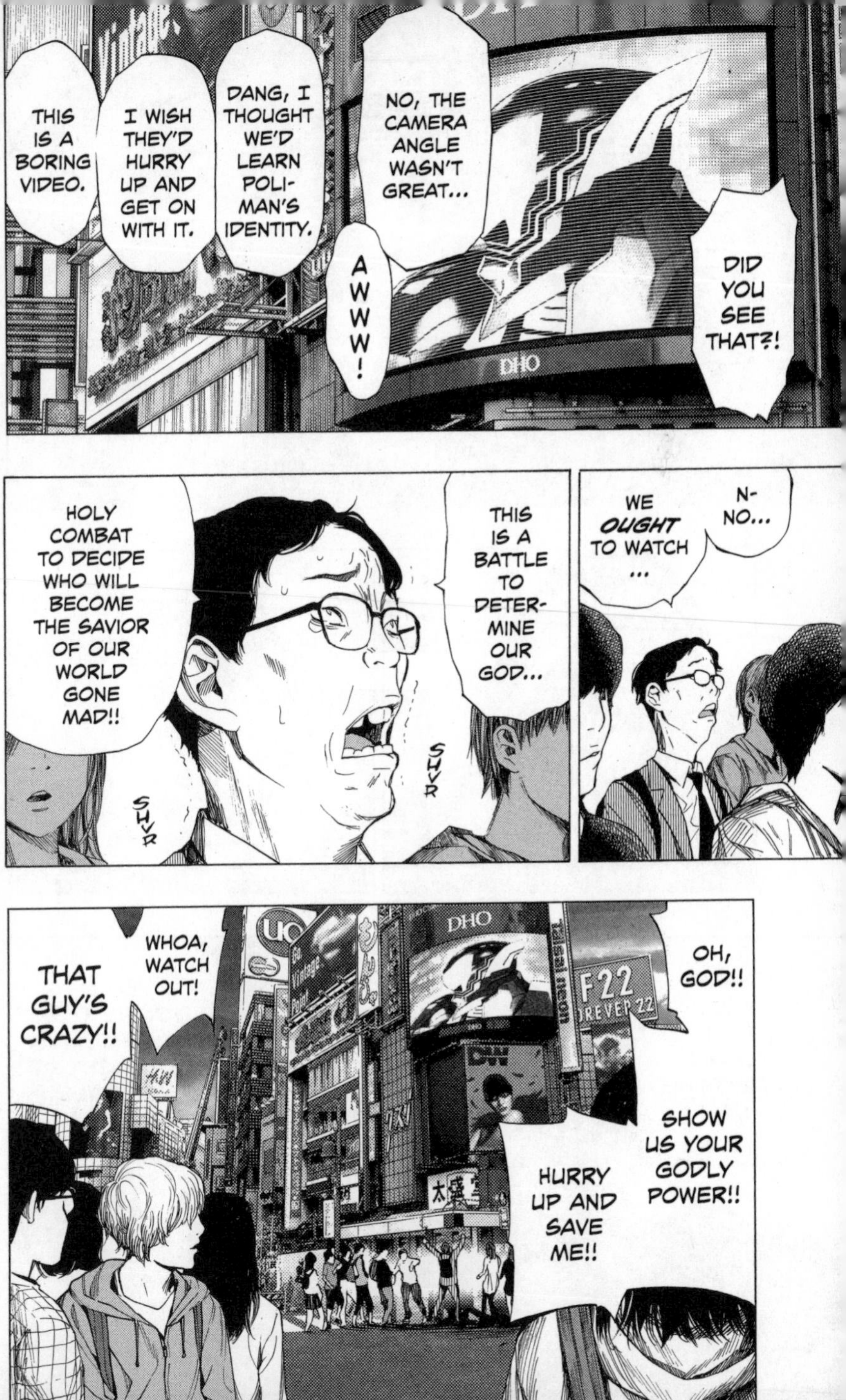
DID YOU SEE THAT?!
AWWW!
NO, THE CAMERA ANGLE WASN'T GREAT...
DANG, I THOUGHT WE'D LEARN POLI-MAN'S IDENTITY.
I WISH THEY'D HURRY UP AND GET ON WITH IT.
THIS IS A BORING VIDEO.
N-NO...
WE *OUGHT* TO WATCH ...
THIS IS A BATTLE TO DETERMINE OUR GOD...
SHVR
HOLY COMBAT TO DECIDE WHO WILL BECOME THE SAVIOR OF OUR WORLD GONE MAD!!
SHVR
OH, GOD!!
SHOW US YOUR GODLY POWER!!
HURRY UP AND SAVE ME!!
WHOA, WATCH OUT!
THAT GUY'S CRAZY!!

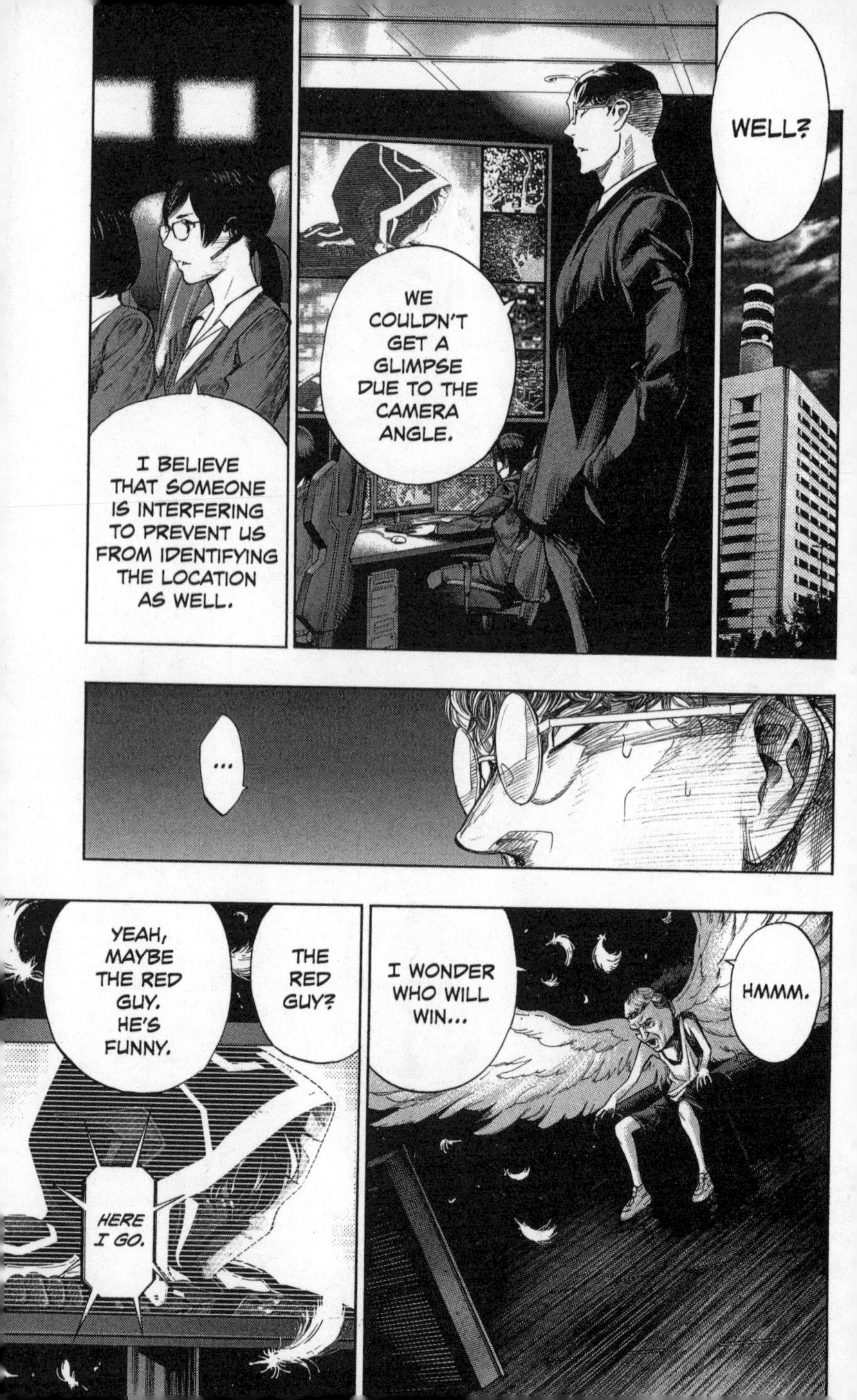
WELL?
WE COULDN'T GET A GLIMPSE DUE TO THE CAMERA ANGLE.
I BELIEVE THAT SOMEONE IS INTERFERING TO PREVENT US FROM IDENTIFYING THE LOCATION AS WELL.
...
HMMM.
I WONDER WHO WILL WIN...
THE RED GUY?
YEAH, MAYBE THE RED GUY. HE'S FUNNY.
HERE I GO.

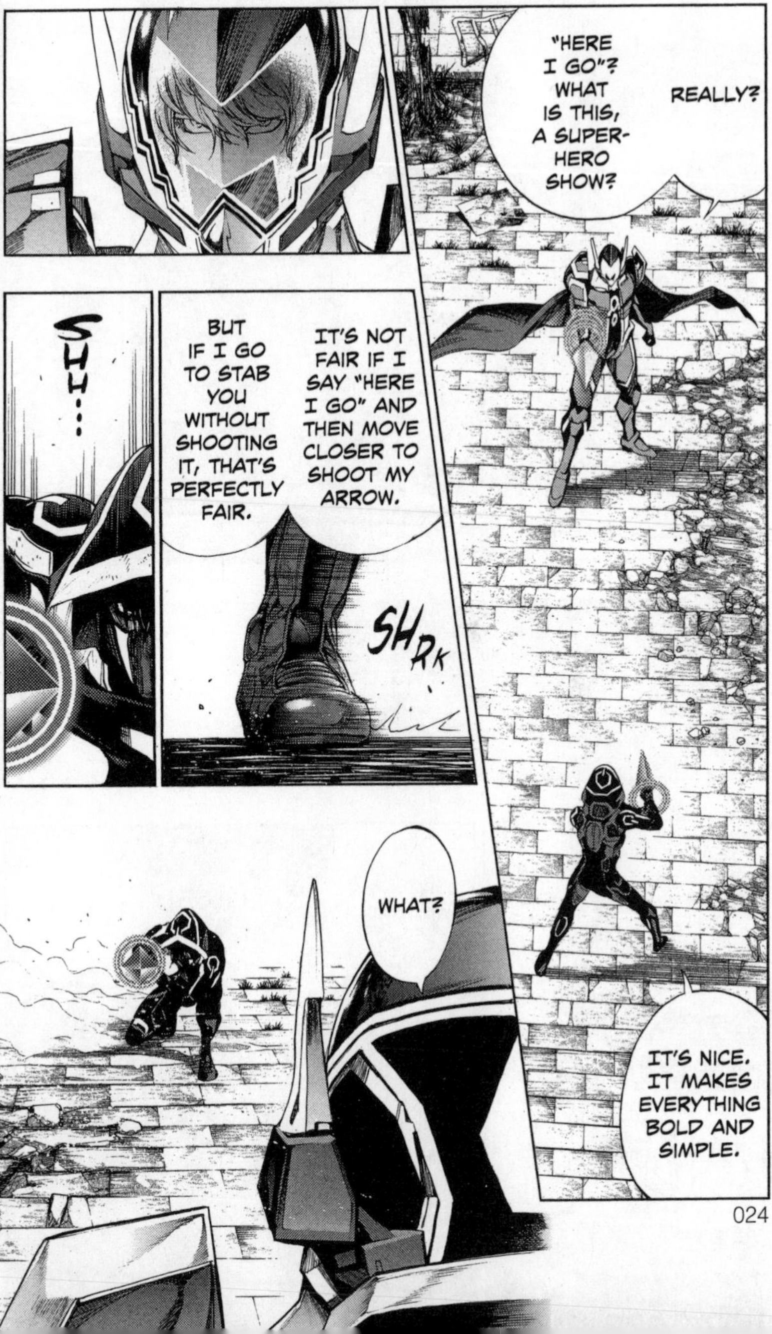
REALLY?
"HERE I GO"? WHAT IS THIS, A SUPER-HERO SHOW?
IT'S NICE. IT MAKES EVERYTHING BOLD AND SIMPLE.
IT'S NOT FAIR IF I SAY "HERE I GO" AND THEN MOVE CLOSER TO SHOOT MY ARROW.
BUT IF I GO TO STAB YOU WITHOUT SHOOTING IT, THAT'S PERFECTLY FAIR.
SHRK
SHH...
WHAT?

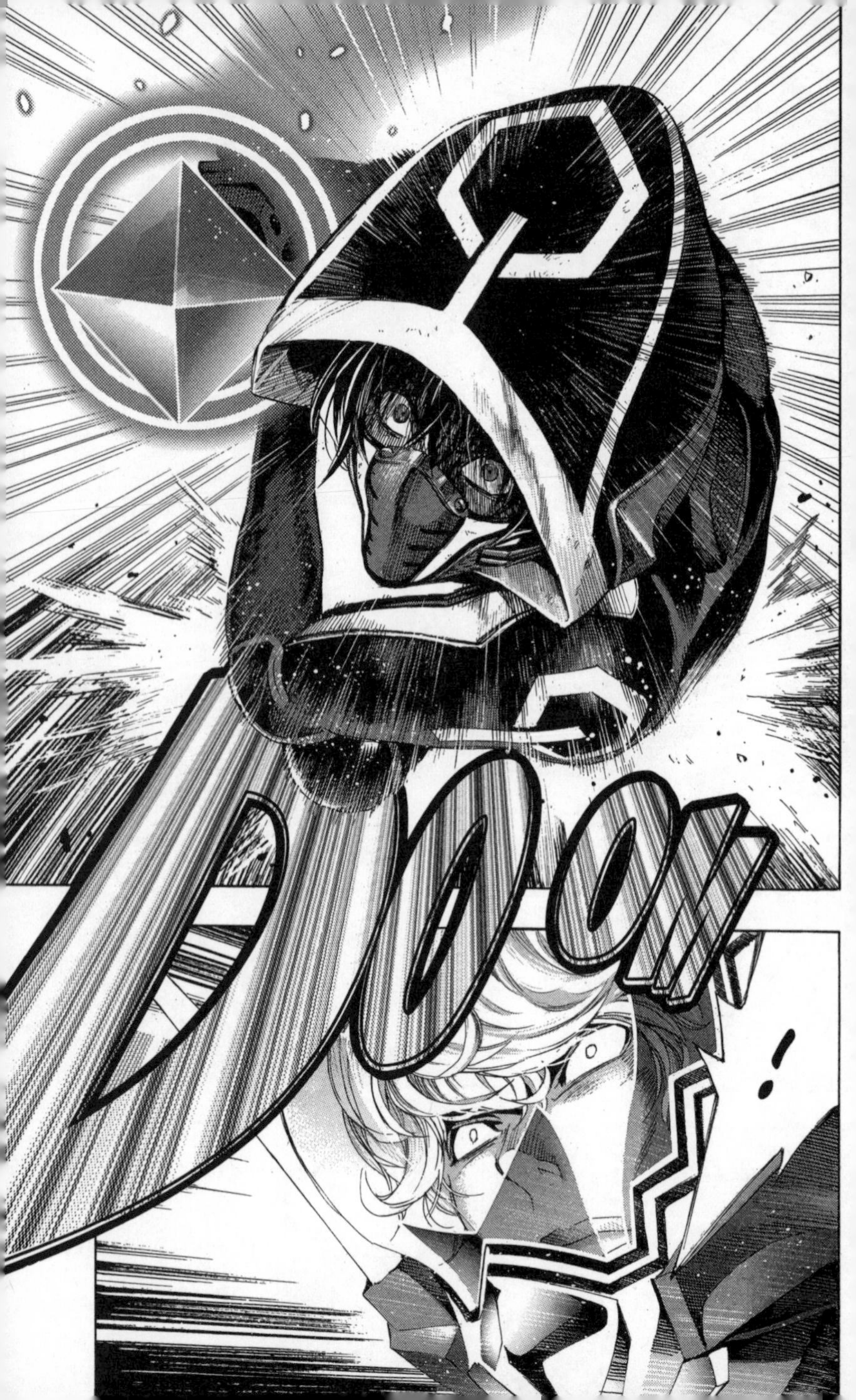

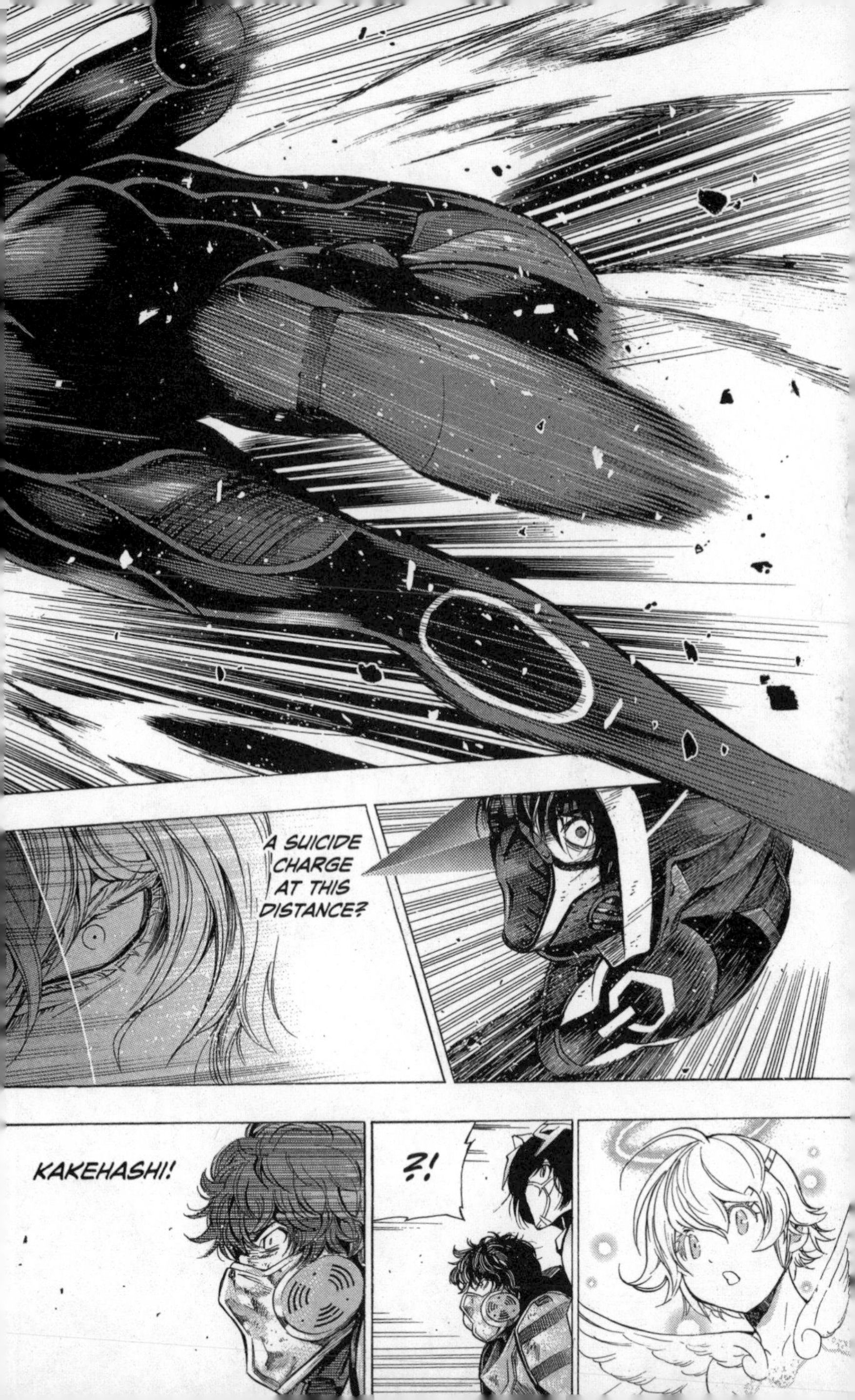
A SUICIDE CHARGE AT THIS DISTANCE?
?!
KAKEHASHI!

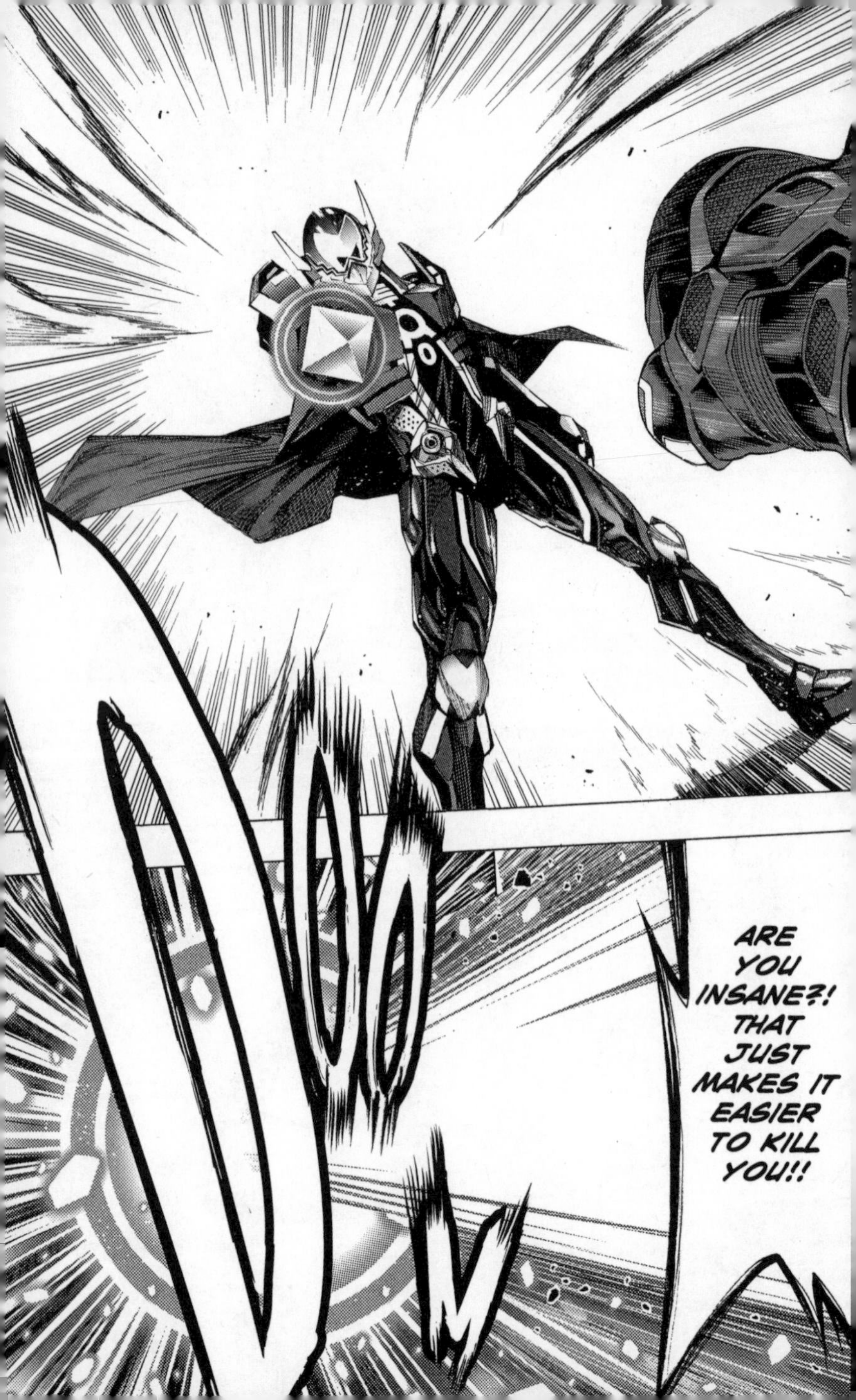
ARE YOU INSANE?! THAT JUST MAKES IT EASIER TO KILL YOU!!

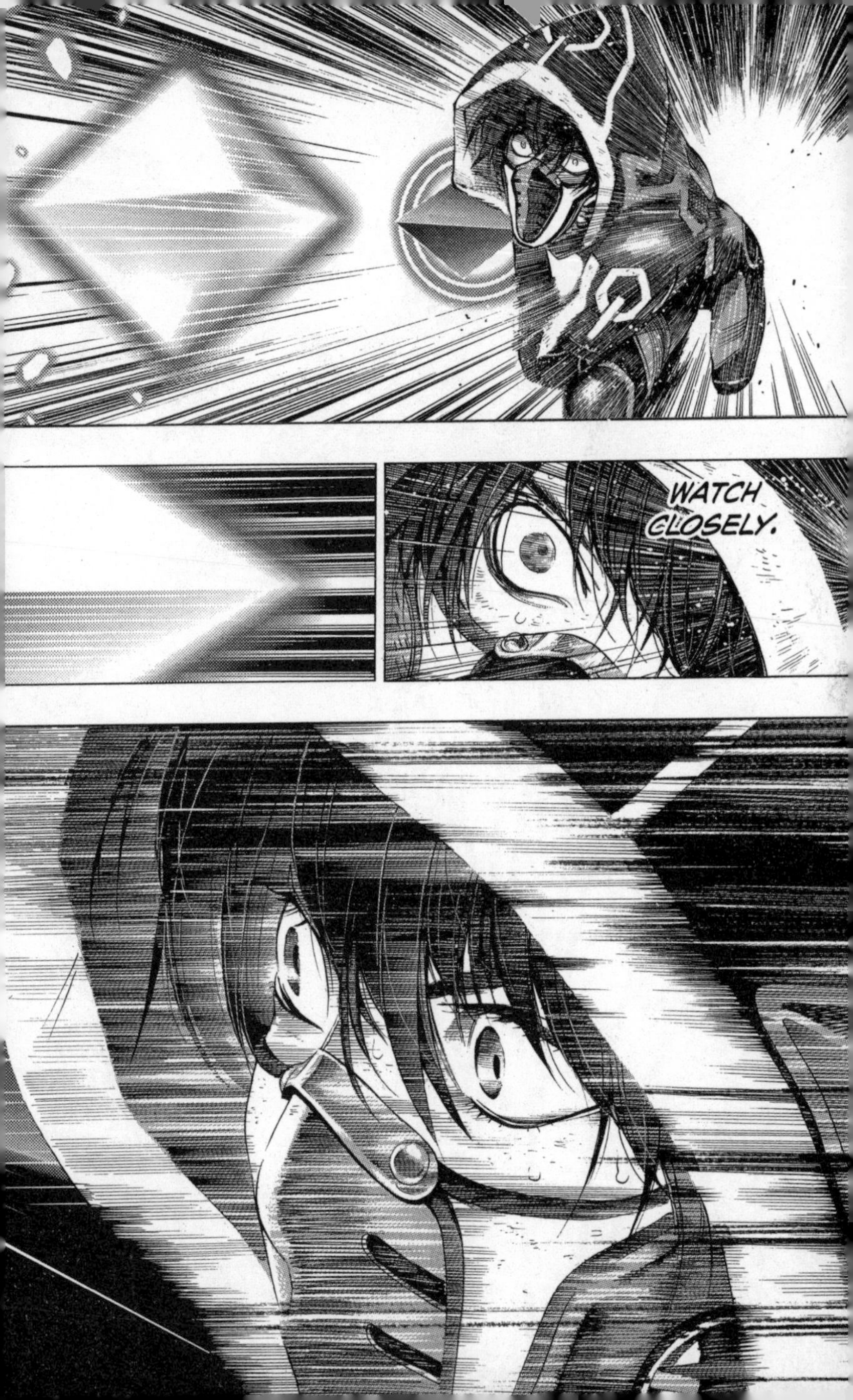
WATCH CLOSELY.

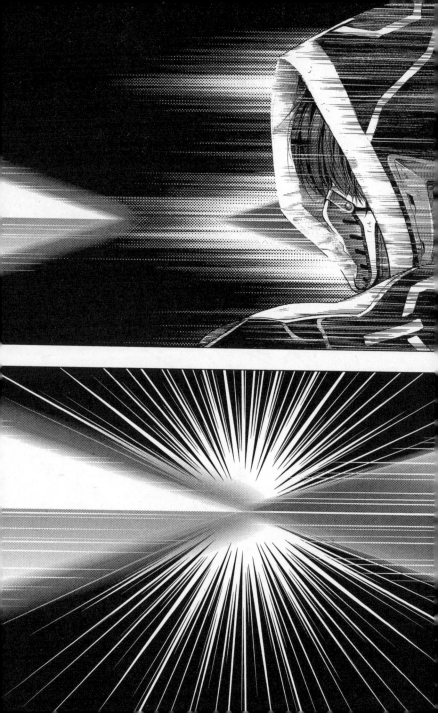

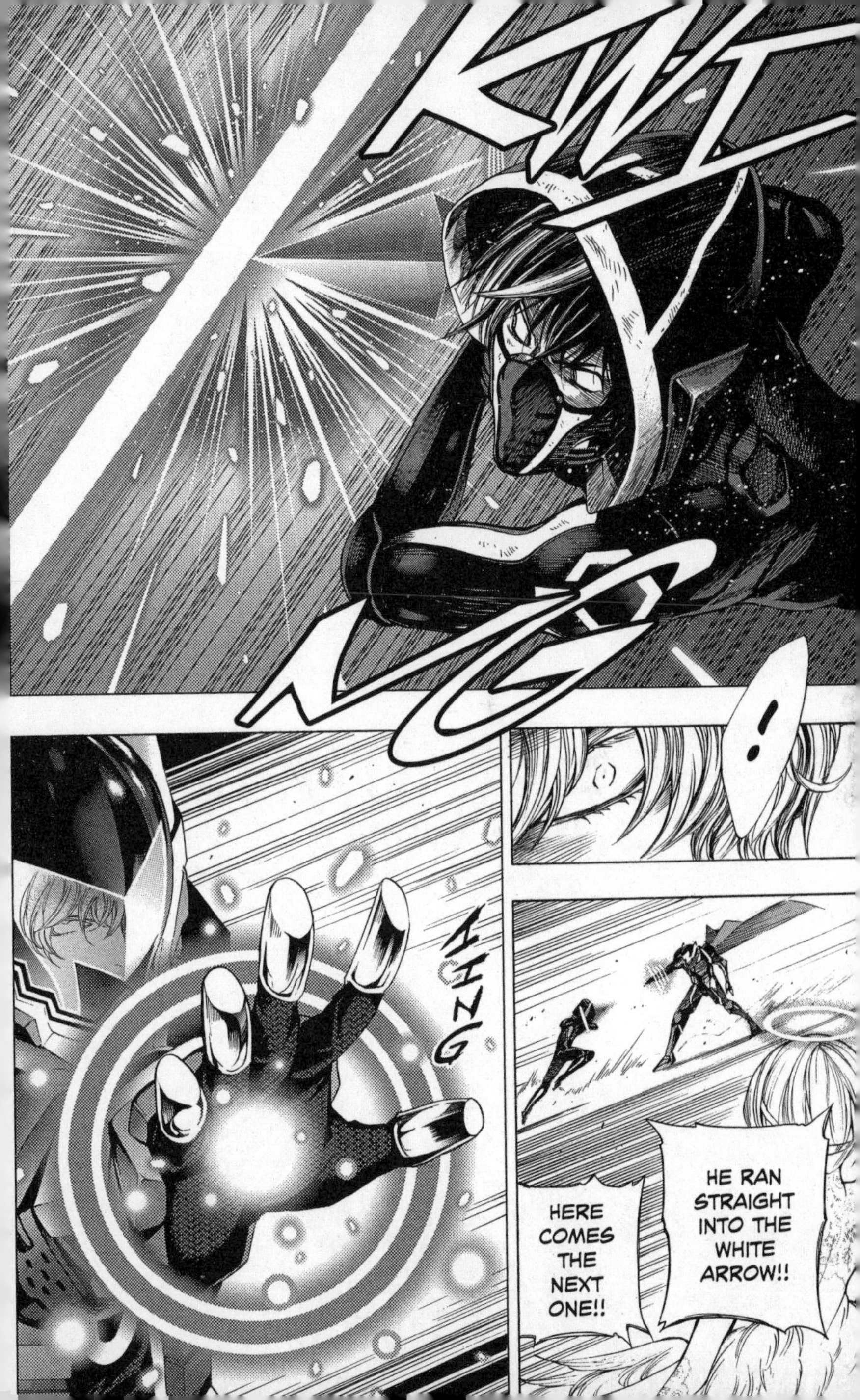
!
HE RAN STRAIGHT INTO THE WHITE ARROW!!
HERE COMES THE NEXT ONE!!

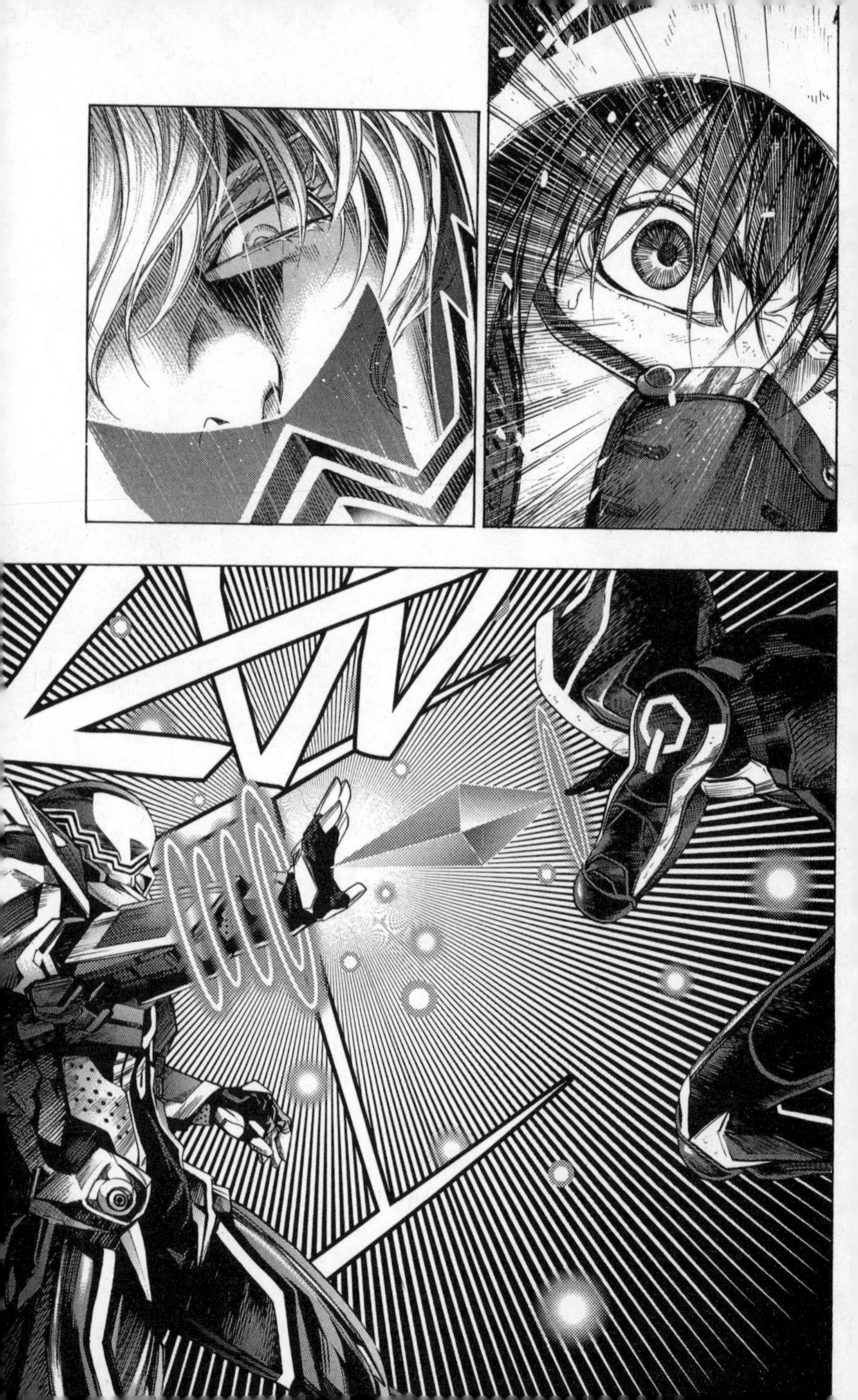

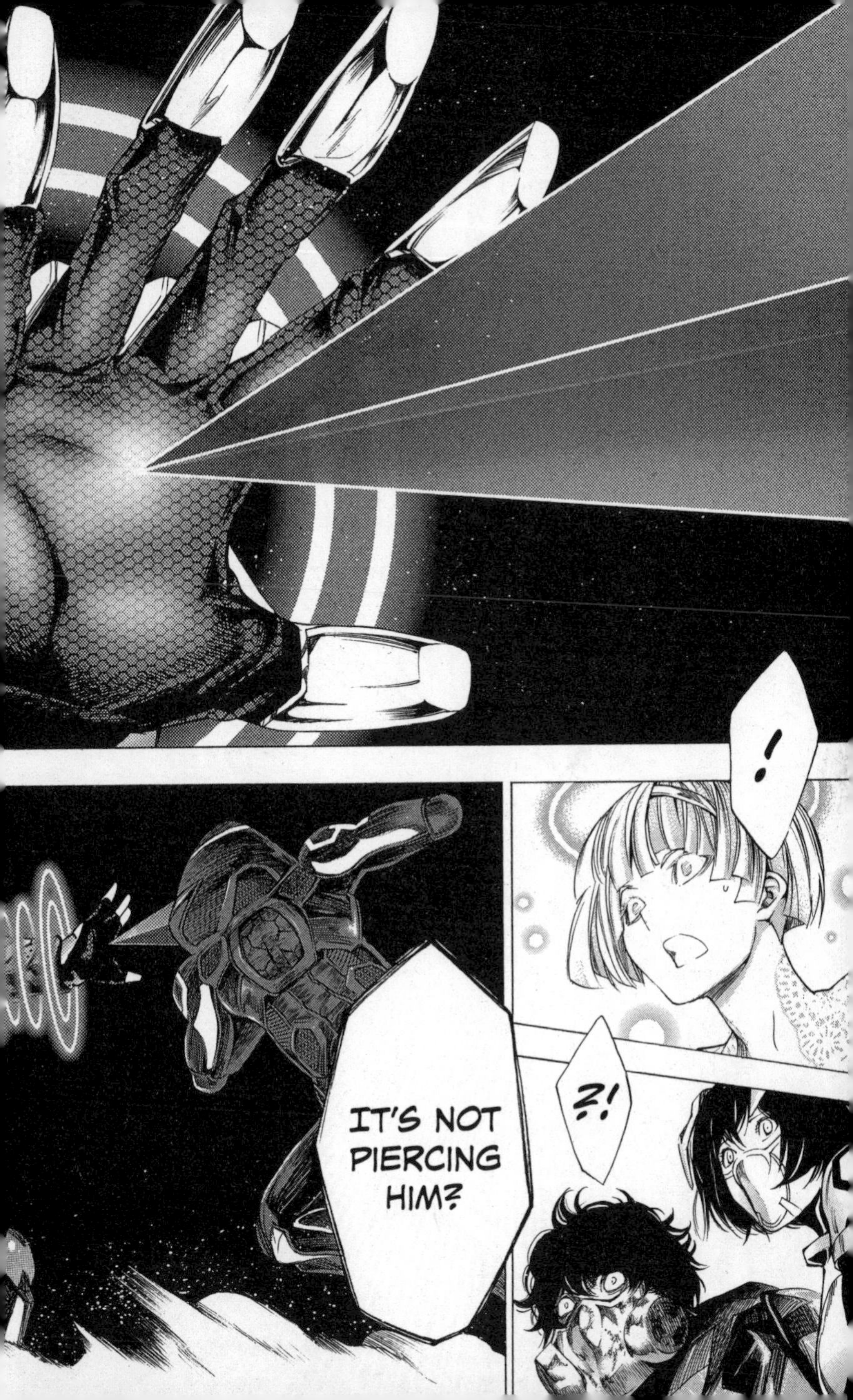
!
?!
IT'S NOT PIERCING HIM?

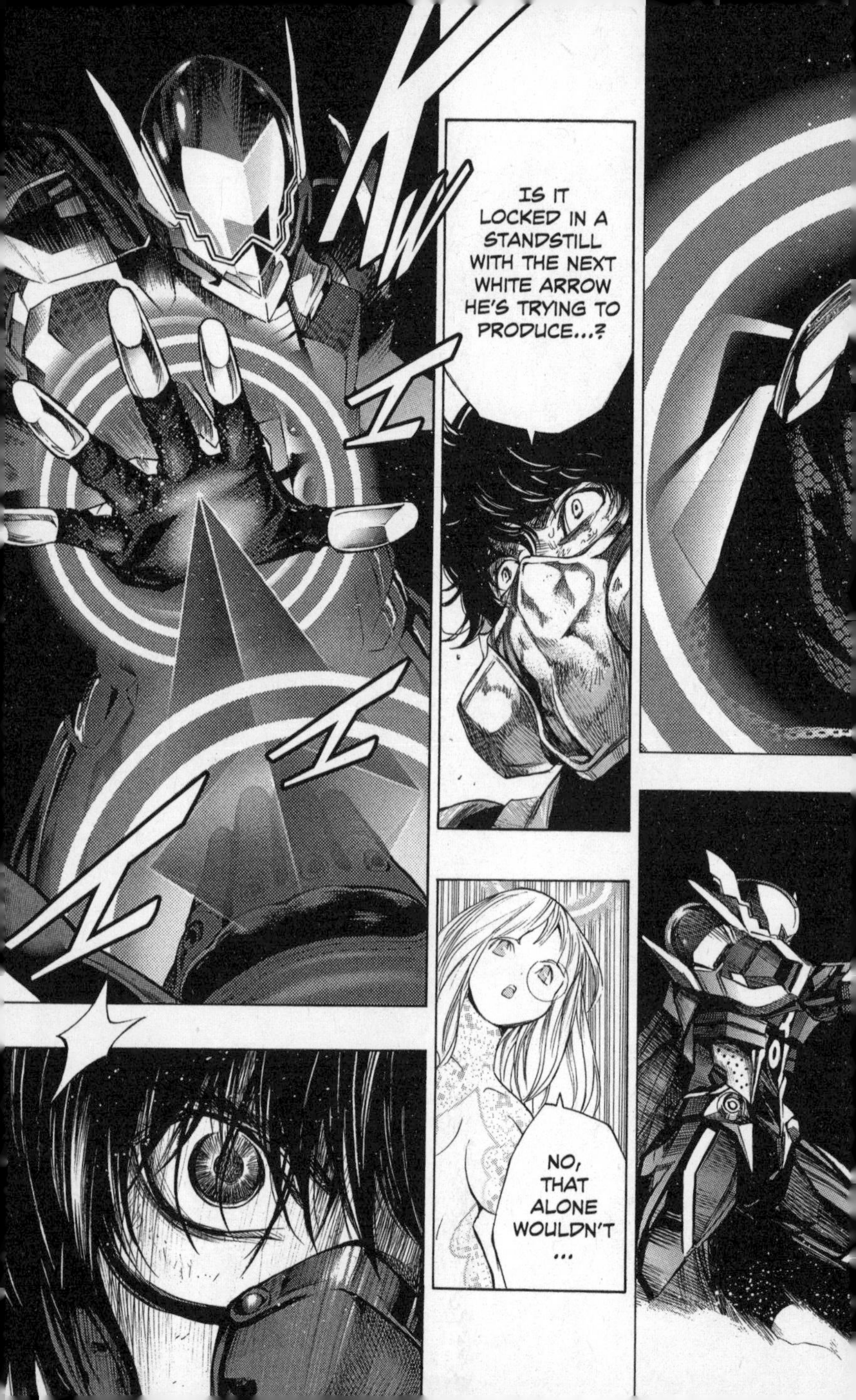
IS IT LOCKED IN A STANDSTILL WITH THE NEXT WHITE ARROW HE'S TRYING TO PRODUCE...?
NO, THAT ALONE WOULDN'T ...

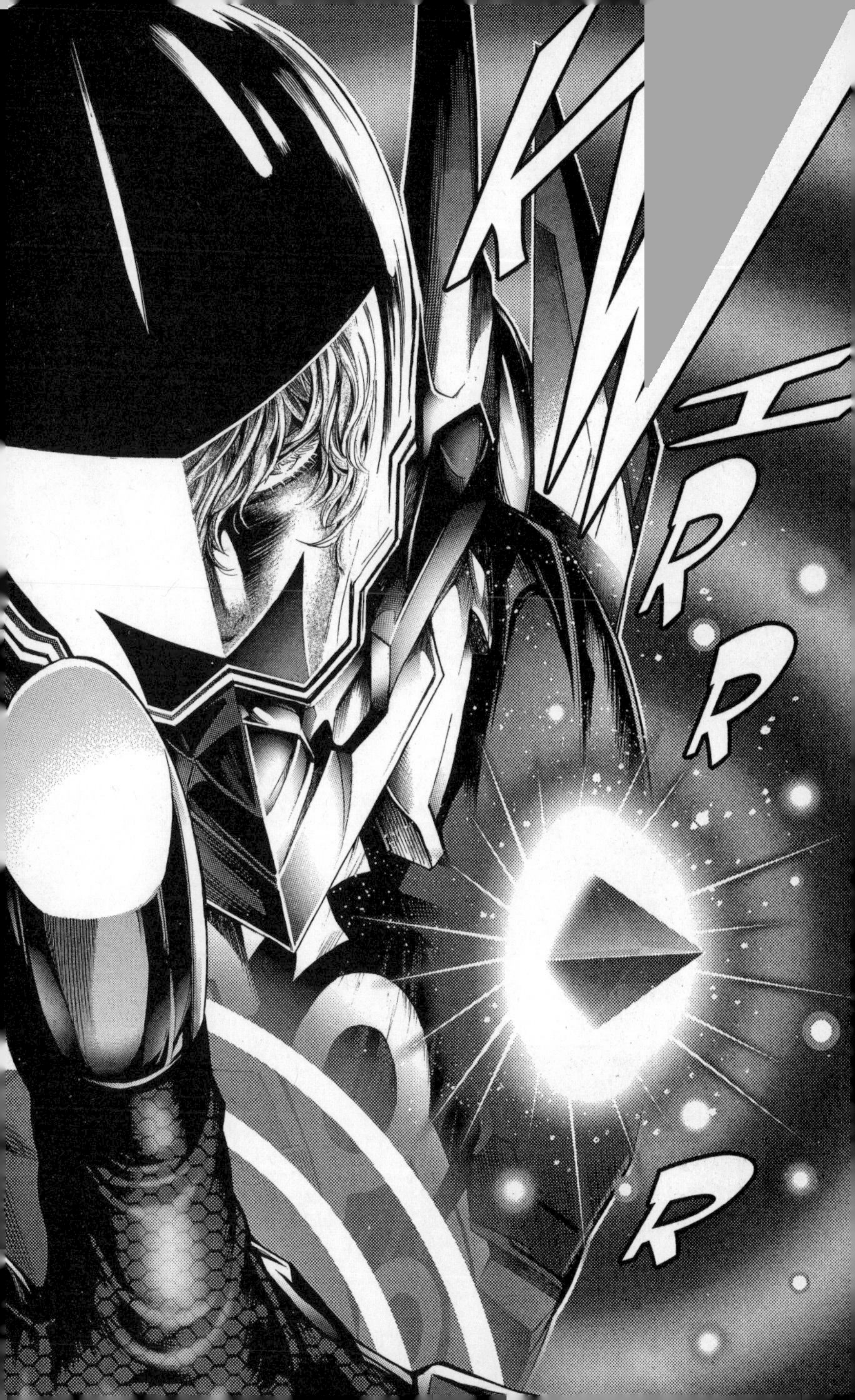
KWIRRR

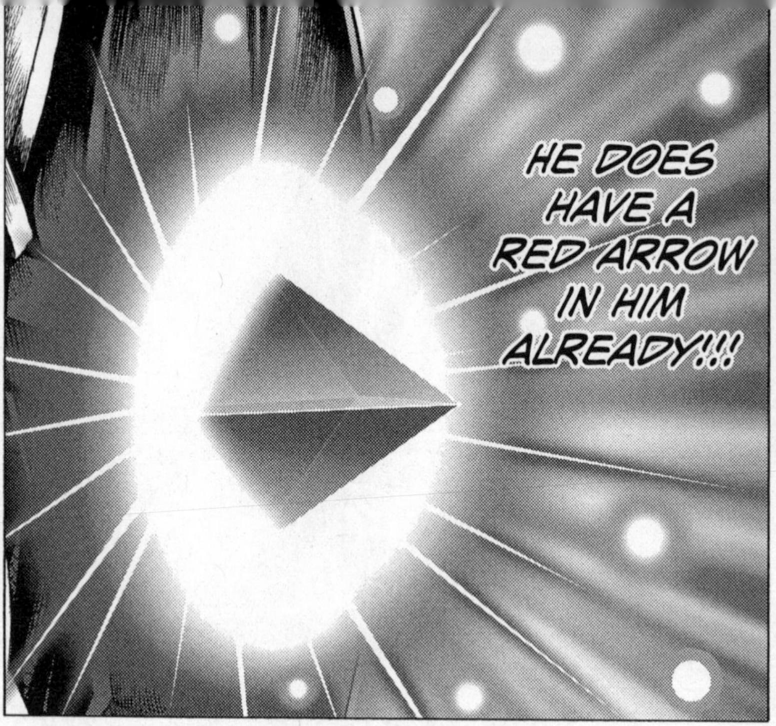
HE DOES HAVE A RED ARROW IN HIM ALREADY!!!

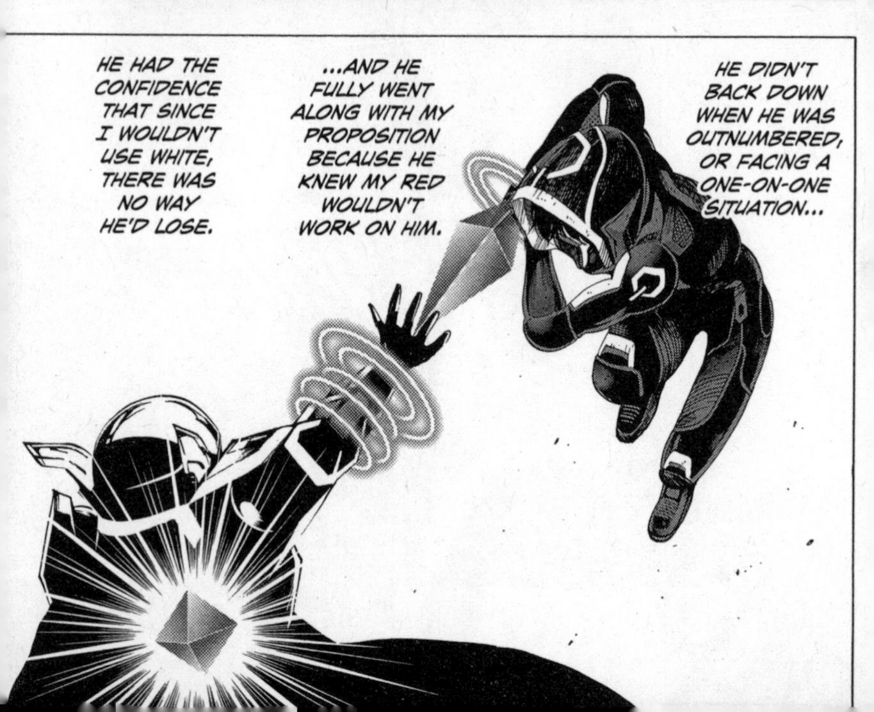
HE DIDN'T BACK DOWN WHEN HE WAS OUTNUMBERED, OR FACING A ONE-ON-ONE SITUATION...
...AND HE FULLY WENT ALONG WITH MY PROPOSITION BECAUSE HE KNEW MY RED WOULDN'T WORK ON HIM.
HE HAD THE CONFIDENCE THAT SINCE I WOULDN'T USE WHITE, THERE WAS NO WAY HE'D LOSE.

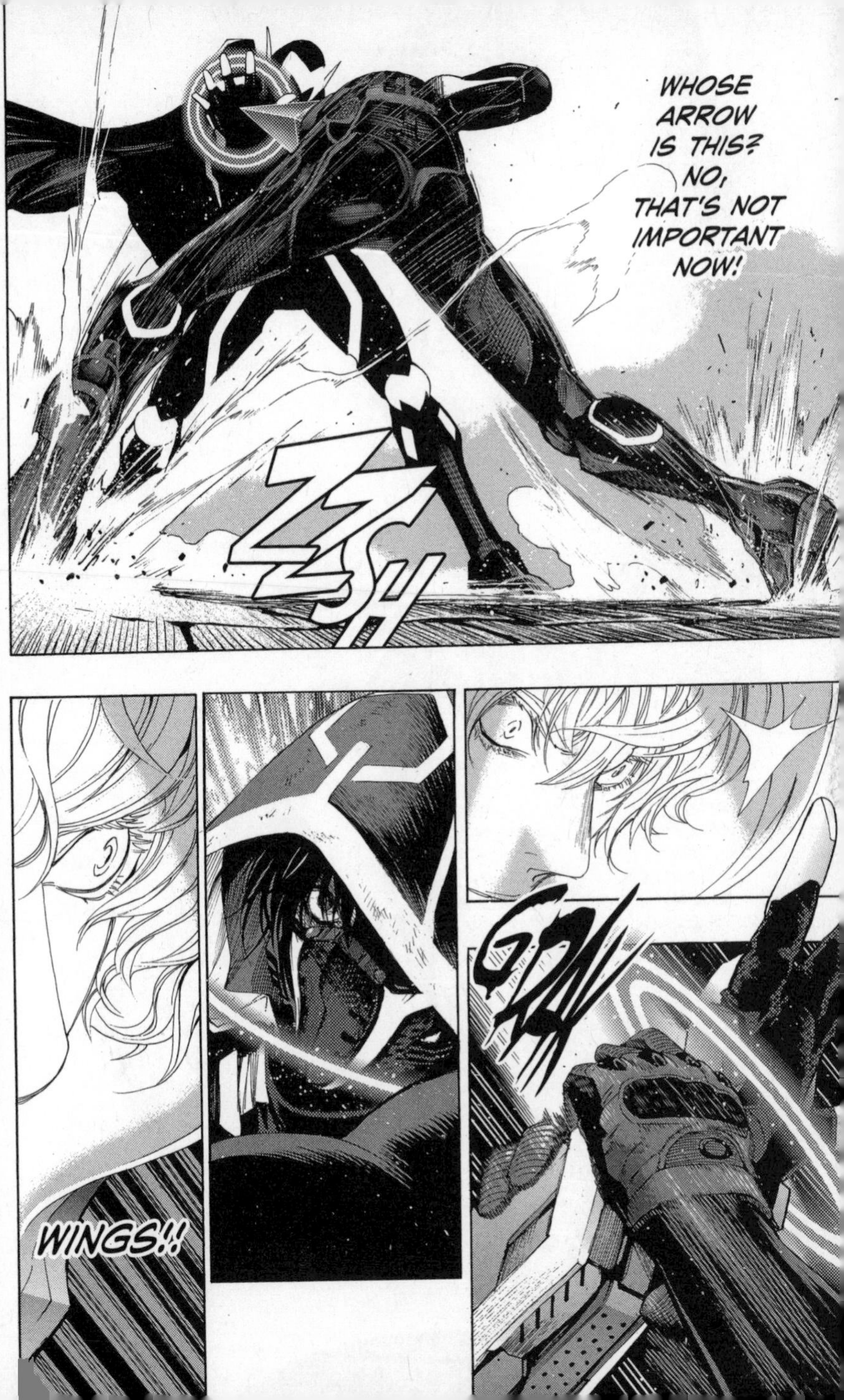
WHOSE ARROW IS THIS? NO, THAT'S NOT IMPORTANT NOW!
ZZSH
WINGS!!

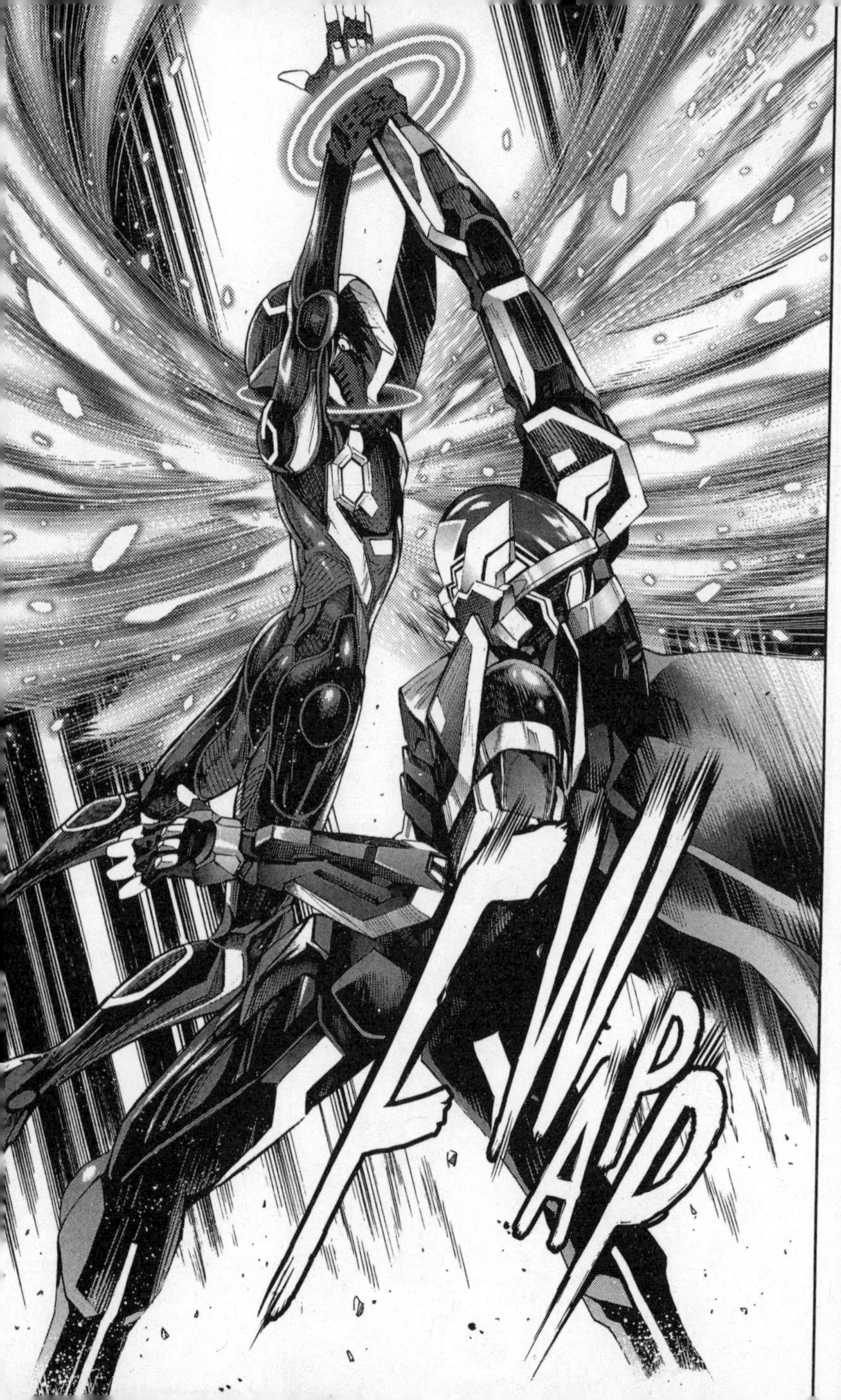

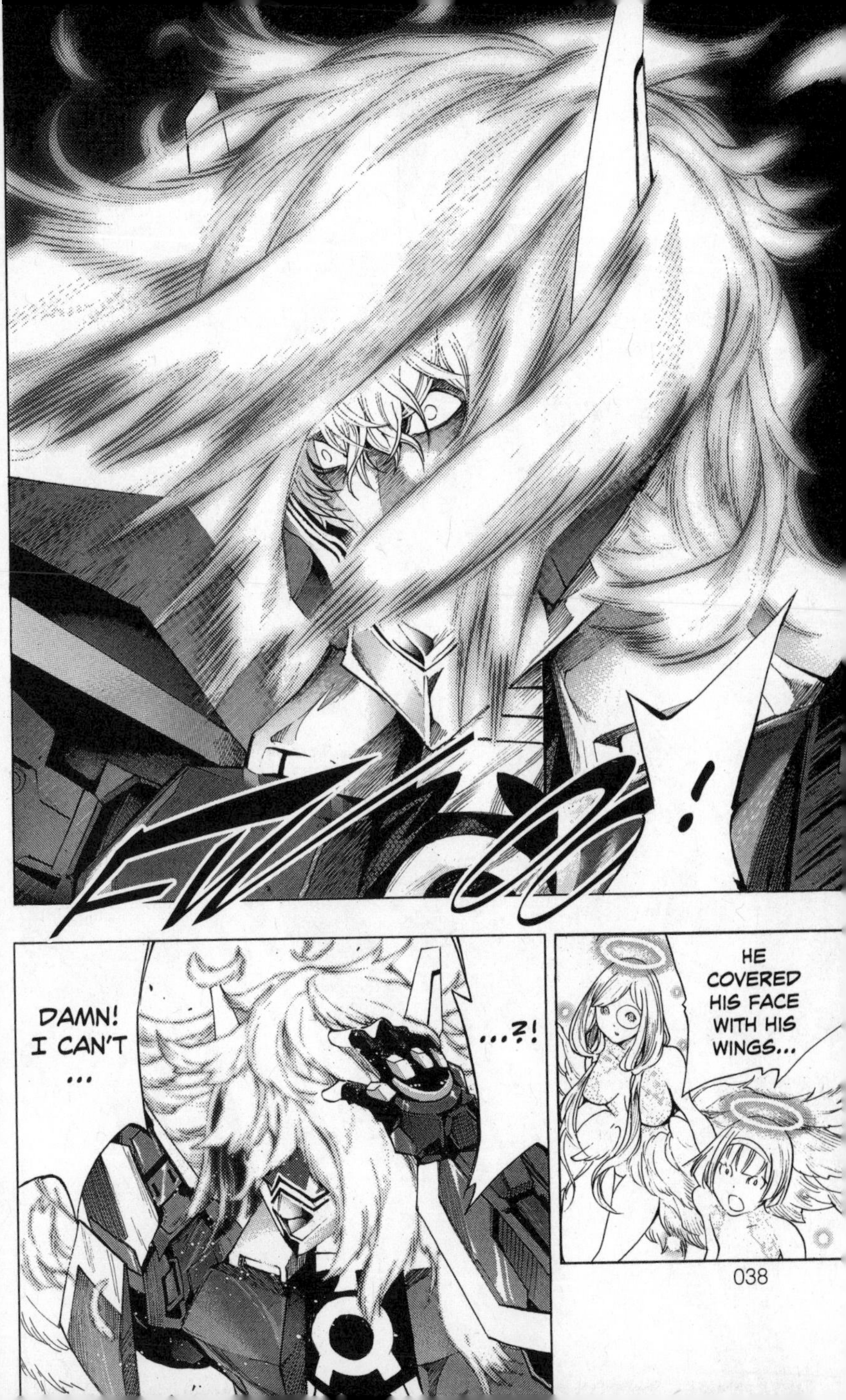
FWOOO
!
HE COVERED HIS FACE WITH HIS WINGS...
...?!
DAMN! I CAN'T ...

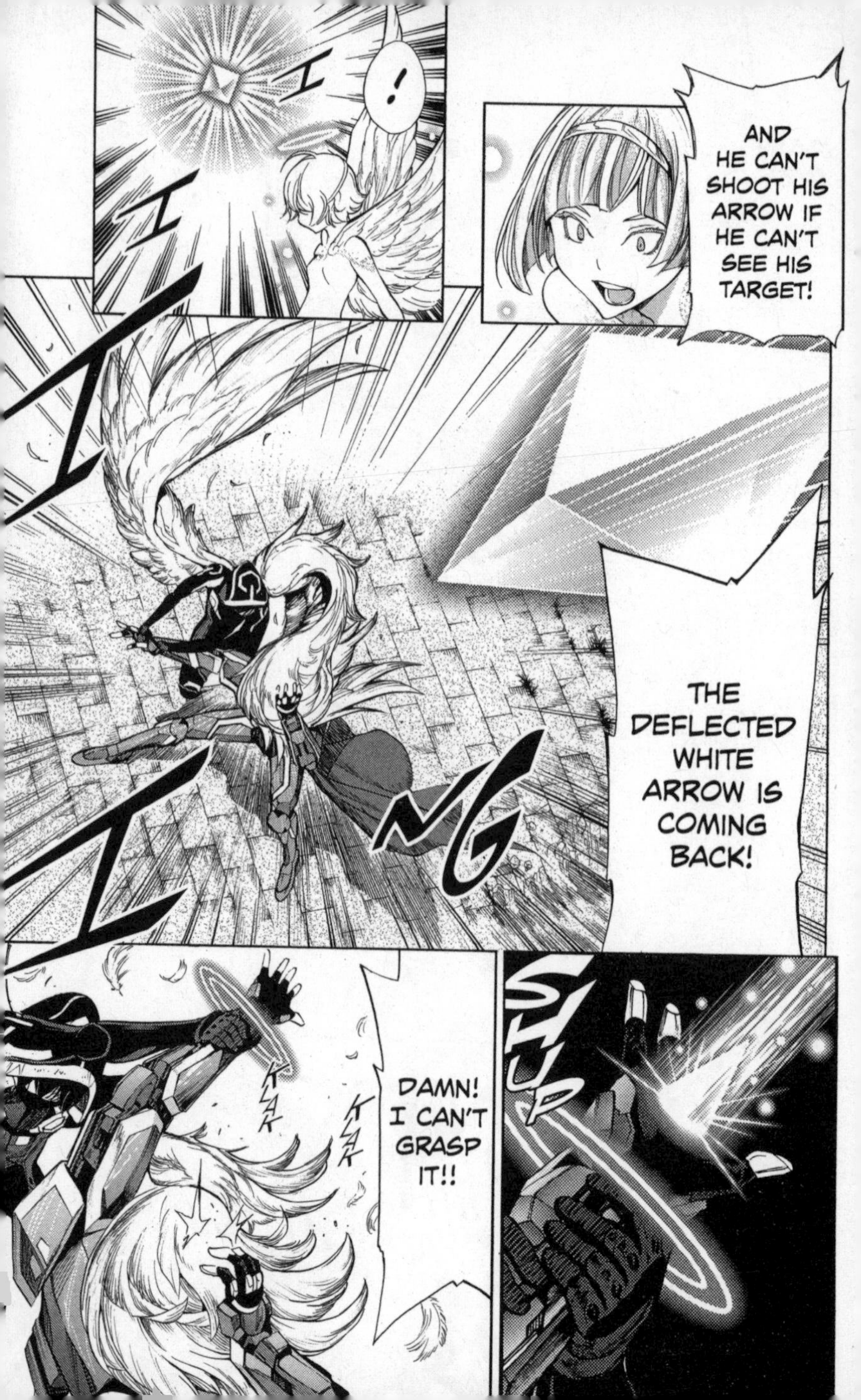
AND HE CAN'T SHOOT HIS ARROW IF HE CAN'T SEE HIS TARGET!
!
THE DEFLECTED WHITE ARROW IS COMING BACK!
NG
SHUP
DAMN! I CAN'T GRASP IT!!
KLAK
KLAK

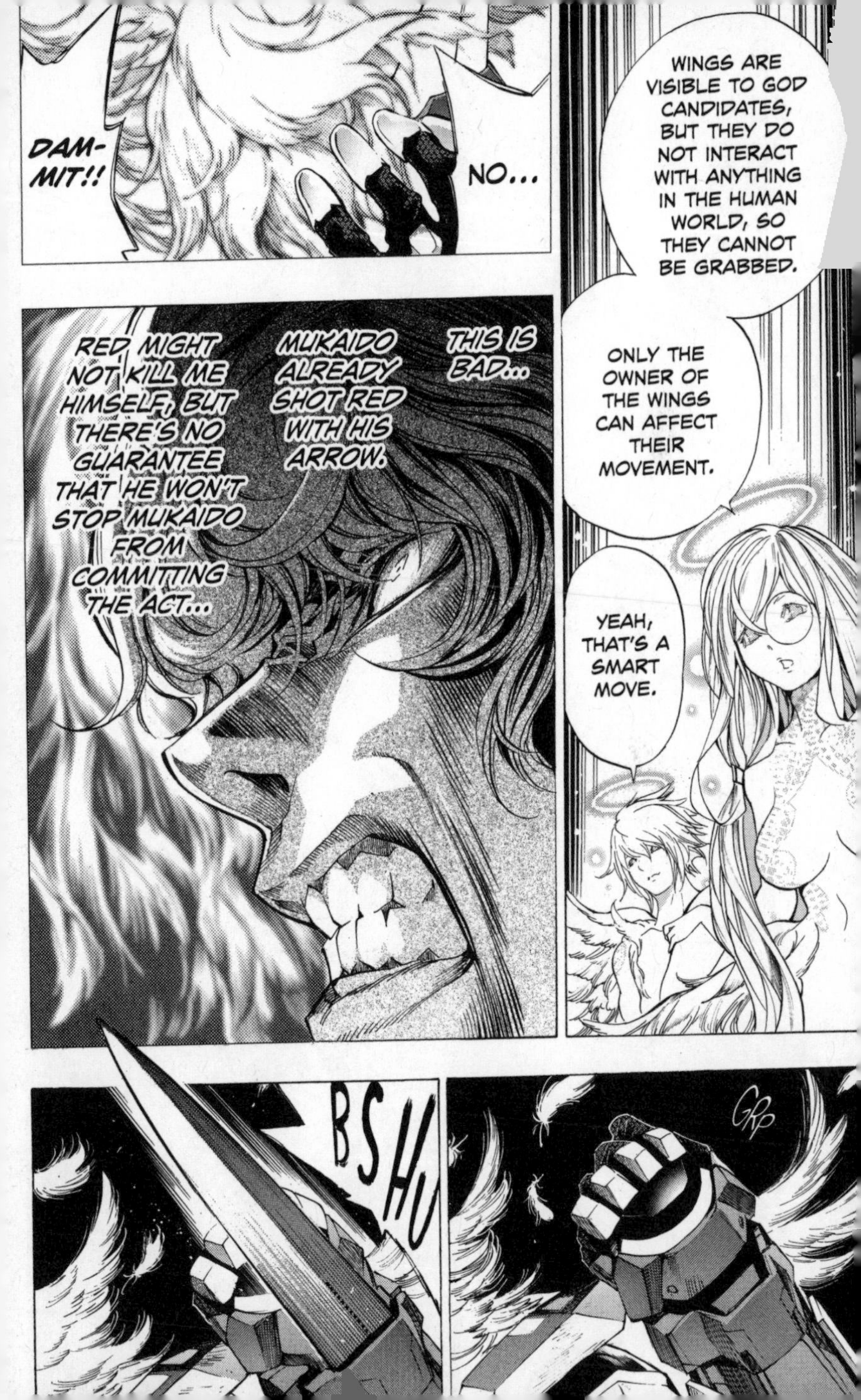
WINGS ARE VISIBLE TO GOD CANDIDATES, BUT THEY DO NOT INTERACT WITH ANYTHING IN THE HUMAN WORLD, SO THEY CANNOT BE GRABBED.
ONLY THE OWNER OF THE WINGS CAN AFFECT THEIR MOVEMENT.
YEAH, THAT'S A SMART MOVE.
NO...
DAM-MIT!!
THIS IS BAD...
MUKAIDO ALREADY SHOT RED WITH HIS ARROW.
RED MIGHT NOT KILL ME HIMSELF, BUT THERE'S NO GUARANTEE THAT HE WON'T STOP MUKAIDO FROM COMMITTING THE ACT...
GRP
BSHU

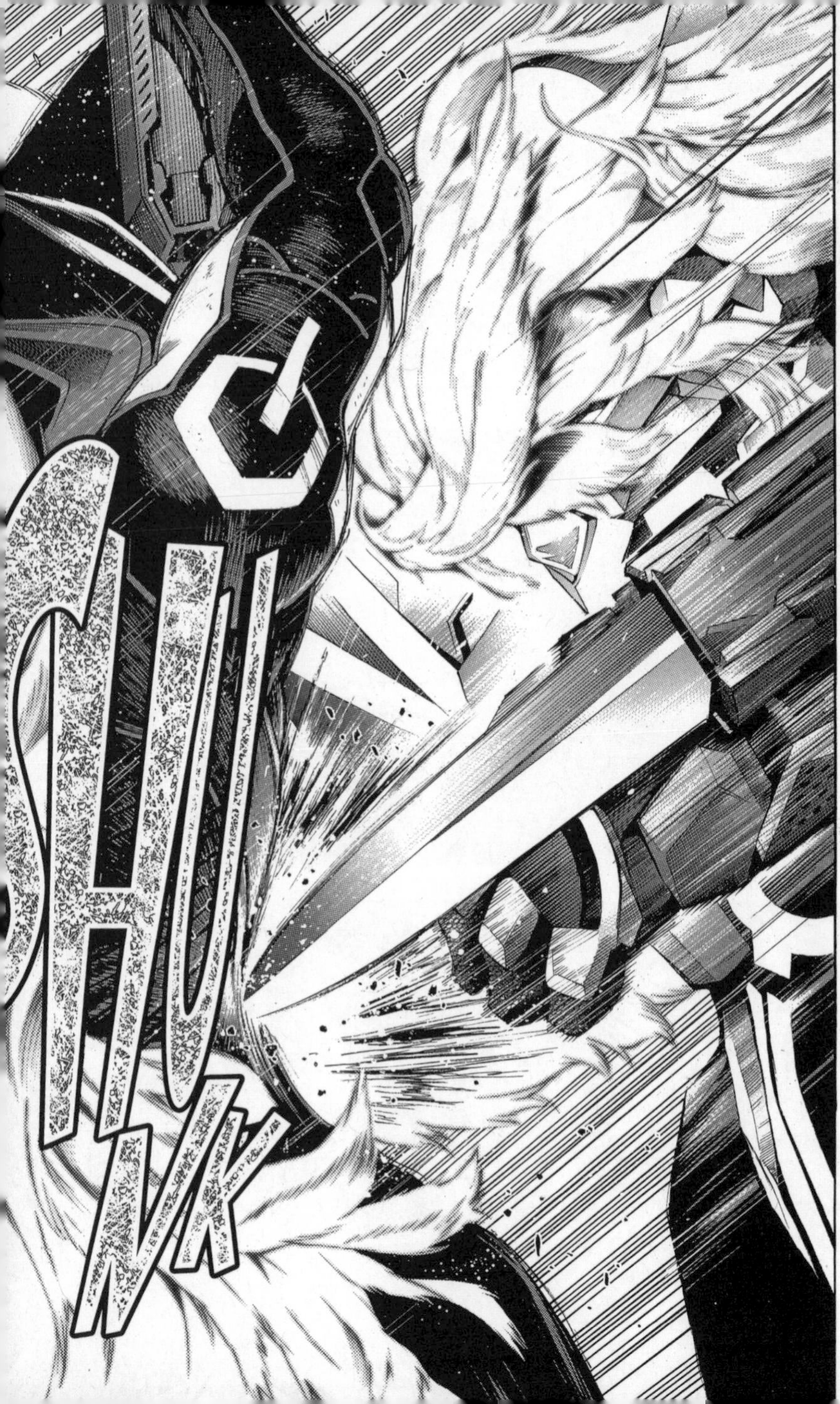
SHUNK

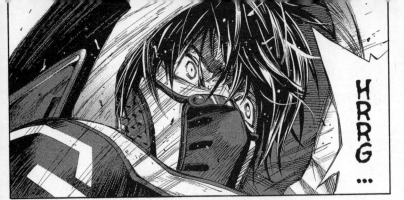

HRRG...

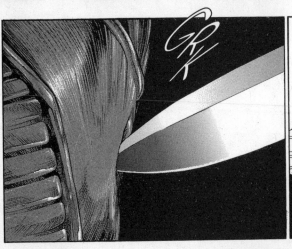

GRK

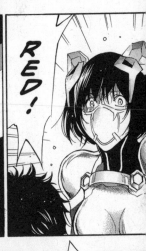

RED!

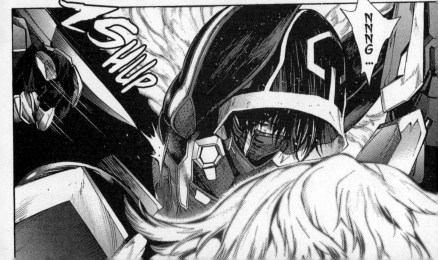

ZSHUP

NNNG...

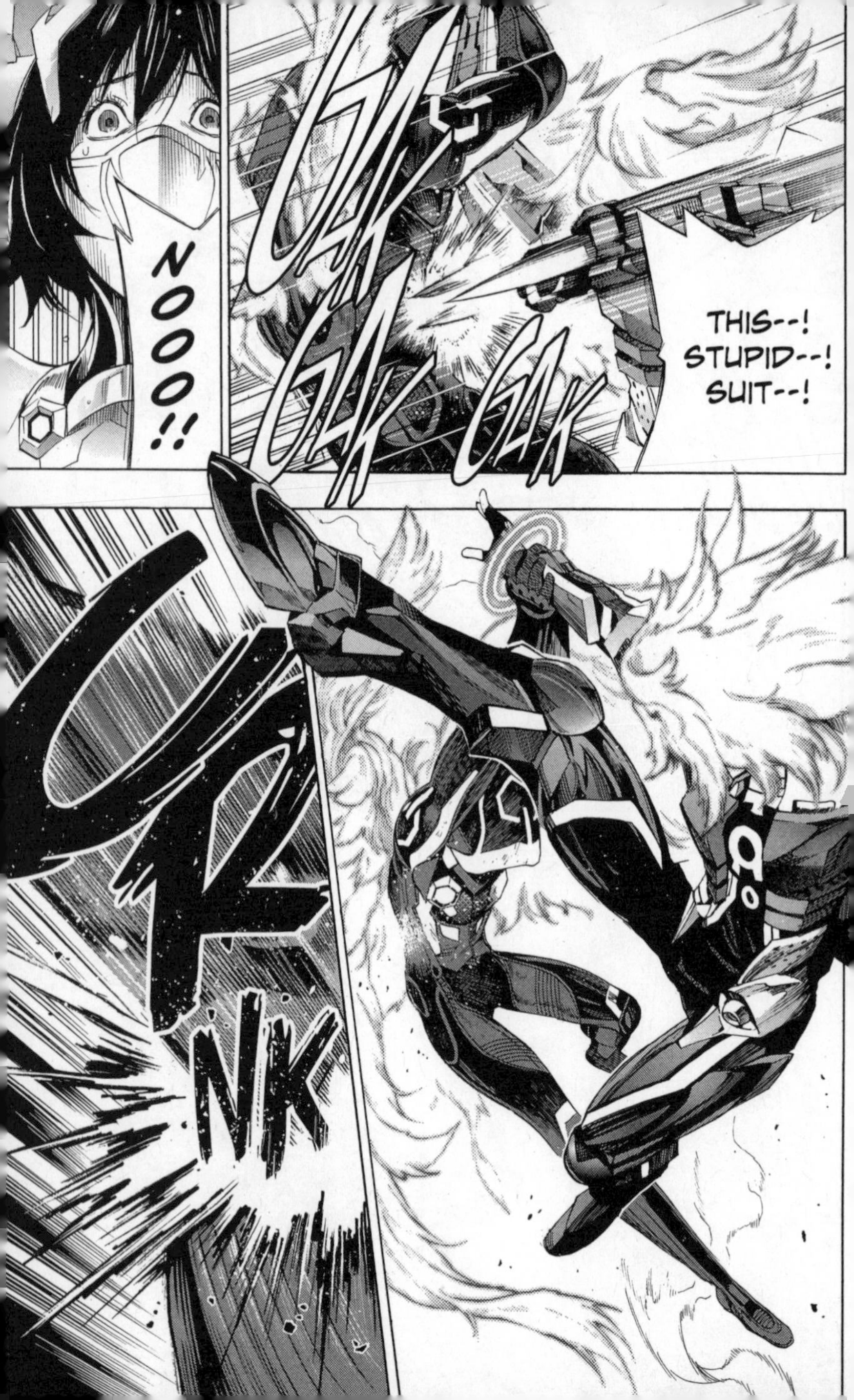
THIS--! STUPID--! SUIT--!
GAK GAK GAK
NOOOO!!

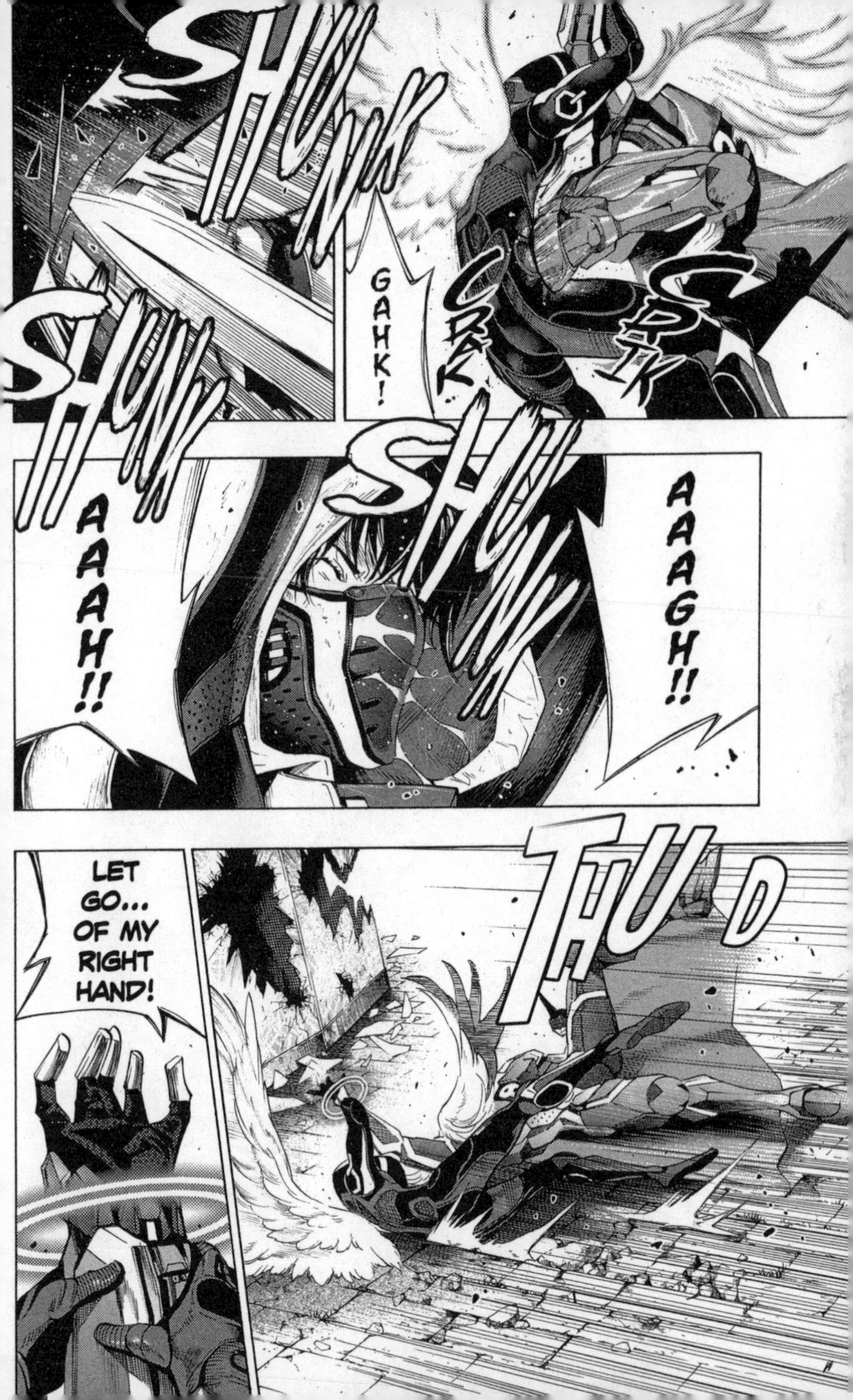

SRIK
CRIK
GAHK!
SHUNK
SHUNK
SHUNK
AAAAGH!!
AAAAH!!
THUD
LET GO... OF MY RIGHT HAND!

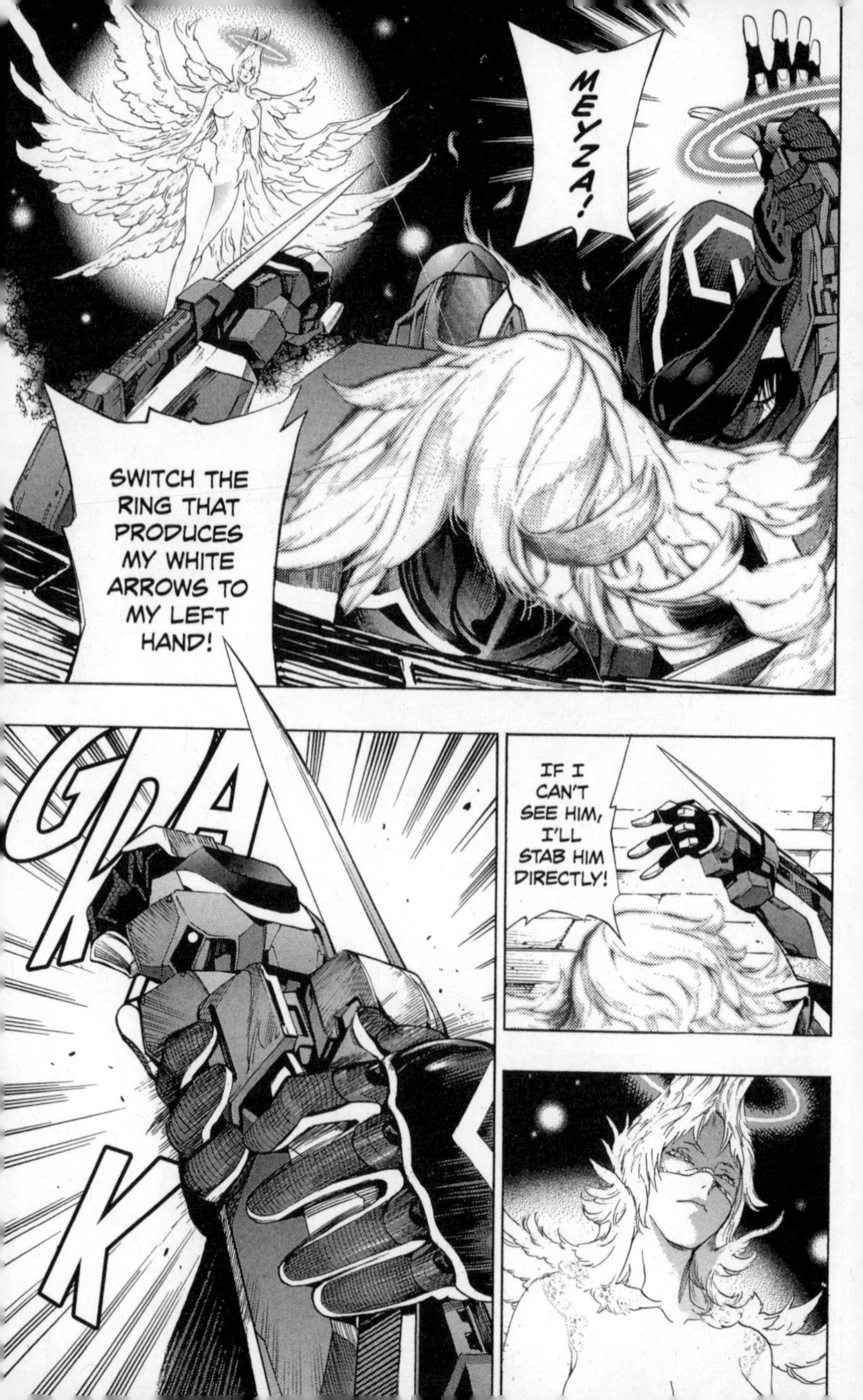
MEYZA!
SWITCH THE RING THAT PRODUCES MY WHITE ARROWS TO MY LEFT HAND!
IF I CAN'T SEE HIM, I'LL STAB HIM DIRECTLY!
GAK

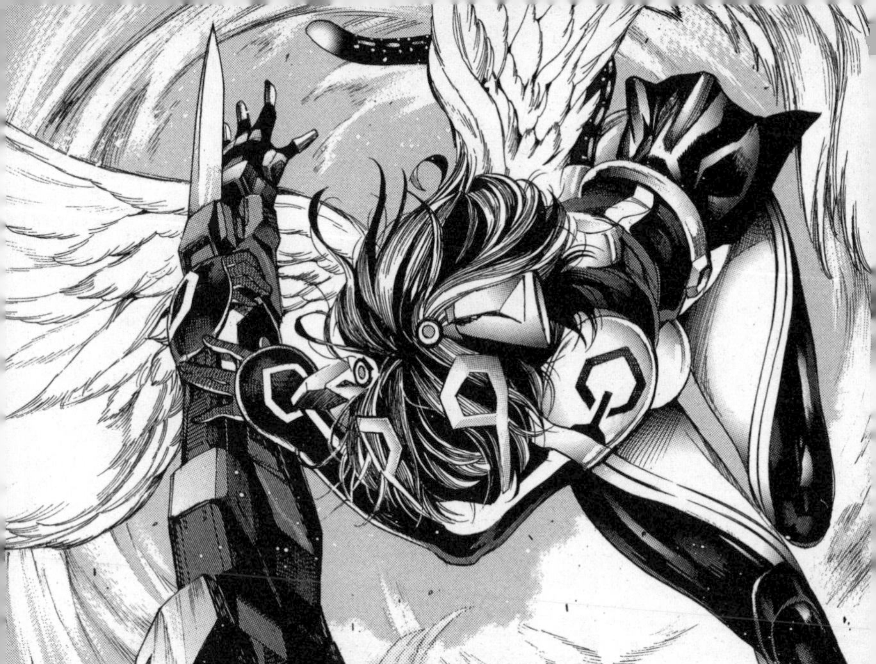

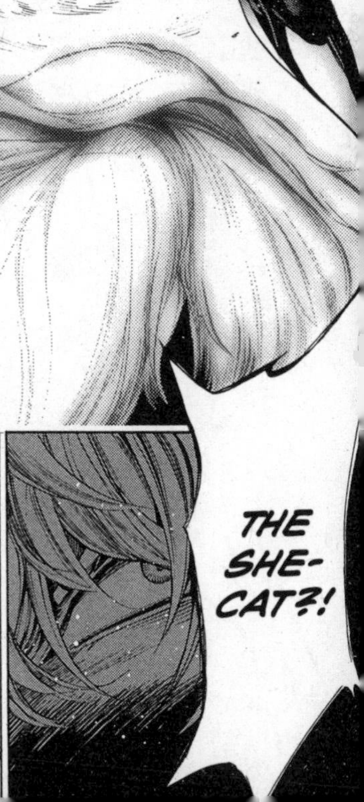
THE SHE-CAT?!

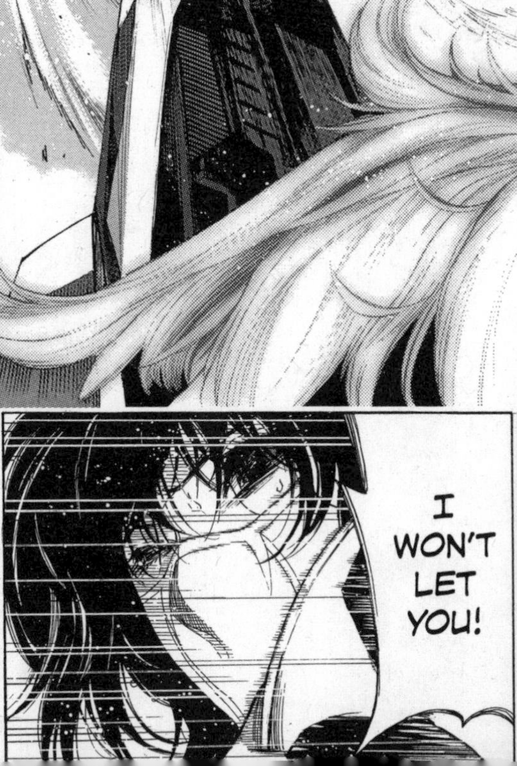
I WON'T LET YOU!

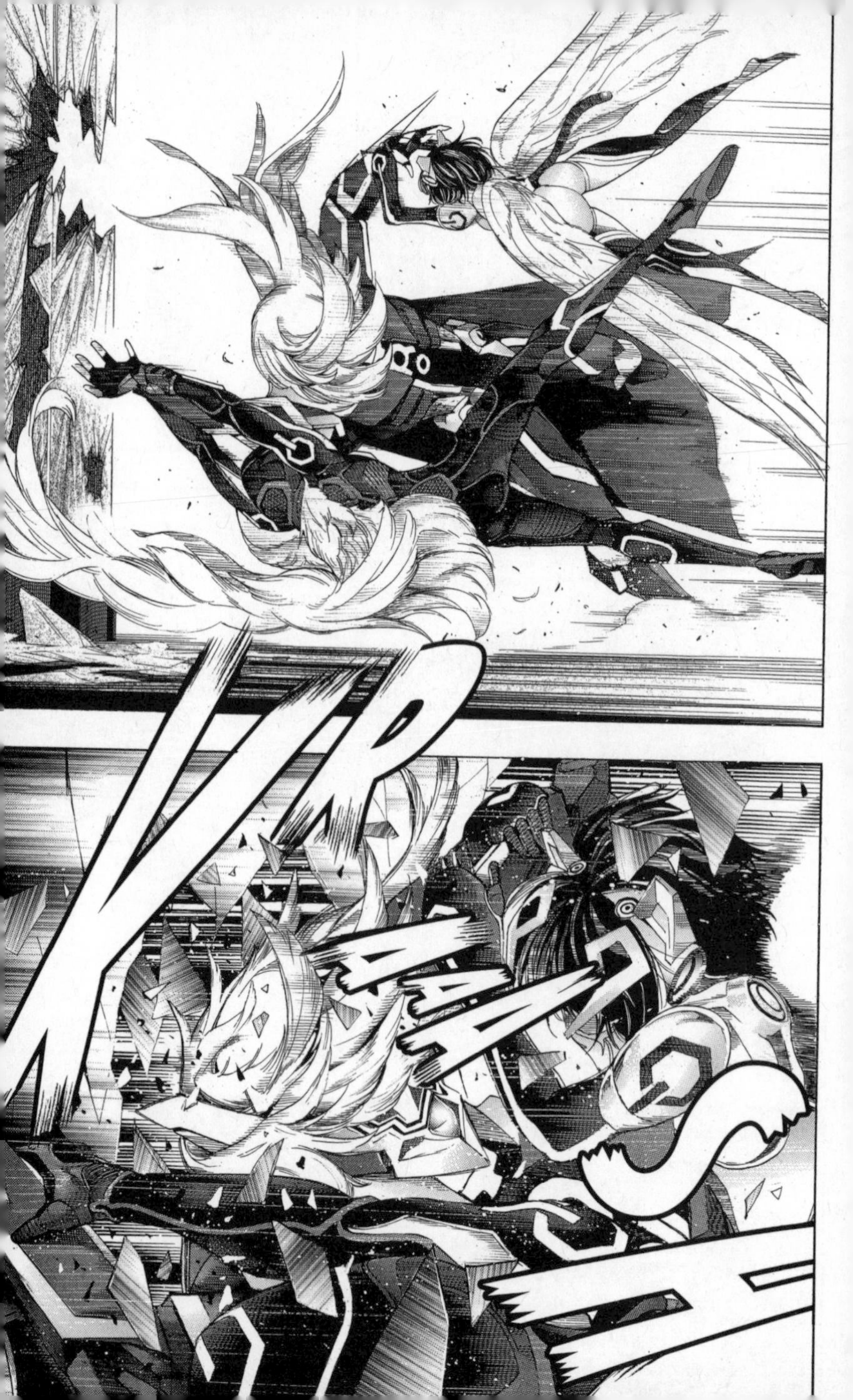
KRAAASH

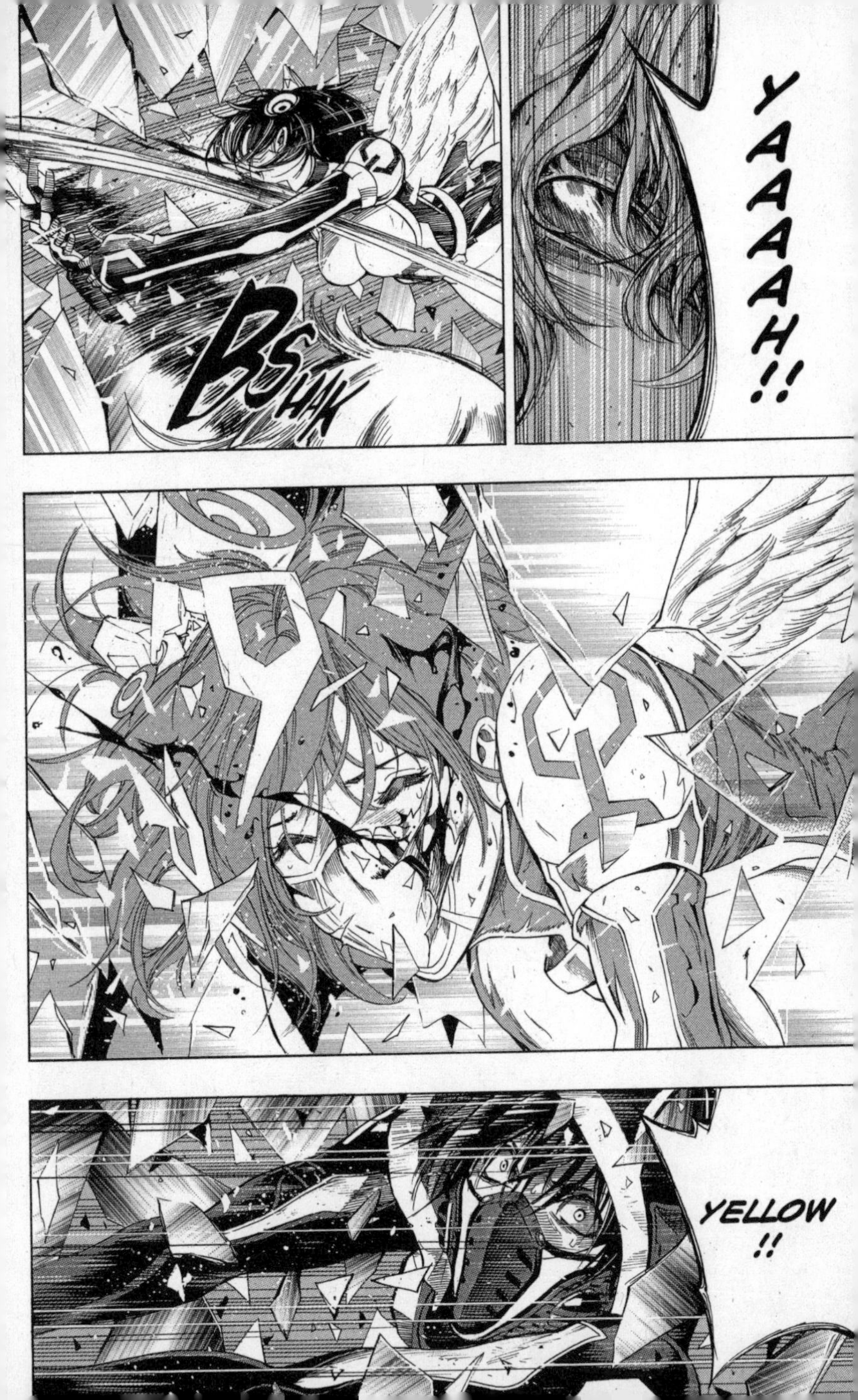
YAAAAAH!!
BSHAK
YELLOW !!

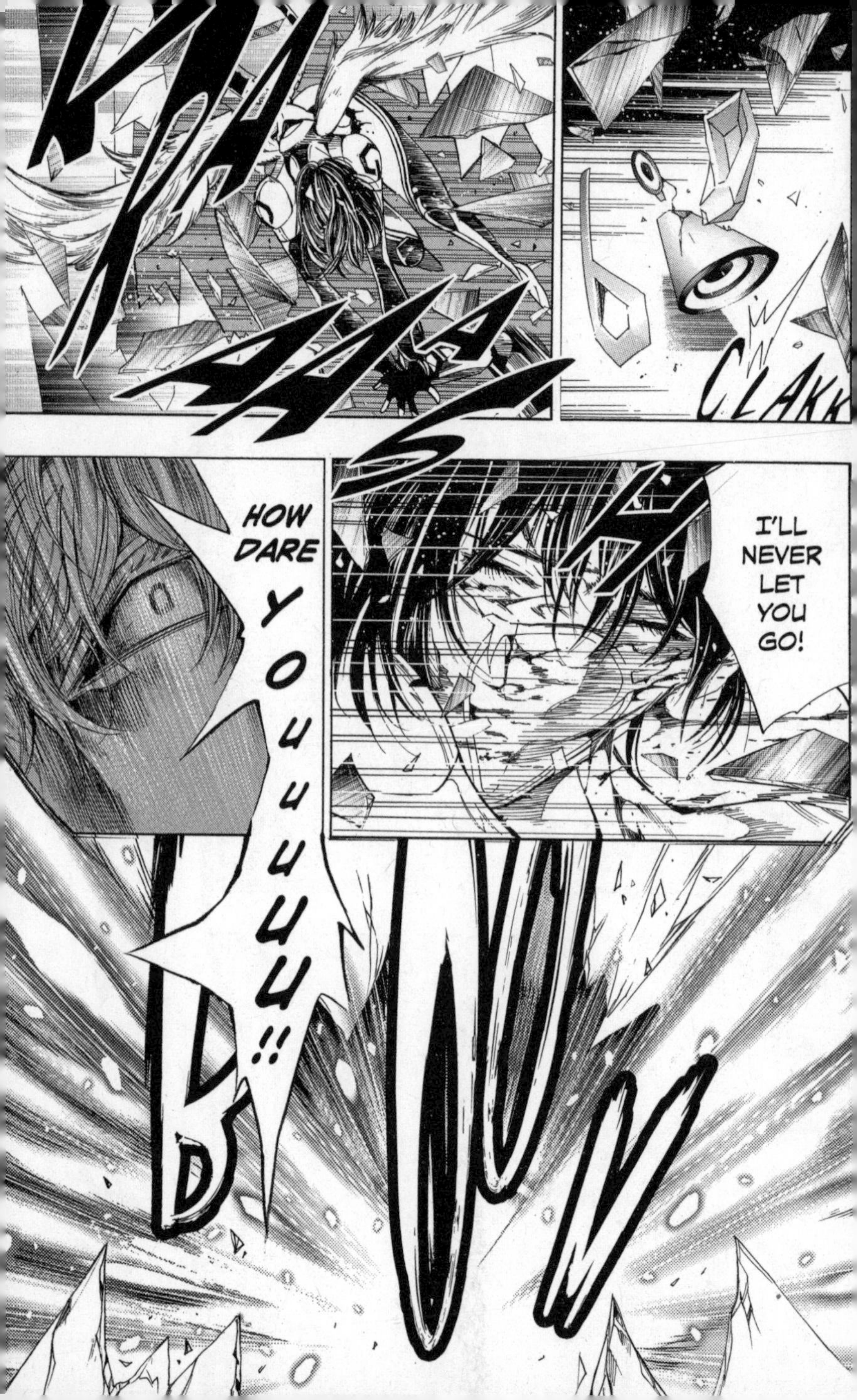
CLAKK
KYAAAHS
I'LL NEVER LET YOU GO!
HOW DARE YOUUUUUU!!

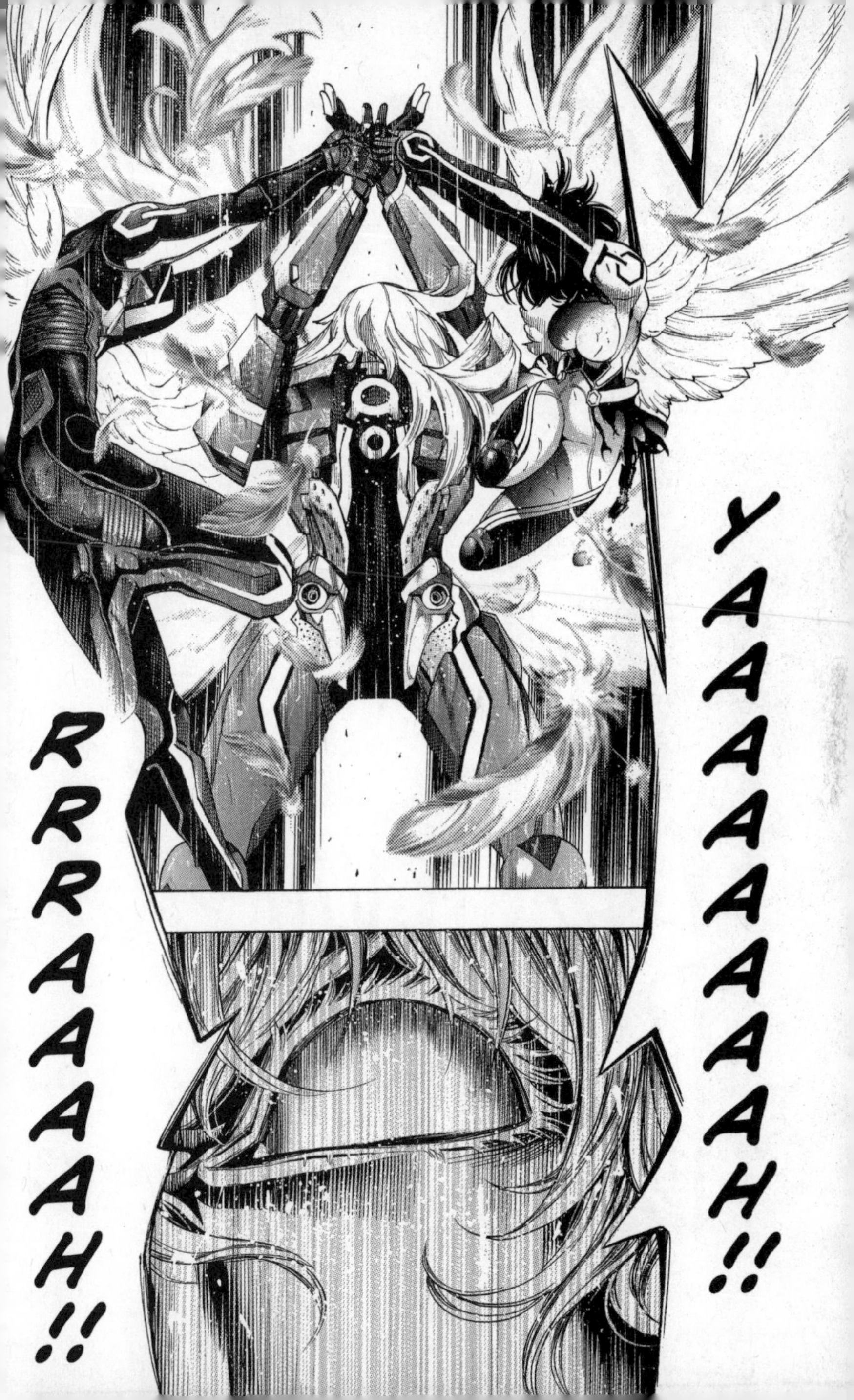
YAAAAAAAAH!!
RRRAAAAH!!

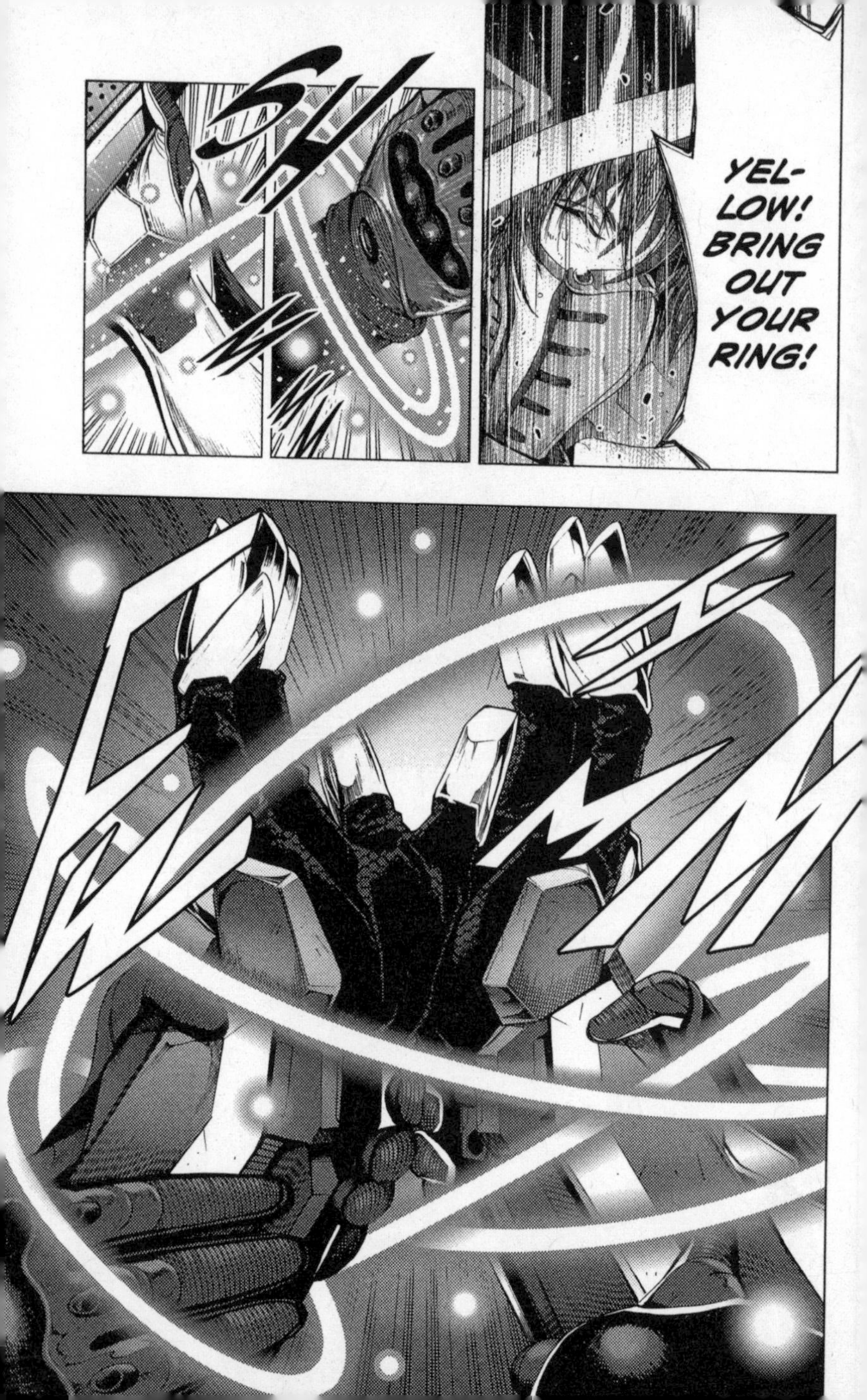
YEL-LOW! BRING OUT YOUR RING!

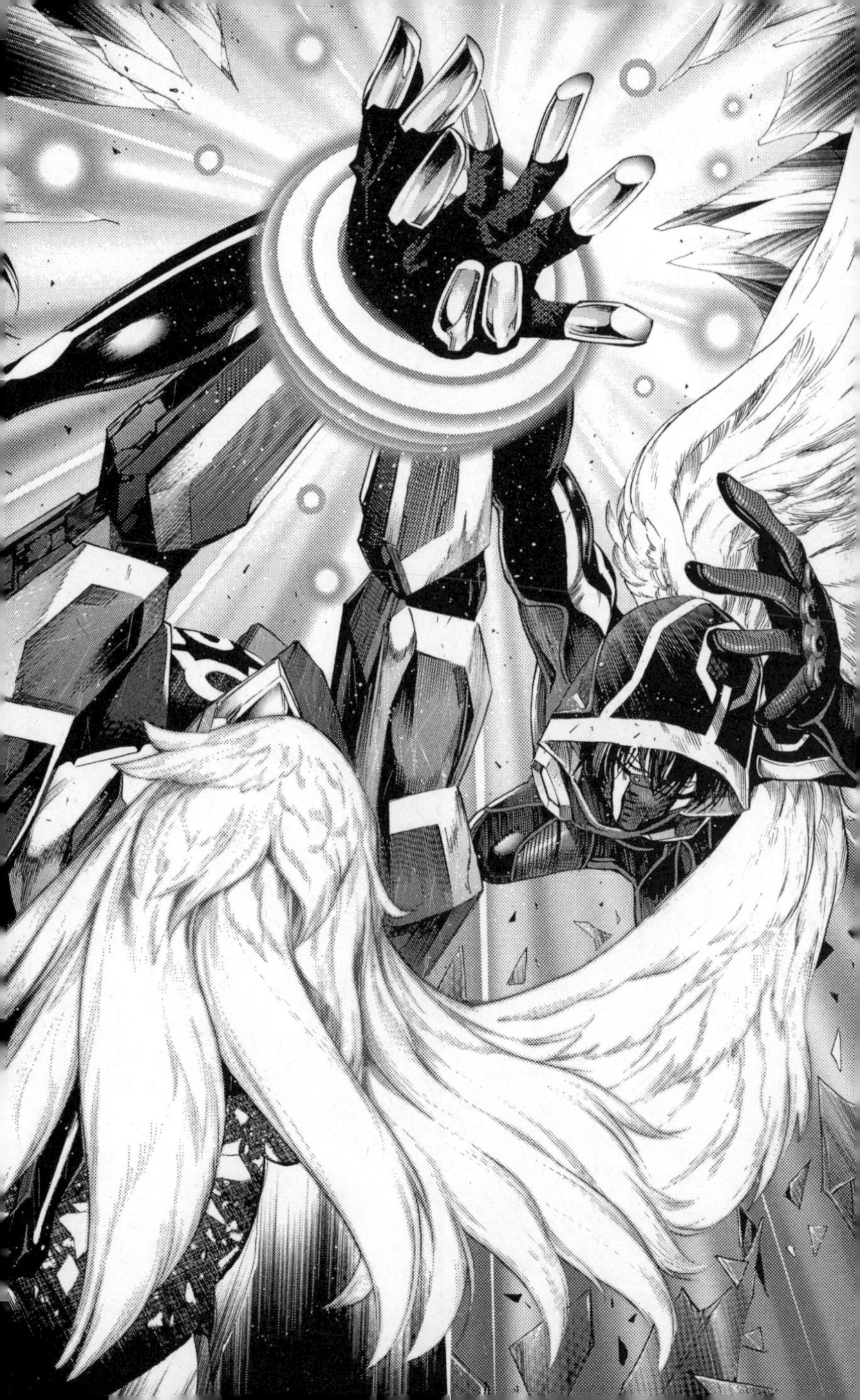

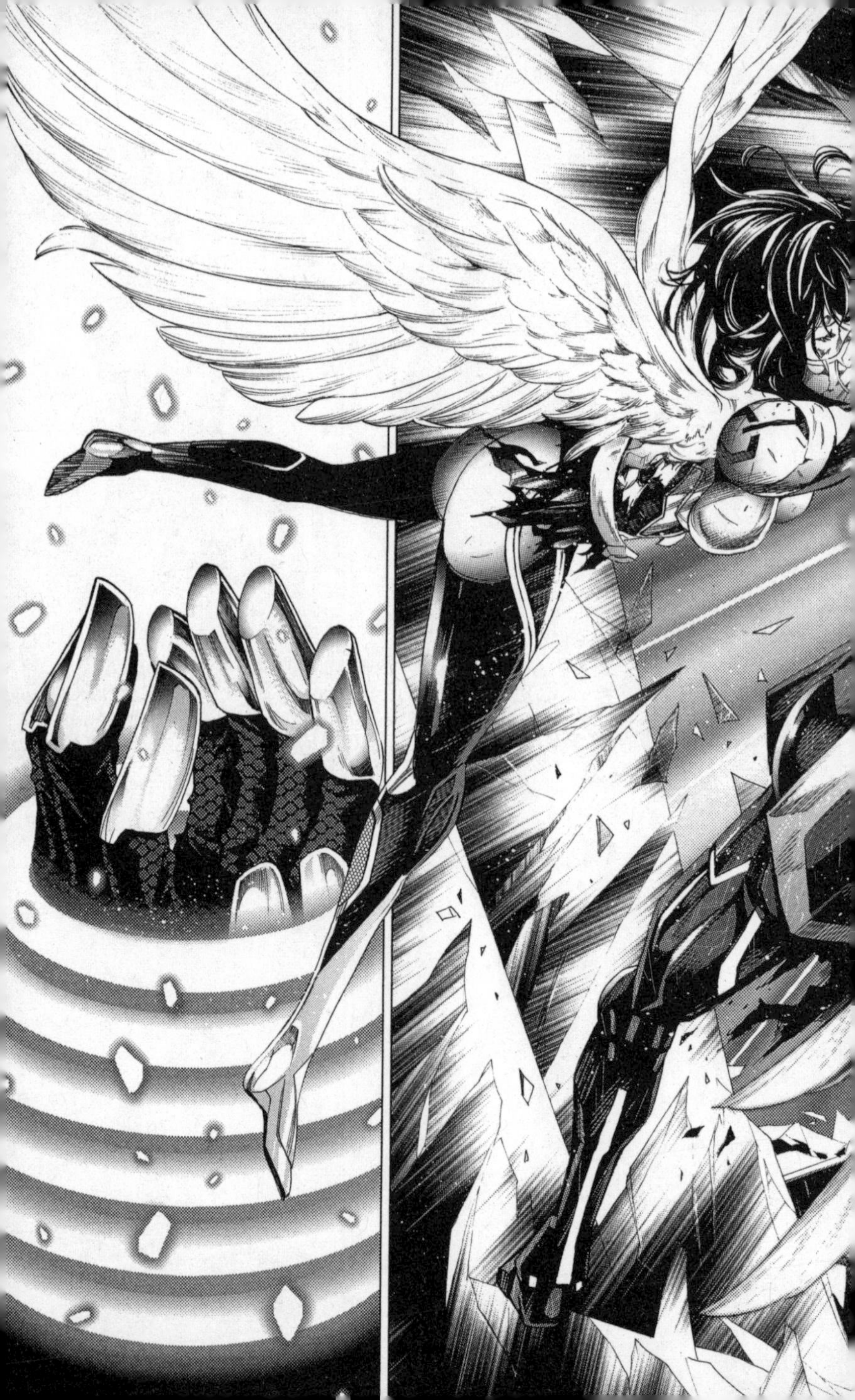

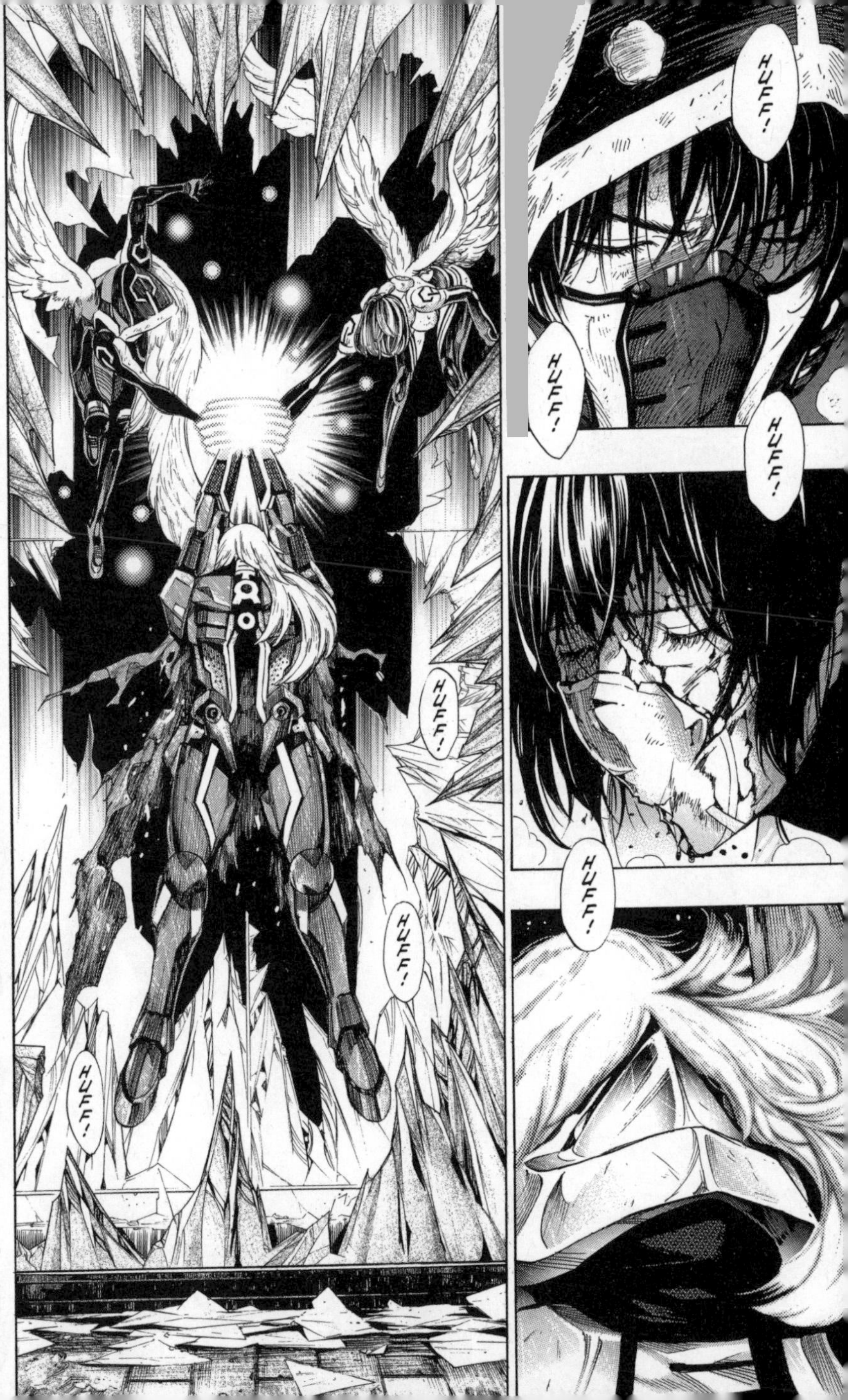
HUFF!
HUFF!
HUFF!
HUFF!
HUFF!
HUFF!
HUFF!

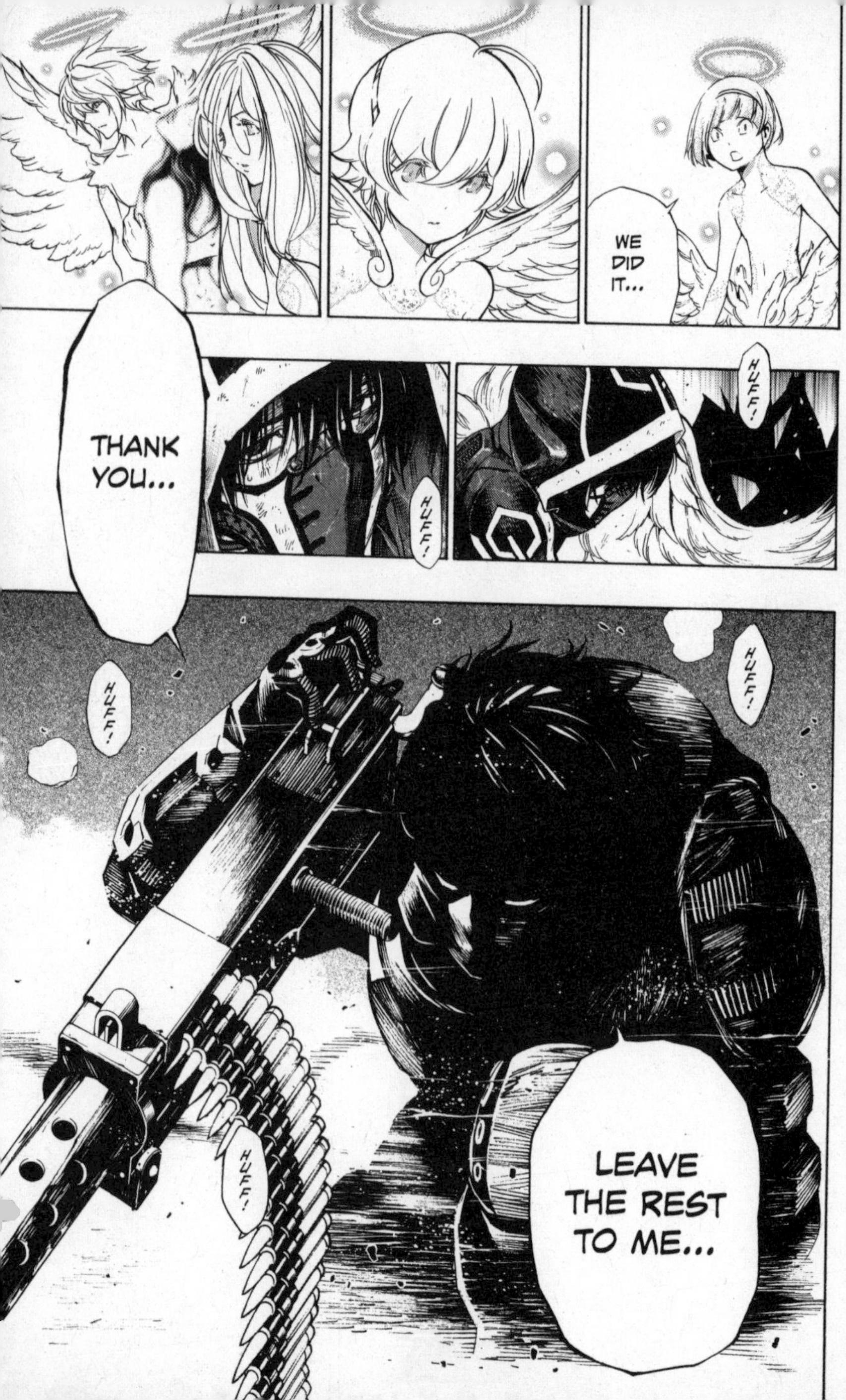
WE DID IT...
HUFF!
HUFF!
THANK YOU...
HUFF!
HUFF!
HUFF!
LEAVE THE REST TO ME...

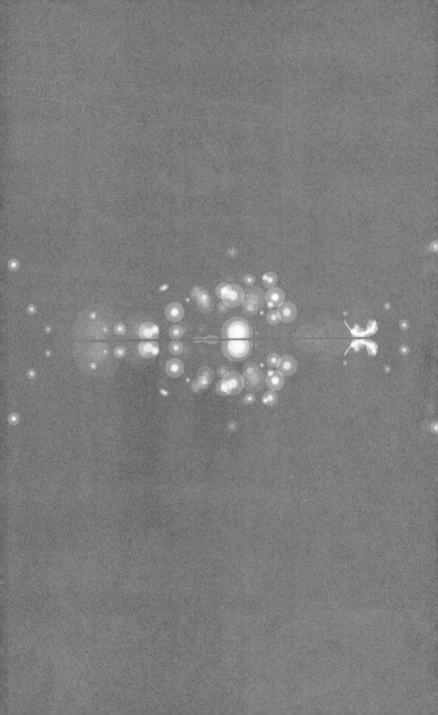

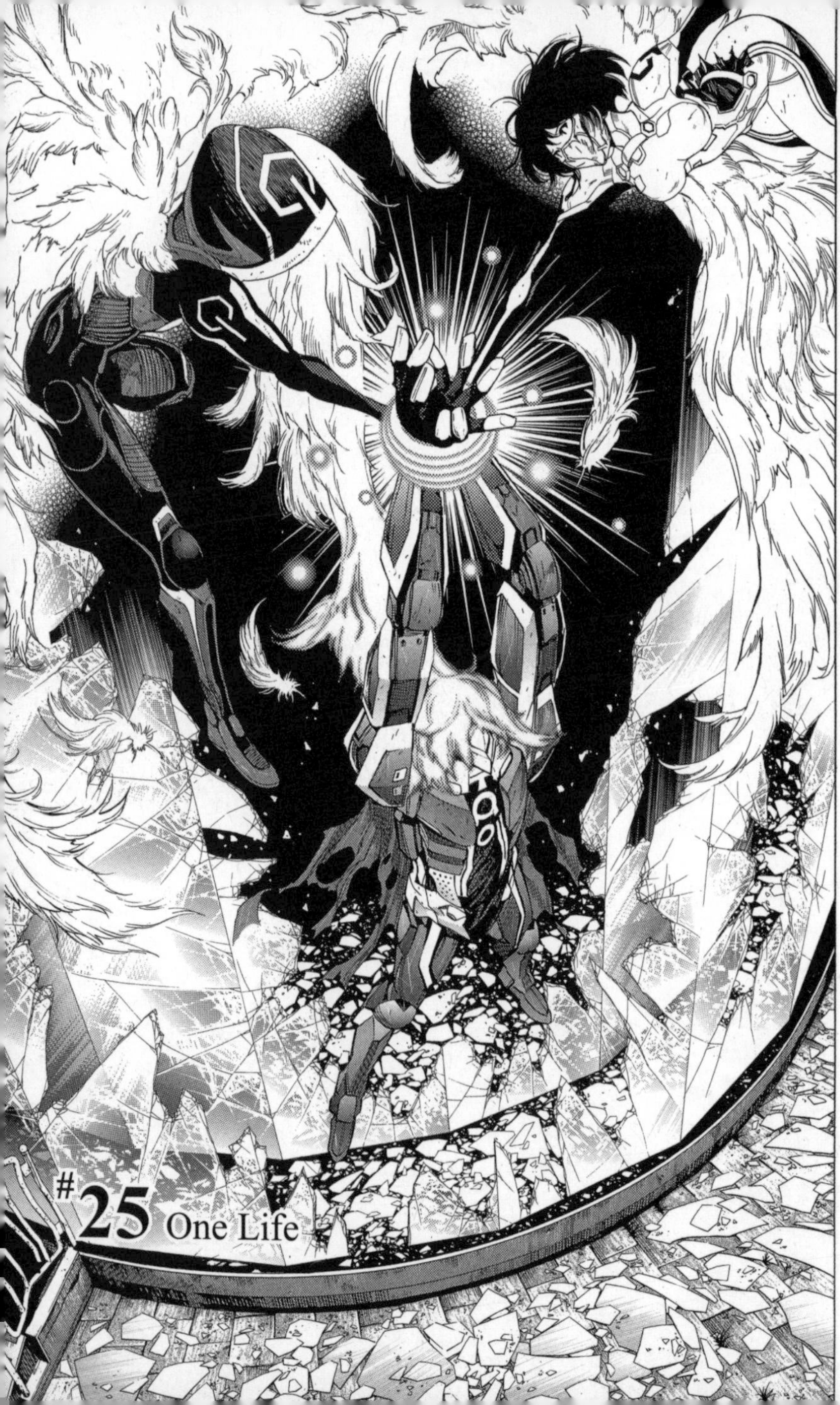
#25 One Life

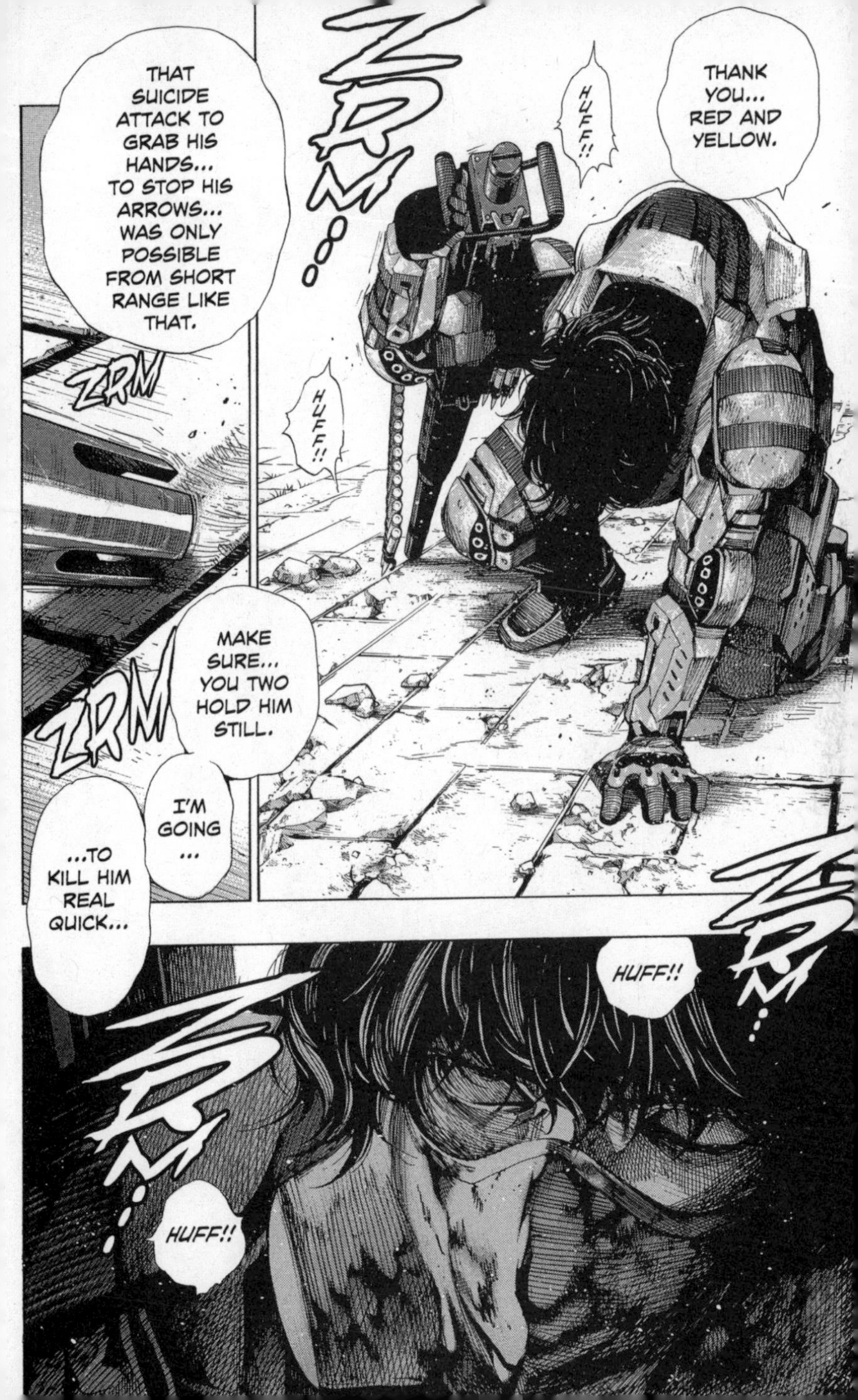
THANK YOU... RED AND YELLOW.
HUFF!!
ZRM...
HUFF!!
MAKE SURE... YOU TWO HOLD HIM STILL.
THAT SUICIDE ATTACK TO GRAB HIS HANDS... TO STOP HIS ARROWS... WAS ONLY POSSIBLE FROM SHORT RANGE LIKE THAT.
ZRM
ZRM
I'M GOING ...
...TO KILL HIM REAL QUICK...
ZRM...
HUFF!!
ZRM...
HUFF!!

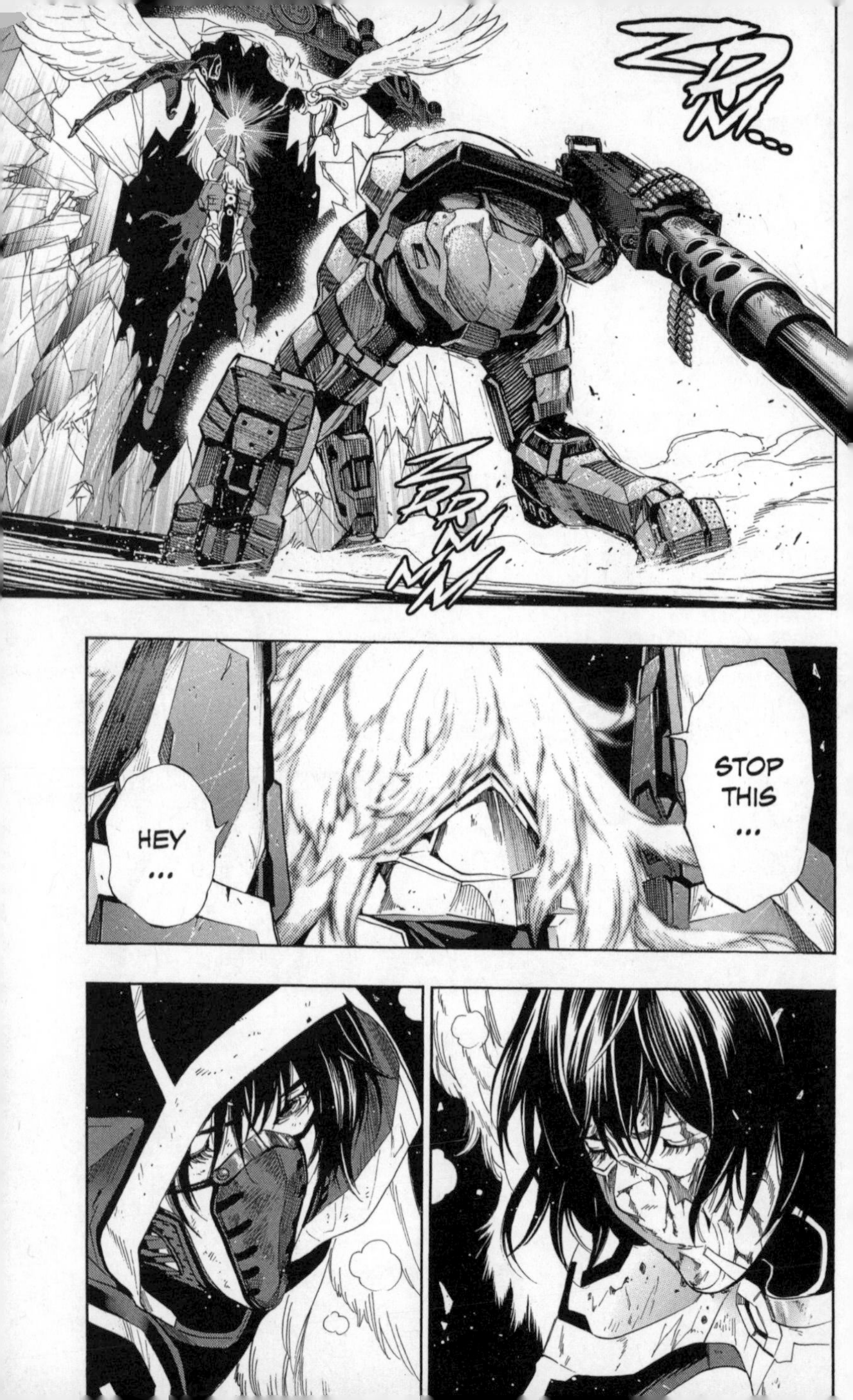
ZDRM...
ZDRMMN
STOP THIS ...
HEY ...

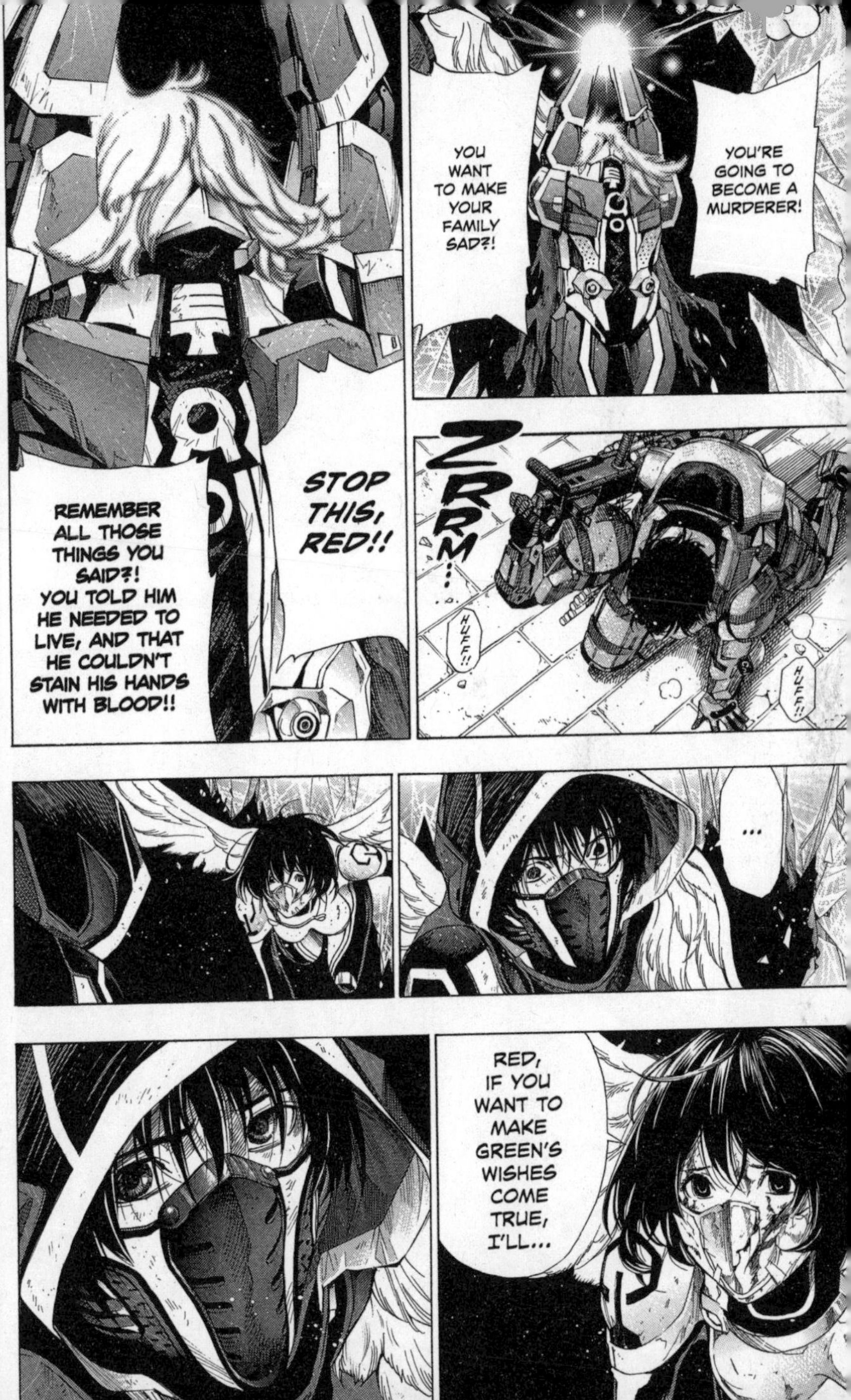

YOU'RE GOING TO BECOME A MURDERER!
YOU WANT TO MAKE YOUR FAMILY SAD?!
ZRRM...
HUFF!!
HUFF!!
STOP THIS, RED!!
REMEMBER ALL THOSE THINGS YOU SAID?! YOU TOLD HIM HE NEEDED TO LIVE, AND THAT HE COULDN'T STAIN HIS HANDS WITH BLOOD!!
...
RED, IF YOU WANT TO MAKE GREEN'S WISHES COME TRUE, I'LL...

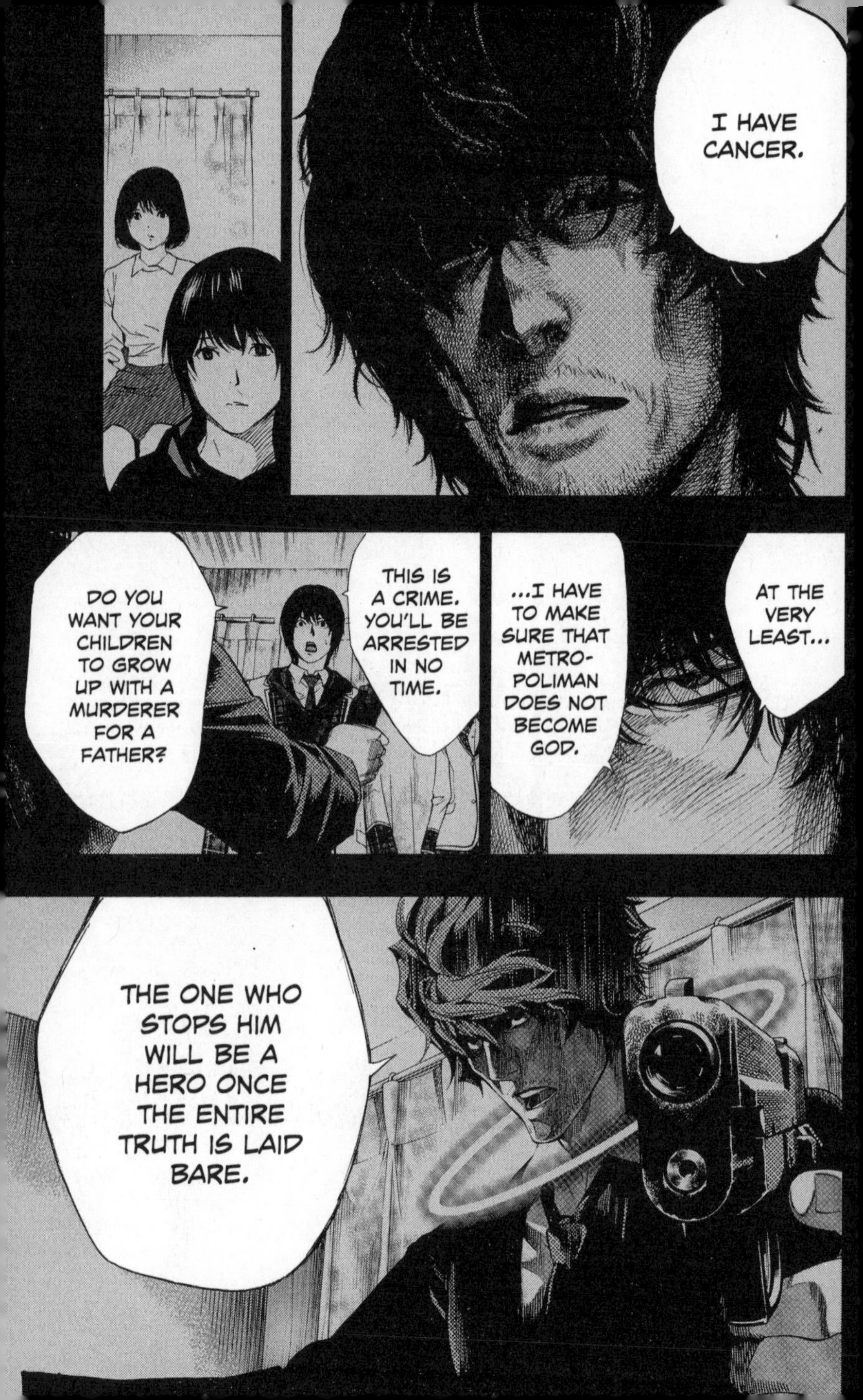
I HAVE CANCER.
AT THE VERY LEAST...
...I HAVE TO MAKE SURE THAT METRO-POLIMAN DOES NOT BECOME GOD.
THIS IS A CRIME. YOU'LL BE ARRESTED IN NO TIME.
DO YOU WANT YOUR CHILDREN TO GROW UP WITH A MURDERER FOR A FATHER?
THE ONE WHO STOPS HIM WILL BE A HERO ONCE THE ENTIRE TRUTH IS LAID BARE.

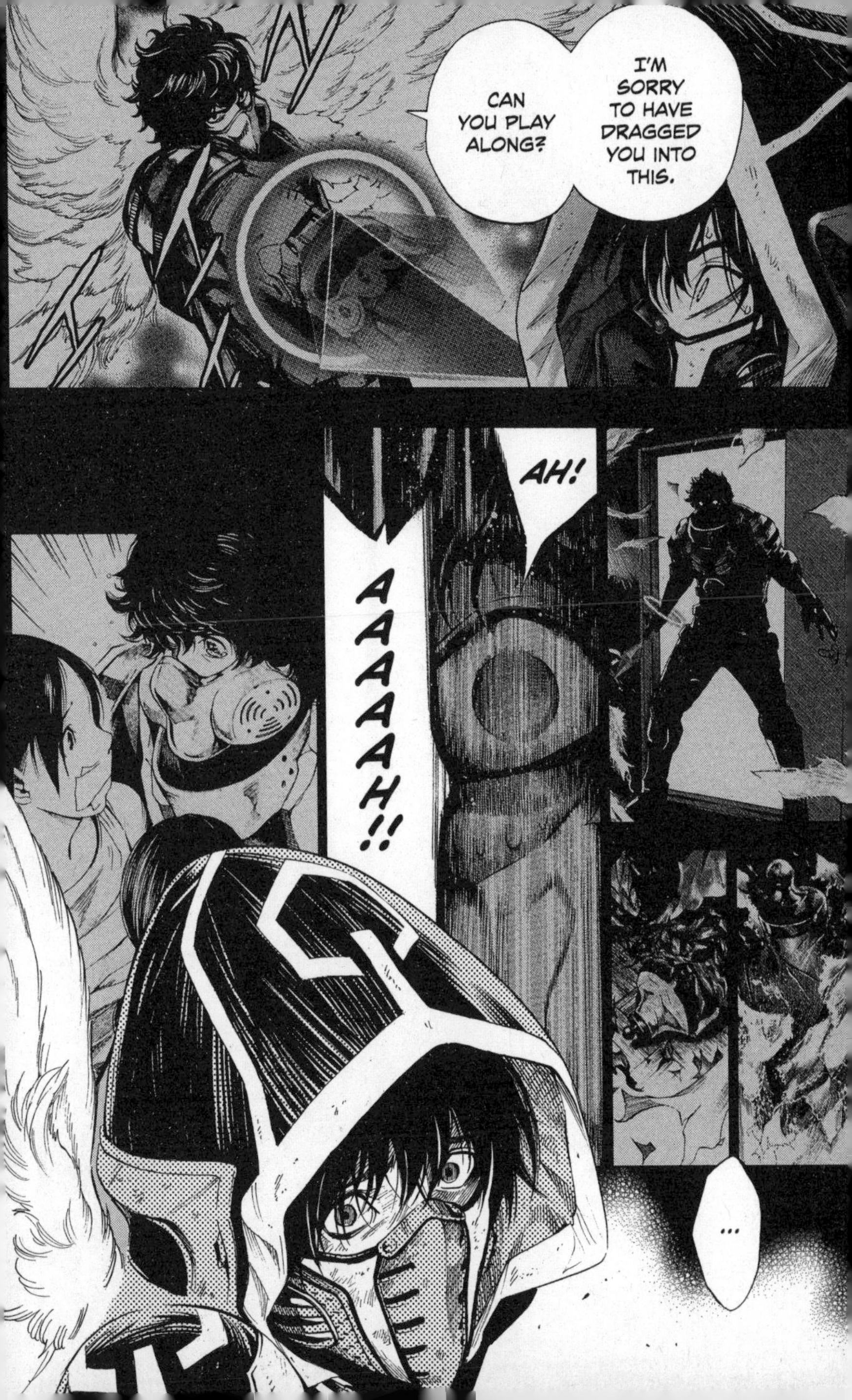
I'M SORRY TO HAVE DRAGGED YOU INTO THIS.
CAN YOU PLAY ALONG?
AH!
AAAAAAH!!
...

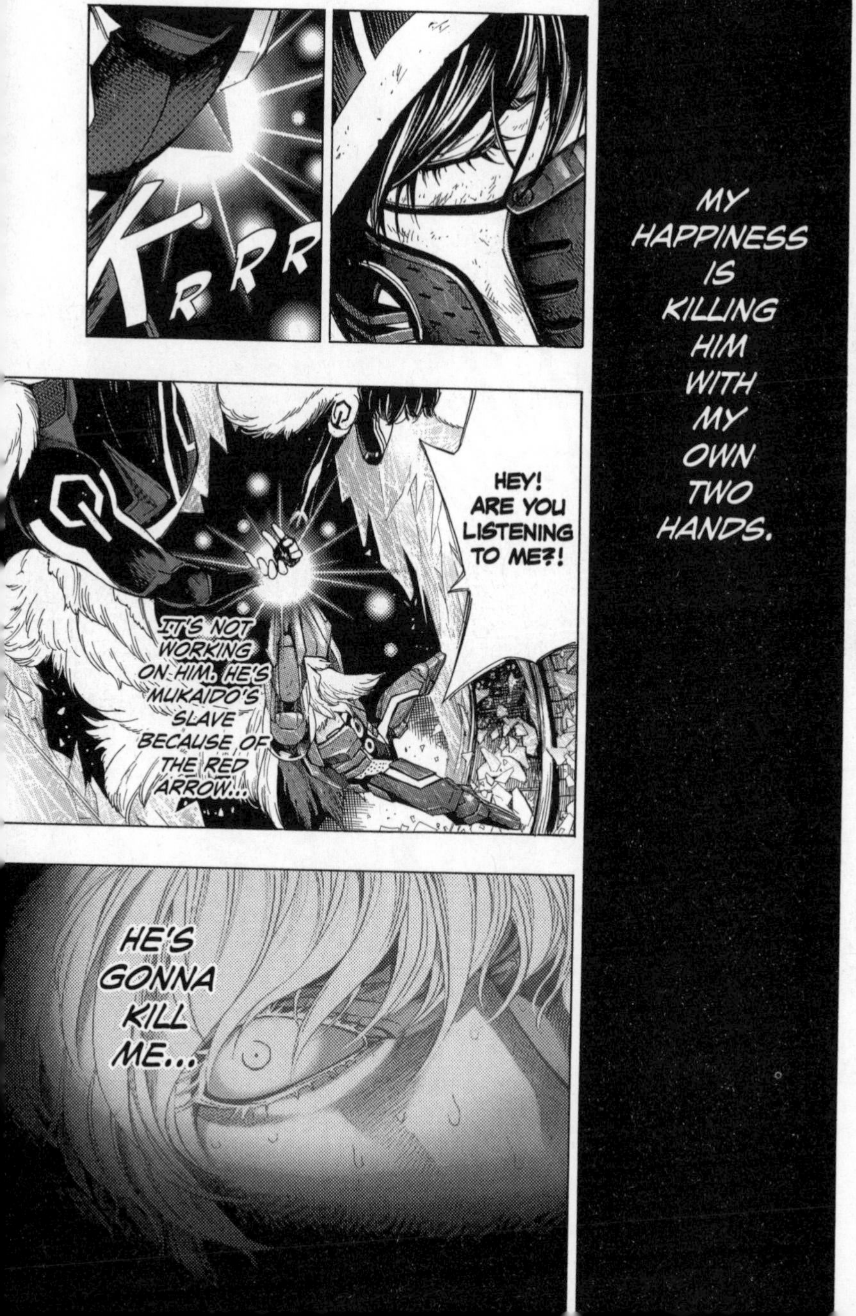
MY HAPPINESS IS KILLING HIM WITH MY OWN TWO HANDS.
KRRRR
HEY! ARE YOU LISTENING TO ME?!
IT'S NOT WORKING ON HIM. HE'S MUKAIDO'S SLAVE BECAUSE OF THE RED ARROW...
HE'S GONNA KILL ME...

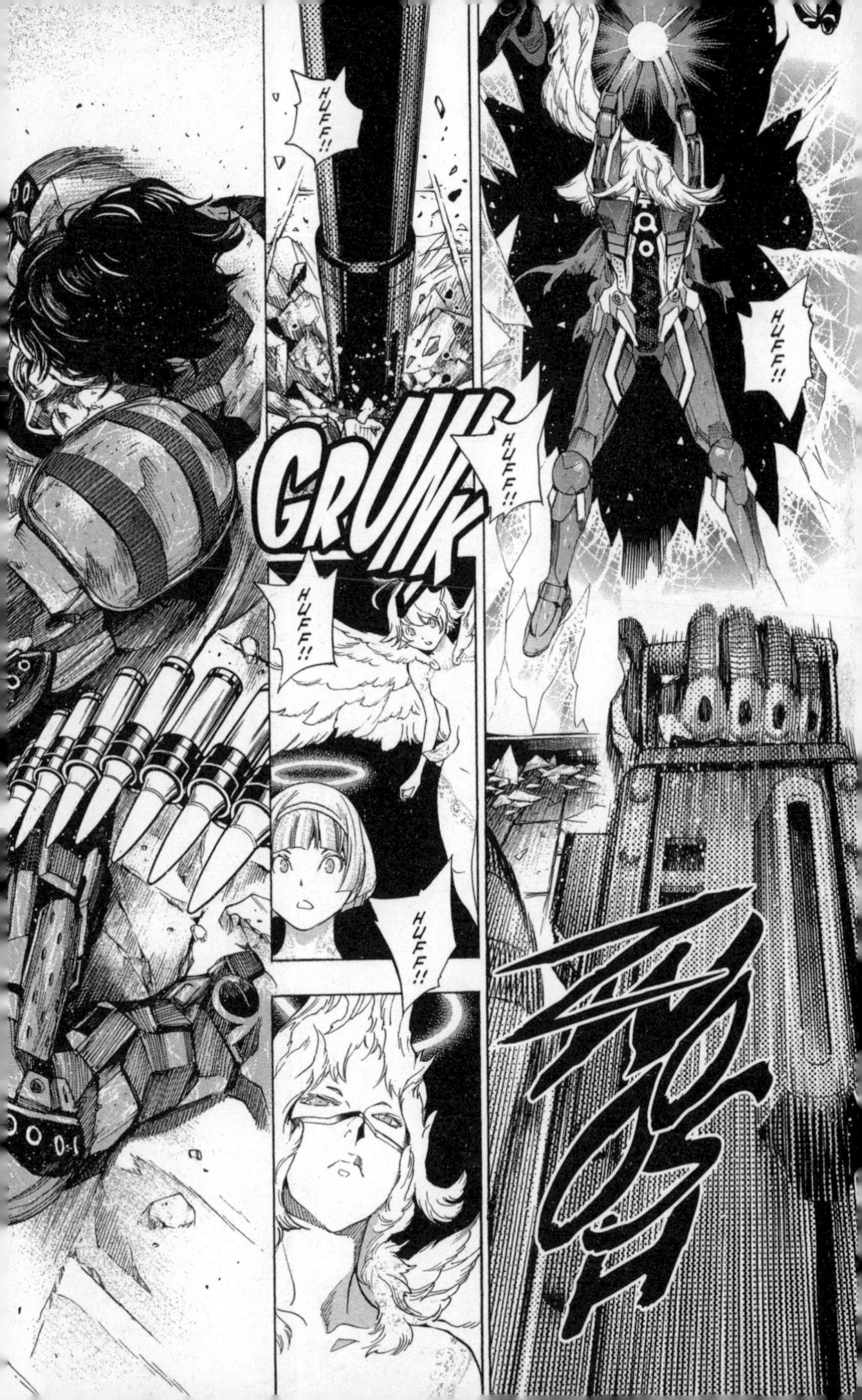
HUFF!!
HUFF!!
HUFF!!
GRUNK
HUFF!!
HUFF!!

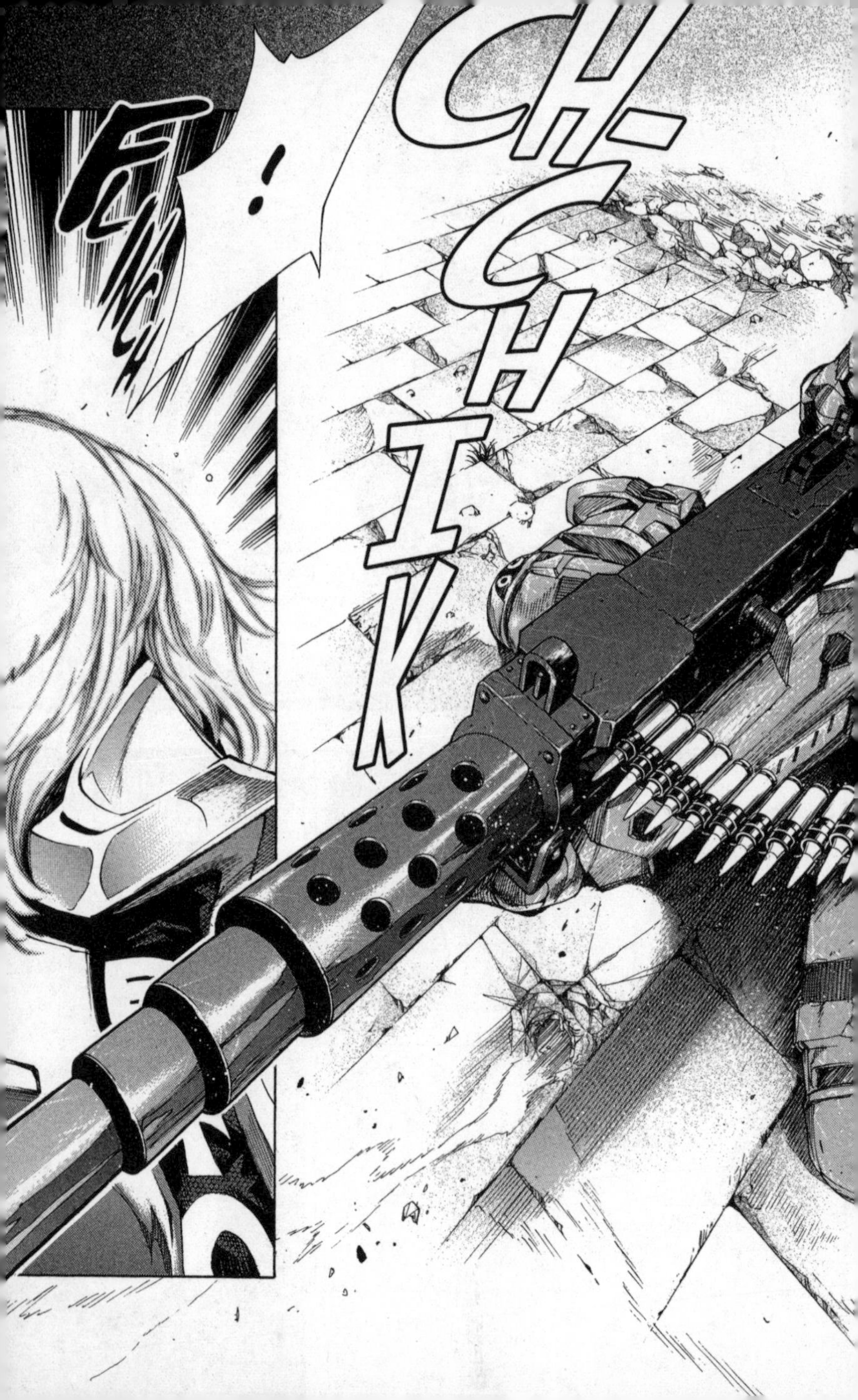
CH-CH-CHIK
!
FLINCH

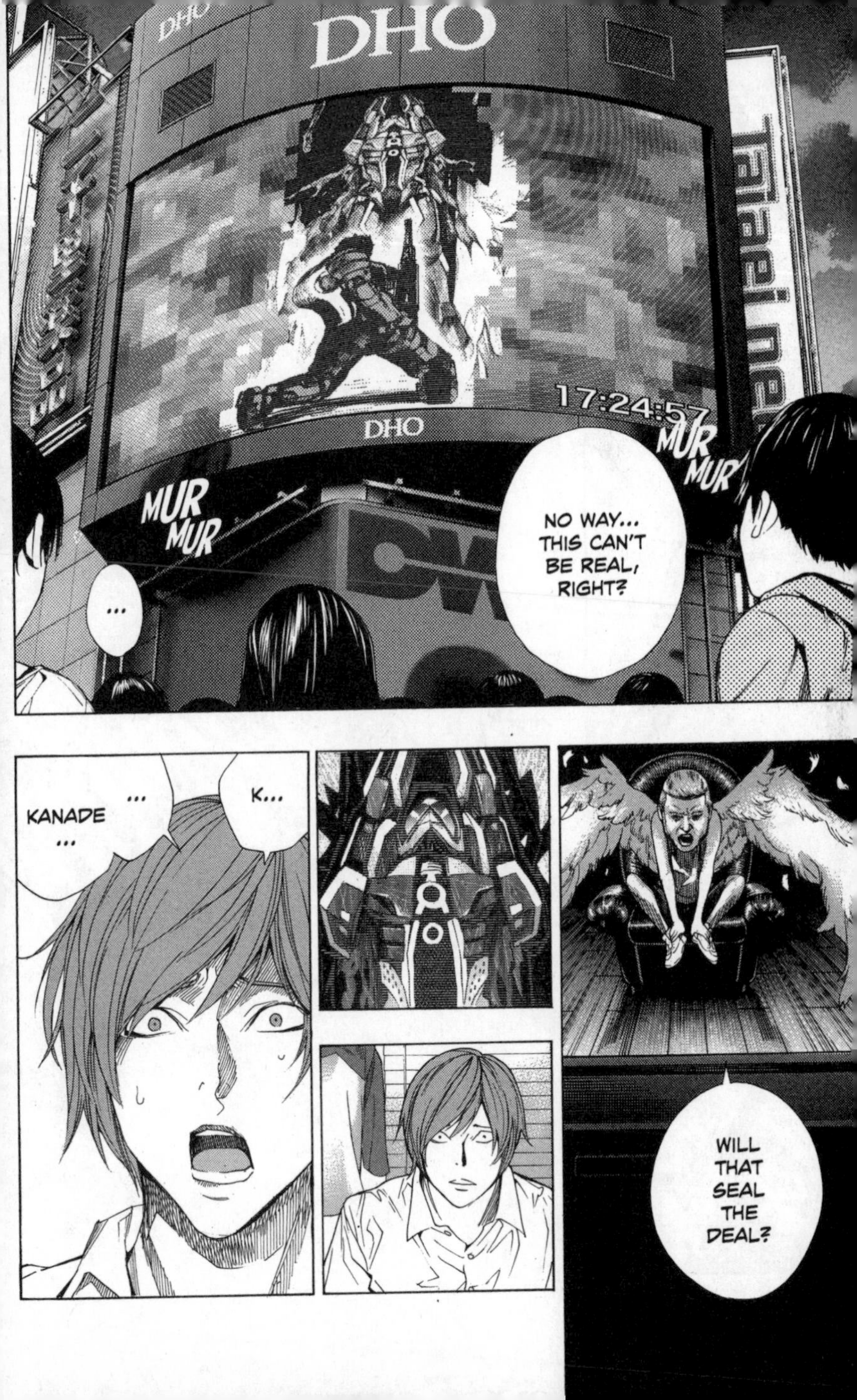
DHO
DHO
17:24:57
DHO
MUR MUR
NO WAY... THIS CAN'T BE REAL, RIGHT?
MUR MUR
...
WILL THAT SEAL THE DEAL?
K...
...
KANADE ...

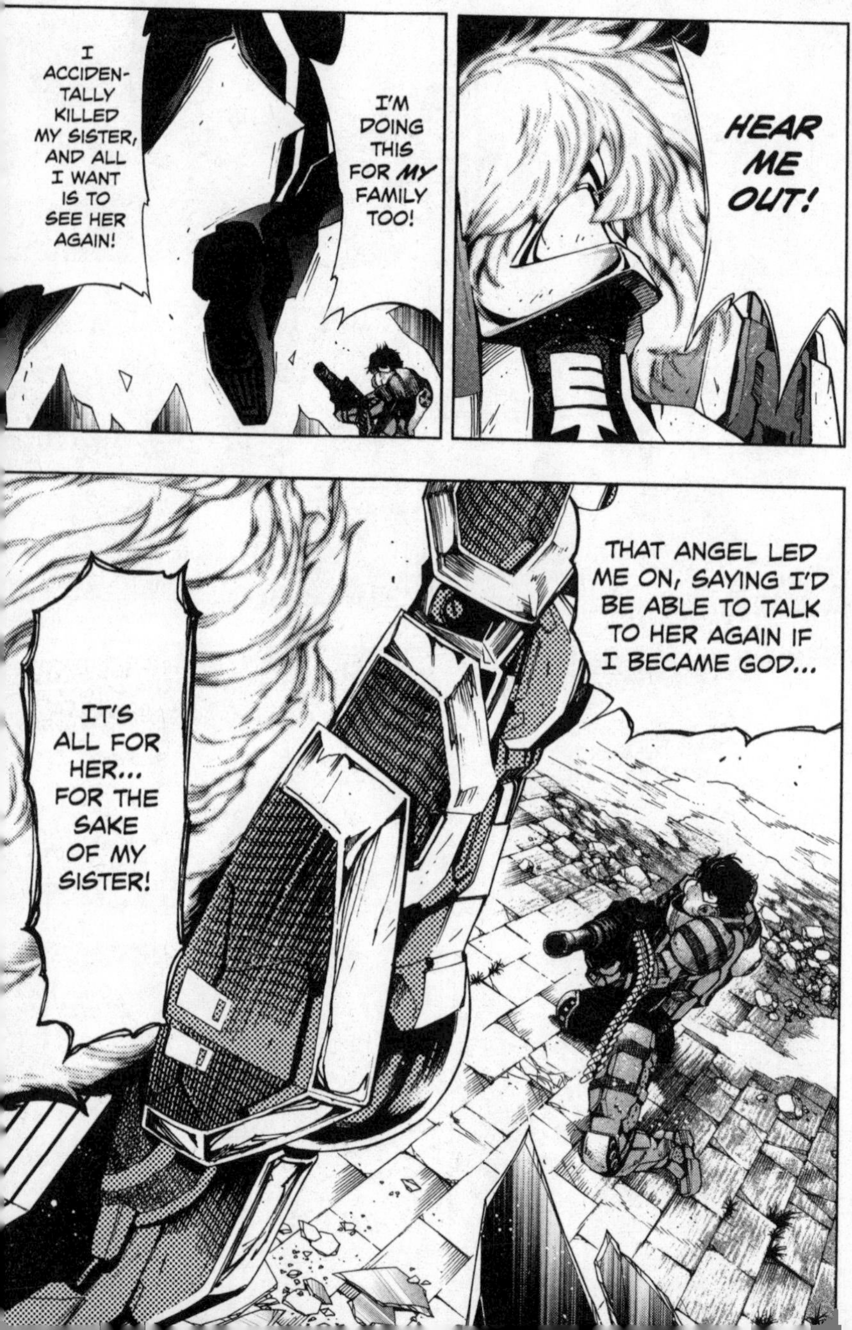
HEAR ME OUT!
I ACCIDENTALLY KILLED MY SISTER, AND ALL I WANT IS TO SEE HER AGAIN!
I'M DOING THIS FOR *MY* FAMILY TOO!
THAT ANGEL LED ME ON, SAYING I'D BE ABLE TO TALK TO HER AGAIN IF I BECAME GOD...
IT'S ALL FOR HER... FOR THE SAKE OF MY SISTER!

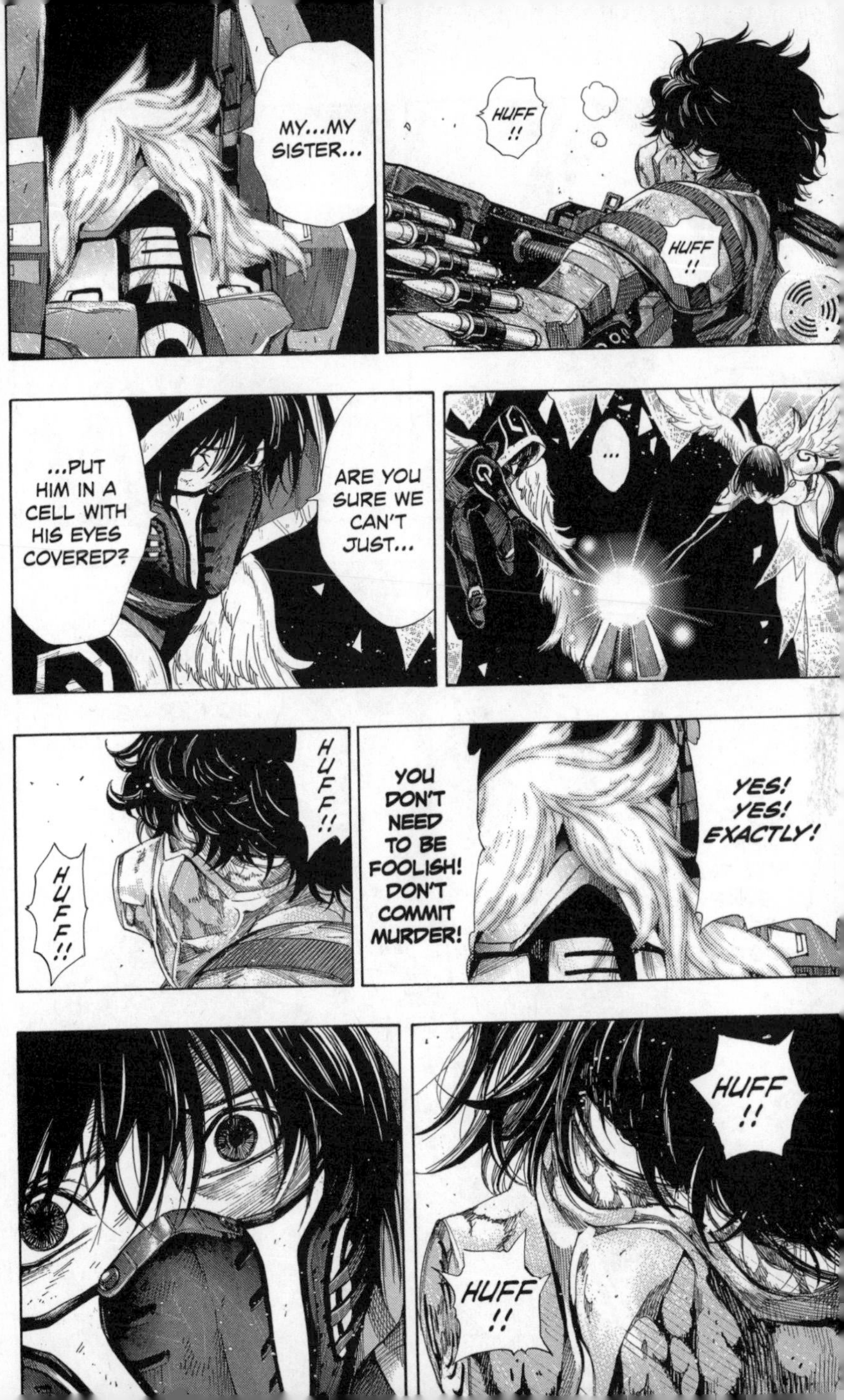
HUFF!!
HUFF!!
MY...MY SISTER...
...
ARE YOU SURE WE CAN'T JUST...
...PUT HIM IN A CELL WITH HIS EYES COVERED?
YES! YES! EXACTLY!
YOU DON'T NEED TO BE FOOLISH! DON'T COMMIT MURDER!
HUFF!!
HUFF!!
HUFF!!
HUFF!!

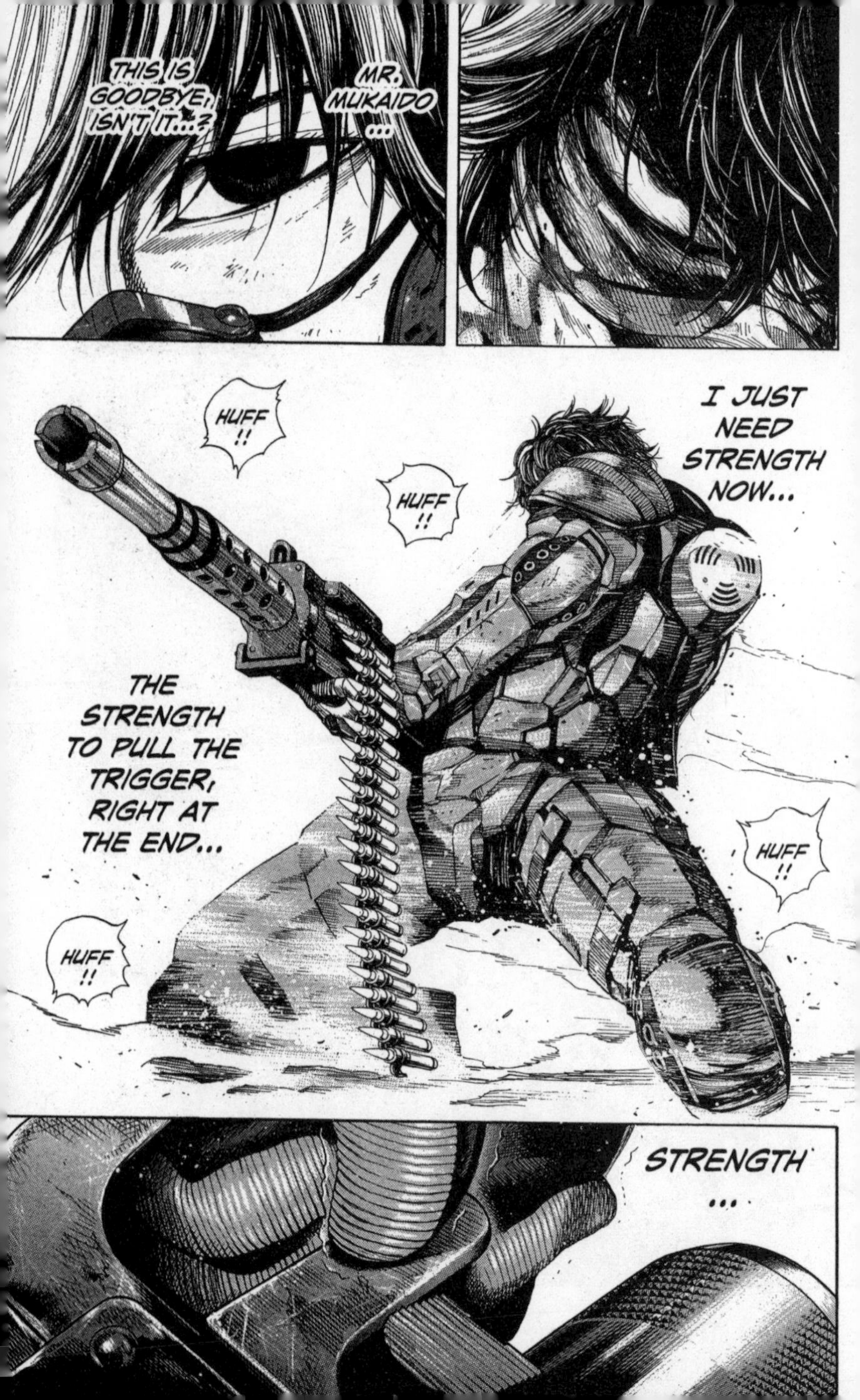
MR. MUKAIDO...
THIS IS GOODBYE, ISN'T IT...?
I JUST NEED STRENGTH NOW...
HUFF!!
HUFF!!
THE STRENGTH TO PULL THE TRIGGER, RIGHT AT THE END...
HUFF!!
HUFF!!
STRENGTH...

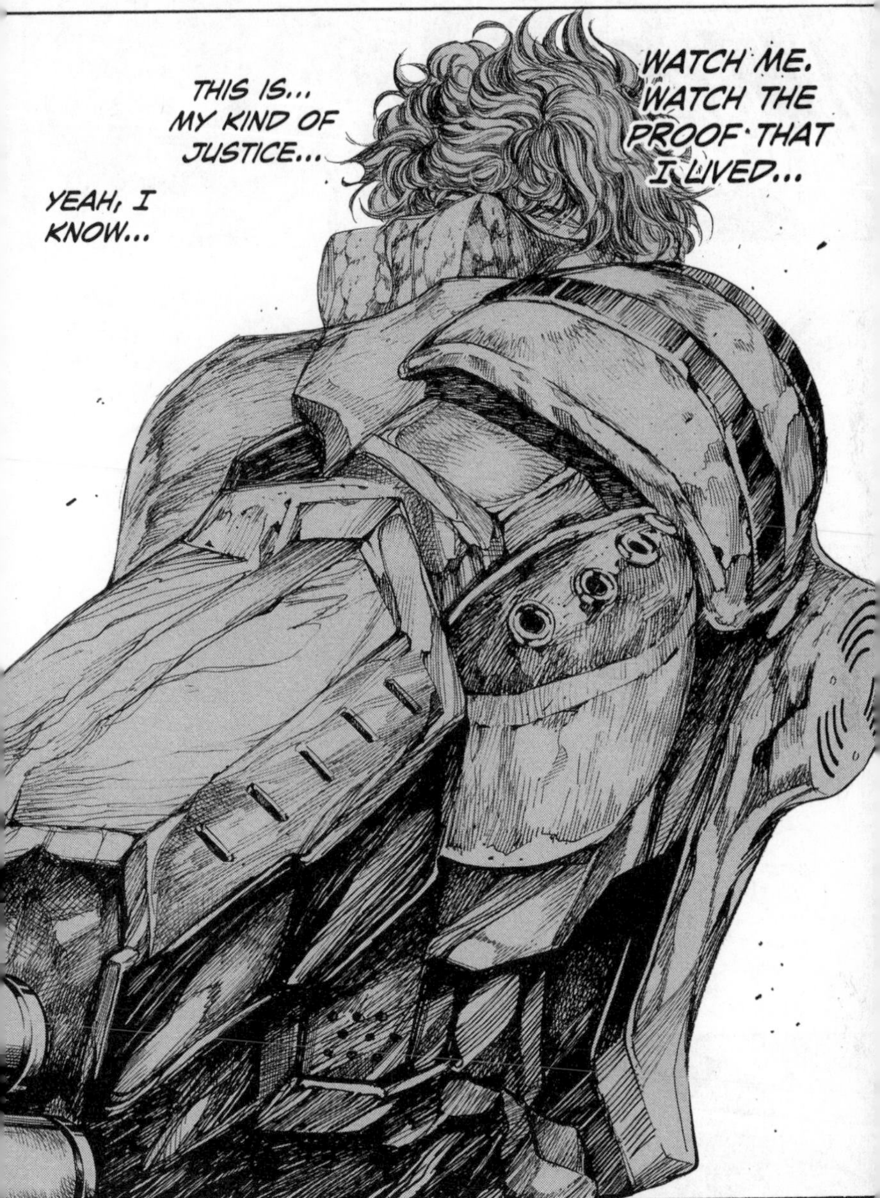

WATCH ME. WATCH THE PROOF THAT I LIVED...
THIS IS... MY KIND OF JUSTICE...
YEAH, I KNOW...

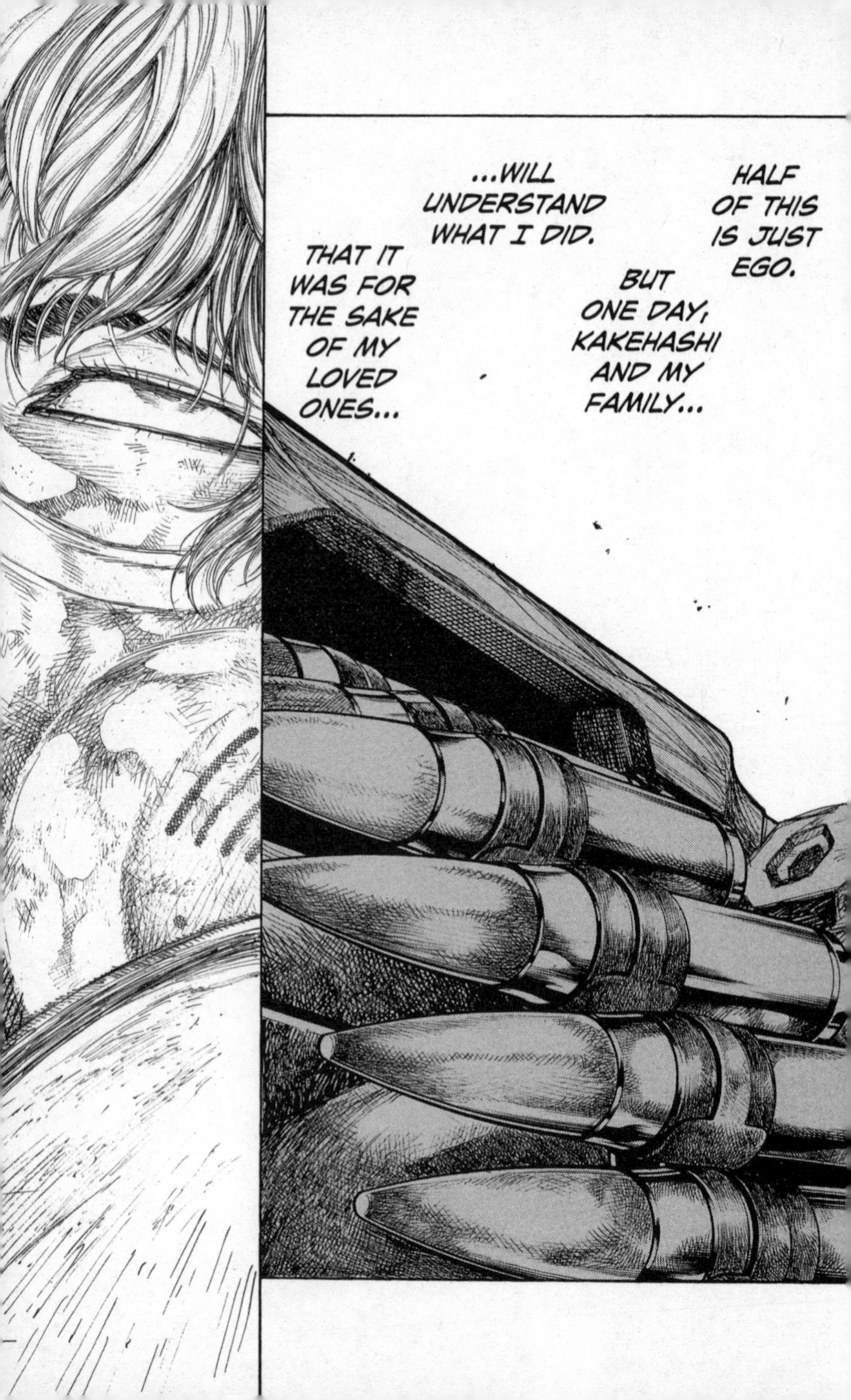
HALF OF THIS IS JUST EGO.
BUT ONE DAY, KAKEHASHI AND MY FAMILY...
...WILL UNDERSTAND WHAT I DID.
THAT IT WAS FOR THE SAKE OF MY LOVED ONES...

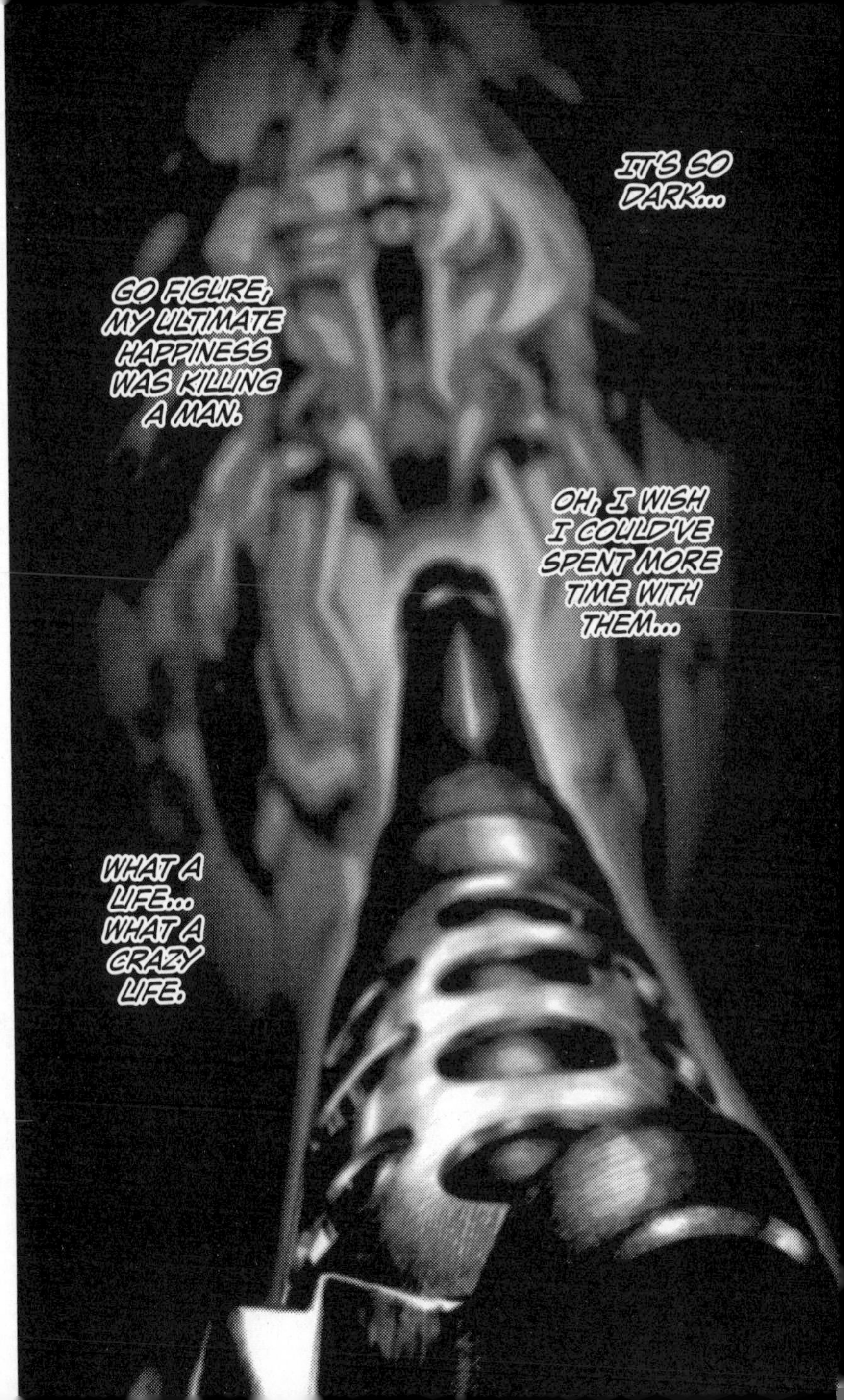
IT'S SO DARK...
GO FIGURE, MY ULTIMATE HAPPINESS WAS KILLING A MAN.
OH, I WISH I COULD'VE SPENT MORE TIME WITH THEM...
WHAT A LIFE... WHAT A CRAZY LIFE.

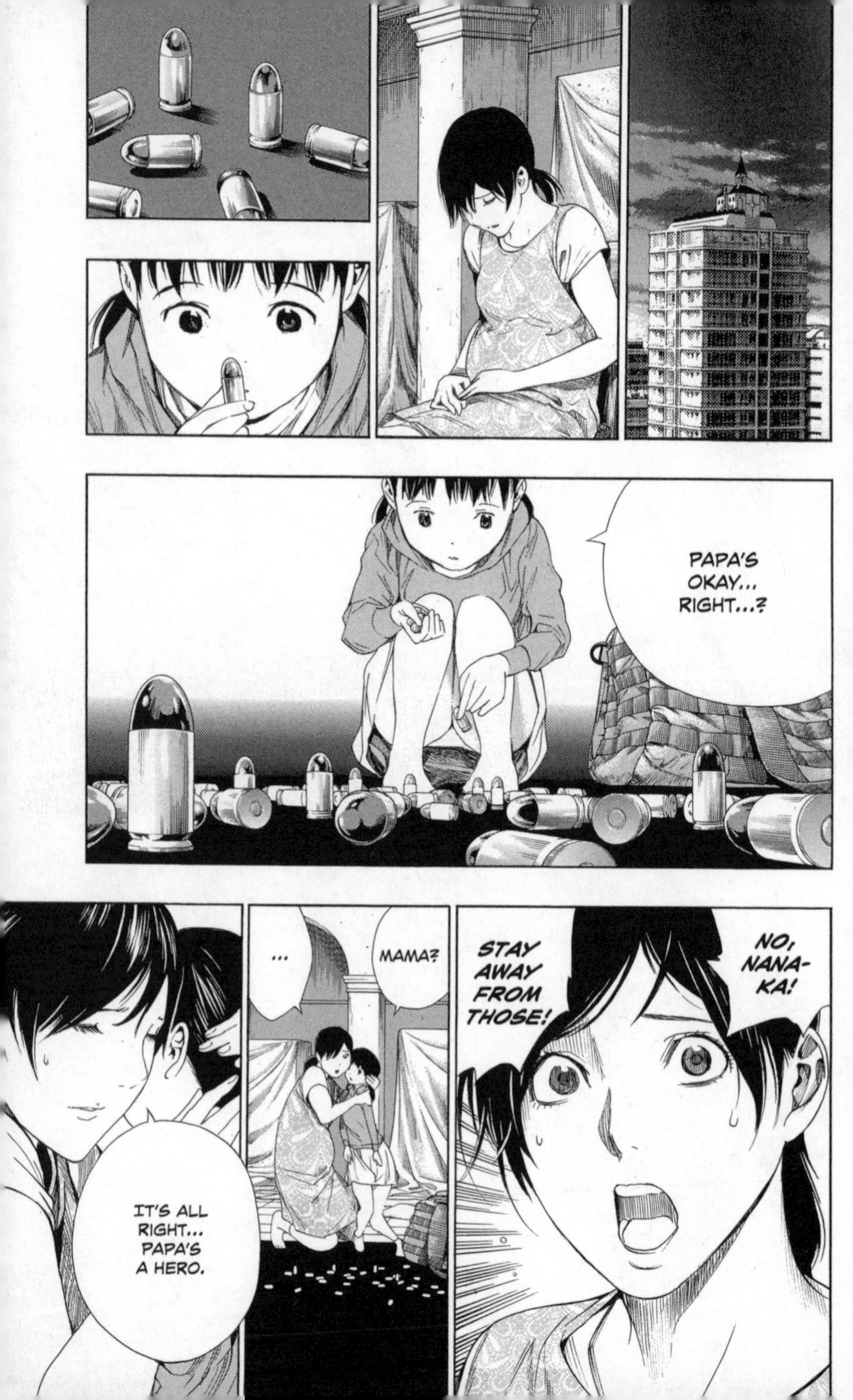
PAPA'S OKAY... RIGHT...?
NO, NANA-KA!
STAY AWAY FROM THOSE!
MAMA?
...
IT'S ALL RIGHT... PAPA'S A HERO.

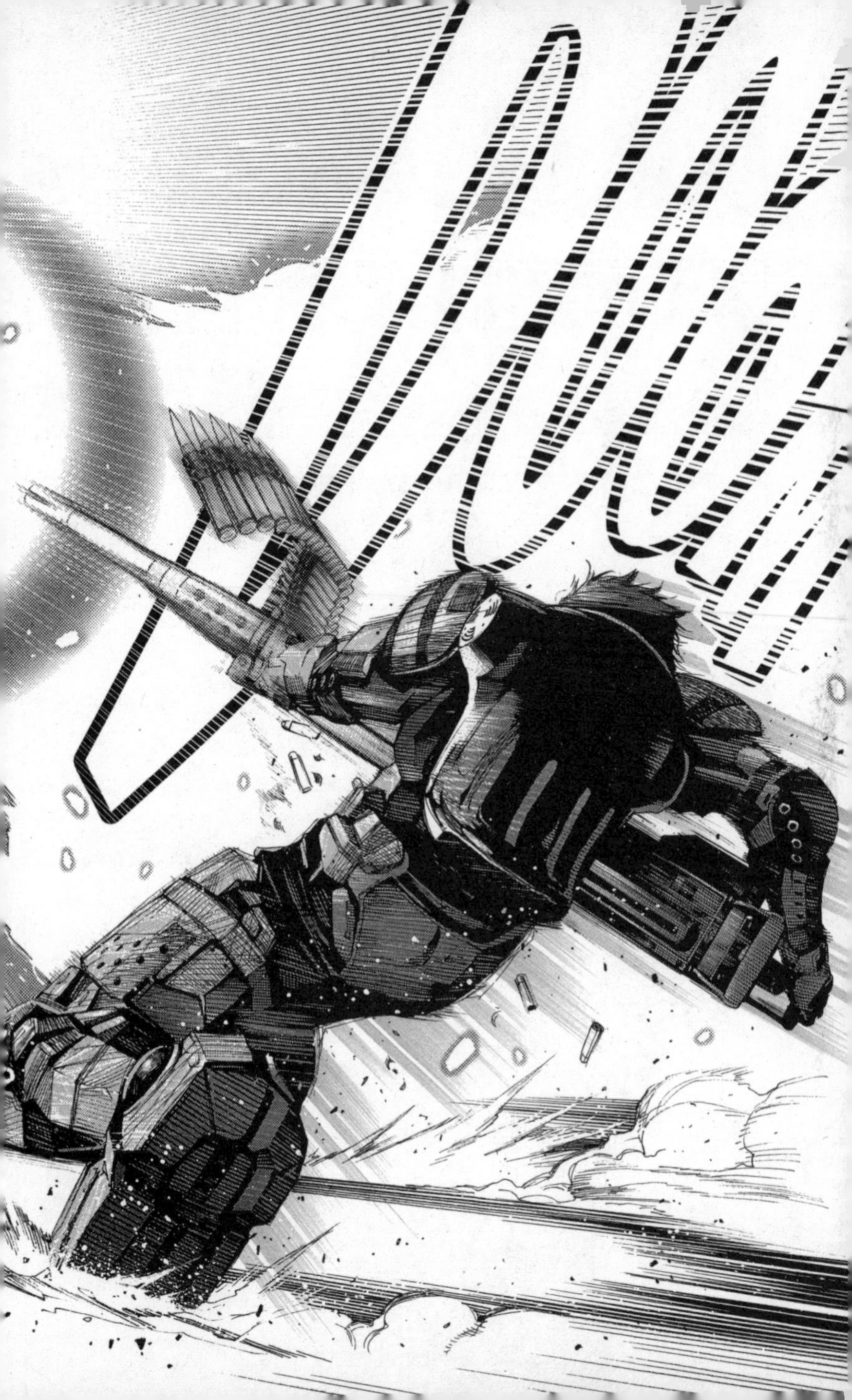

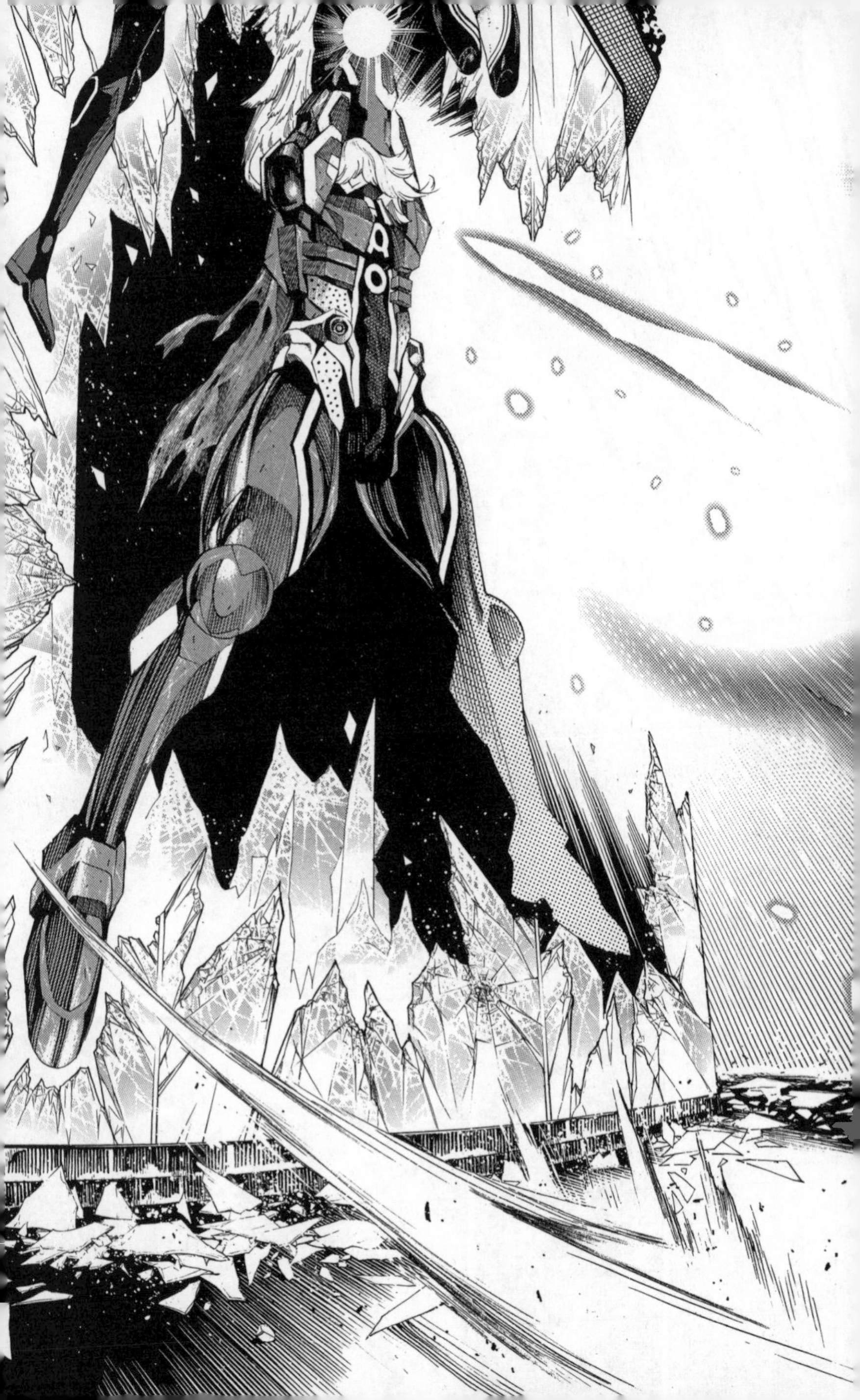

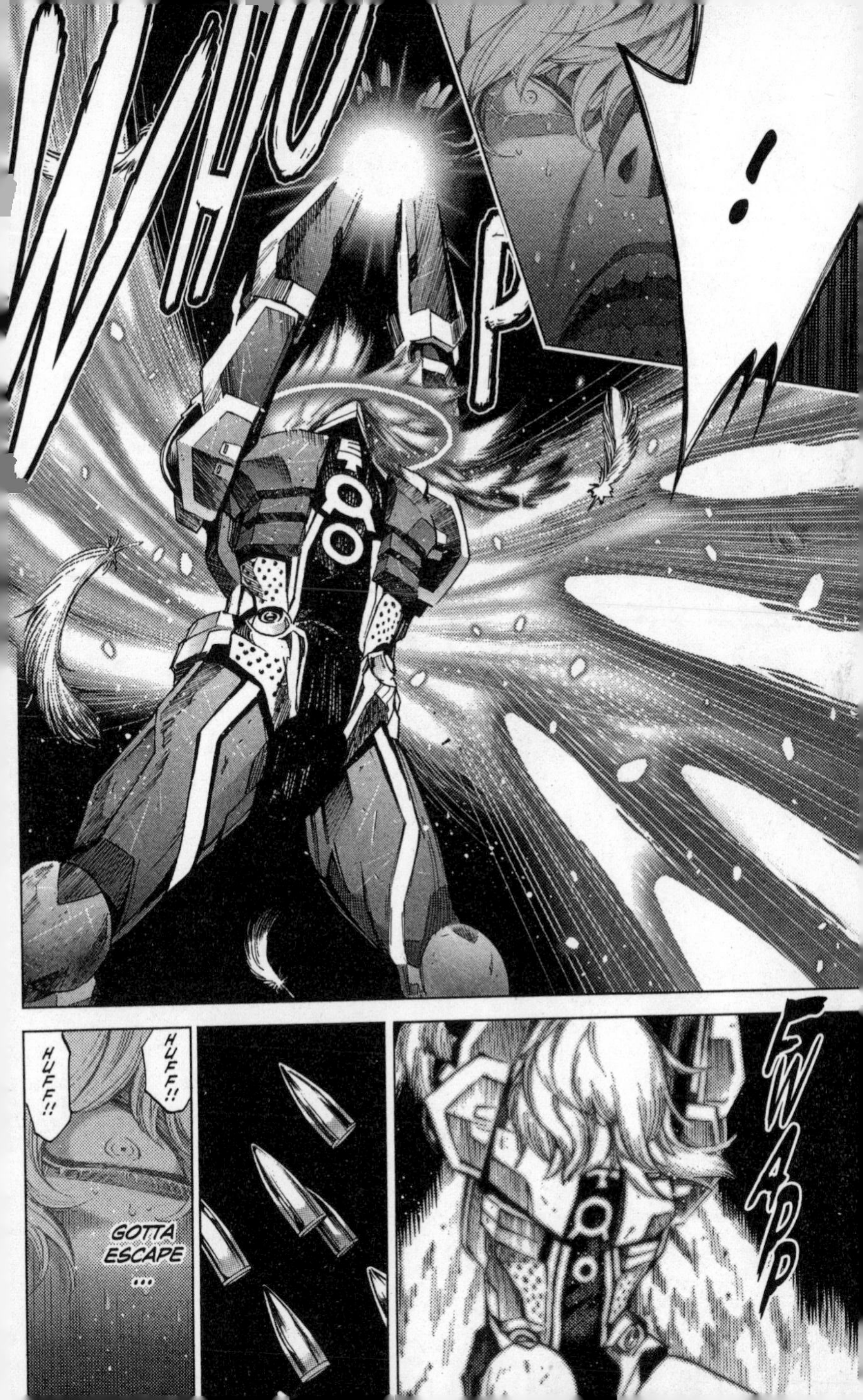
!
WHUP
FWADD
HUFF!!
HUFF!!
GOTTA ESCAPE ...

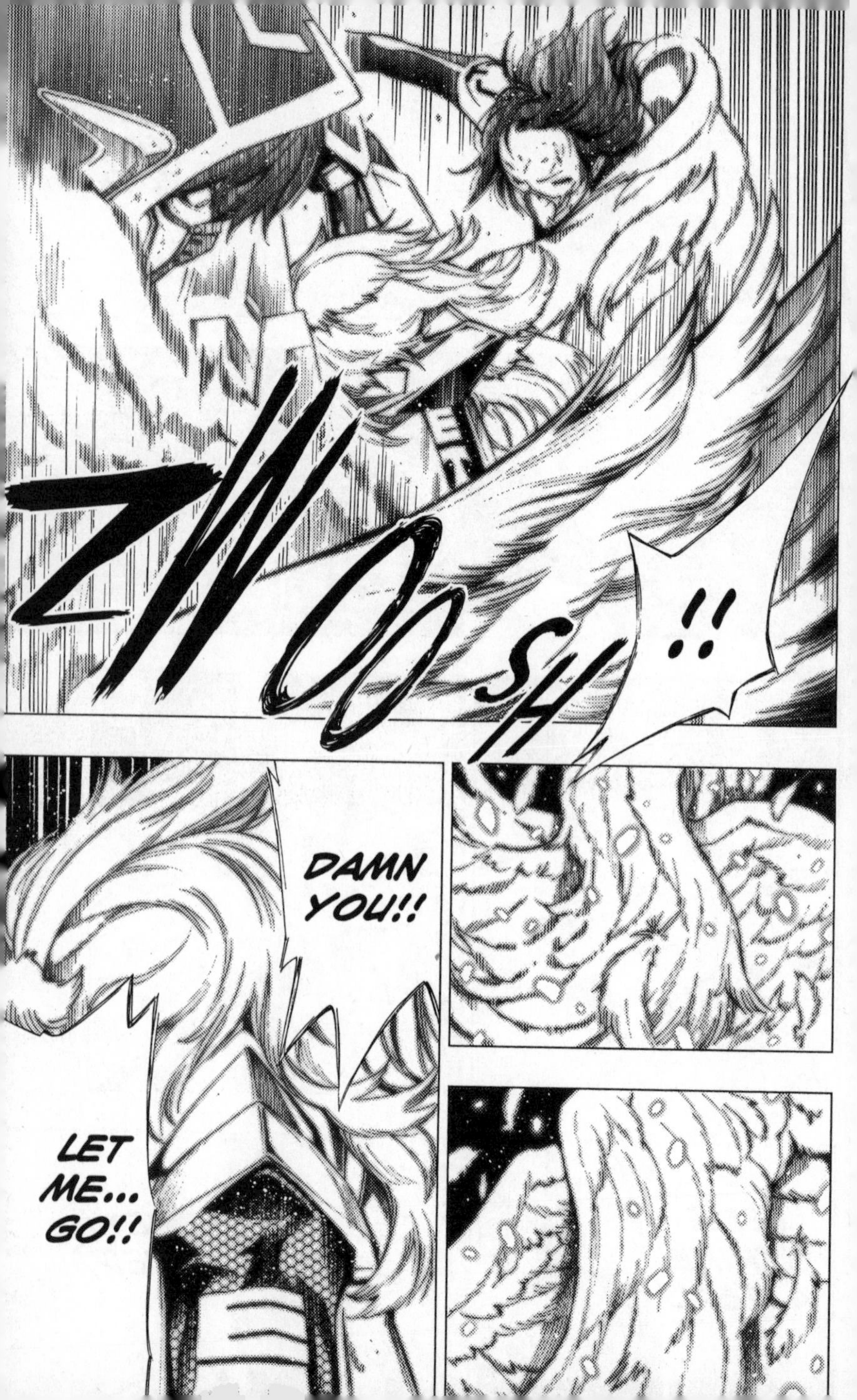
ZWOOSH!!
DAMN YOU!!
LET ME... GO!!

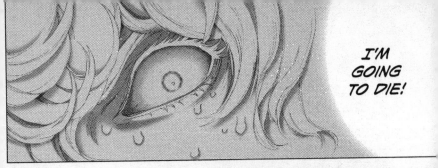

I'M GOING TO DIE!
BASED ON THE SOUND, HE'S FIRING FROM VERY CLOSE BY...
HOW LONG UNTIL IT HITS ME?!
HUFF!!
HUFF!!
HUFF!!
HUFF!!
HEY! RED!
LET'S STRIKE A DEAL!

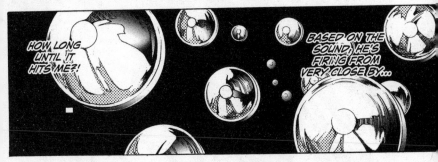

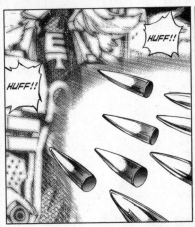

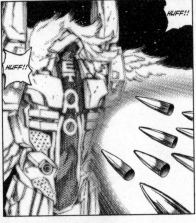

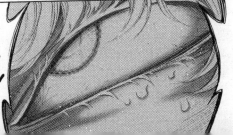

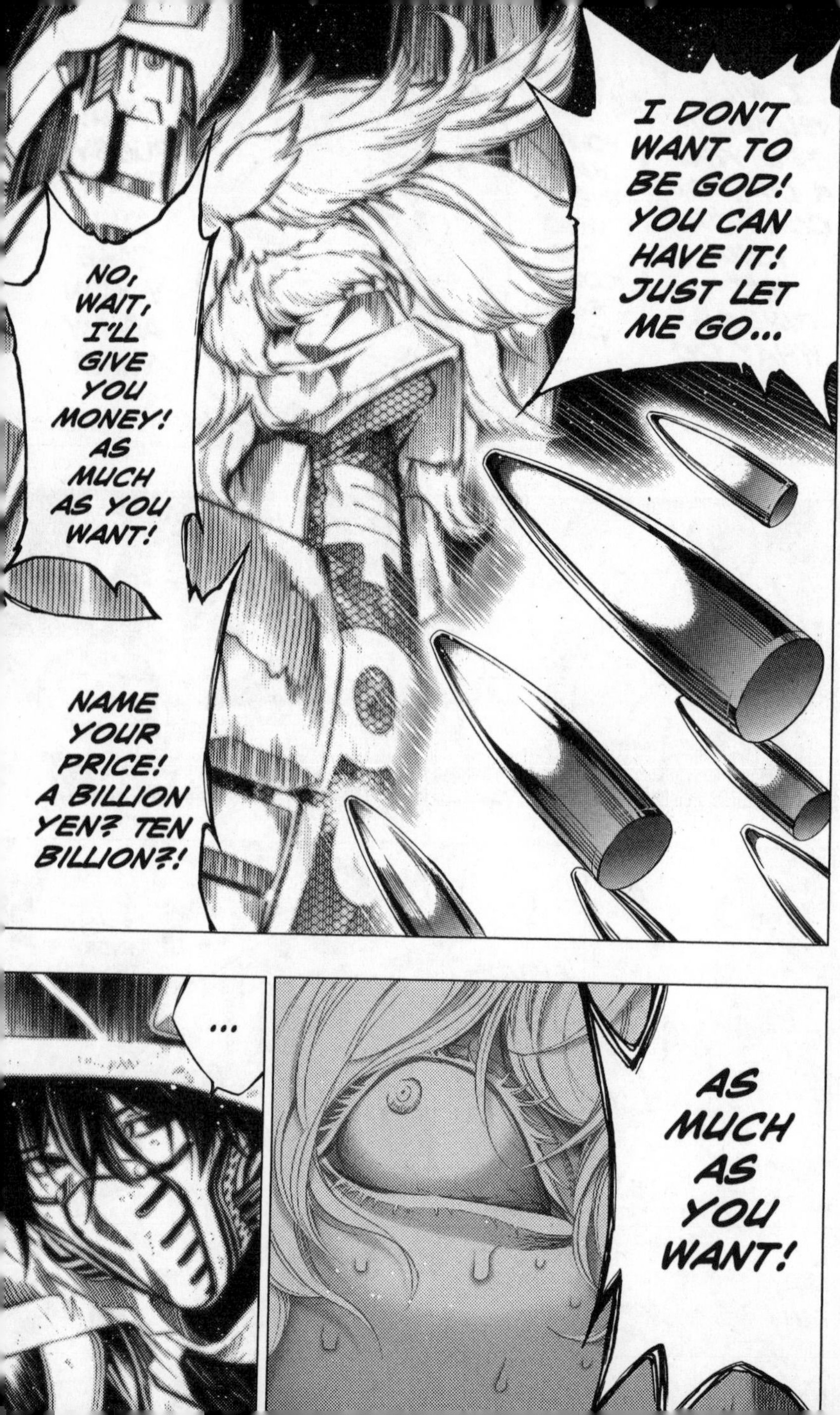
I DON'T WANT TO BE GOD! YOU CAN HAVE IT! JUST LET ME GO...
NO, WAIT, I'LL GIVE YOU MONEY! AS MUCH AS YOU WANT!
NAME YOUR PRICE! A BILLION YEN?! TEN BILLION?!
AS MUCH AS YOU WANT!
...

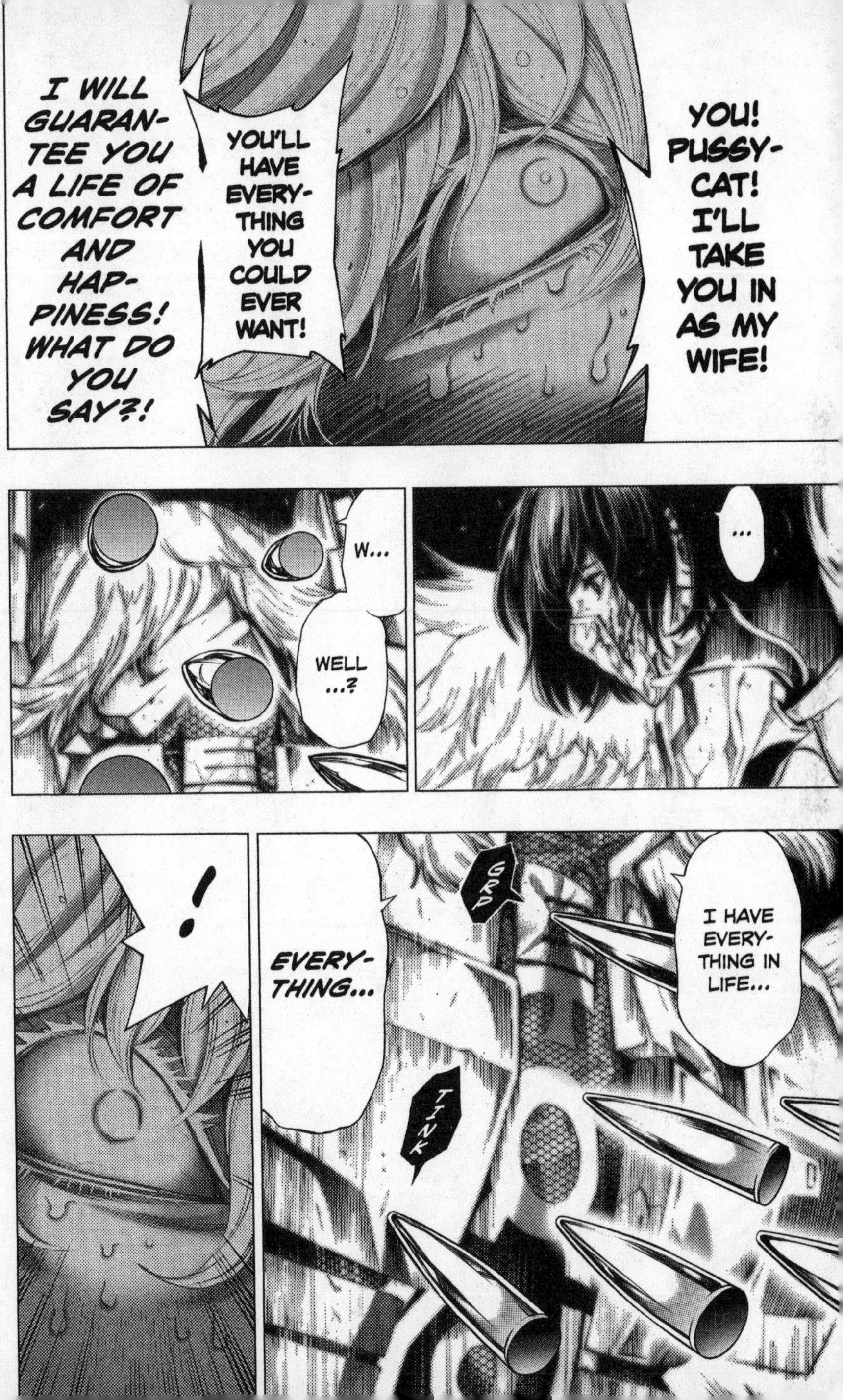

YOU! PUSSYCAT! I'LL TAKE YOU IN AS MY WIFE!
YOU'LL HAVE EVERYTHING YOU COULD EVER WANT!
I WILL GUARANTEE YOU A LIFE OF COMFORT AND HAPPINESS! WHAT DO YOU SAY?!
...
W...
WELL ...?
I HAVE EVERYTHING IN LIFE...
GRP
EVERYTHING...
TINK
!

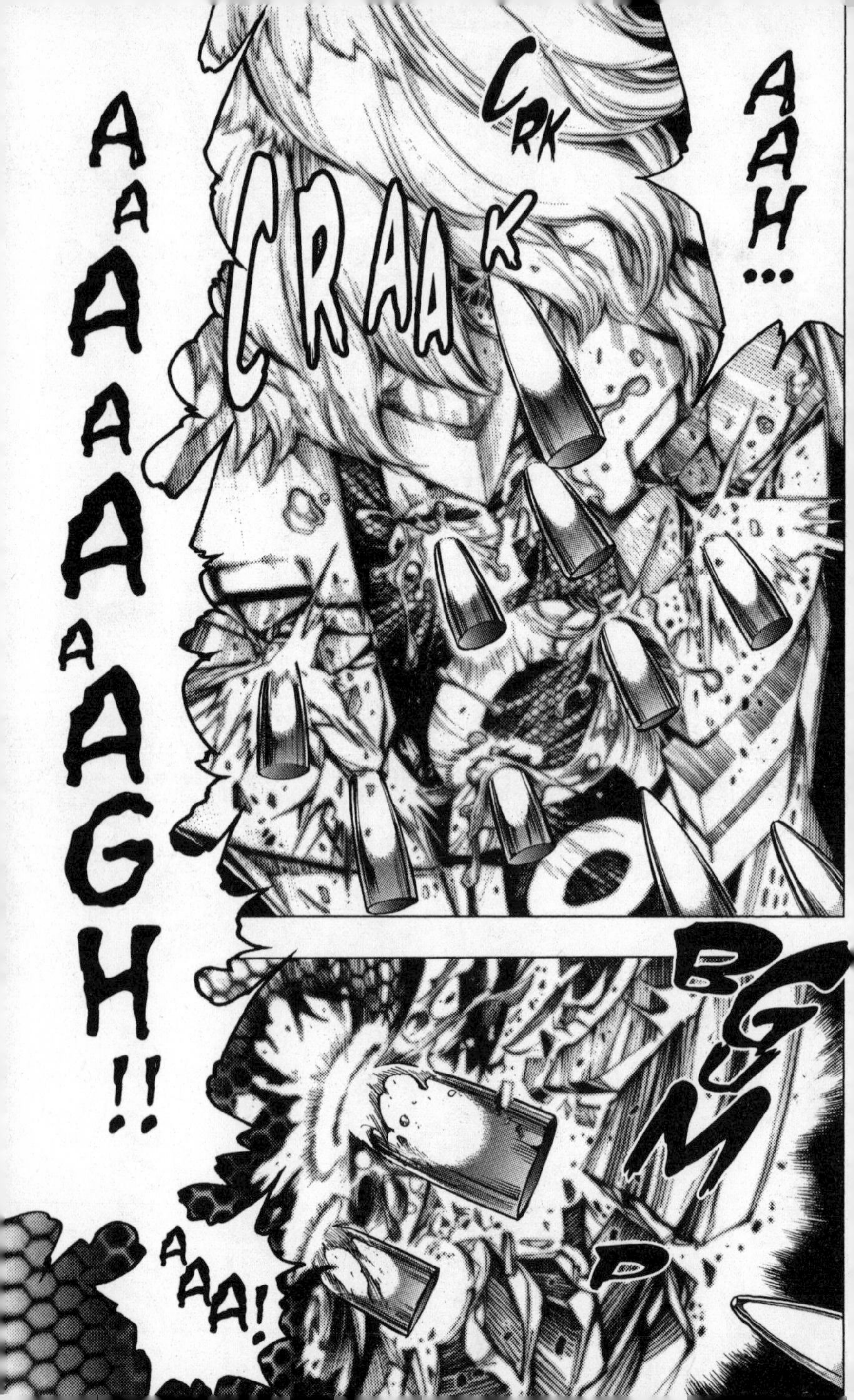
AAH...
CRK
CRAAK
AAAAAAAGH!!
BGUMP
AAAA!

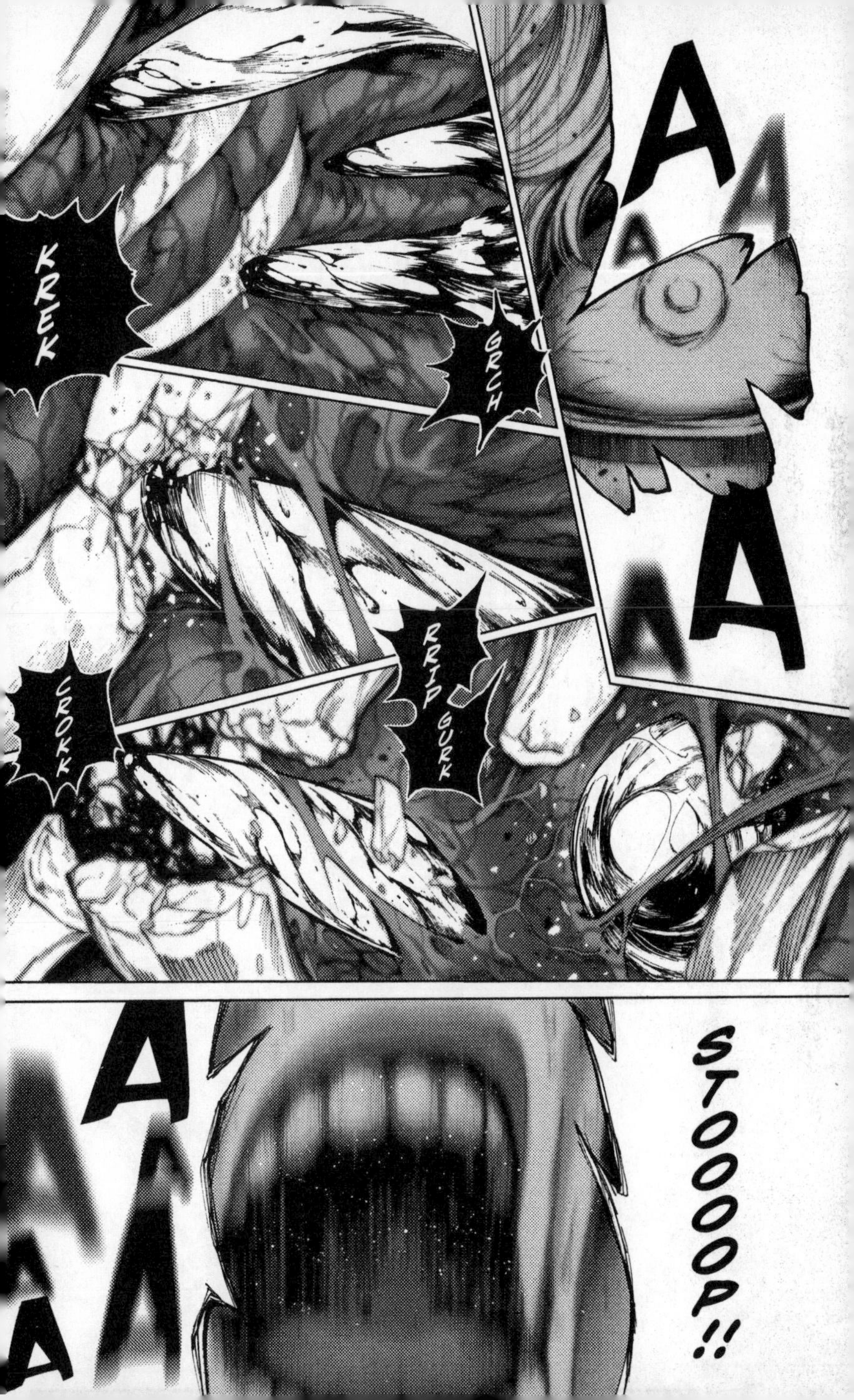
AAAAA
GRCH
KREK
RRIP
GURK
CROKK
STOOOOOP!!
AAAAA

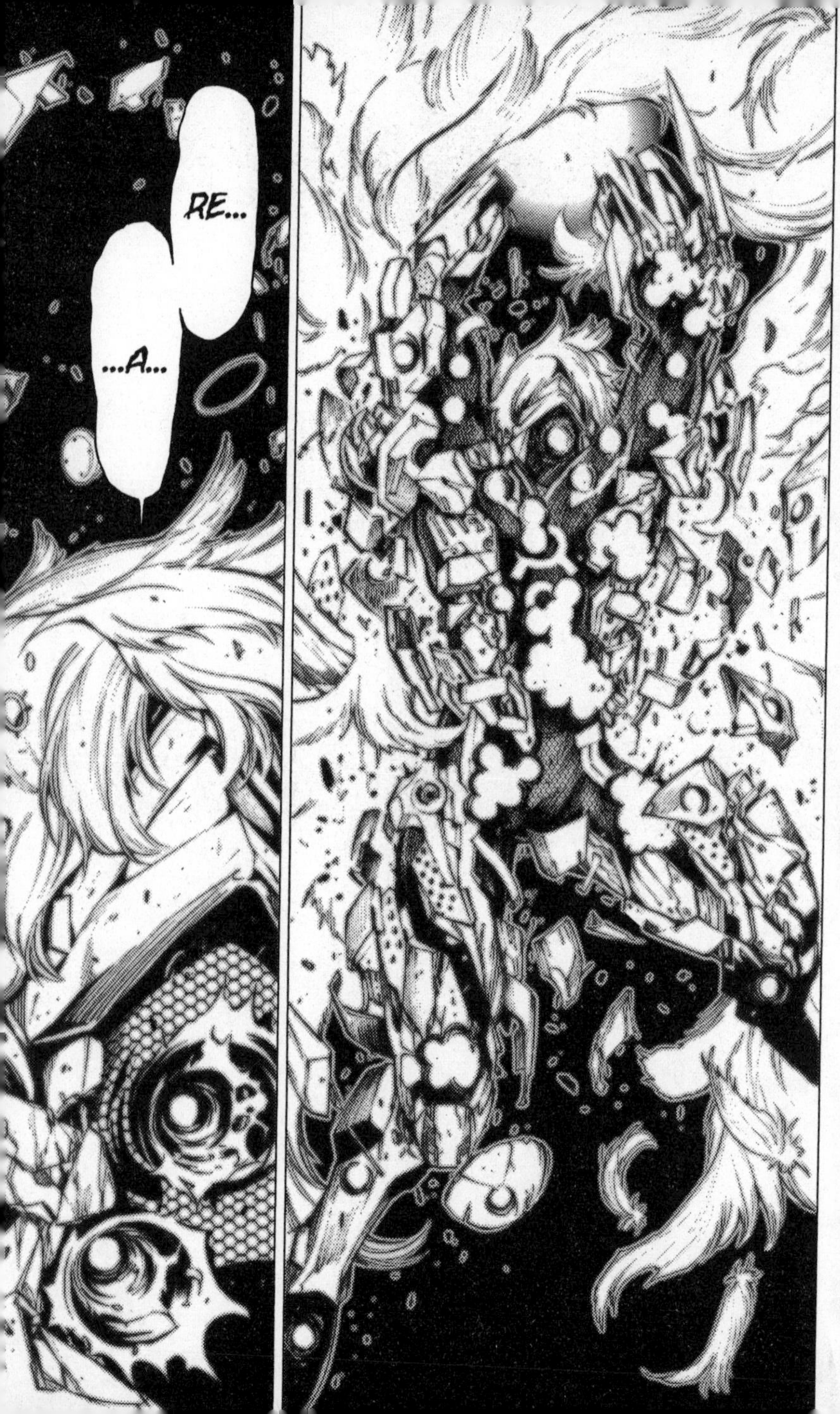
RE...
...A...

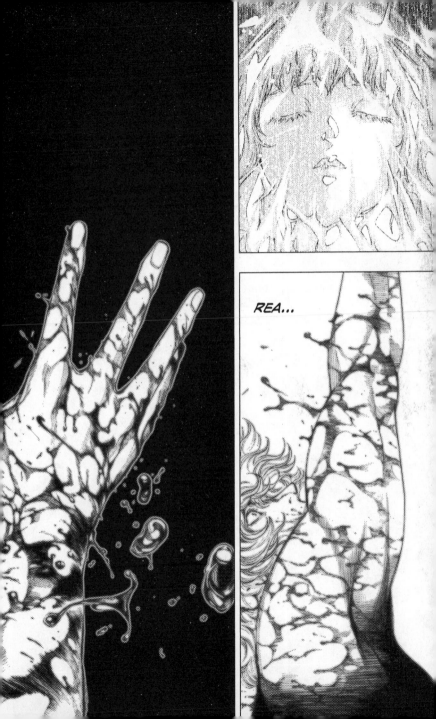

REA...

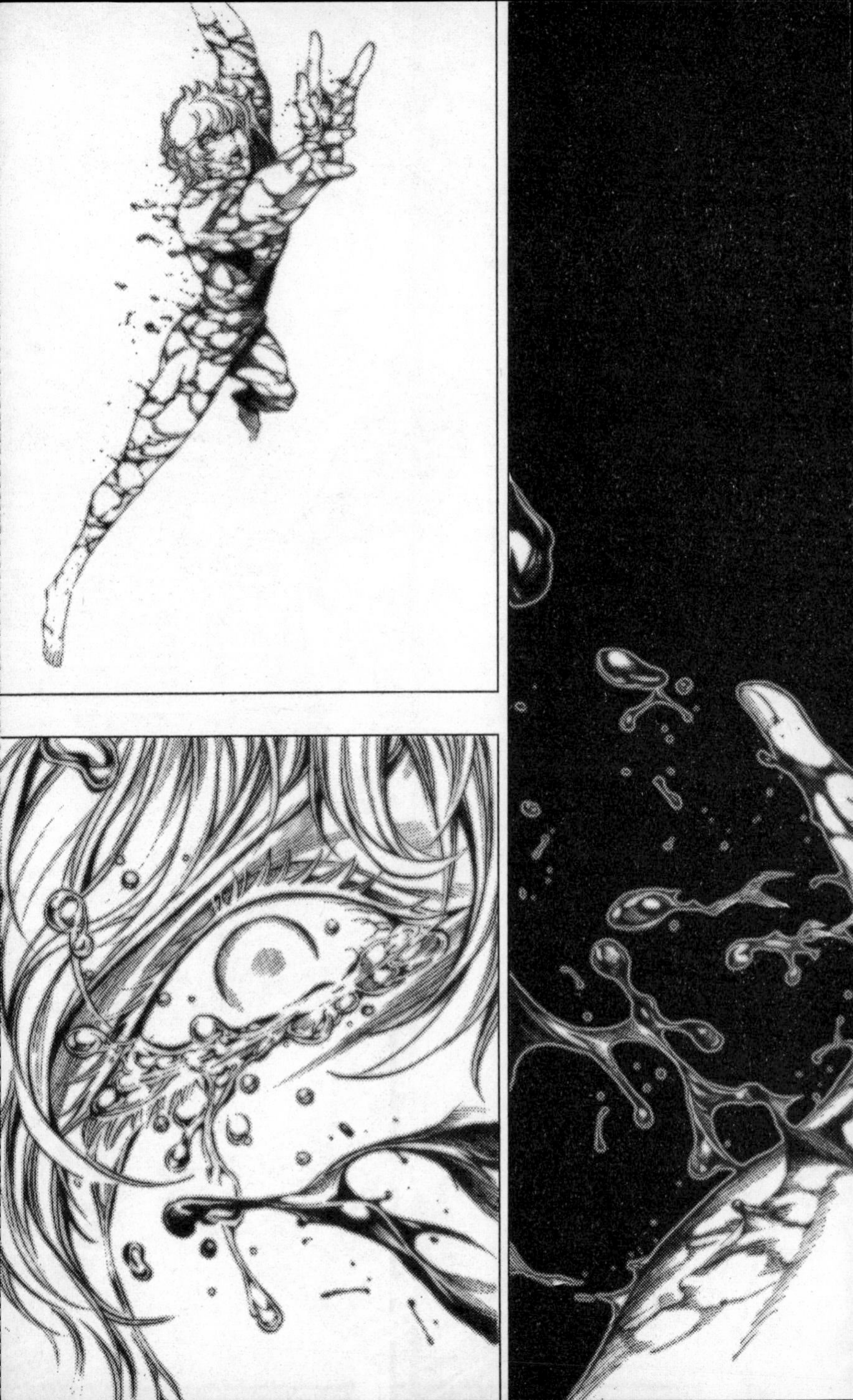

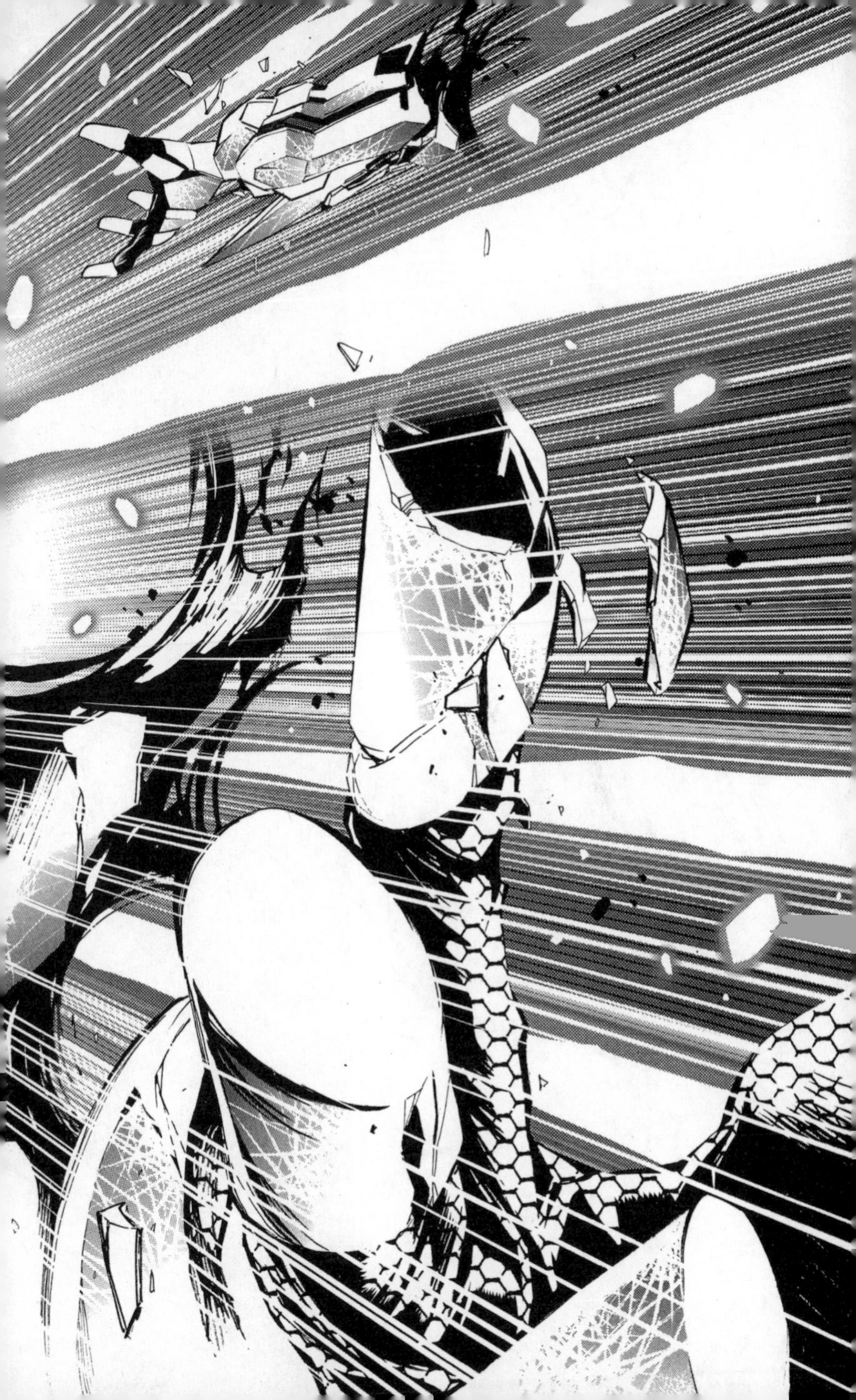

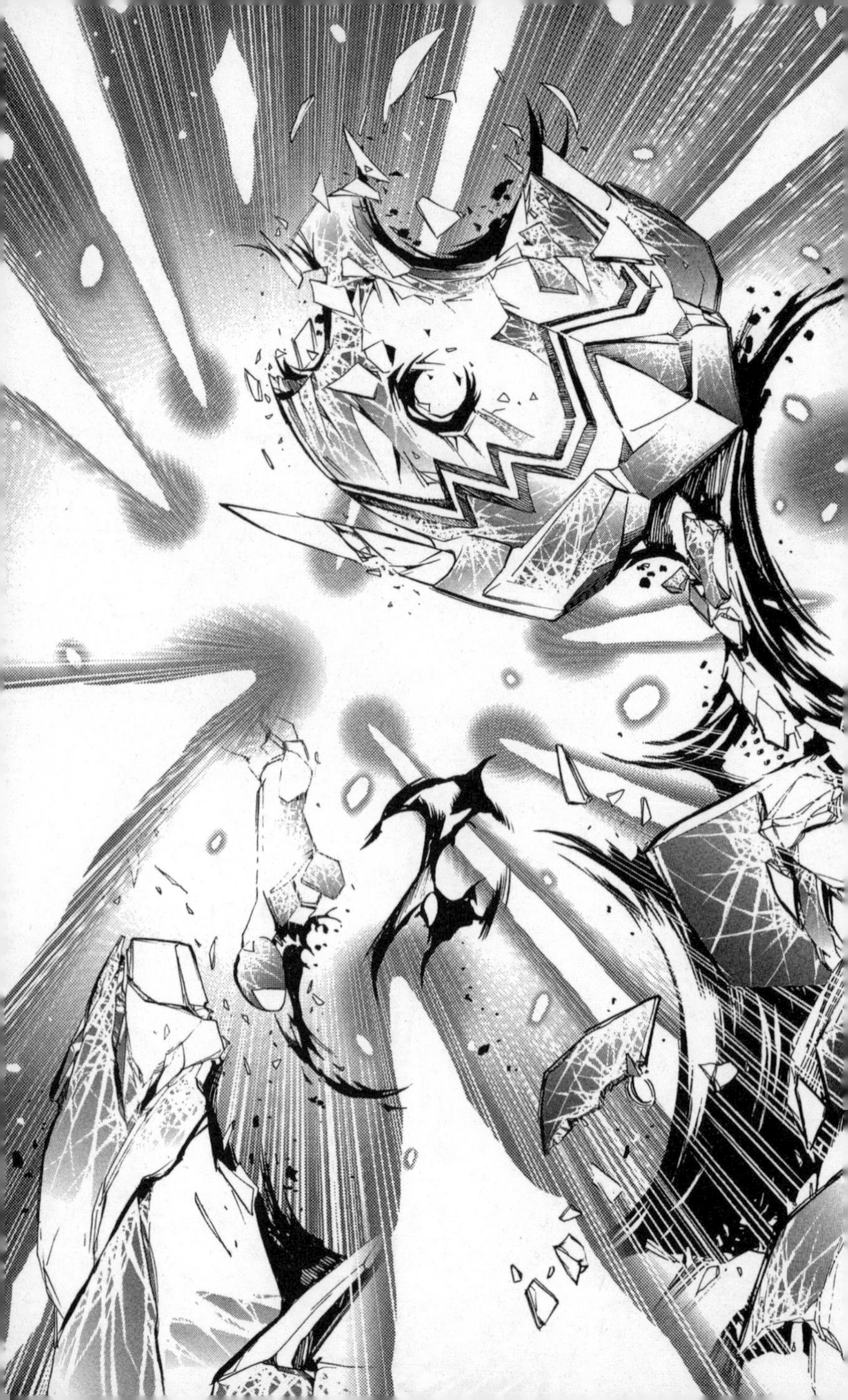

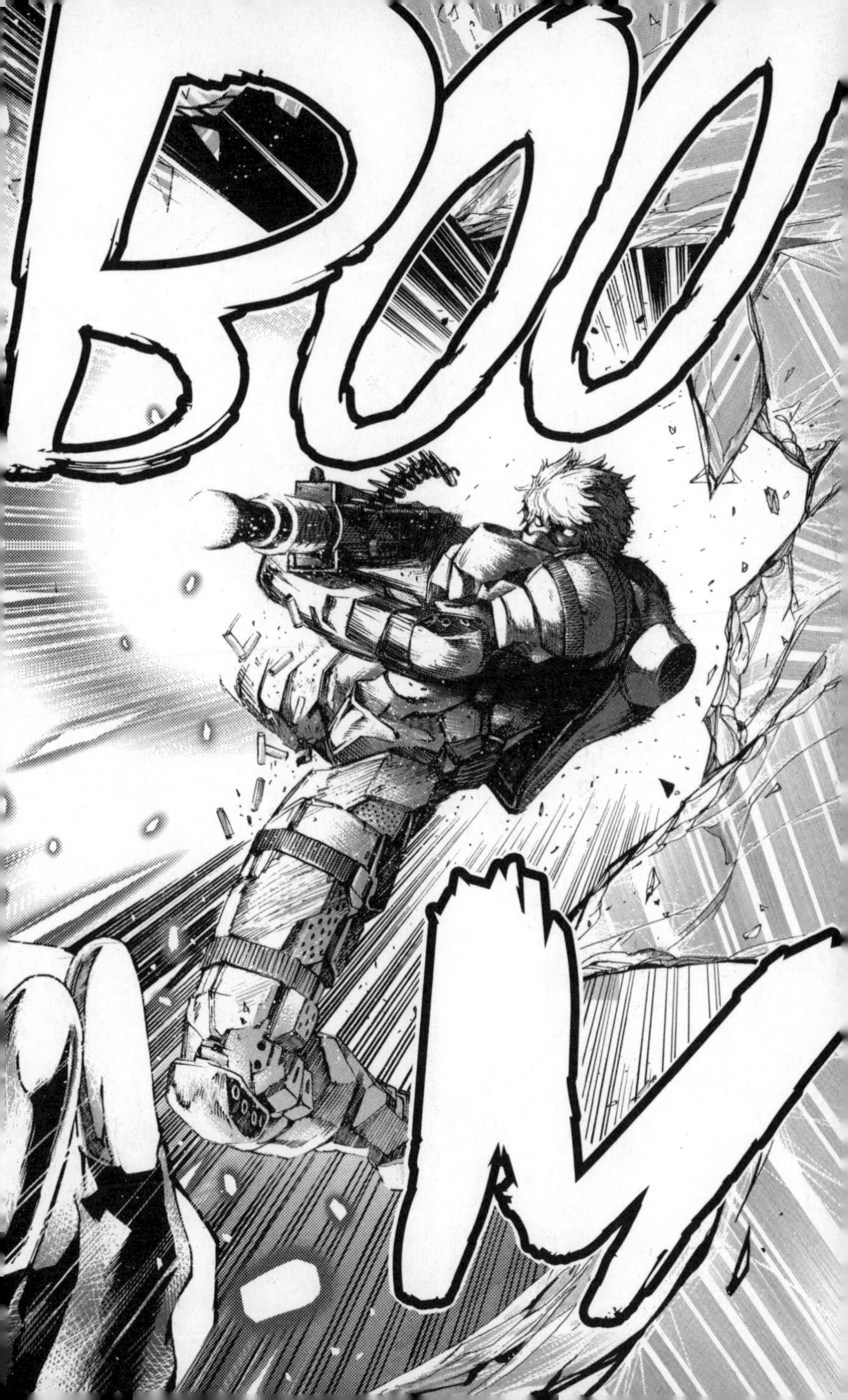
BOOM

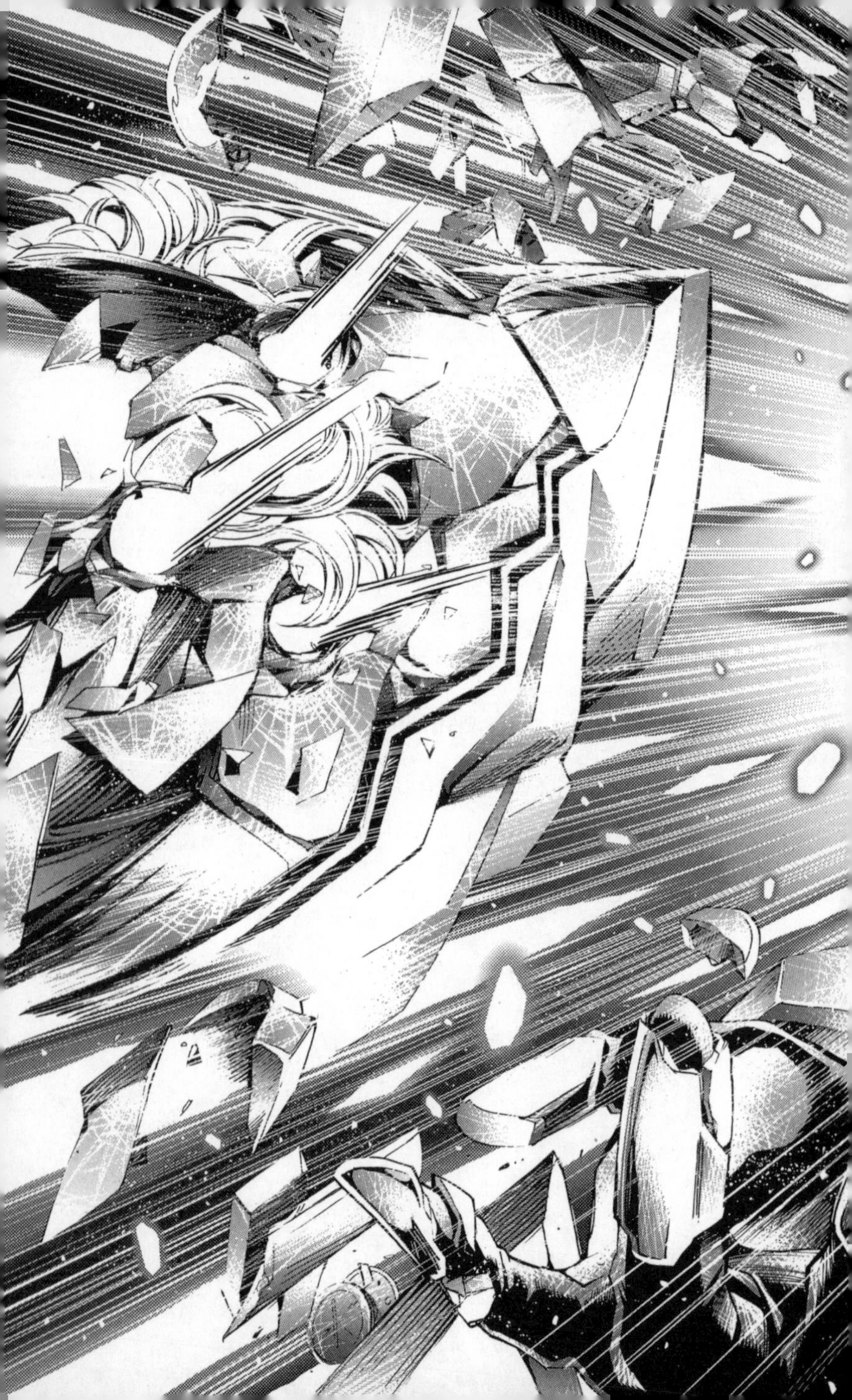

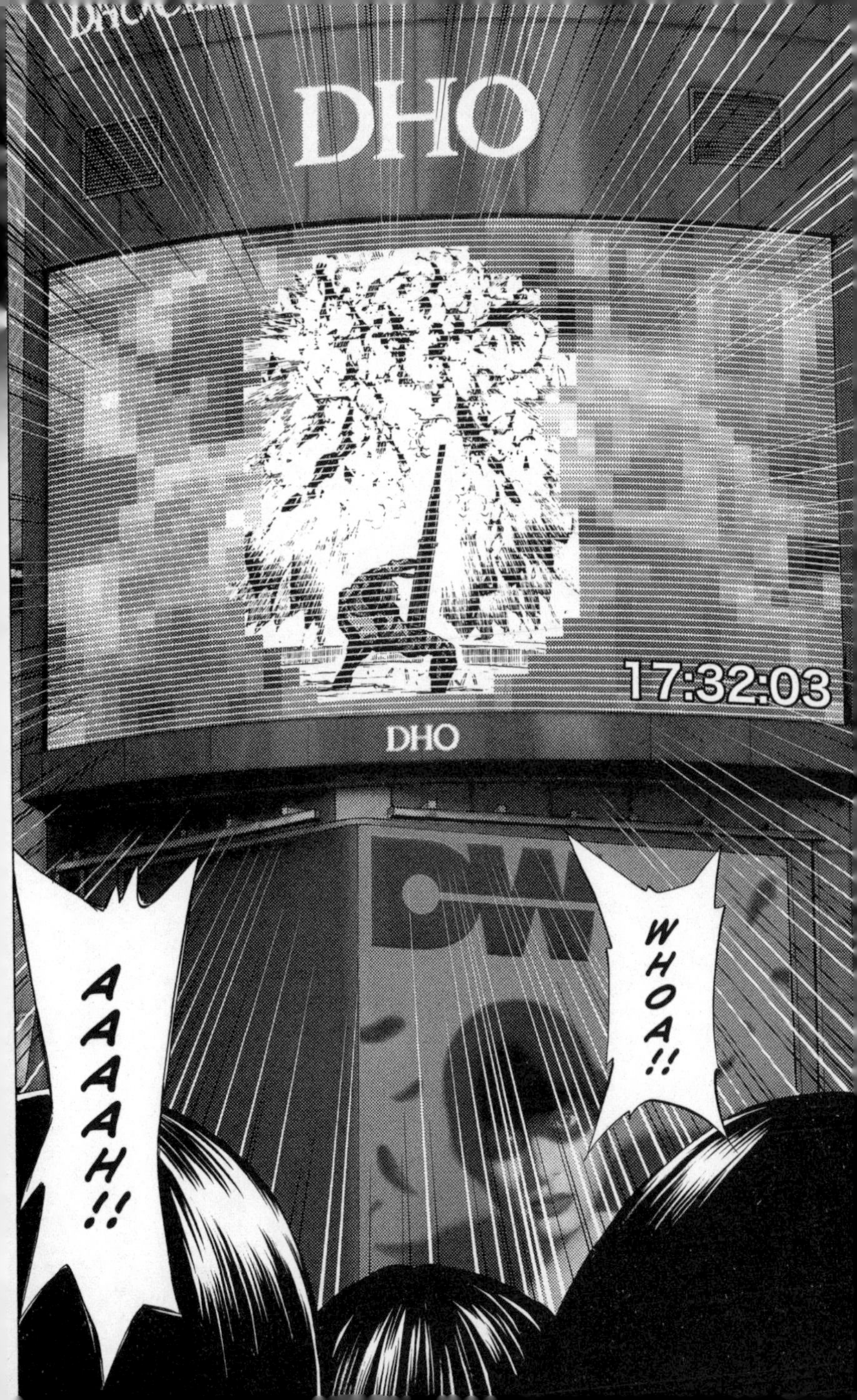
DHO
17:32:03
DHO
WHOA!!
AAAAAH!!

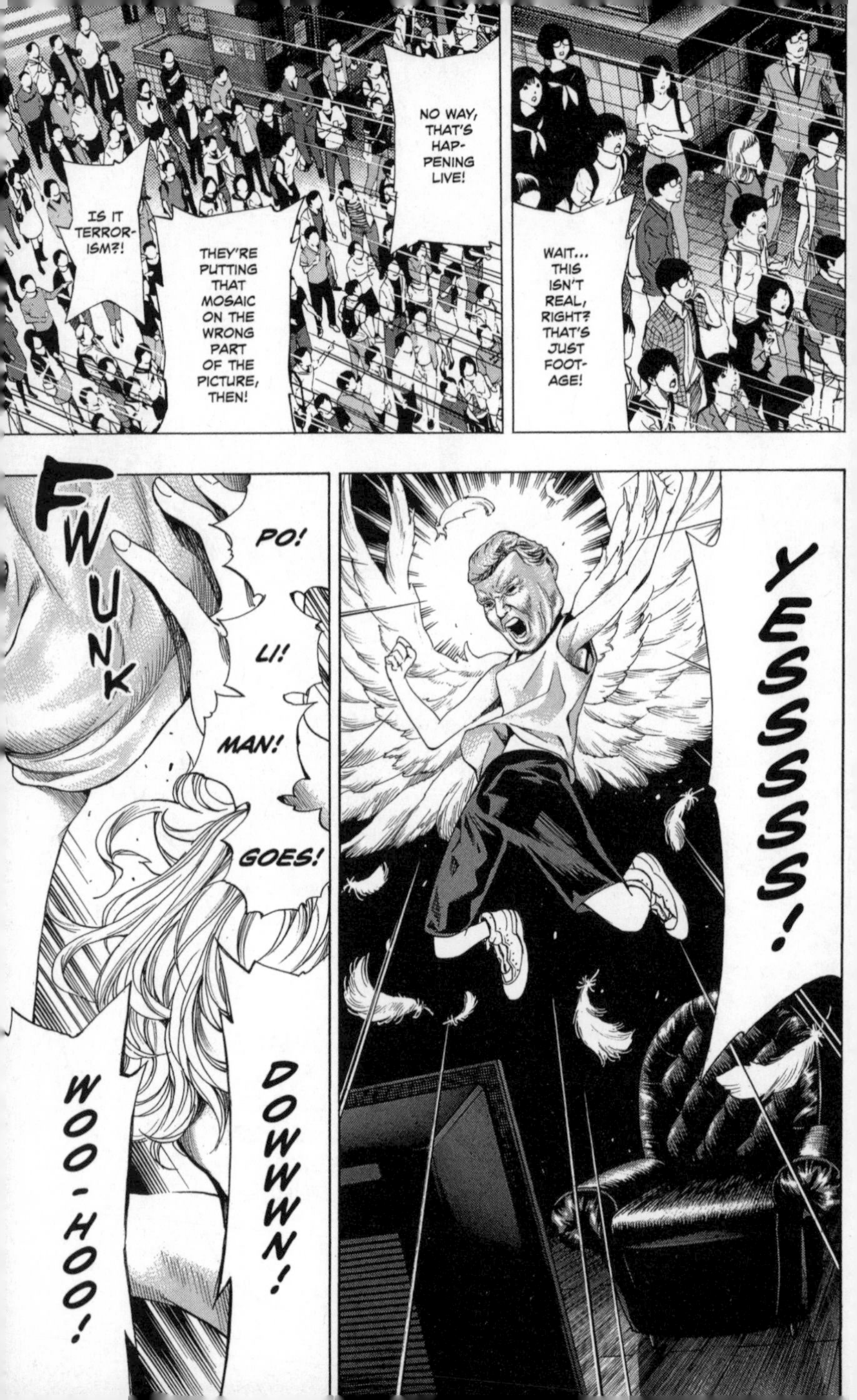
WAIT... THIS ISN'T REAL, RIGHT? THAT'S JUST FOOTAGE!
NO WAY, THAT'S HAPPENING LIVE!
THEY'RE PUTTING THAT MOSAIC ON THE WRONG PART OF THE PICTURE, THEN!
IS IT TERRORISM?!
YESSSSSS!
FWUNK
PO!
LI!
MAN!
GOES!
DOWWWN!
WOO-HOO!

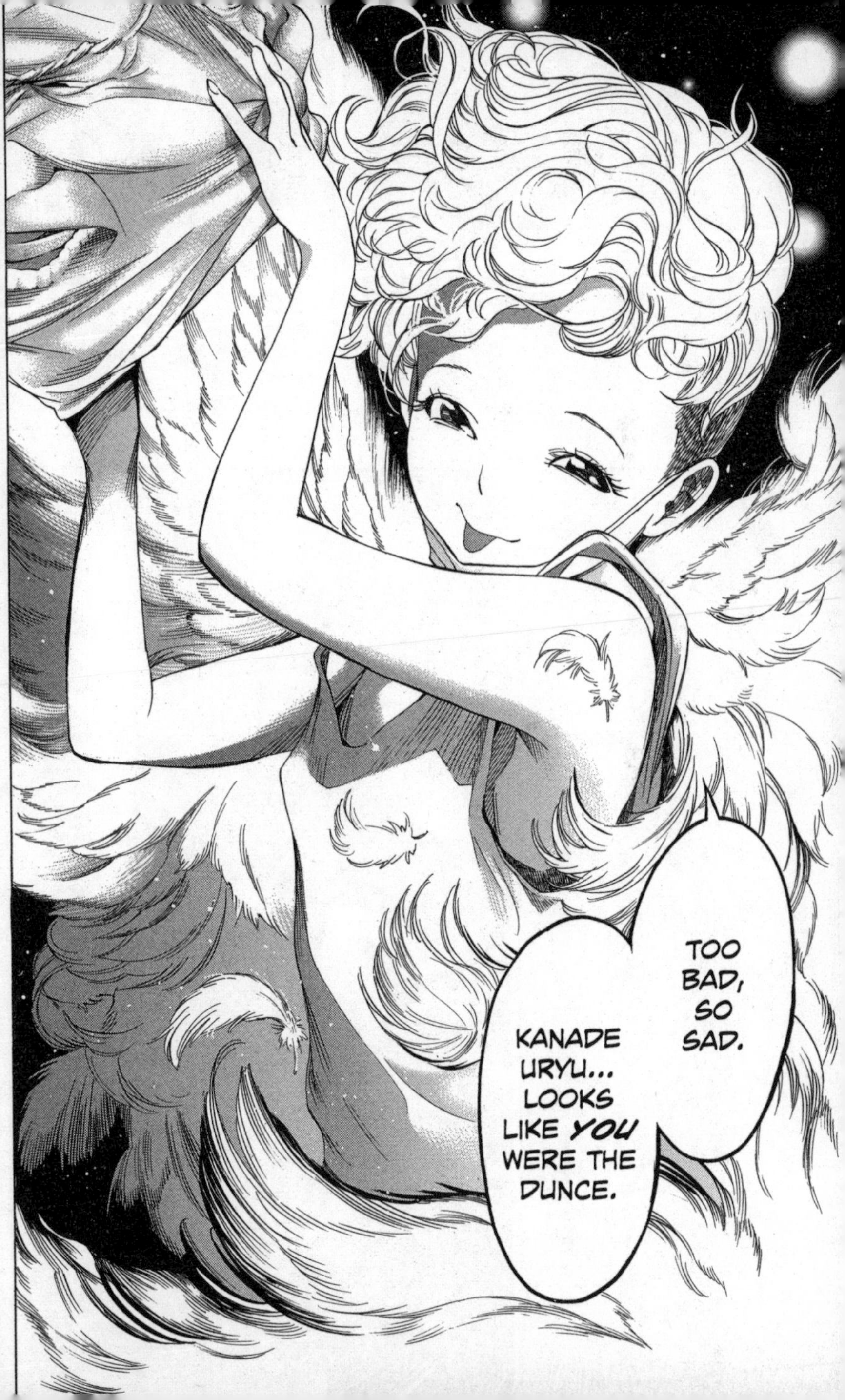
TOO BAD, SO SAD.
KANADE URYU... LOOKS LIKE *YOU* WERE THE DUNCE.

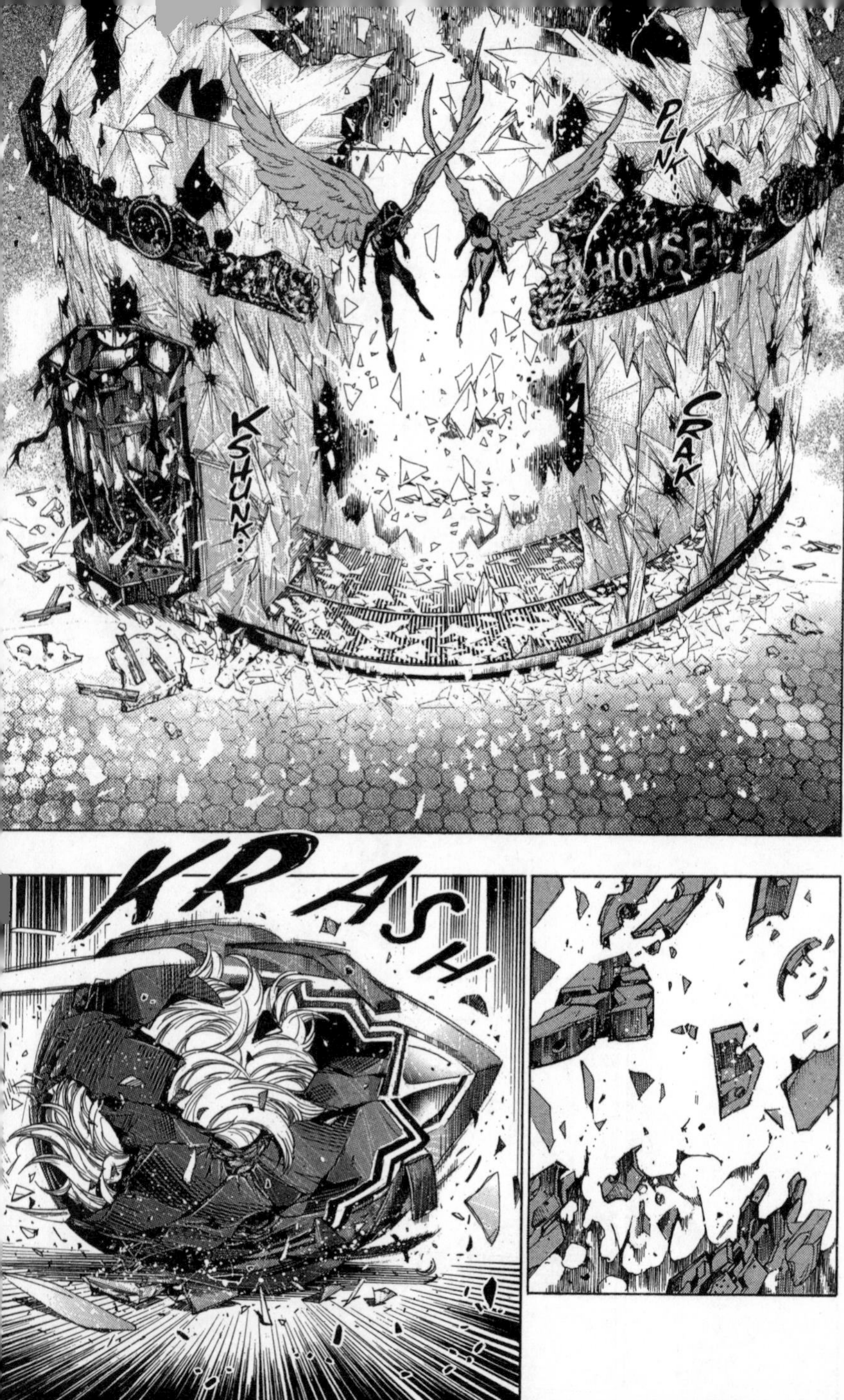
PLINK...
HOUSE
CRAK
KSHUNK...
KRASH

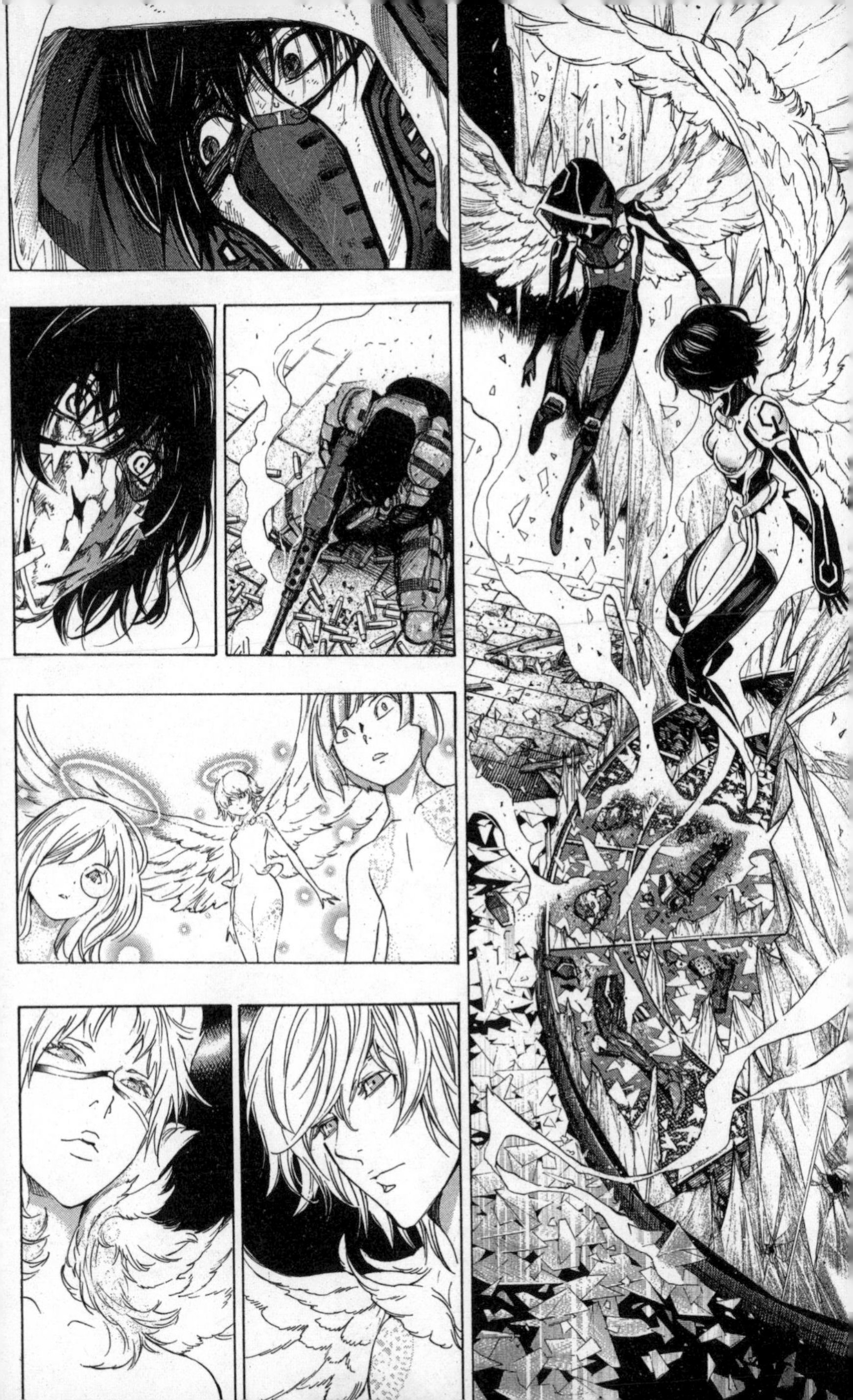

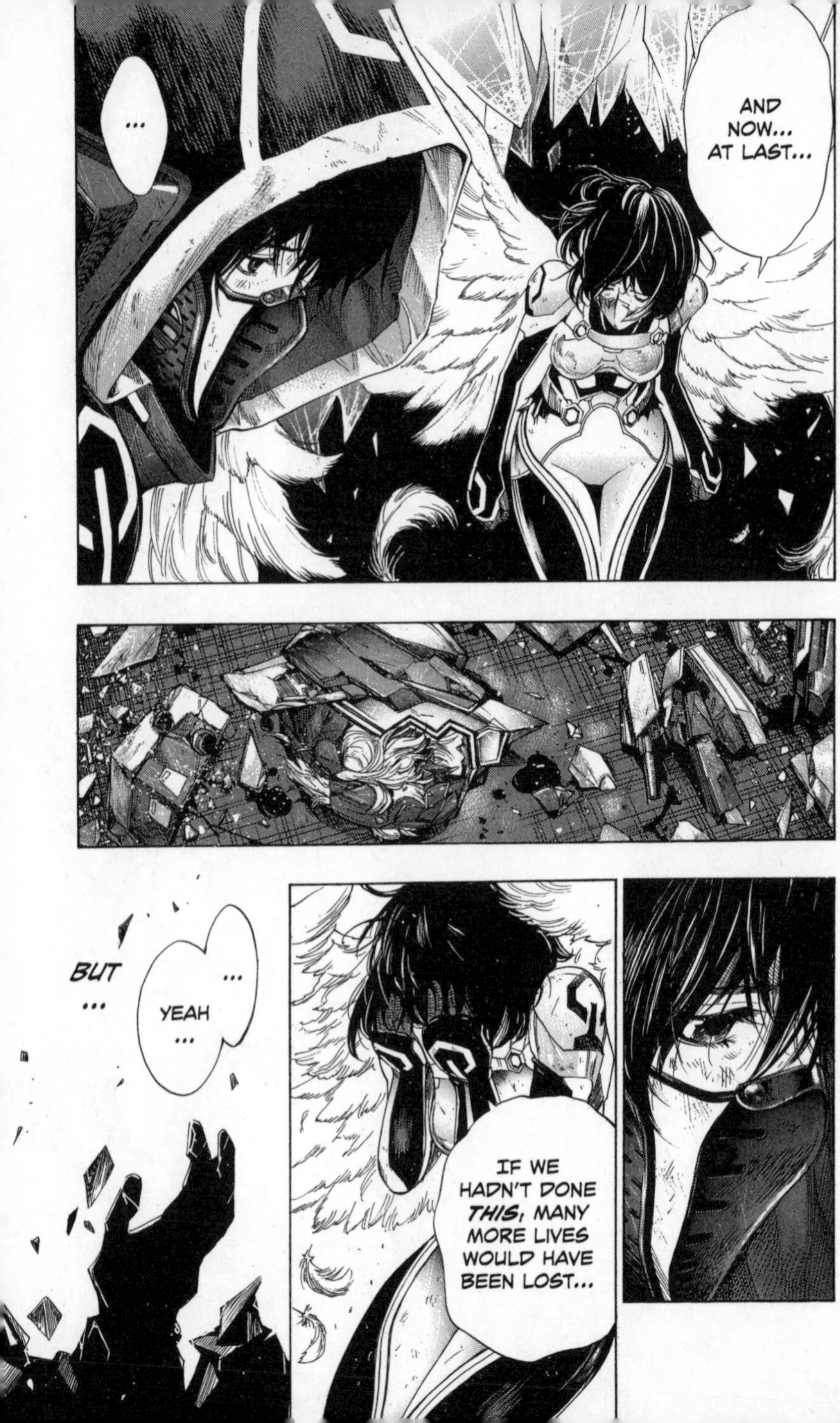
AND NOW... AT LAST...
...
IF WE HADN'T DONE *THIS*, MANY MORE LIVES WOULD HAVE BEEN LOST...
... YEAH ...
BUT ...

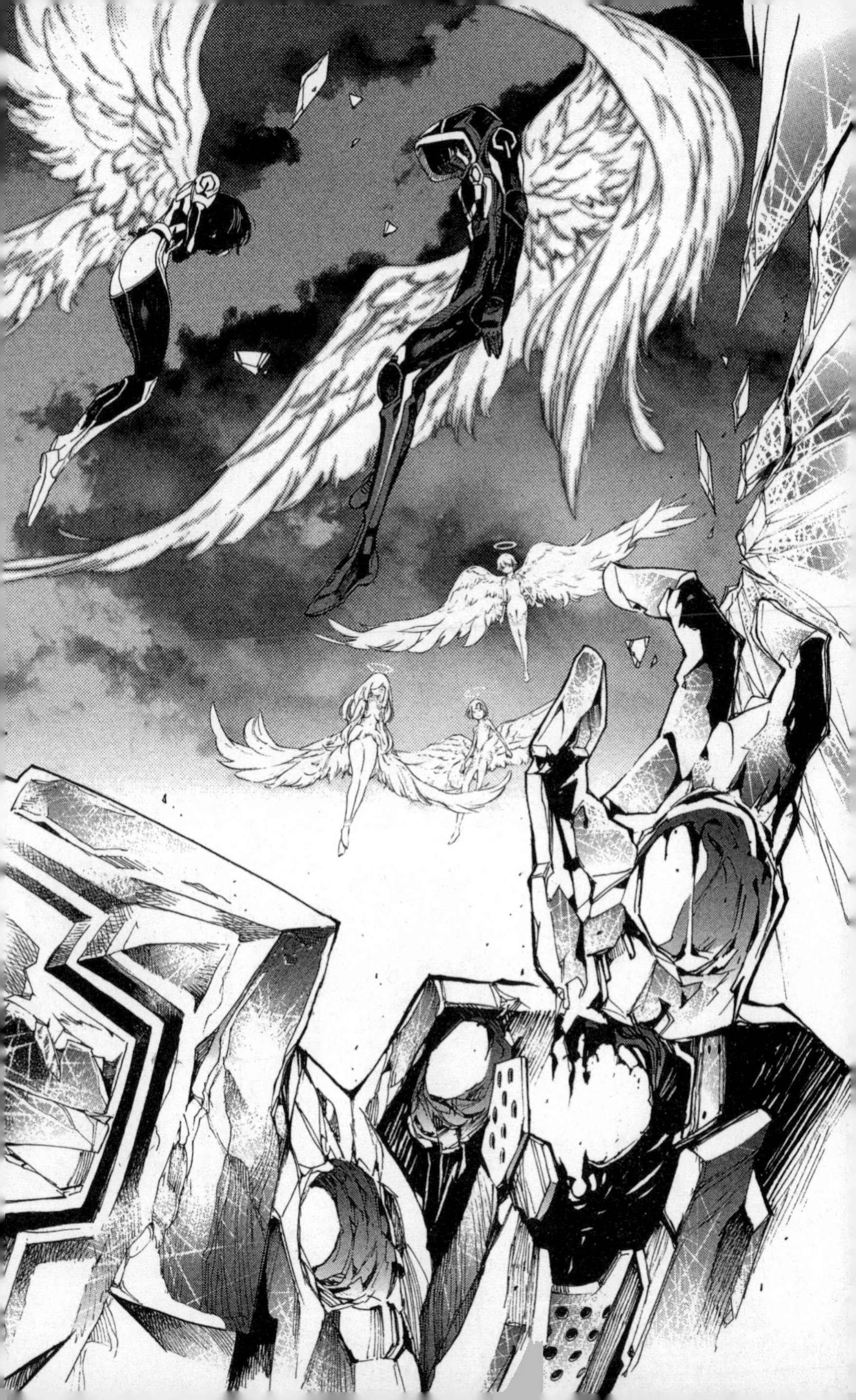

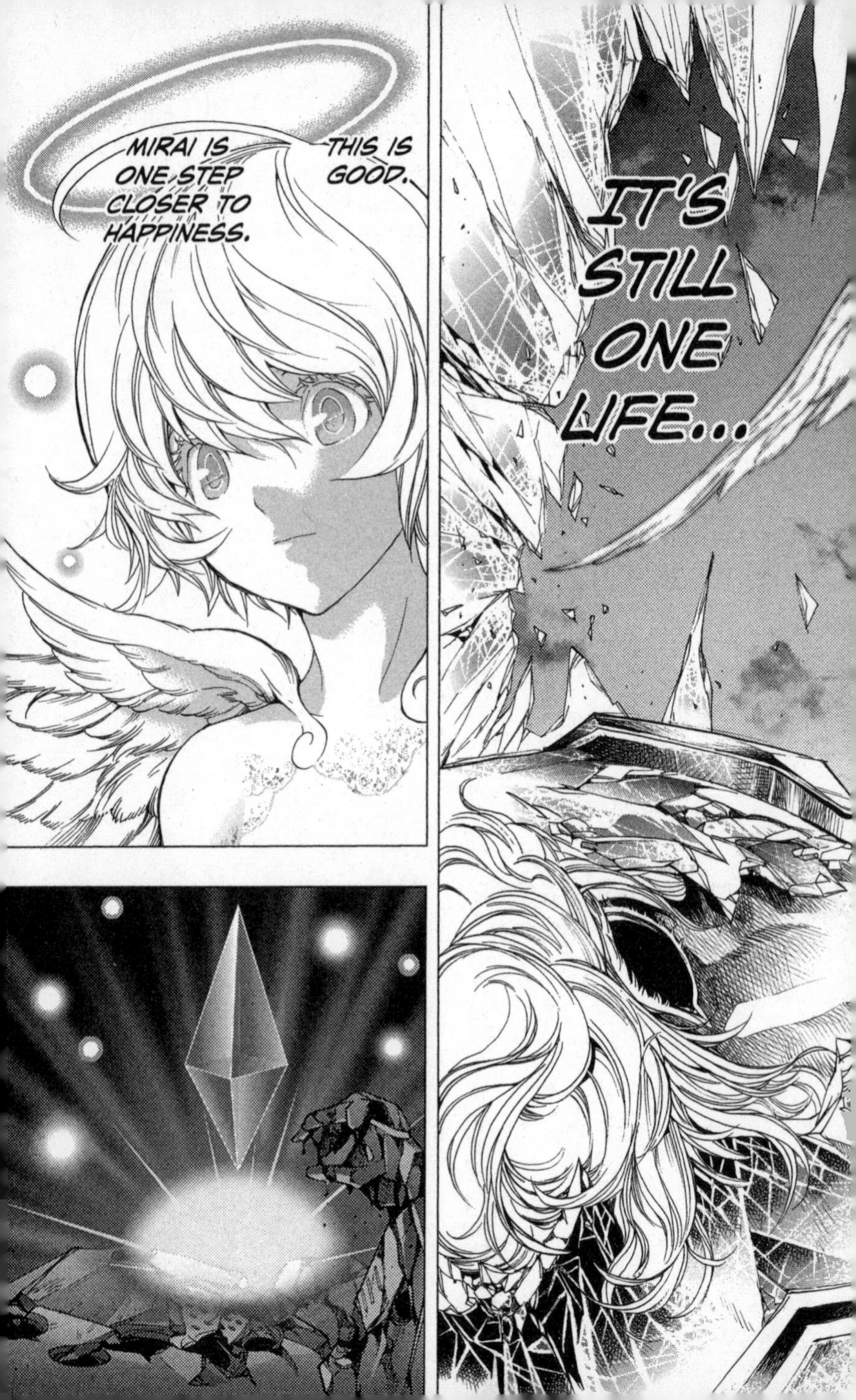
IT'S STILL ONE LIFE...
THIS IS GOOD.
MIRAI IS ONE STEP CLOSER TO HAPPINESS.

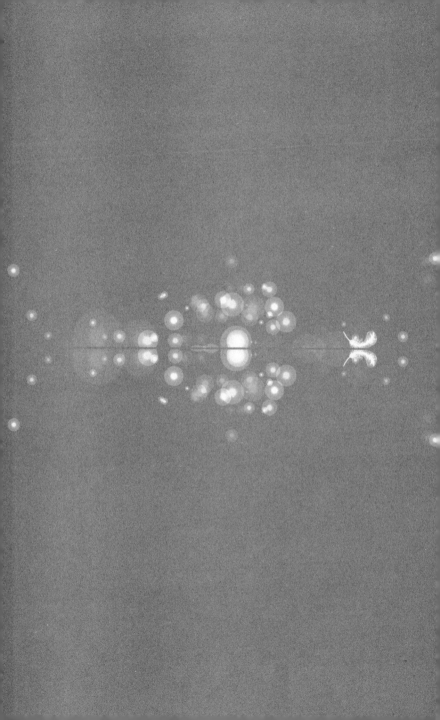

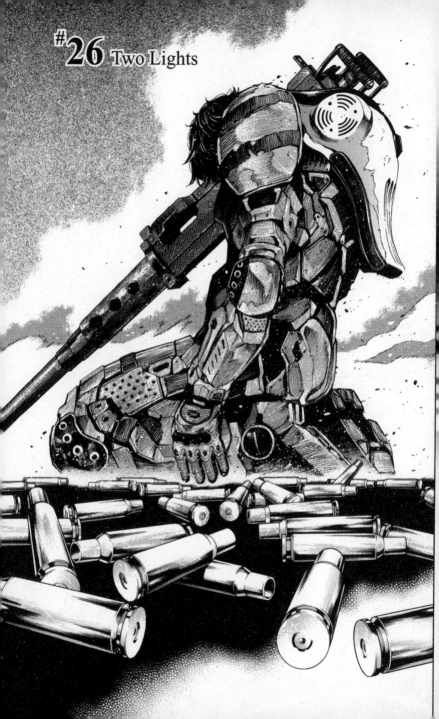

#26 Two Lights

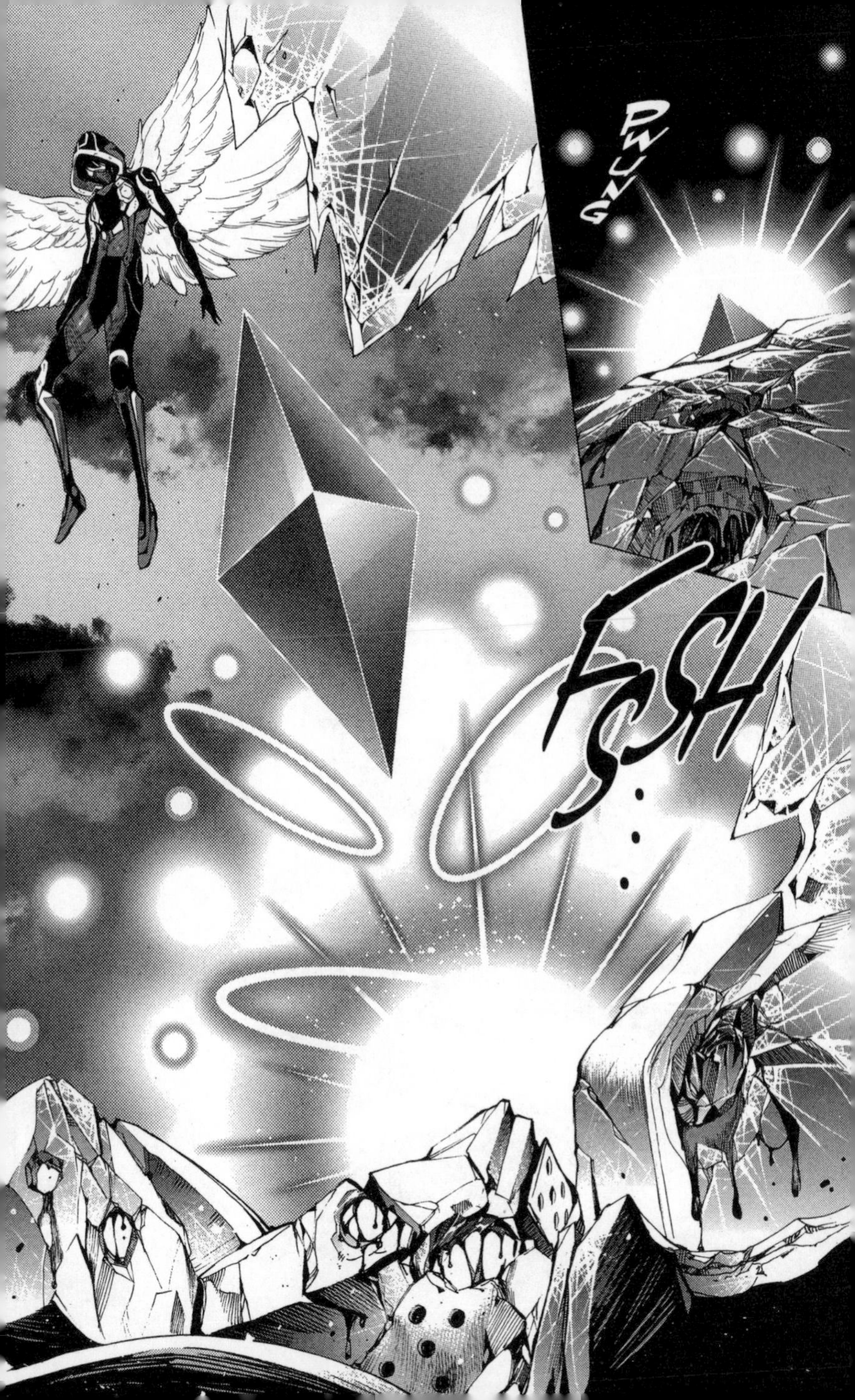
PWUNG
FSSH

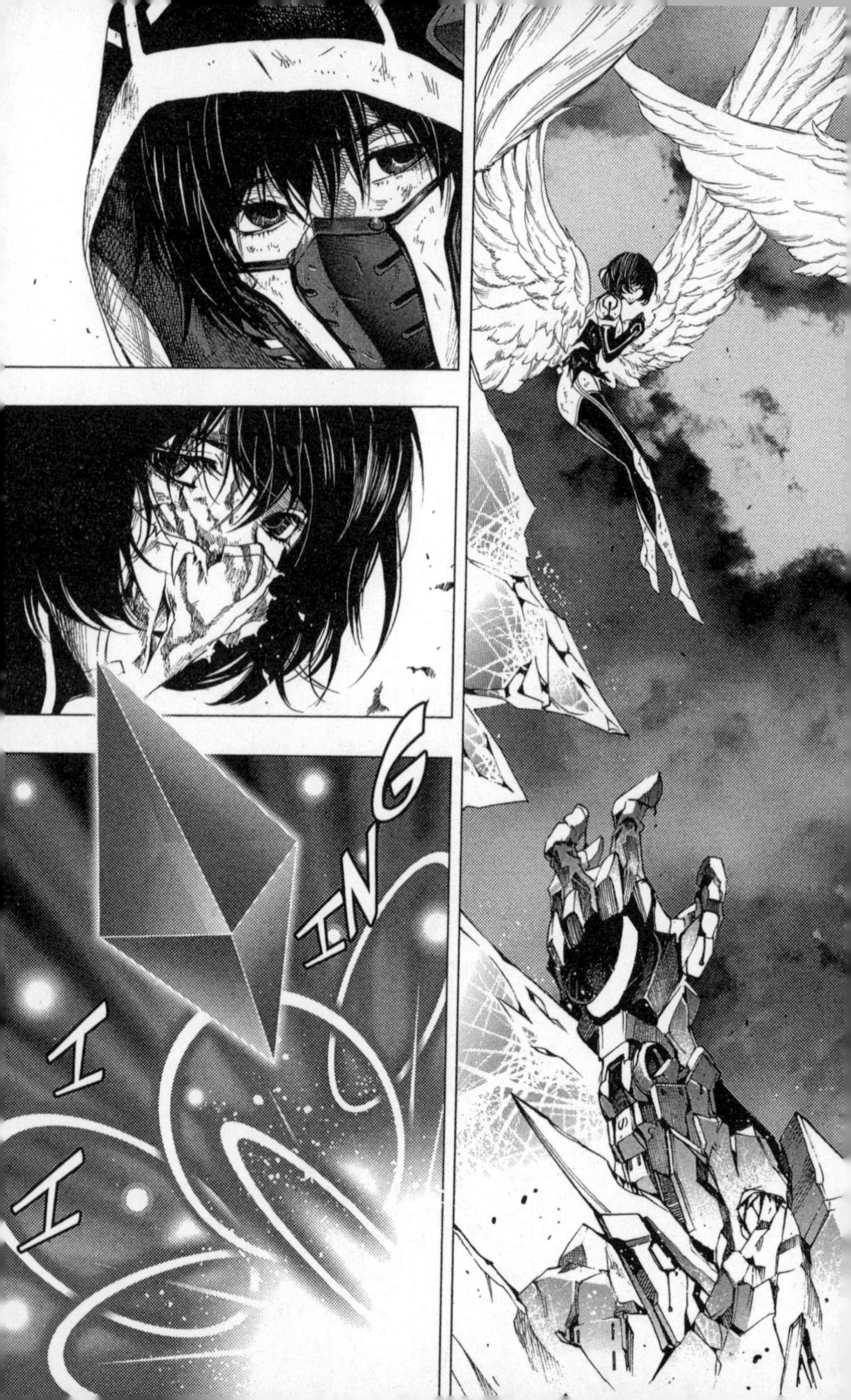
HIING

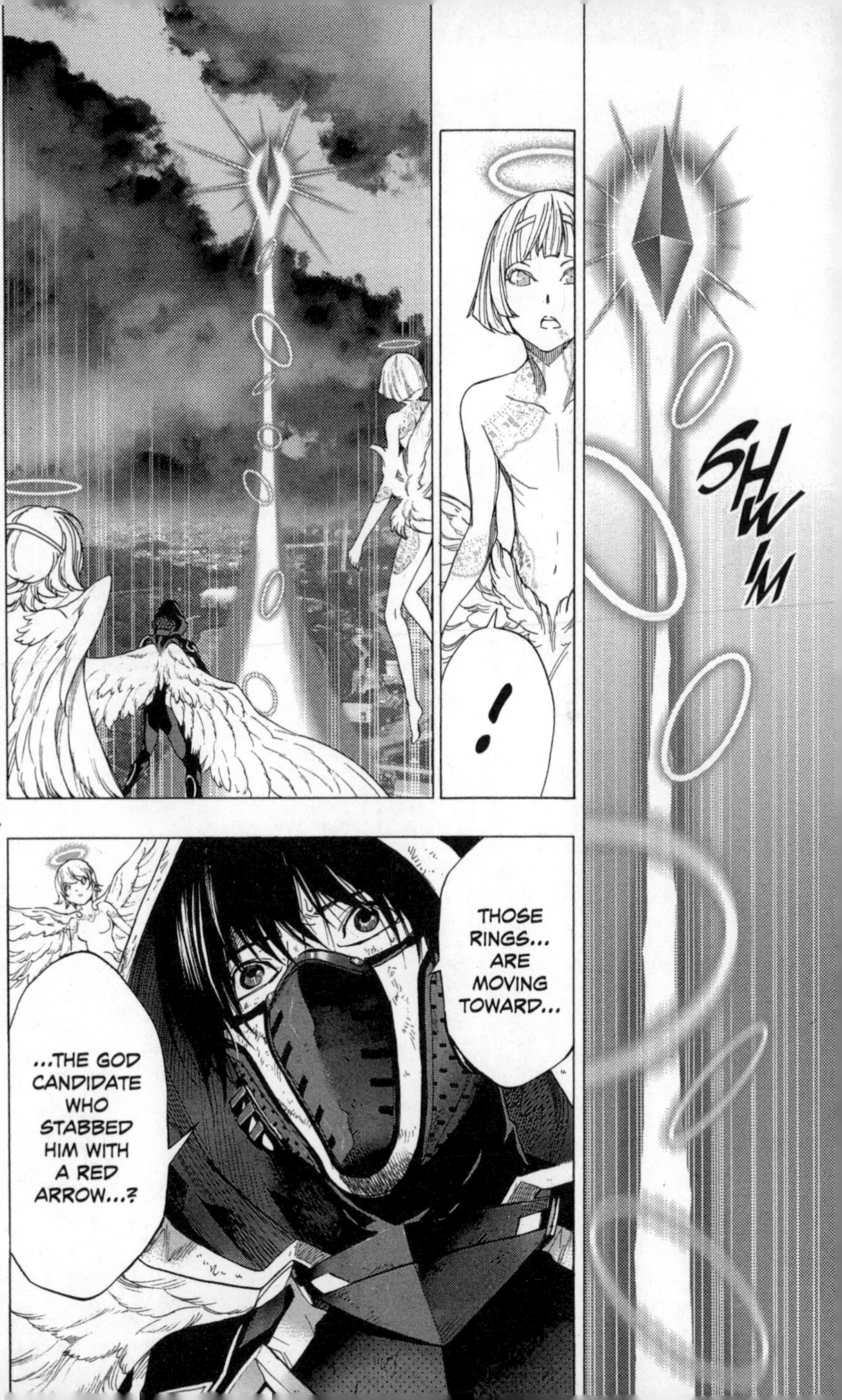
SHWIM
!
THOSE RINGS... ARE MOVING TOWARD...
...THE GOD CANDIDATE WHO STABBED HIM WITH A RED ARROW...?

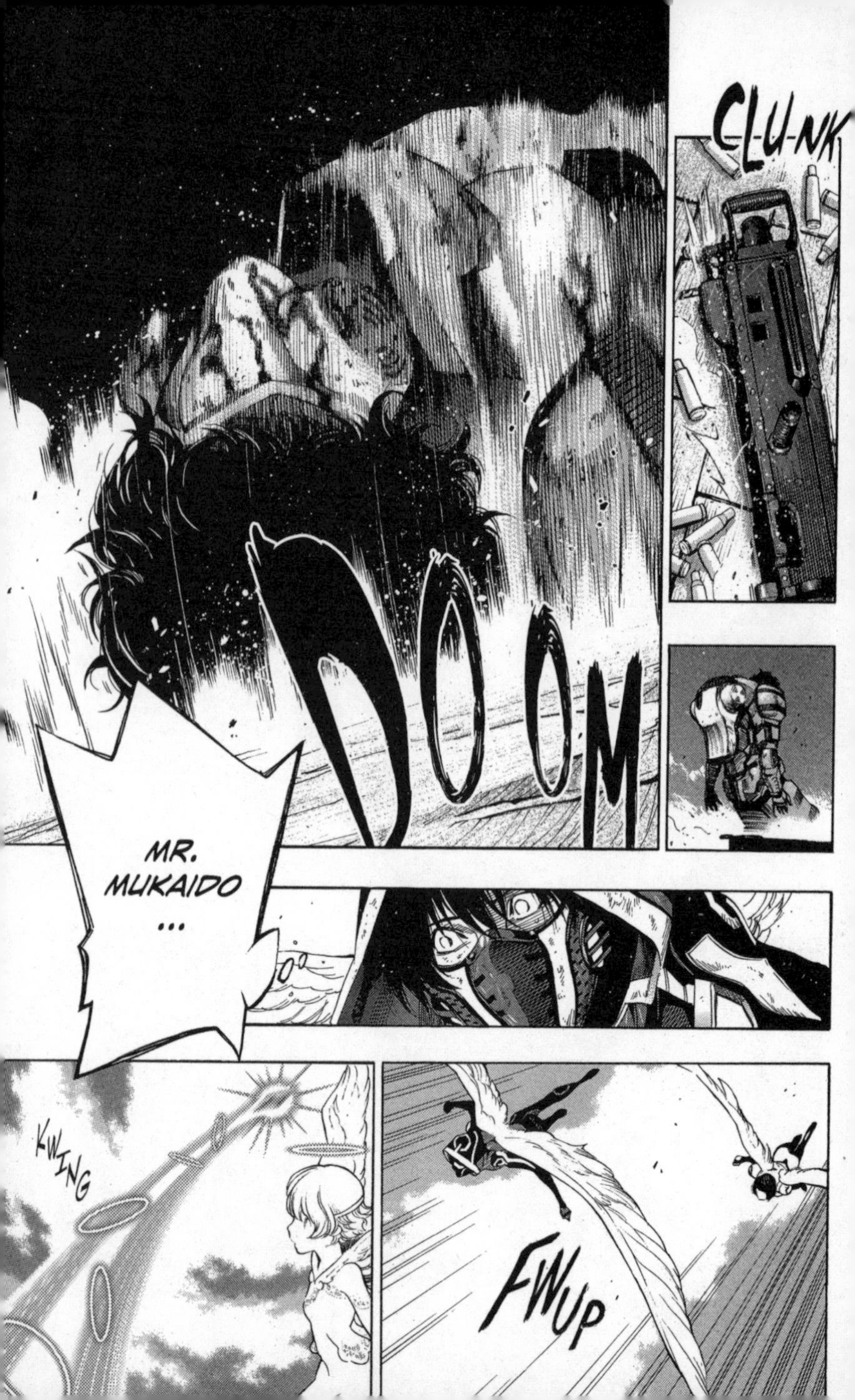
CLU-NK
DOOM
MR. MUKAIDO ...
FWUP
KWING

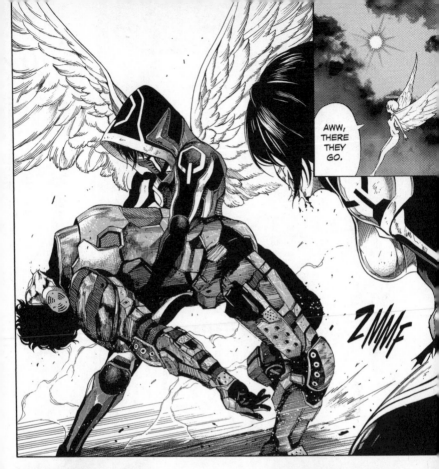

AWW, THERE THEY GO.

ZMMMF

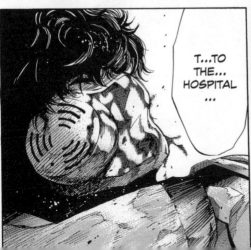

T...TO THE... HOSPITAL ...

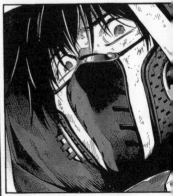

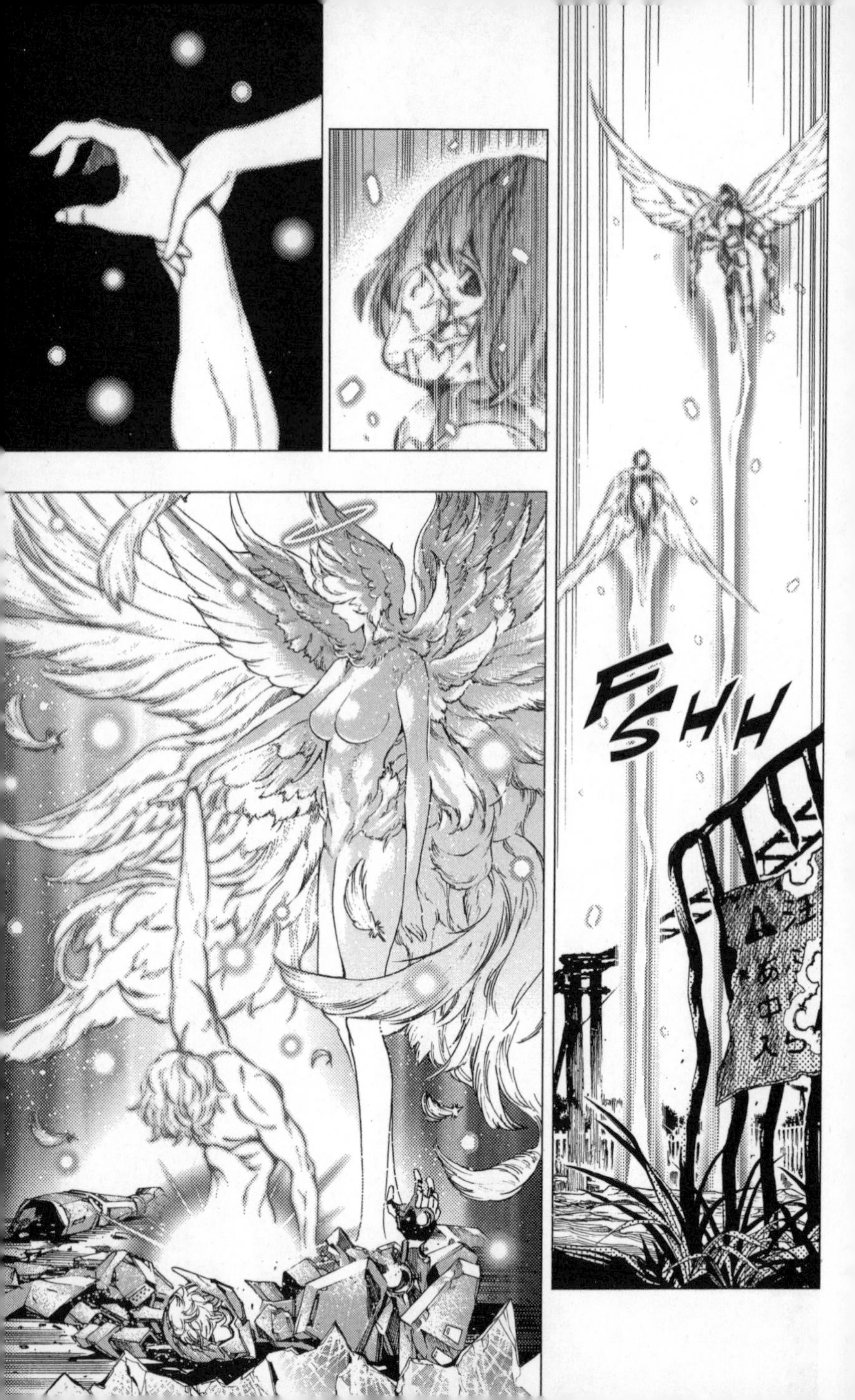
FSHH

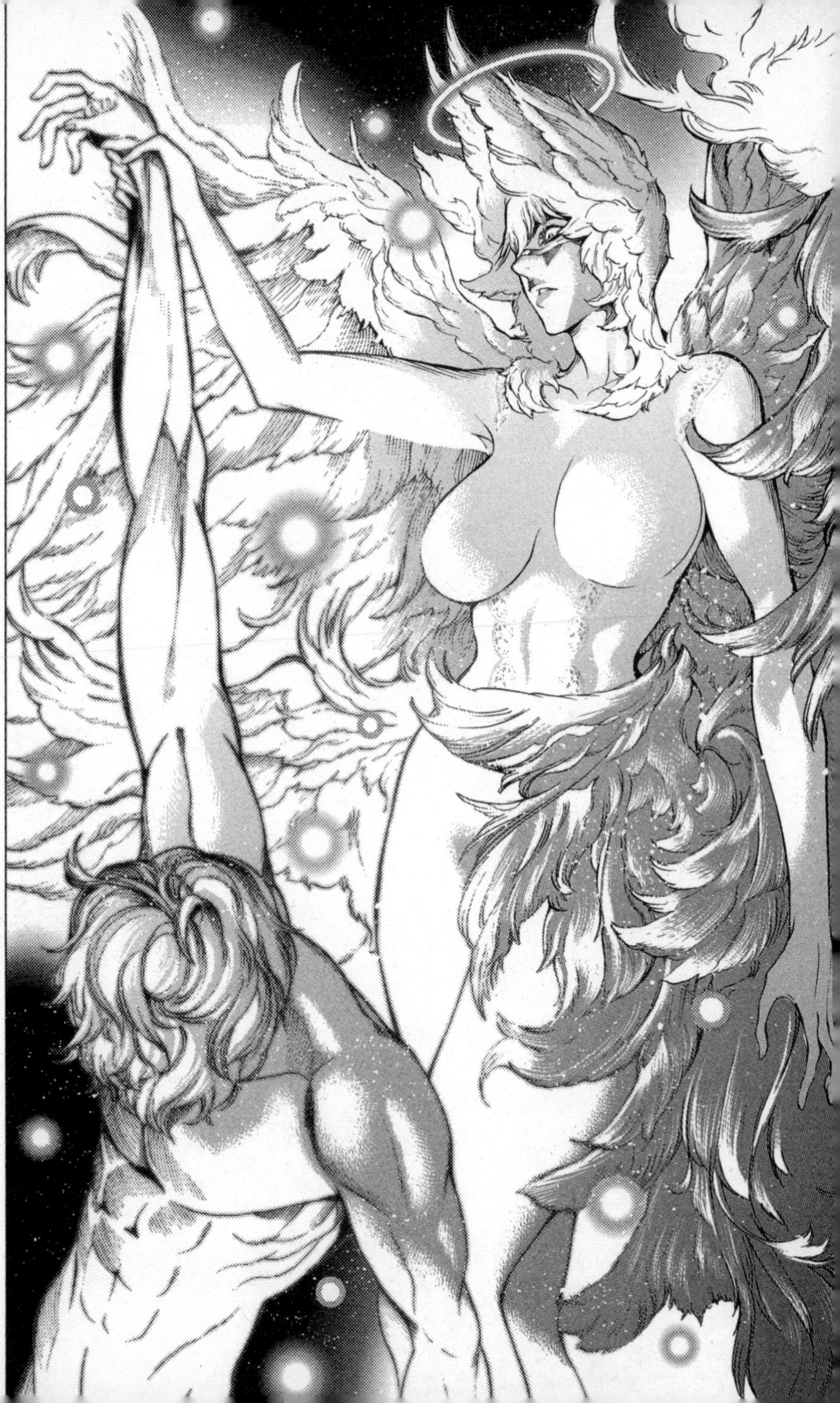

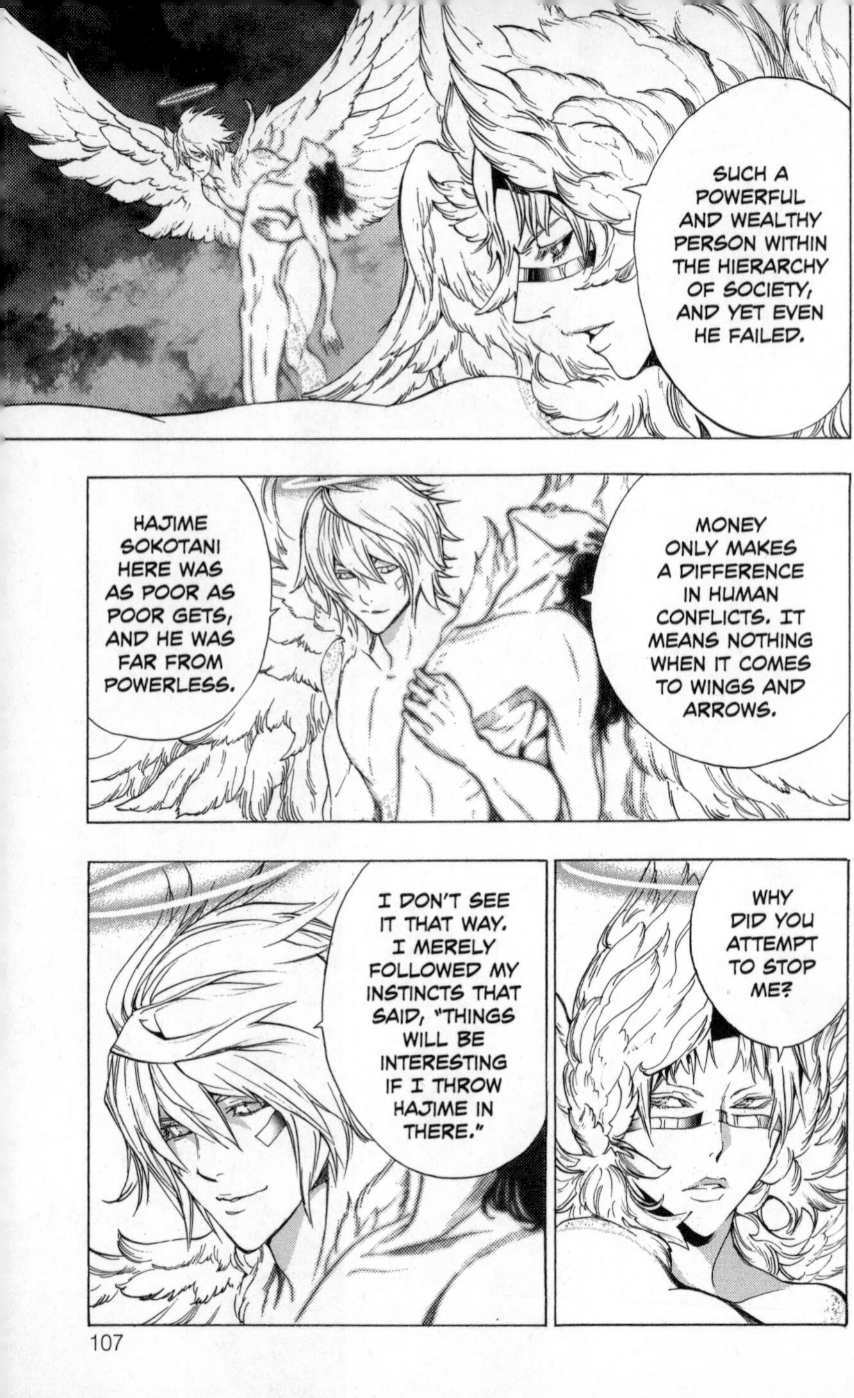
SUCH A POWERFUL AND WEALTHY PERSON WITHIN THE HIERARCHY OF SOCIETY, AND YET EVEN HE FAILED.
MONEY ONLY MAKES A DIFFERENCE IN HUMAN CONFLICTS. IT MEANS NOTHING WHEN IT COMES TO WINGS AND ARROWS.
HAJIME SOKOTANI HERE WAS AS POOR AS POOR GETS, AND HE WAS FAR FROM POWERLESS.
WHY DID YOU ATTEMPT TO STOP ME?
I DON'T SEE IT THAT WAY. I MERELY FOLLOWED MY INSTINCTS THAT SAID, "THINGS WILL BE INTERESTING IF I THROW HAJIME IN THERE."

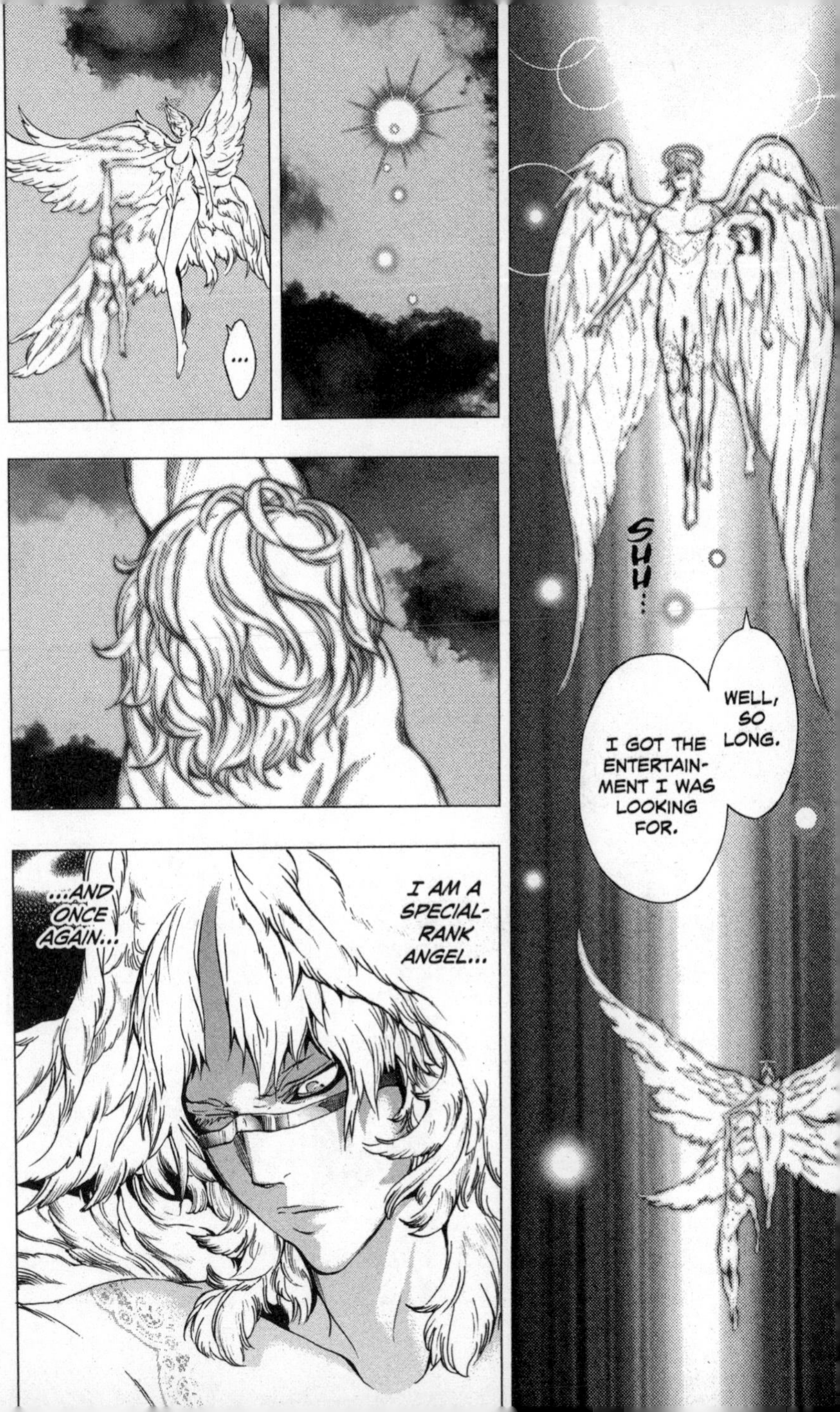
SHH...
WELL, SO LONG.
I GOT THE ENTERTAINMENT I WAS LOOKING FOR.
...
I AM A SPECIAL-RANK ANGEL...
...AND ONCE AGAIN...

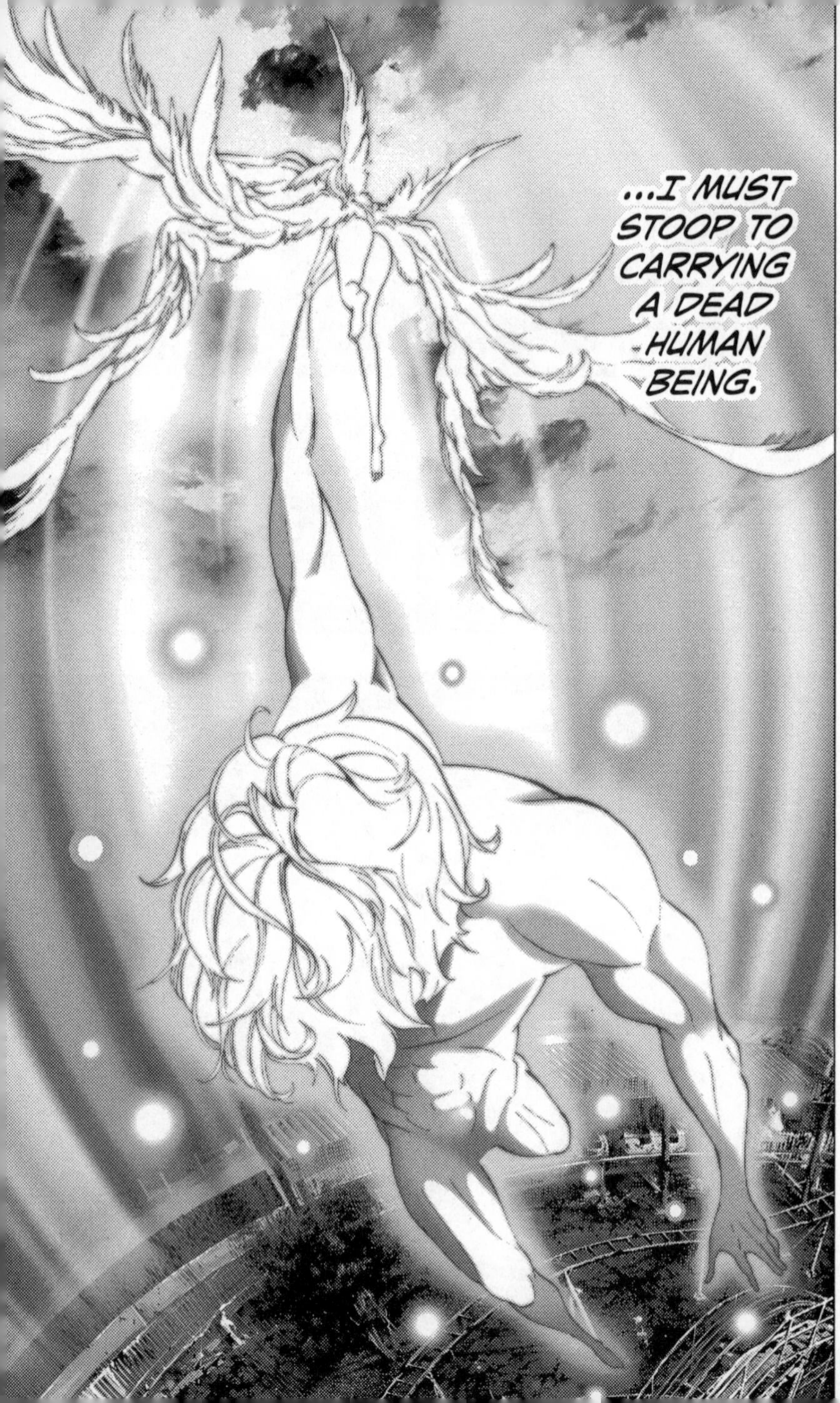
...I MUST STOOP TO CARRYING A DEAD HUMAN BEING.

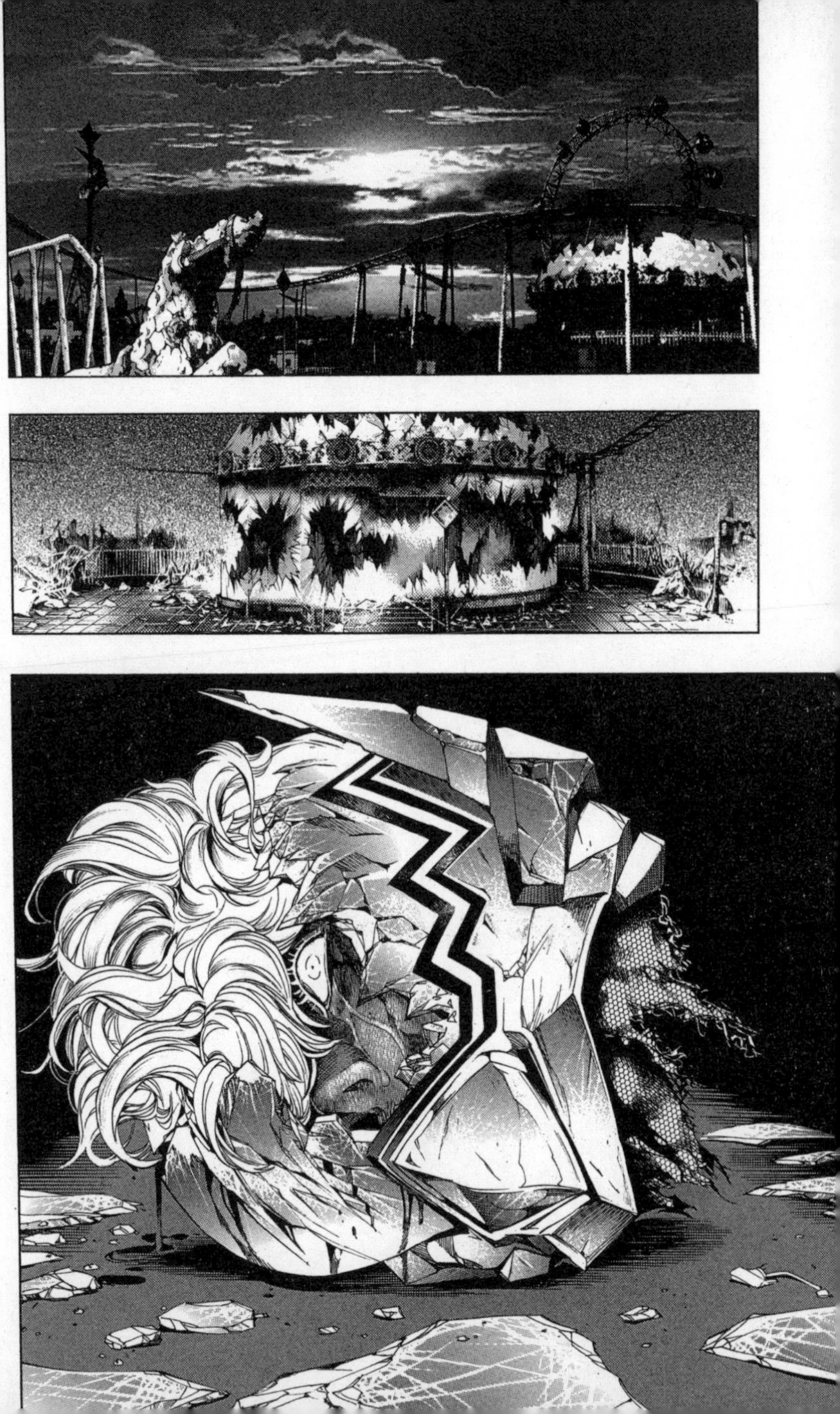

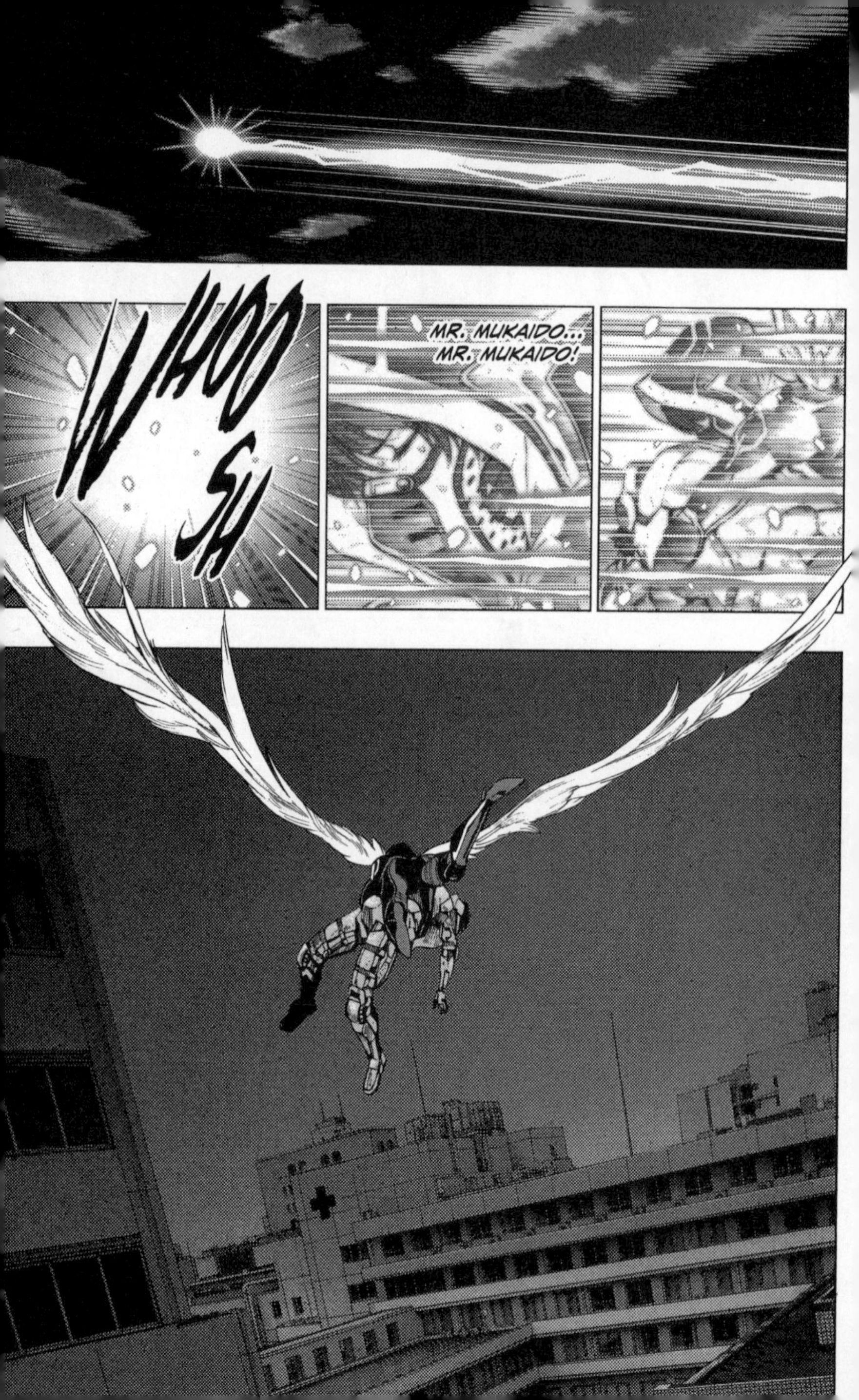
MR. MUKAIDO...
MR. MUKAIDO!
WHOOSH

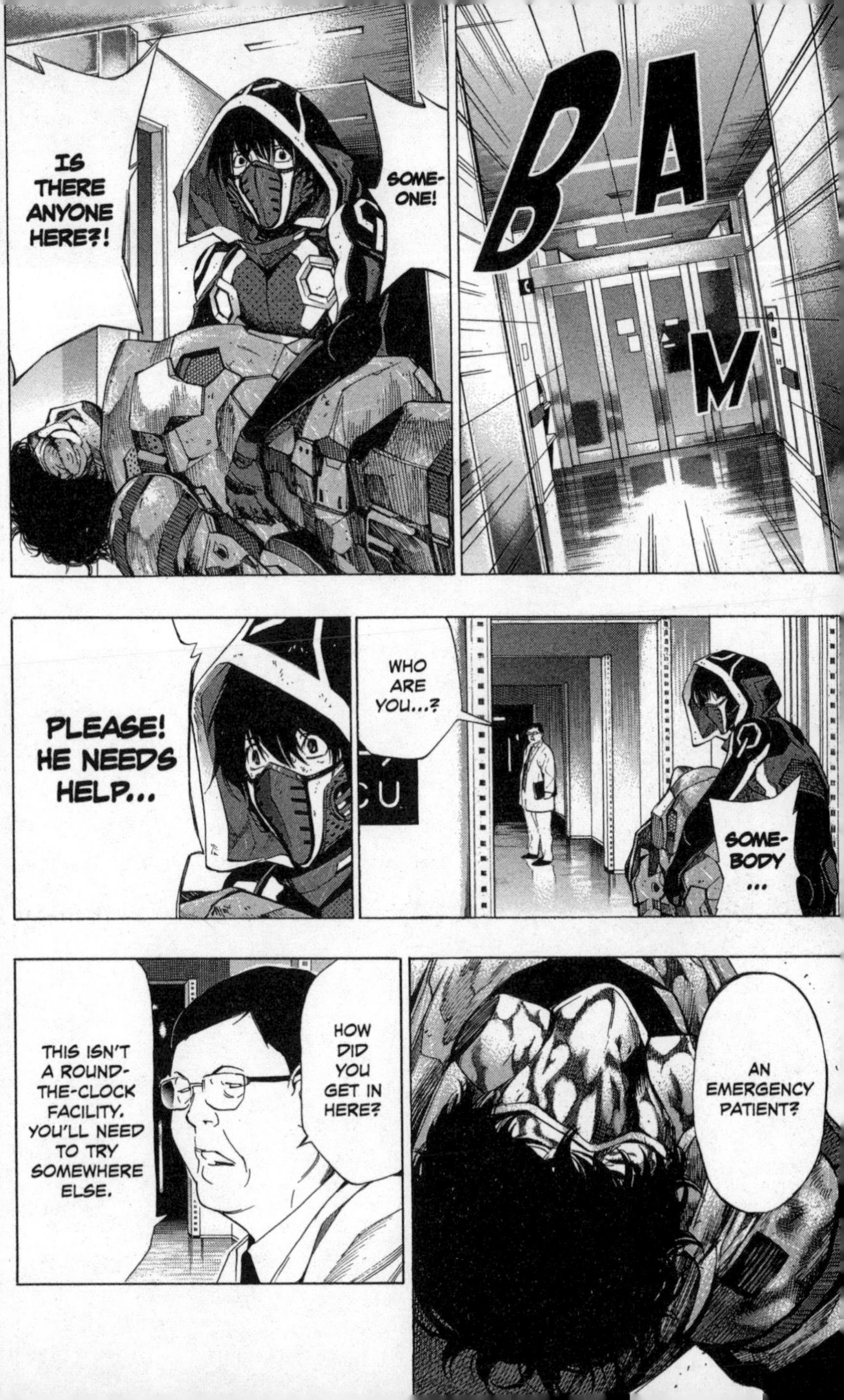
BAM
IS THERE ANYONE HERE?!
SOME-ONE!
SOME-BODY ...
WHO ARE YOU...?
PLEASE! HE NEEDS HELP...
AN EMERGENCY PATIENT?
HOW DID YOU GET IN HERE?
THIS ISN'T A ROUND-THE-CLOCK FACILITY. YOU'LL NEED TO TRY SOMEWHERE ELSE.

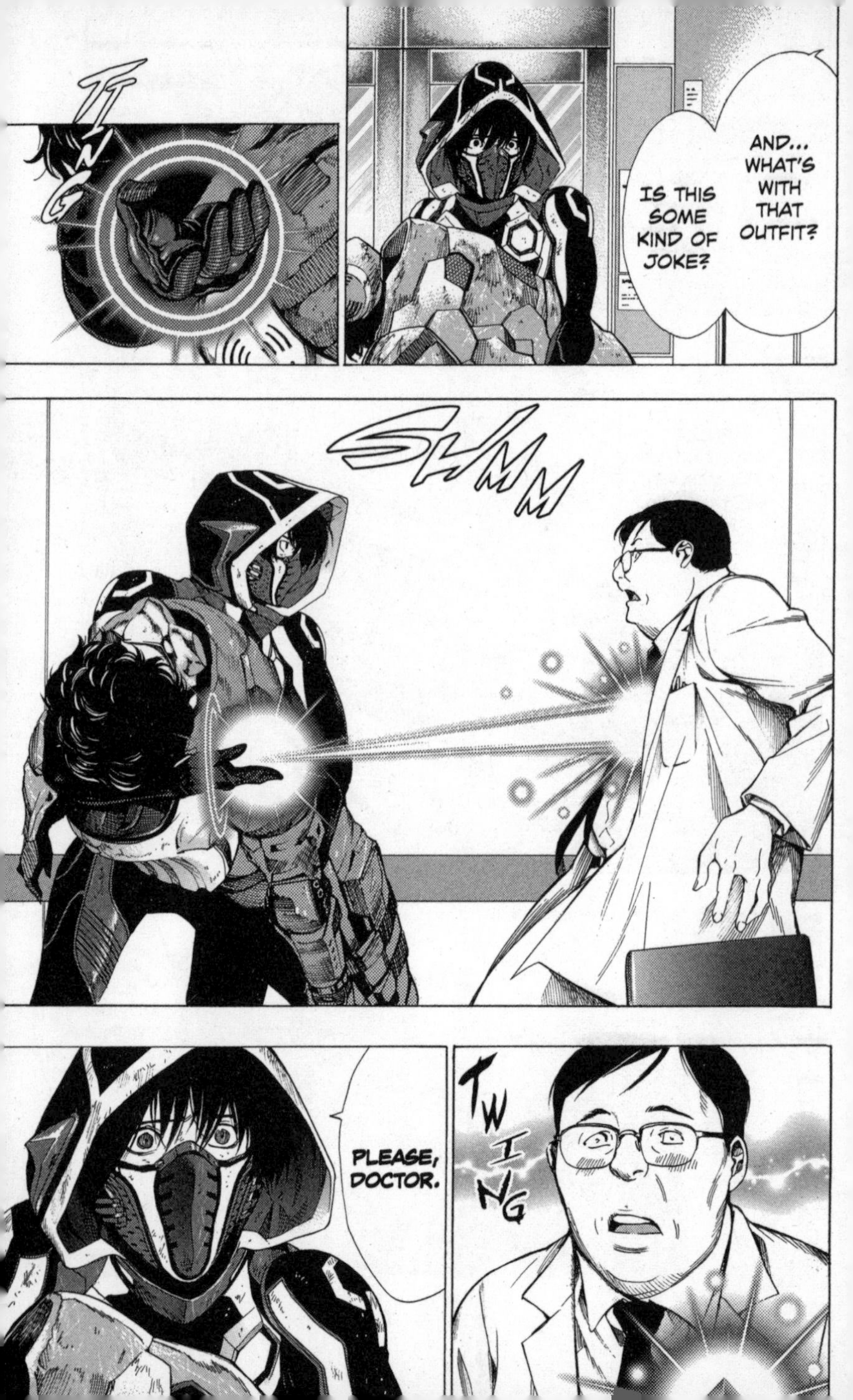
AND... WHAT'S WITH THAT OUTFIT?
IS THIS SOME KIND OF JOKE?
TING
SHMMM
TWING
PLEASE, DOCTOR.

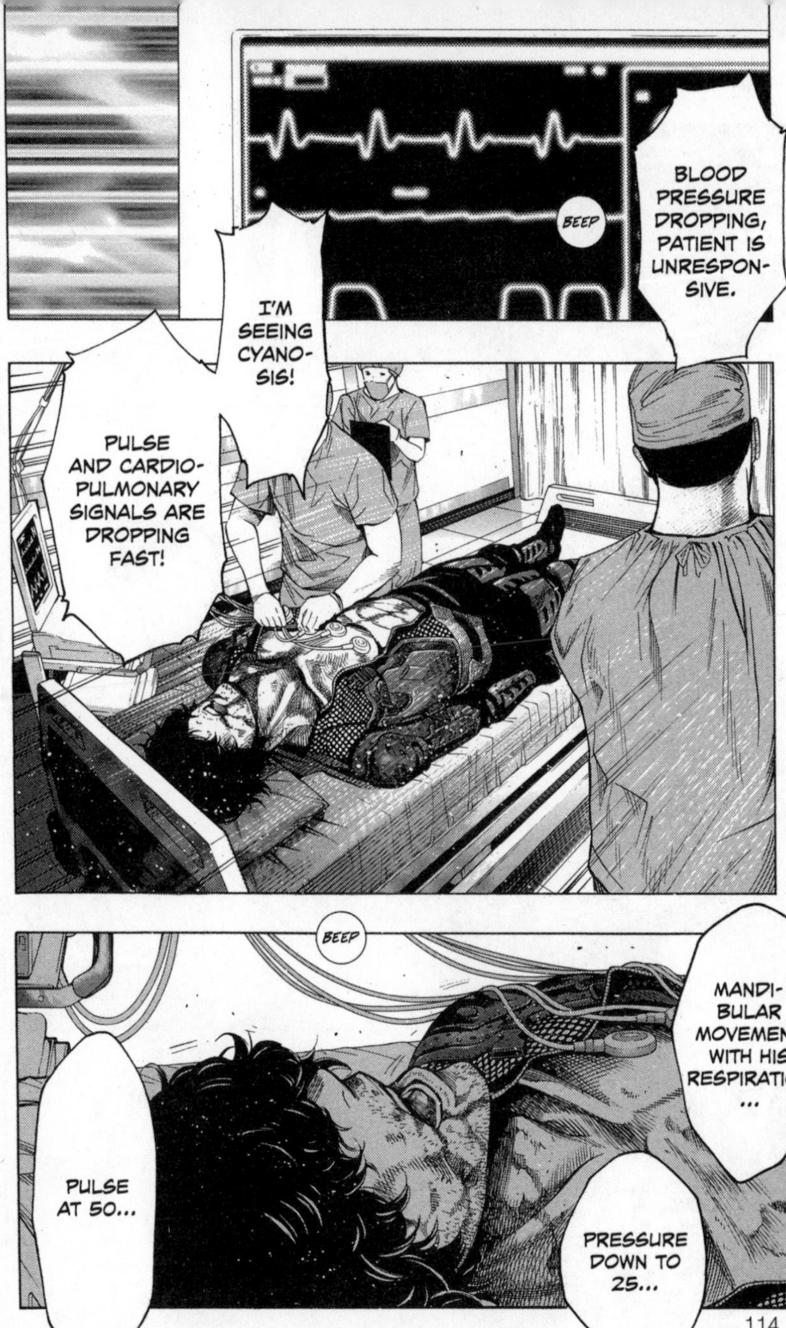
BLOOD PRESSURE DROPPING, PATIENT IS UNRESPON-SIVE.
BEEP
I'M SEEING CYANO-SIS!
PULSE AND CARDIO-PULMONARY SIGNALS ARE DROPPING FAST!
BEEP
MANDI-BULAR MOVEMENT WITH HIS RESPIRATION ...
PRESSURE DOWN TO 25...
PULSE AT 50...

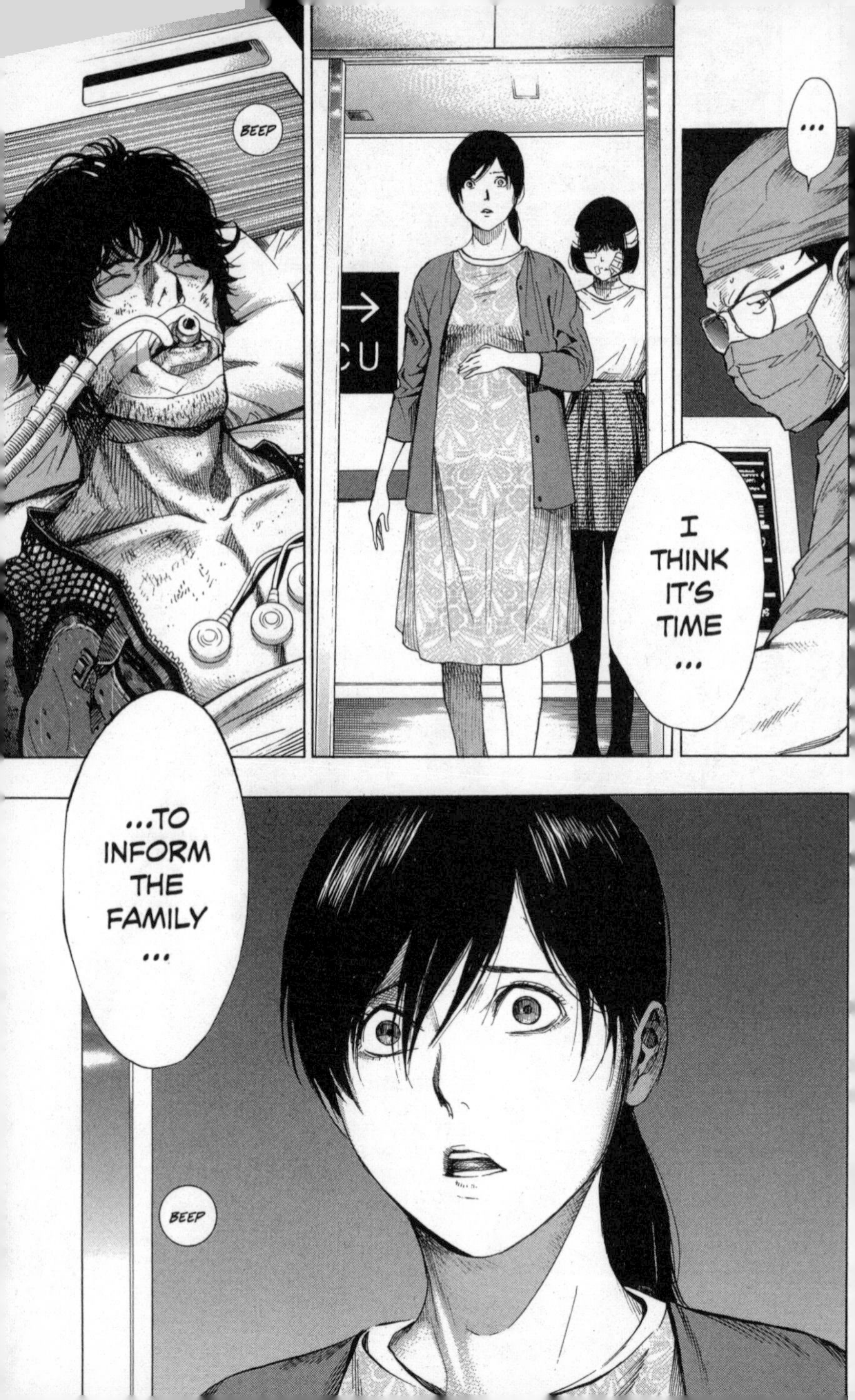
...
I THINK IT'S TIME ...
BEEP
...TO INFORM THE FAMILY ...
BEEP

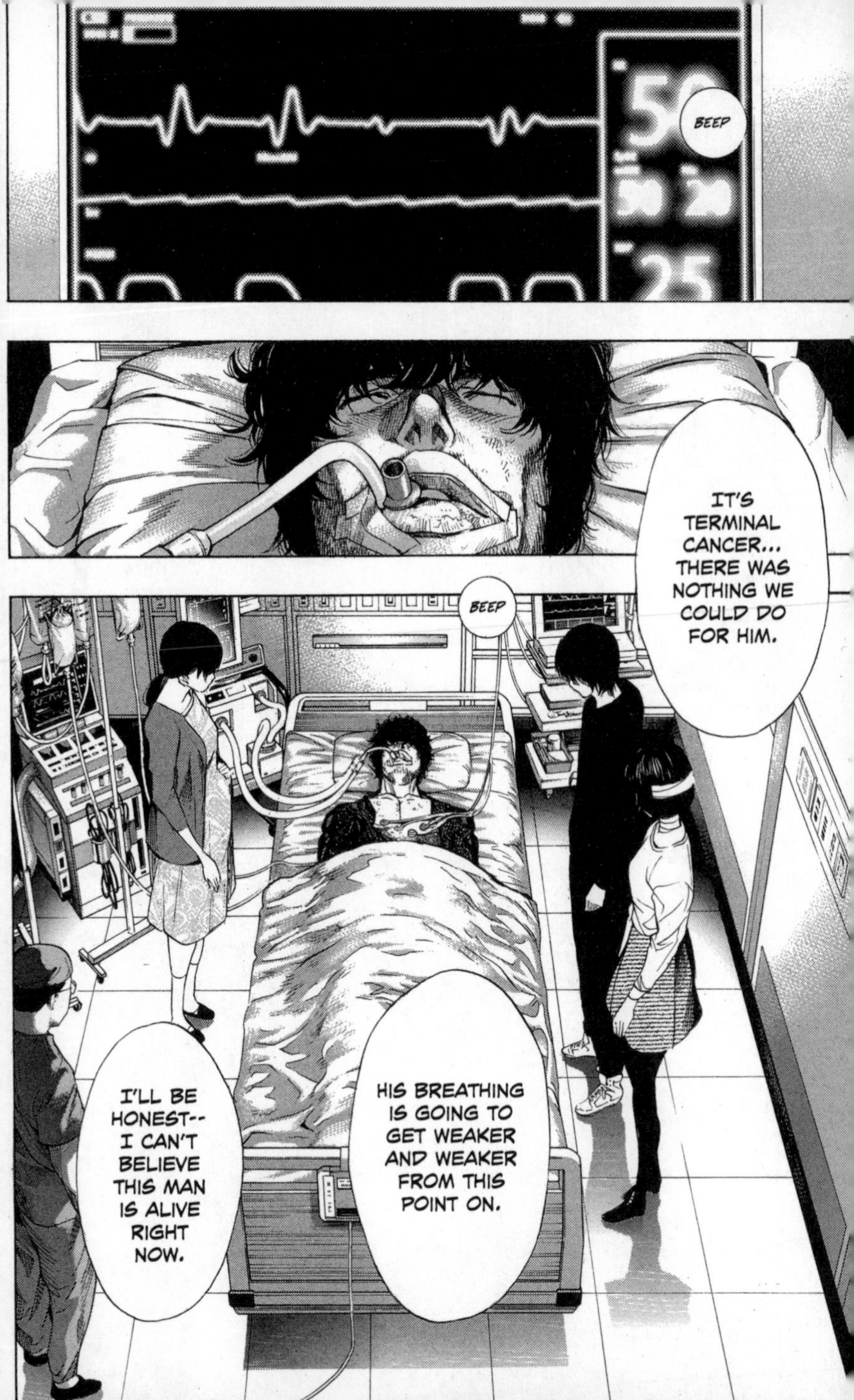
BEEP
IT'S TERMINAL CANCER... THERE WAS NOTHING WE COULD DO FOR HIM.
BEEP
HIS BREATHING IS GOING TO GET WEAKER AND WEAKER FROM THIS POINT ON.
I'LL BE HONEST-- I CAN'T BELIEVE THIS MAN IS ALIVE RIGHT NOW.

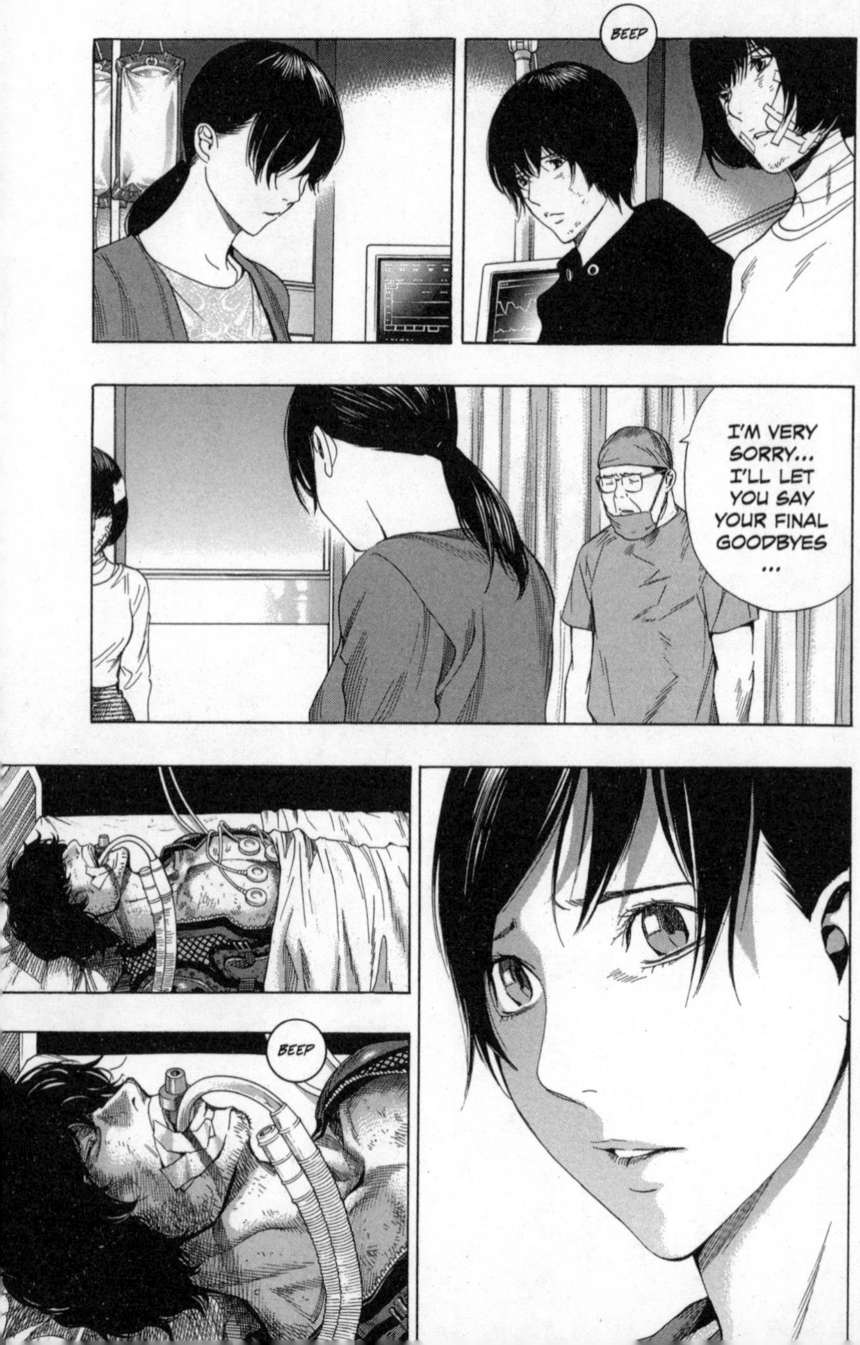
BEEP
I'M VERY SORRY... I'LL LET YOU SAY YOUR FINAL GOODBYES ...
BEEP

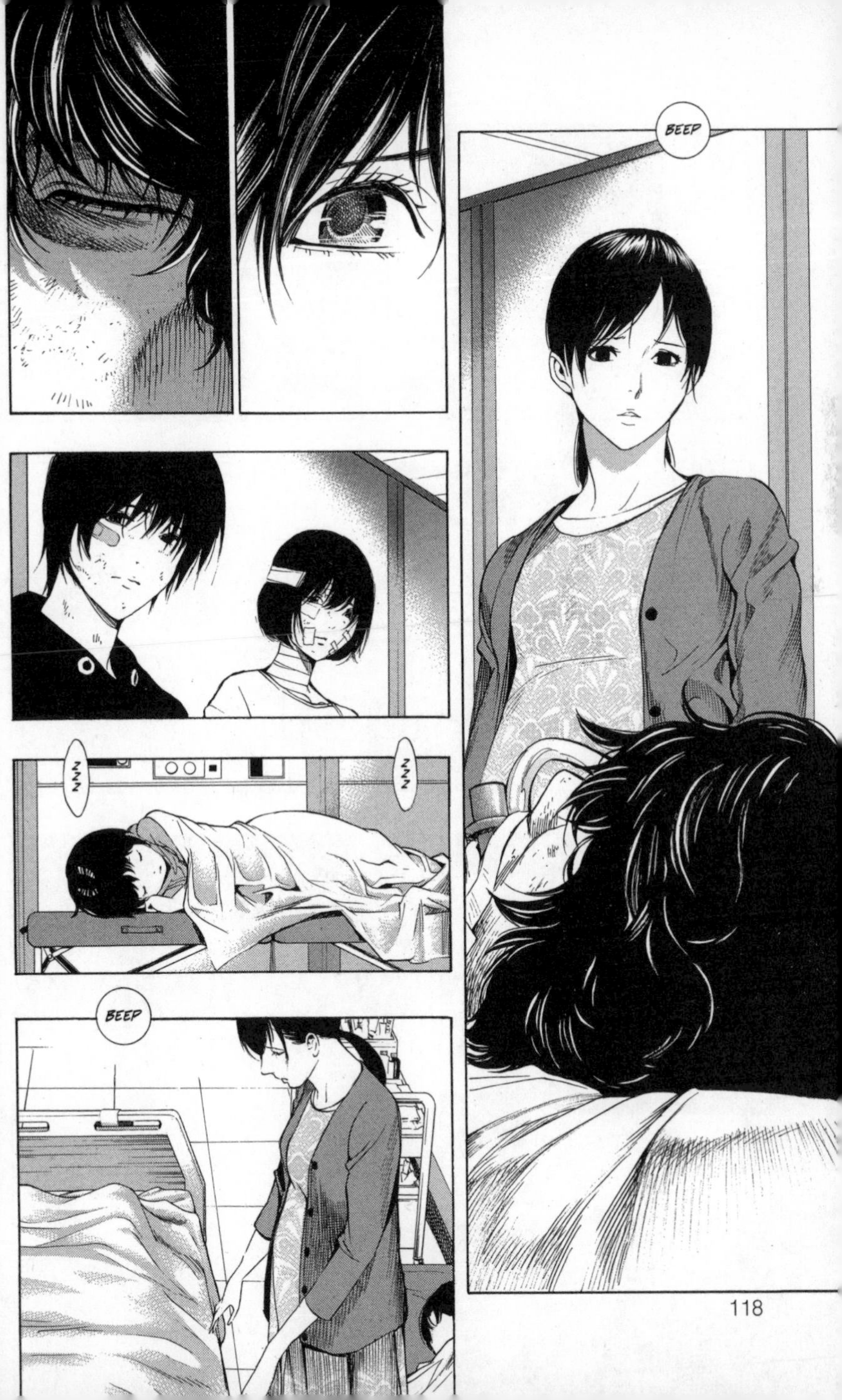
BEEP
ZZZ
ZZZ
BEEP

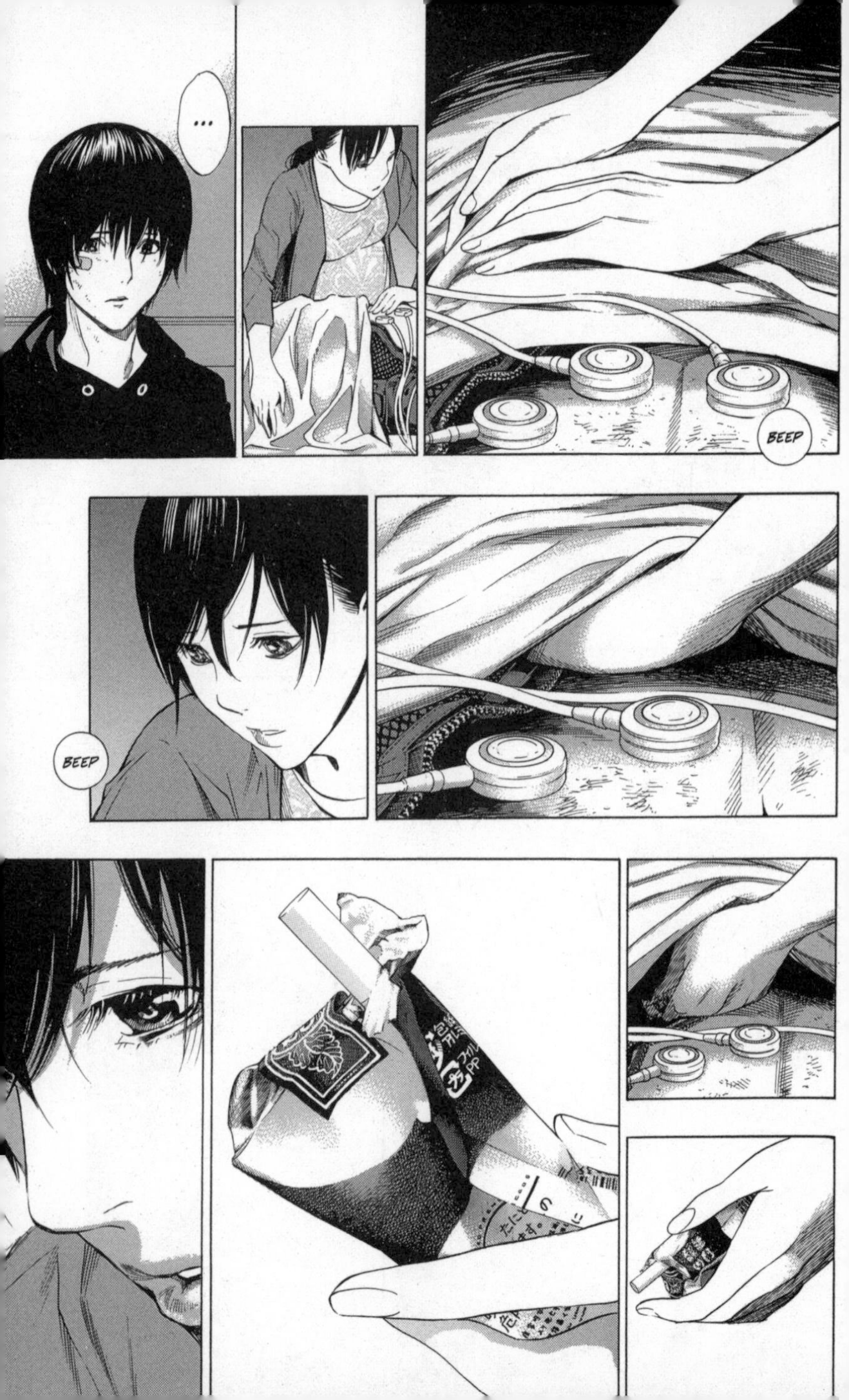
BEEP
...
BEEP

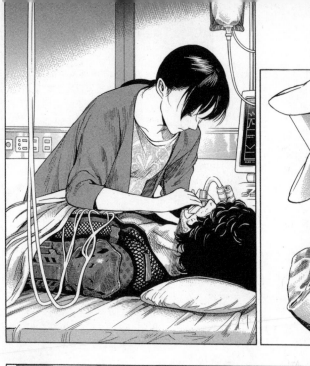

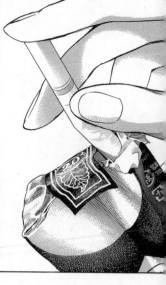

BEEP

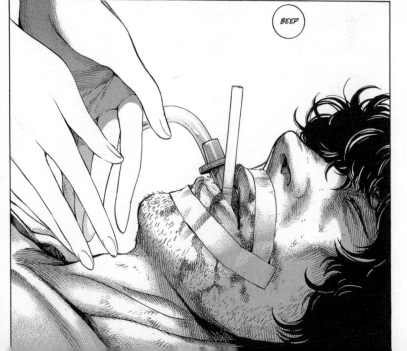

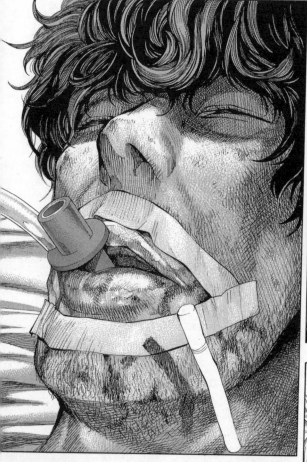

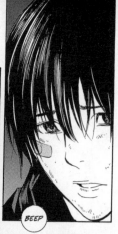

BEEP

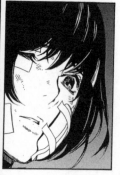

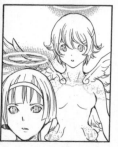

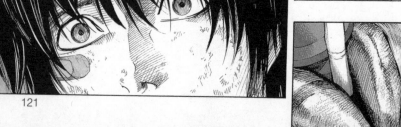

121

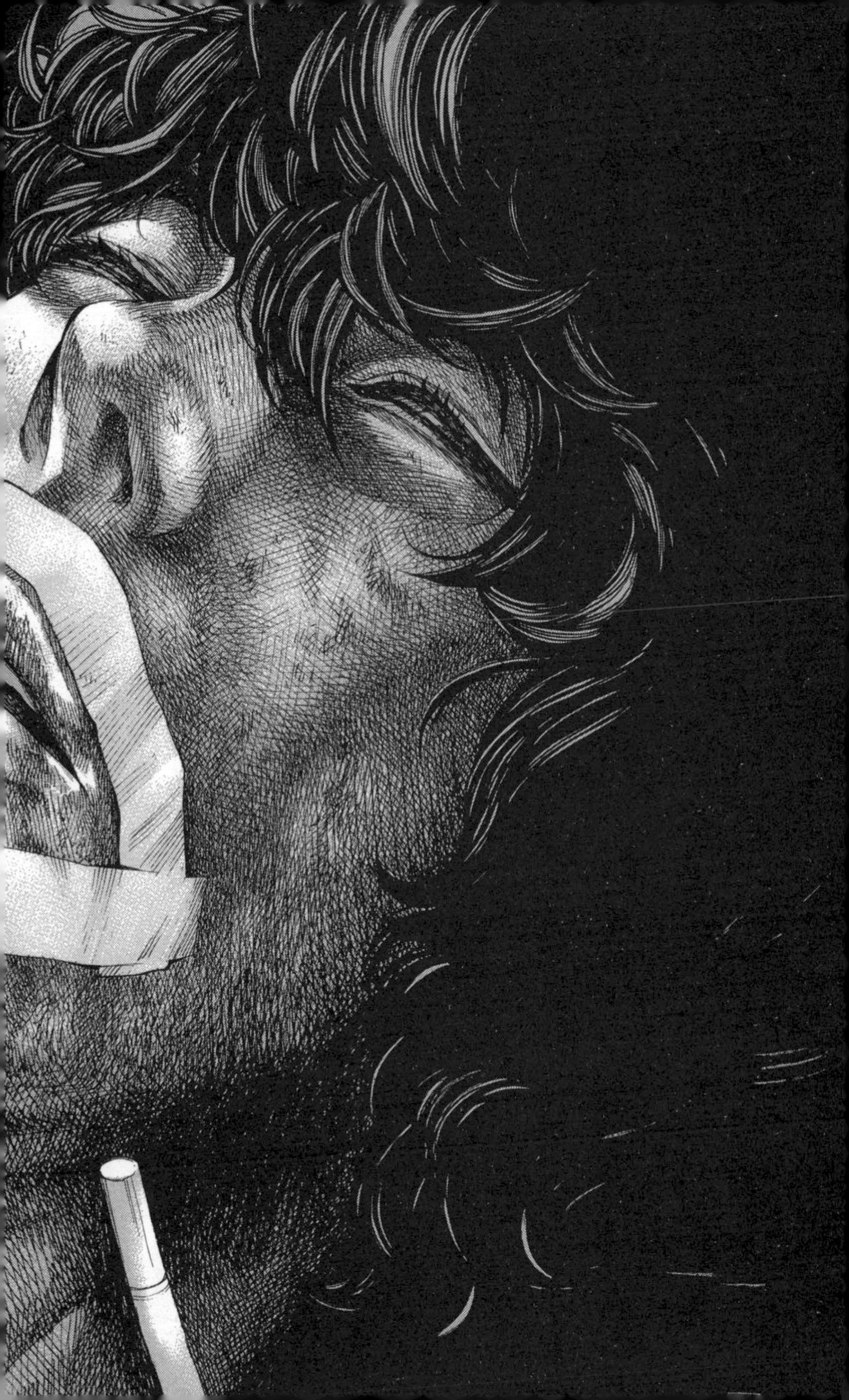

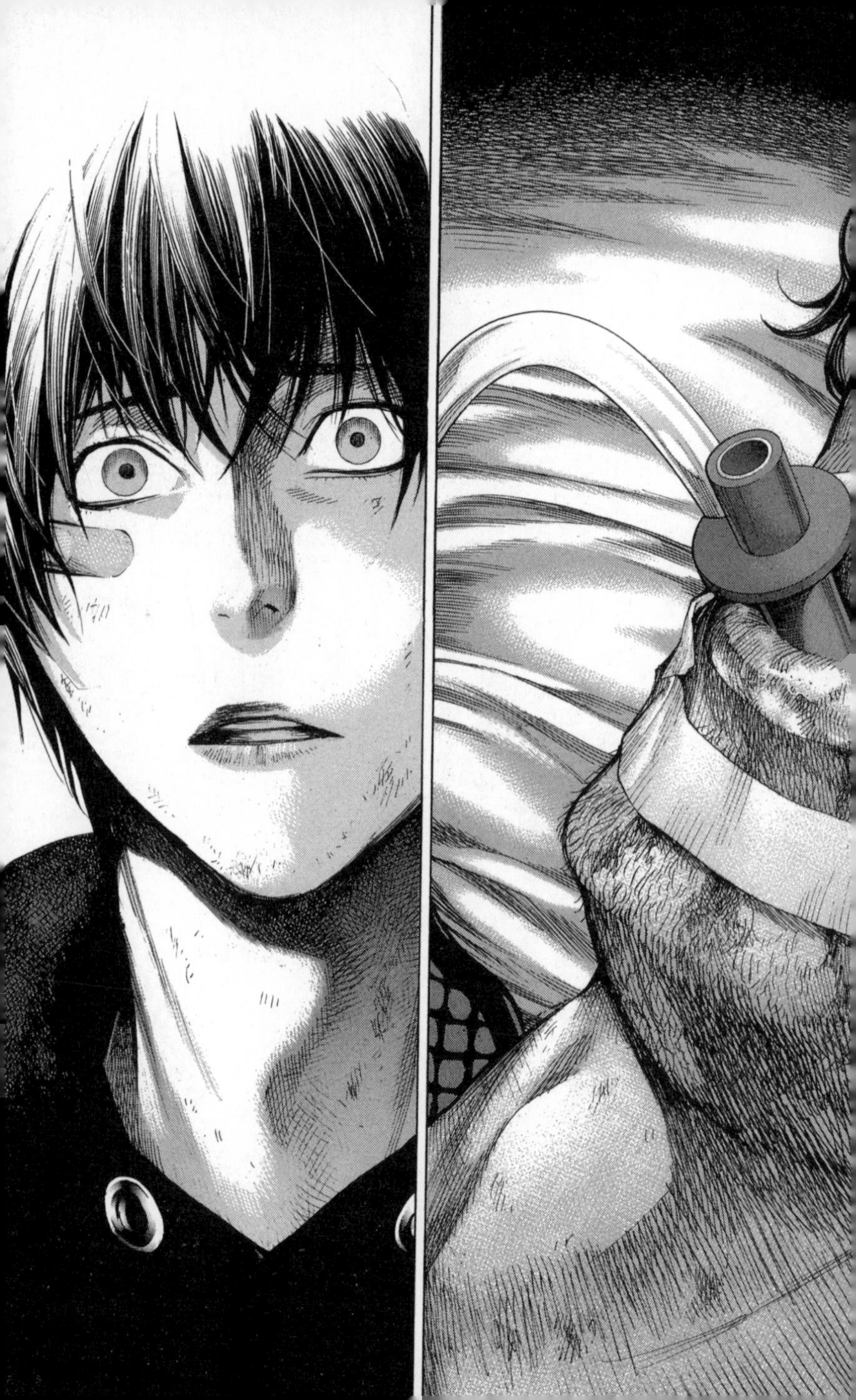

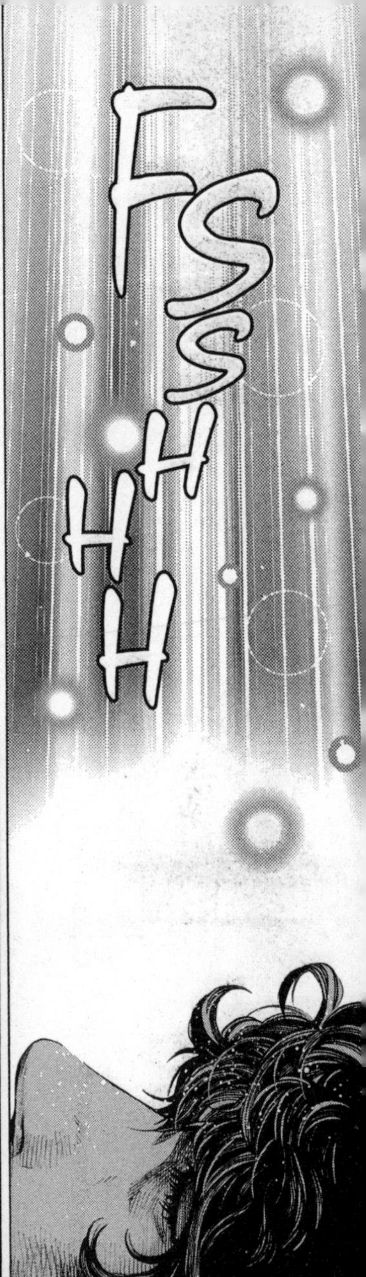
FSSHHHH
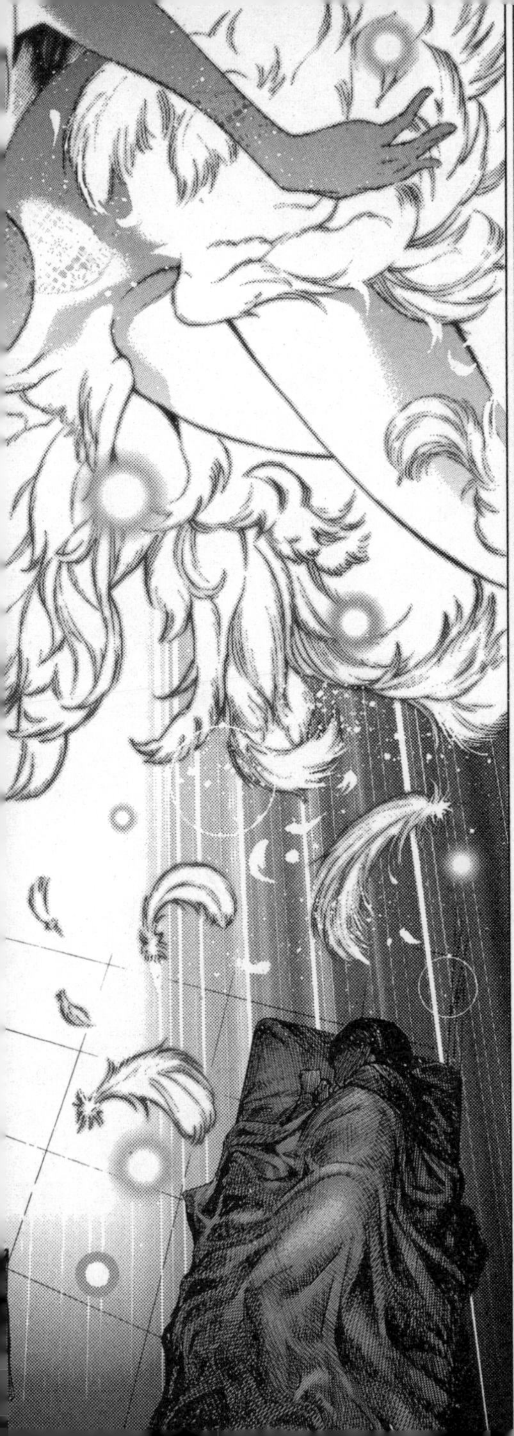

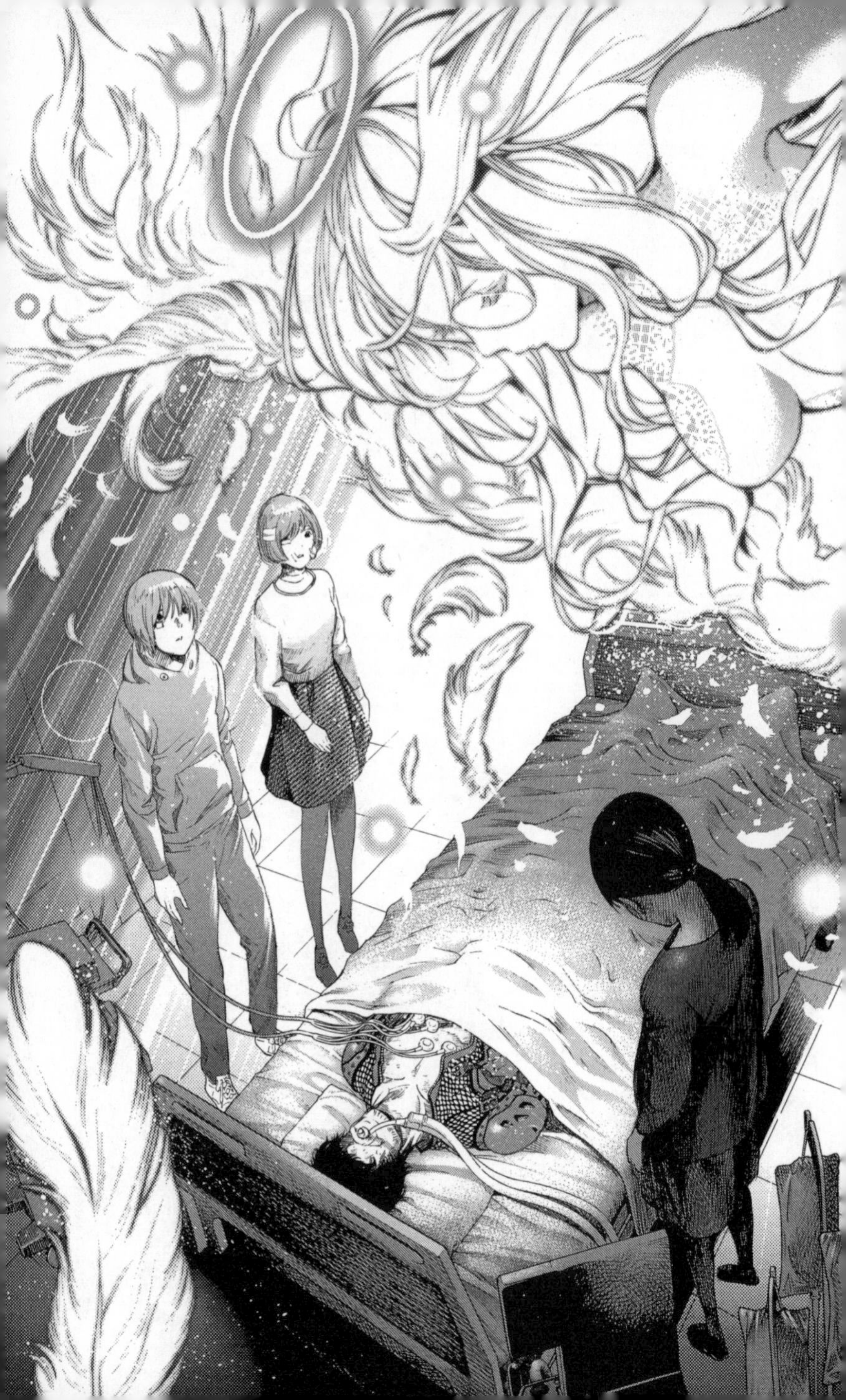

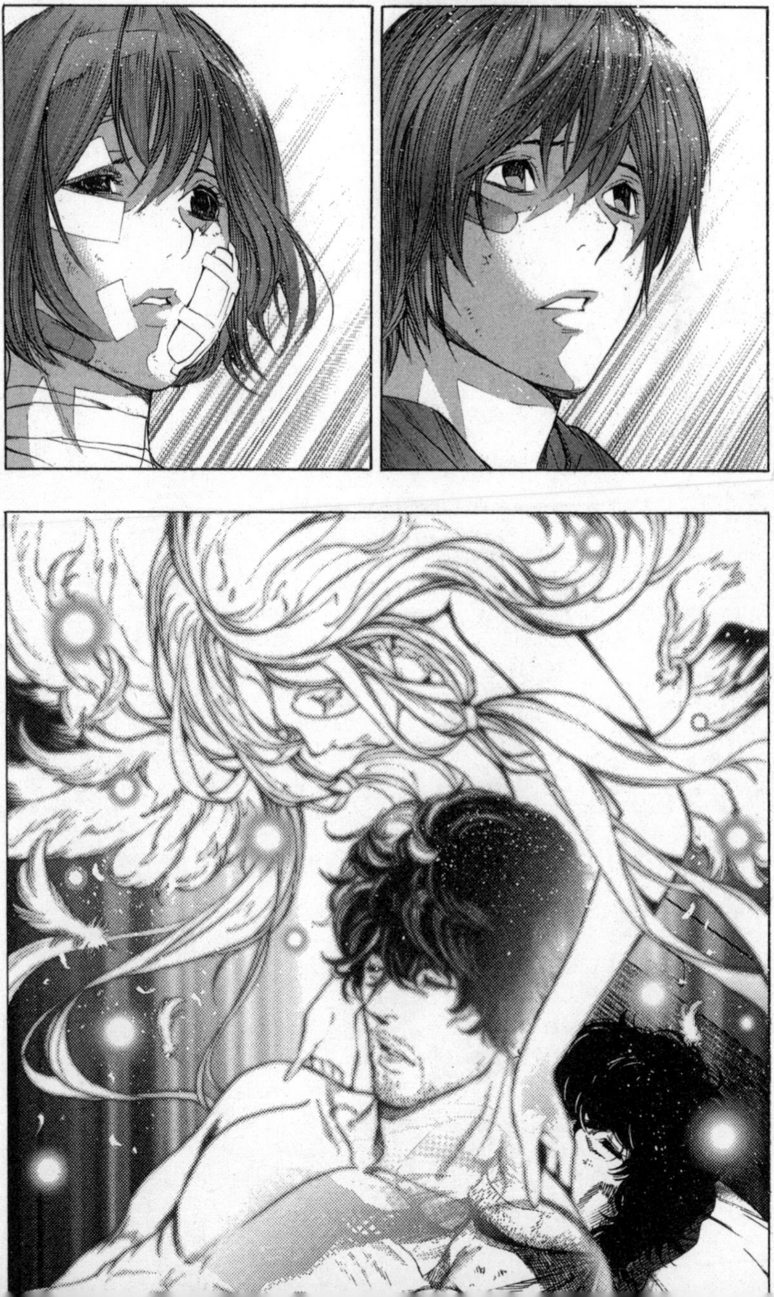

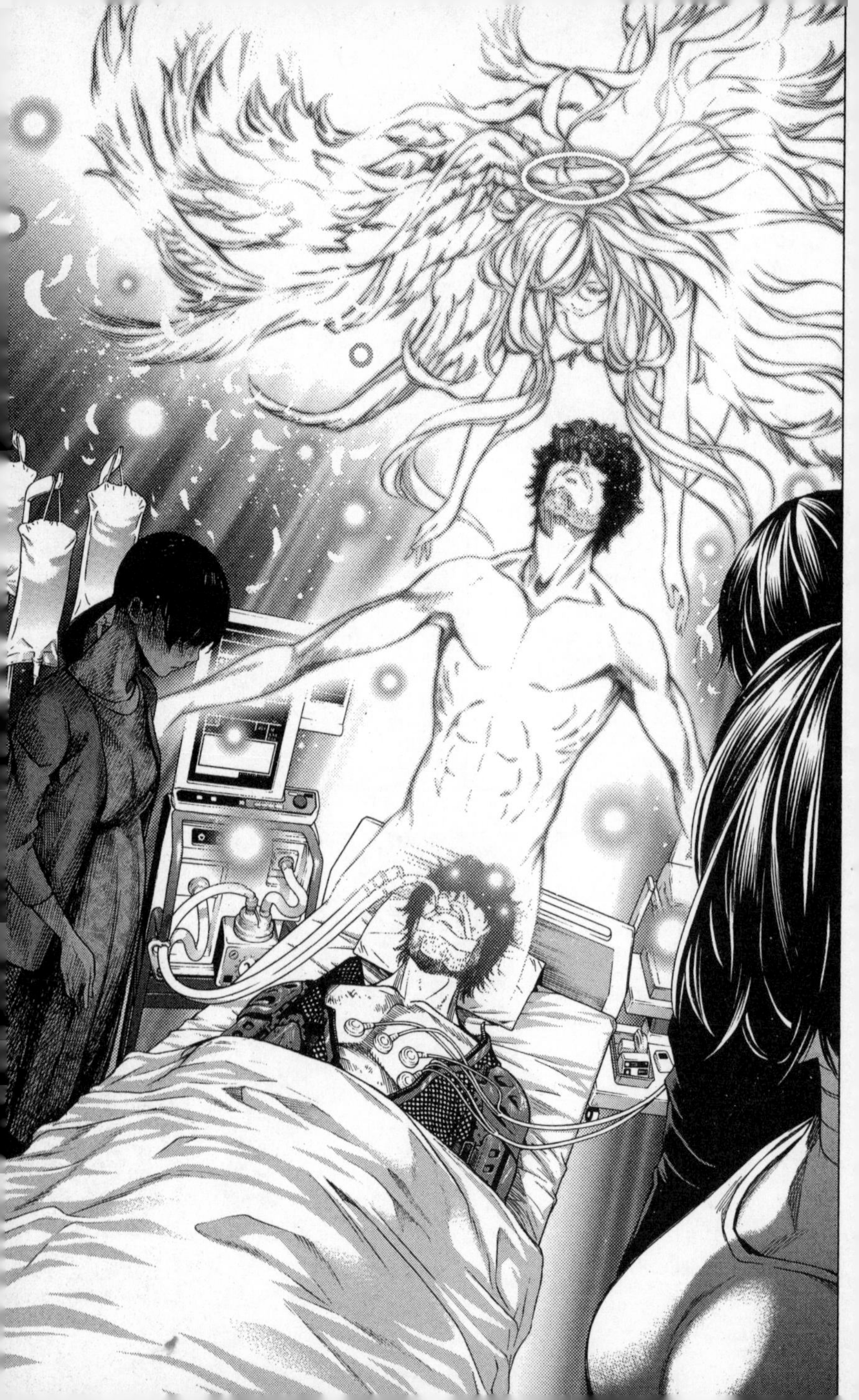

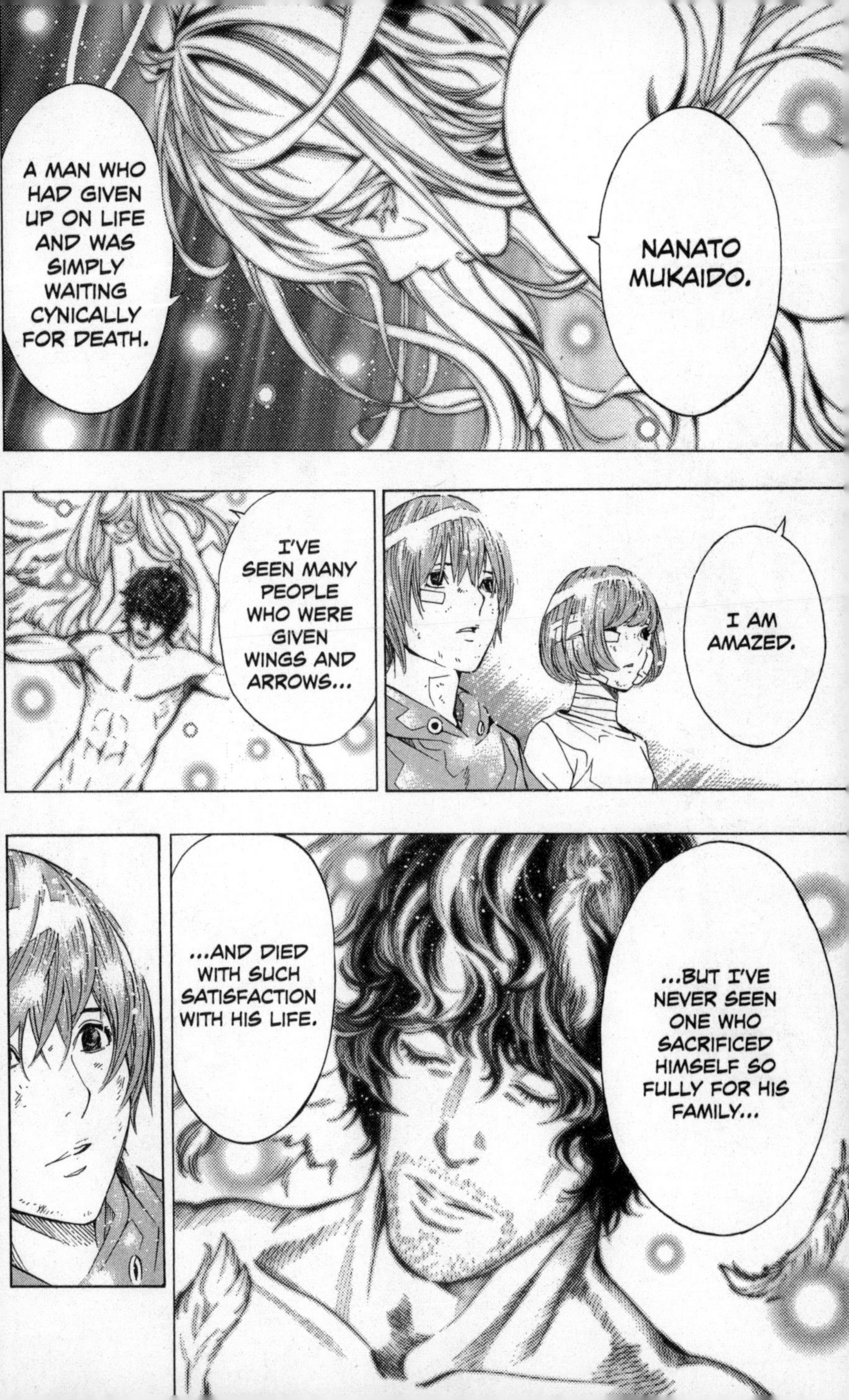
NANATO MUKAIDO.
A MAN WHO HAD GIVEN UP ON LIFE AND WAS SIMPLY WAITING CYNICALLY FOR DEATH.
I AM AMAZED.
I'VE SEEN MANY PEOPLE WHO WERE GIVEN WINGS AND ARROWS...
...BUT I'VE NEVER SEEN ONE WHO SACRIFICED HIMSELF SO FULLY FOR HIS FAMILY...
...AND DIED WITH SUCH SATISFACTION WITH HIS LIFE.

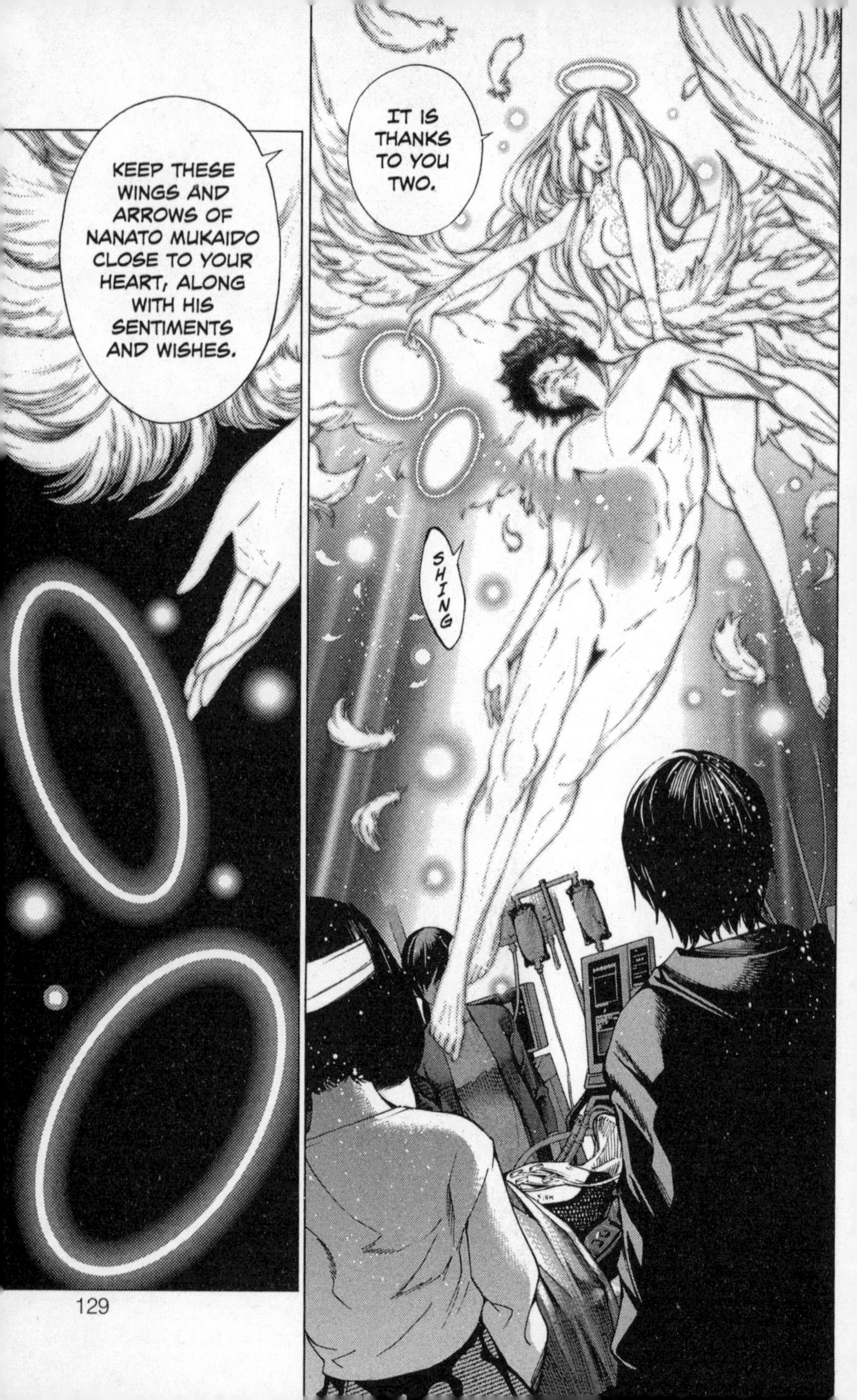
IT IS THANKS TO YOU TWO.
SHING
KEEP THESE WINGS AND ARROWS OF NANATO MUKAIDO CLOSE TO YOUR HEART, ALONG WITH HIS SENTIMENTS AND WISHES.

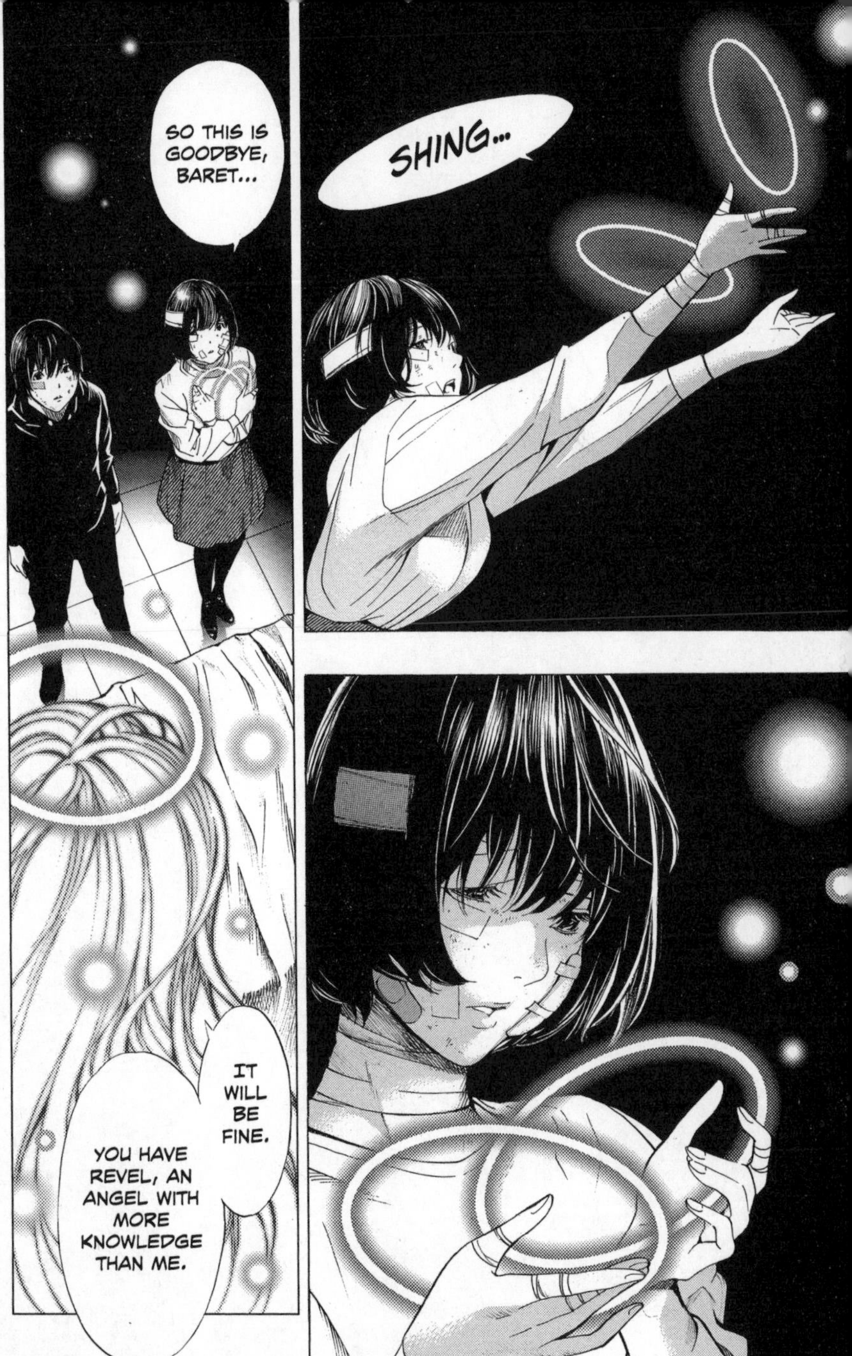
SHING...
SO THIS IS GOODBYE, BARET...
IT WILL BE FINE.
YOU HAVE REVEL, AN ANGEL WITH MORE KNOWLEDGE THAN ME.

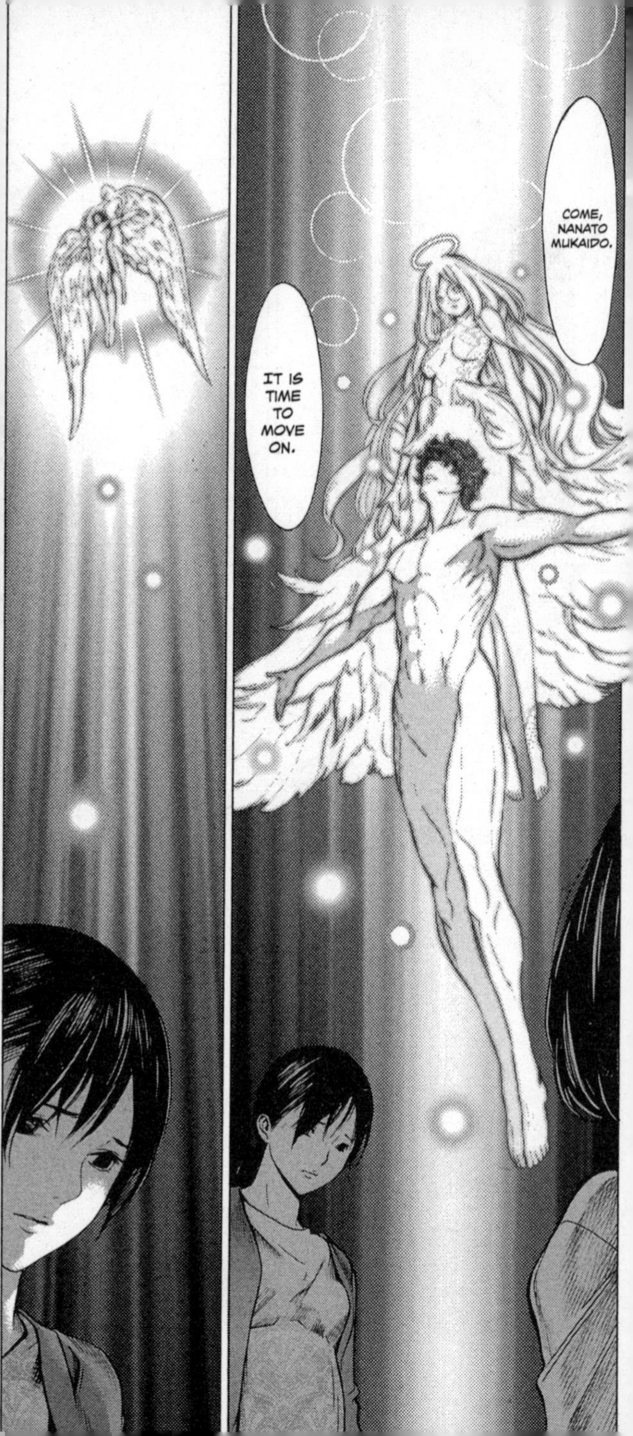
COME, NANATO MUKAIDO.
IT IS TIME TO MOVE ON.

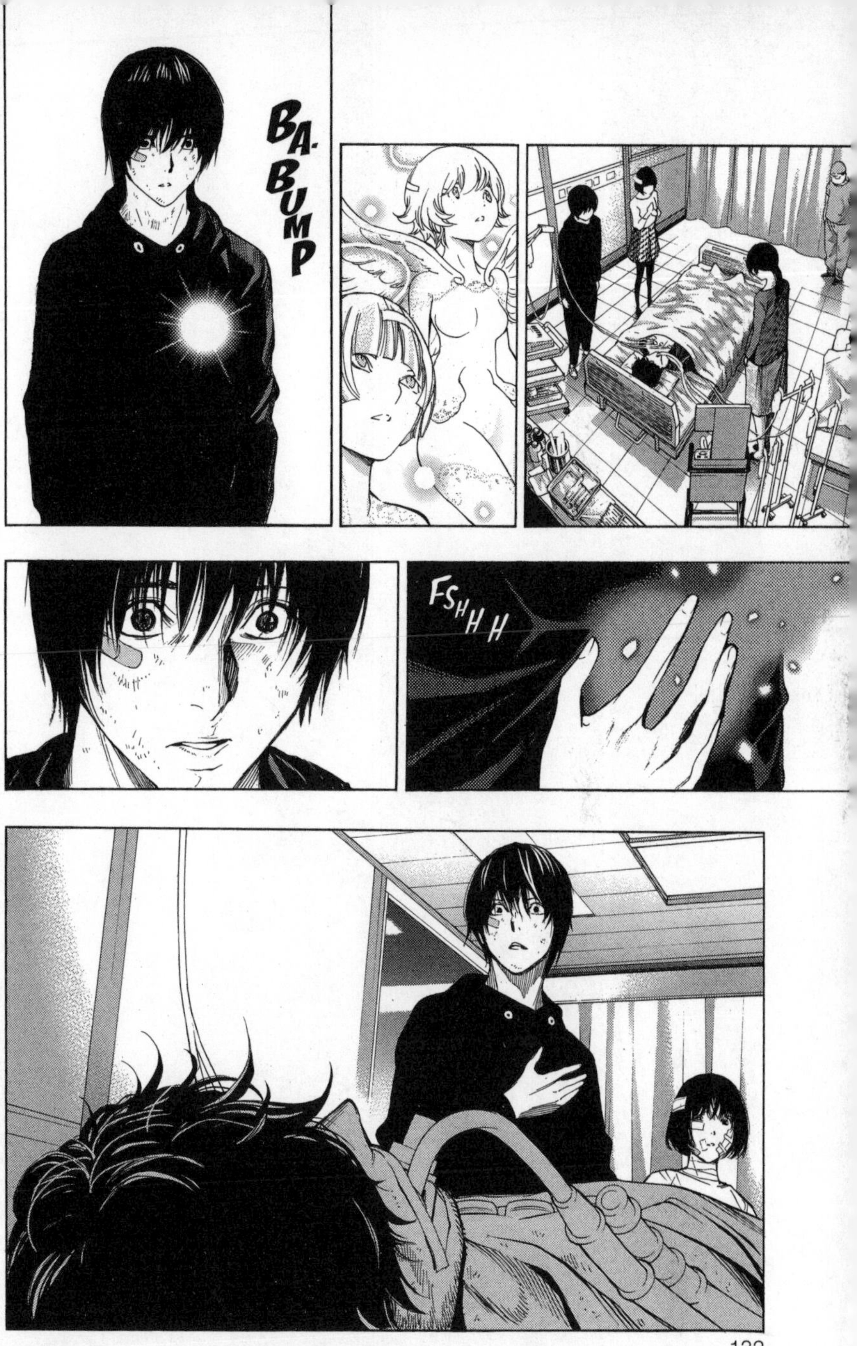
BA-BUMP
FSHHH

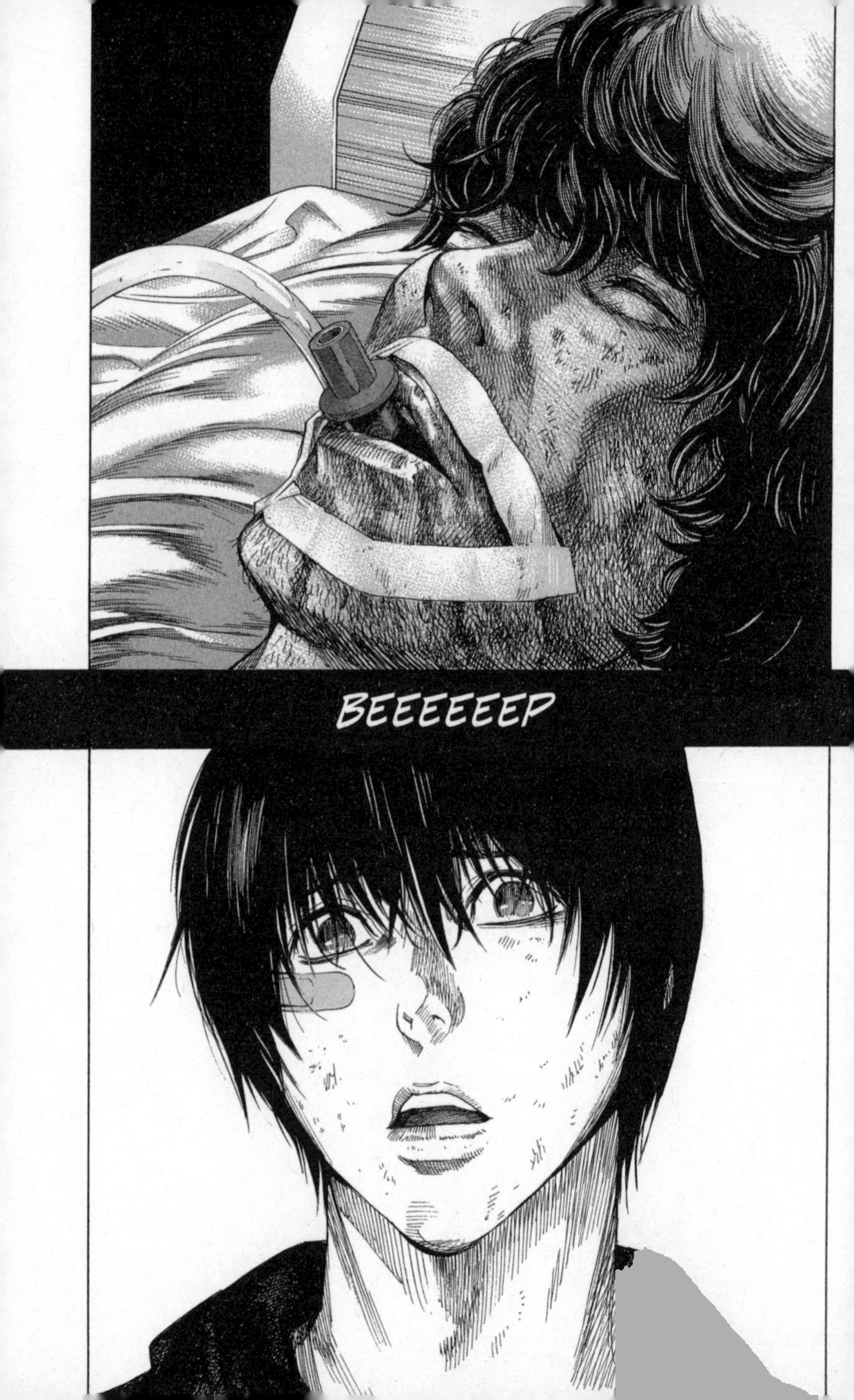
BEEEEEEP

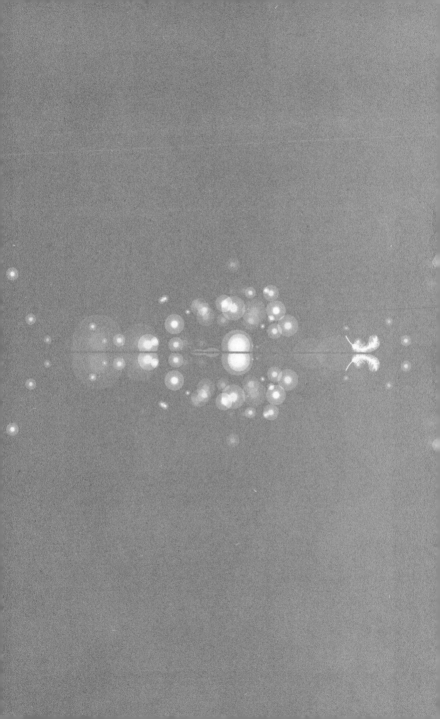

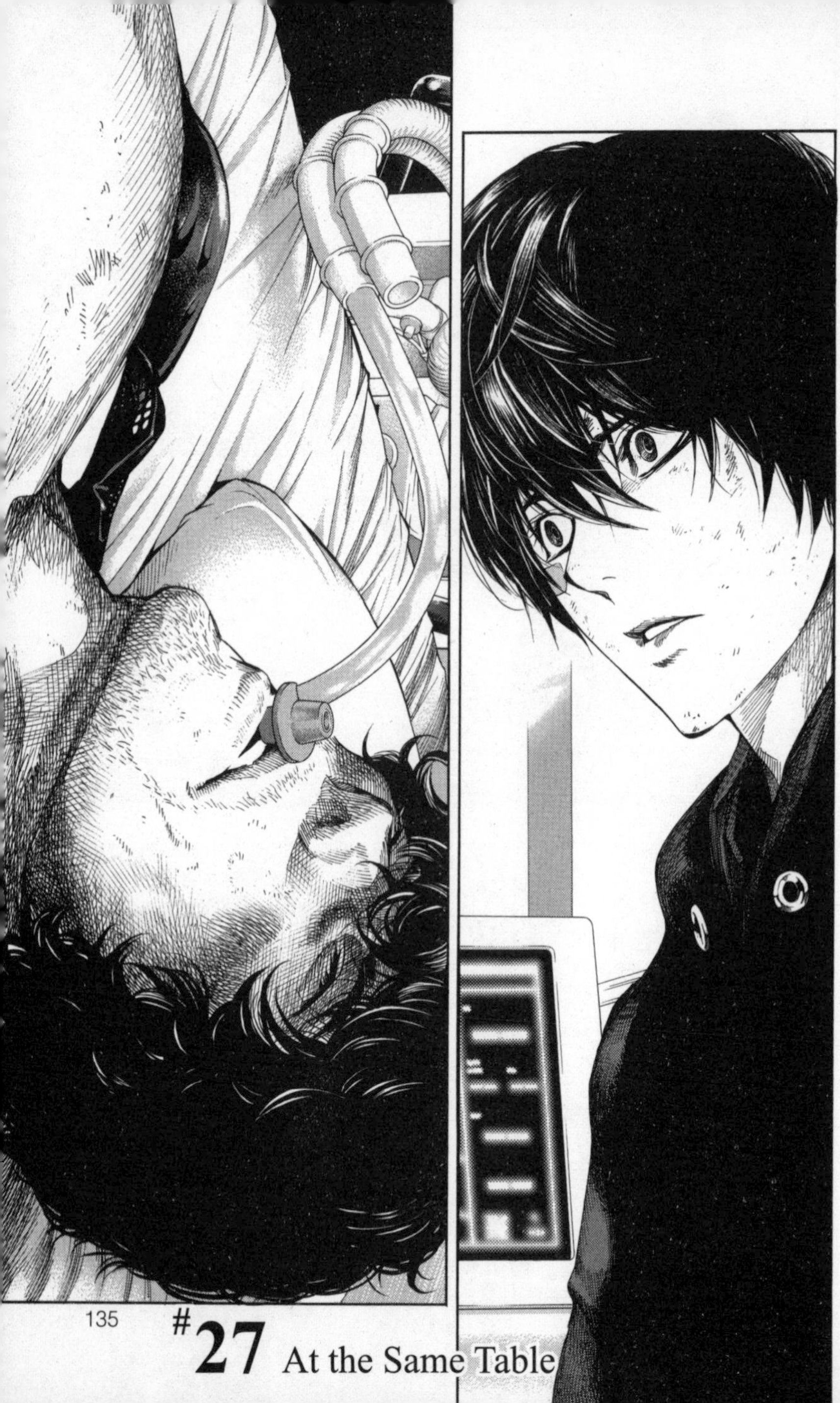

#27 At the Same Table

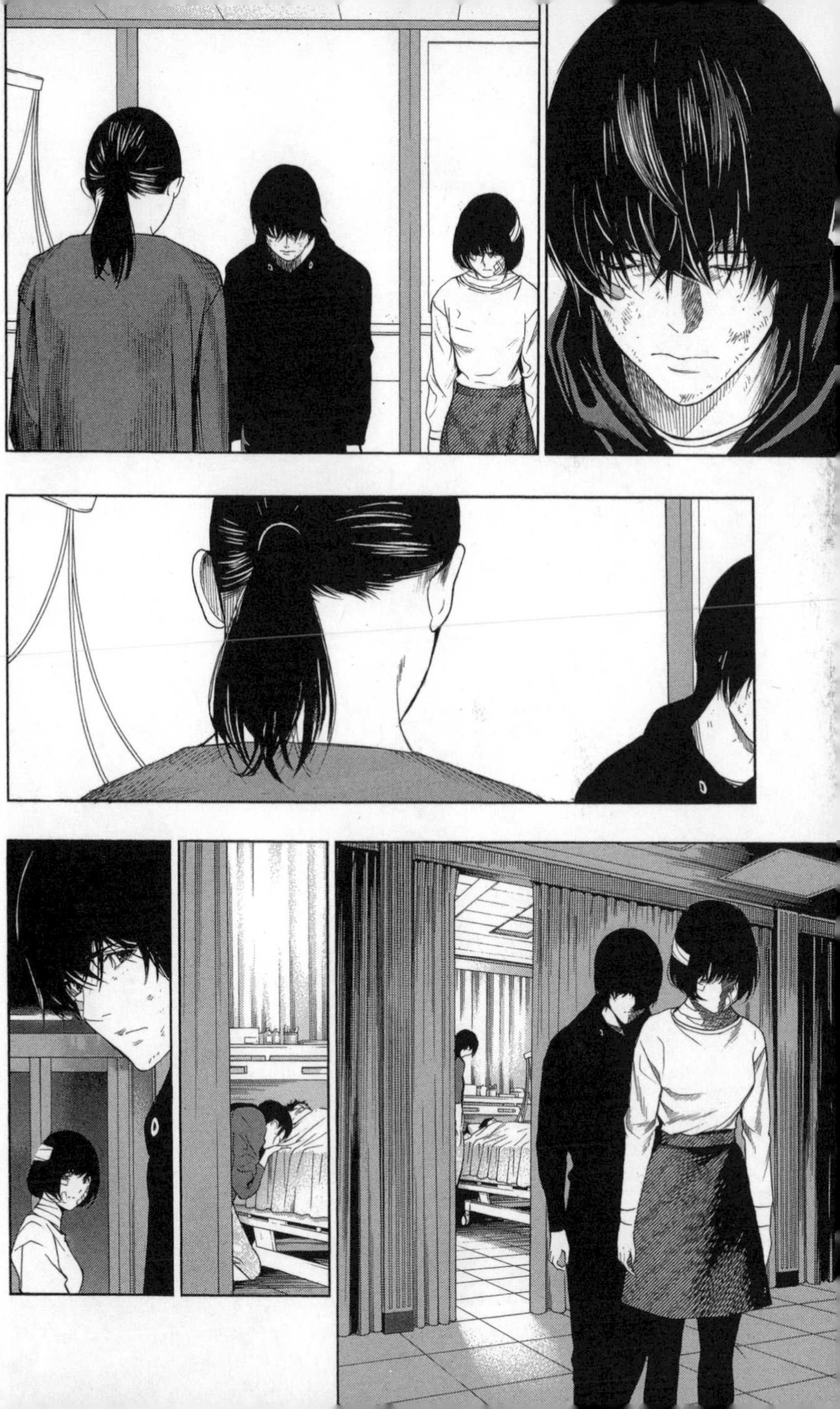

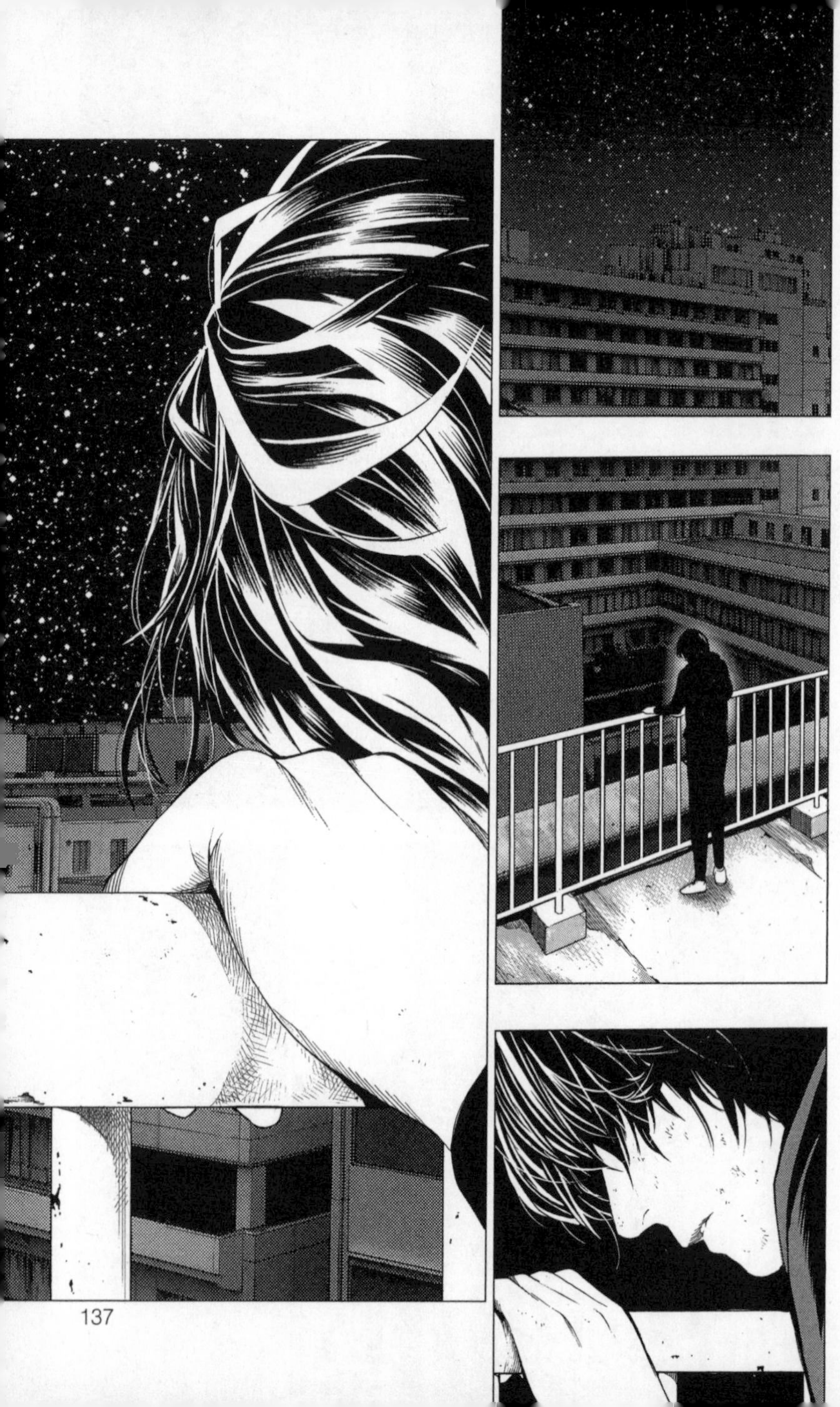

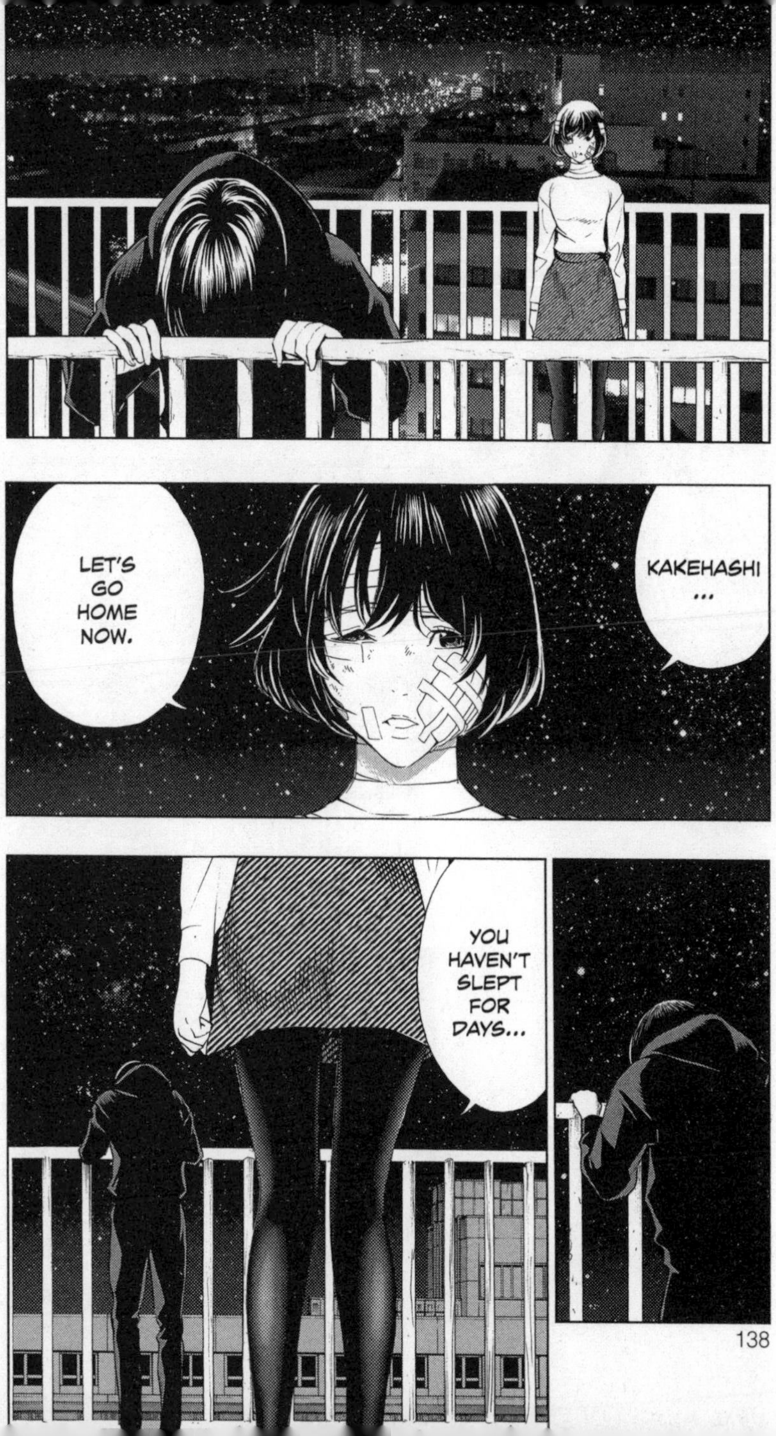
KAKEHASHI ...
LET'S GO HOME NOW.
YOU HAVEN'T SLEPT FOR DAYS...

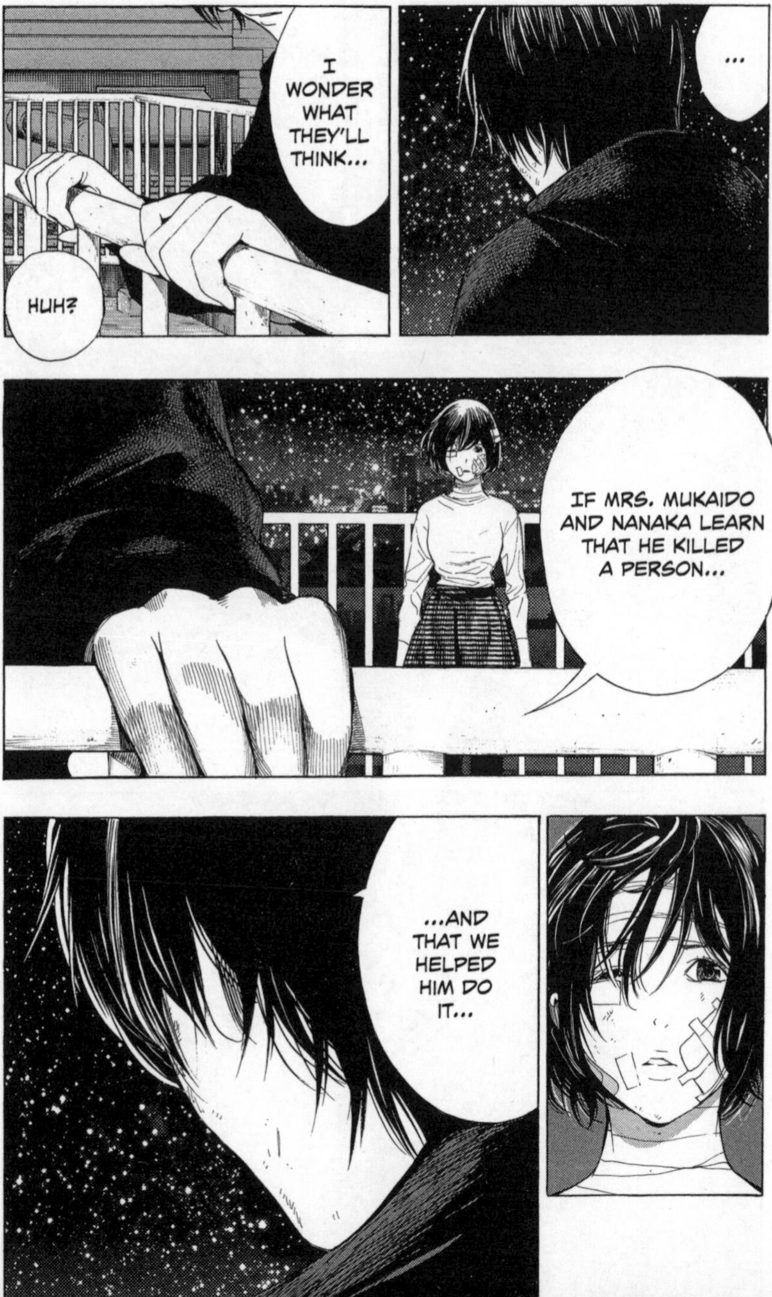
...
I WONDER WHAT THEY'LL THINK...
HUH?
IF MRS. MUKAIDO AND NANAKA LEARN THAT HE KILLED A PERSON...
...AND THAT WE HELPED HIM DO IT...

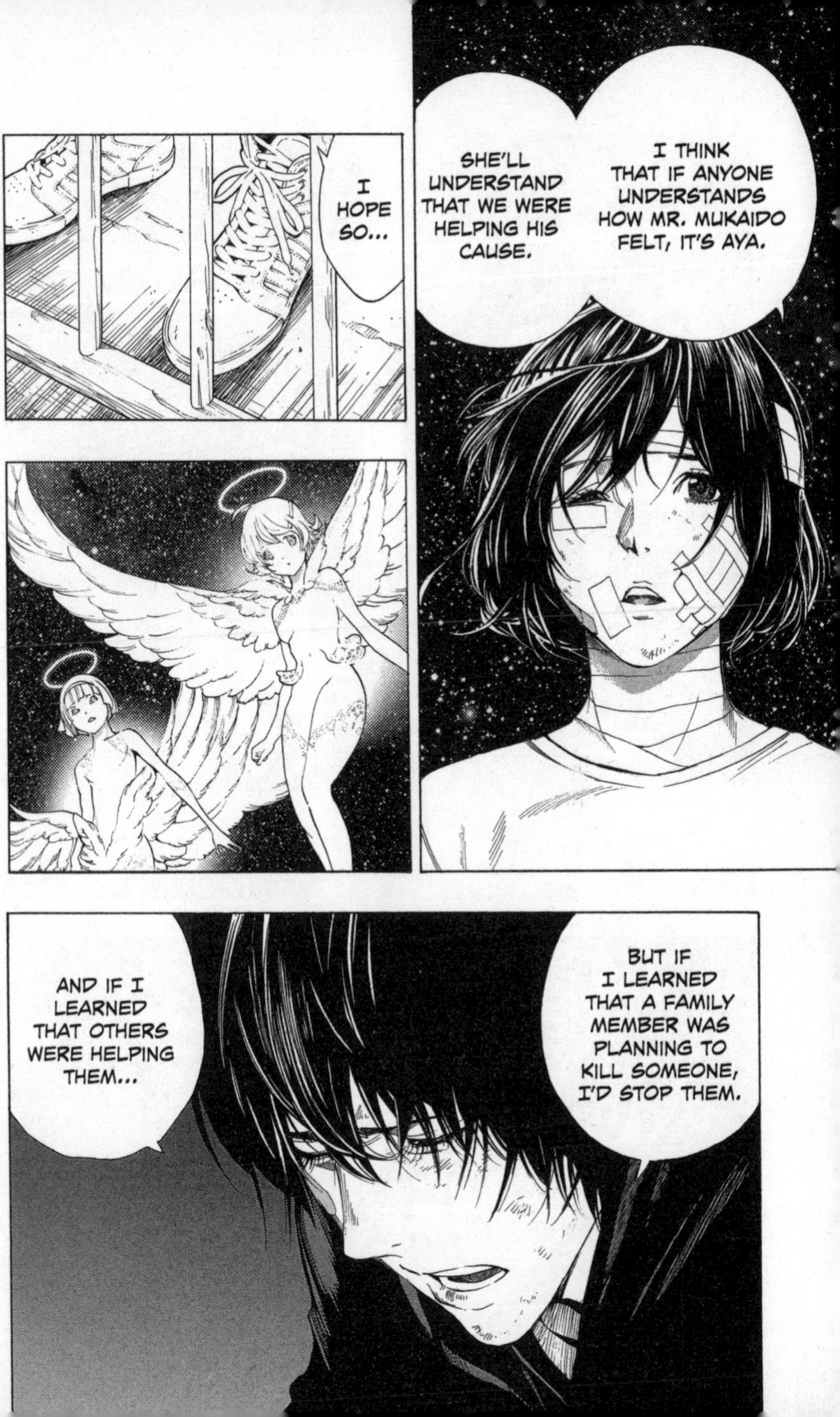
I THINK THAT IF ANYONE UNDERSTANDS HOW MR. MUKAIDO FELT, IT'S AYA.
SHE'LL UNDERSTAND THAT WE WERE HELPING HIS CAUSE.
I HOPE SO...
BUT IF I LEARNED THAT A FAMILY MEMBER WAS PLANNING TO KILL SOMEONE, I'D STOP THEM.
AND IF I LEARNED THAT OTHERS WERE HELPING THEM...

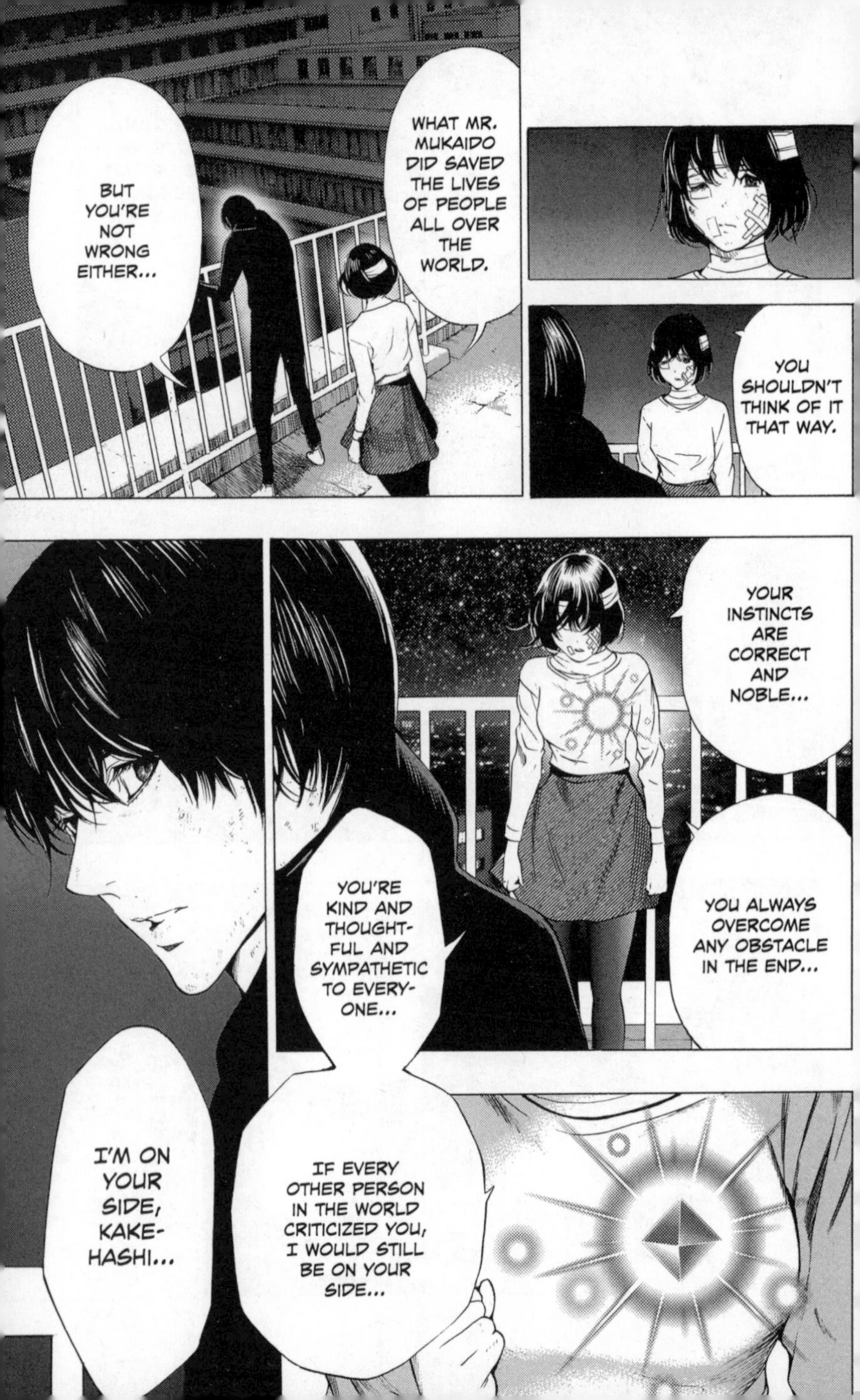
YOU SHOULDN'T THINK OF IT THAT WAY.
WHAT MR. MUKAIDO DID SAVED THE LIVES OF PEOPLE ALL OVER THE WORLD.
BUT YOU'RE NOT WRONG EITHER...
YOUR INSTINCTS ARE CORRECT AND NOBLE...
YOU ALWAYS OVERCOME ANY OBSTACLE IN THE END...
YOU'RE KIND AND THOUGHT-FUL AND SYMPATHETIC TO EVERY-ONE...
IF EVERY OTHER PERSON IN THE WORLD CRITICIZED YOU, I WOULD STILL BE ON YOUR SIDE...
I'M ON YOUR SIDE, KAKE-HASHI...

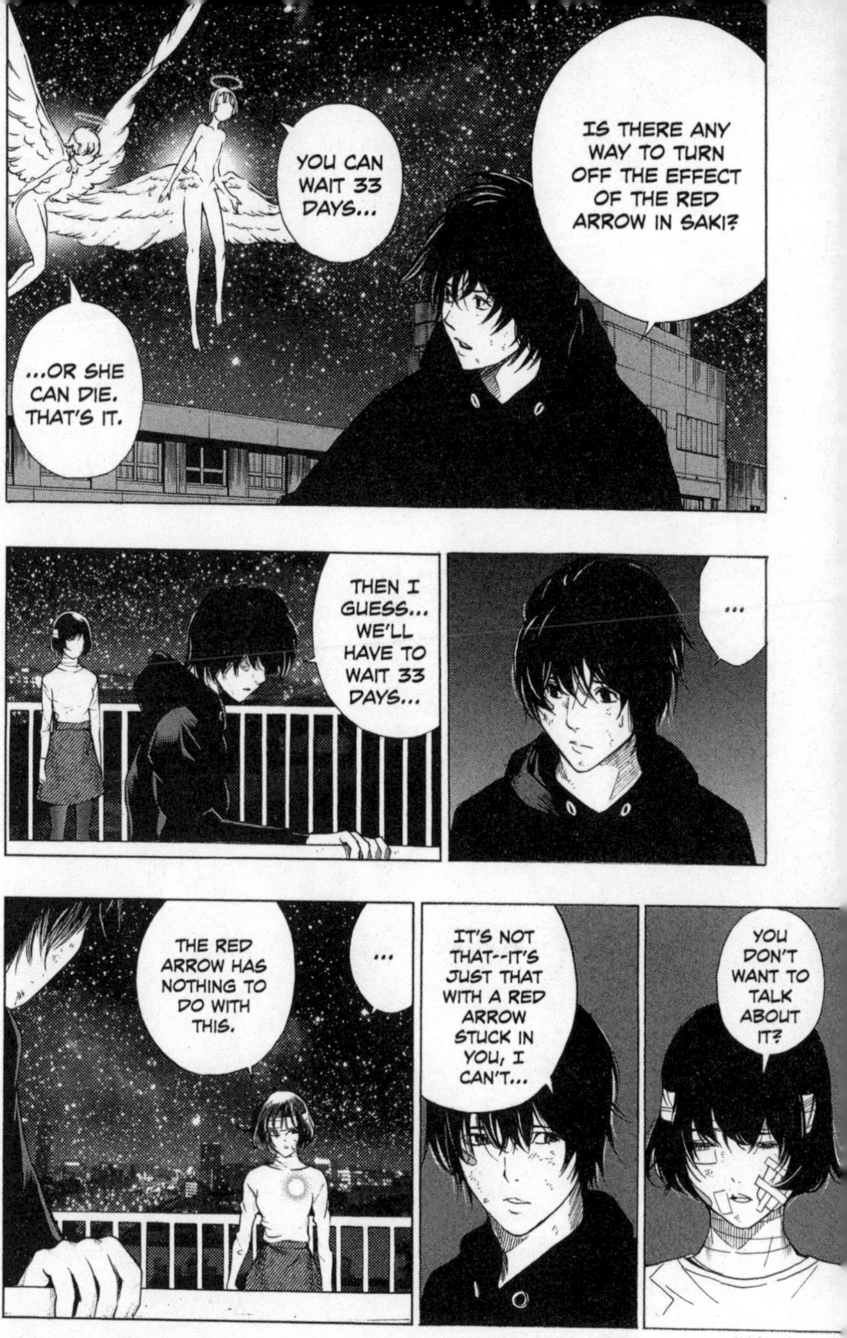
IS THERE ANY WAY TO TURN OFF THE EFFECT OF THE RED ARROW IN SAKI?
YOU CAN WAIT 33 DAYS...
...OR SHE CAN DIE. THAT'S IT.
...
THEN I GUESS... WE'LL HAVE TO WAIT 33 DAYS...
YOU DON'T WANT TO TALK ABOUT IT?
IT'S NOT THAT--IT'S JUST THAT WITH A RED ARROW STUCK IN YOU, I CAN'T...
...
THE RED ARROW HAS NOTHING TO DO WITH THIS.

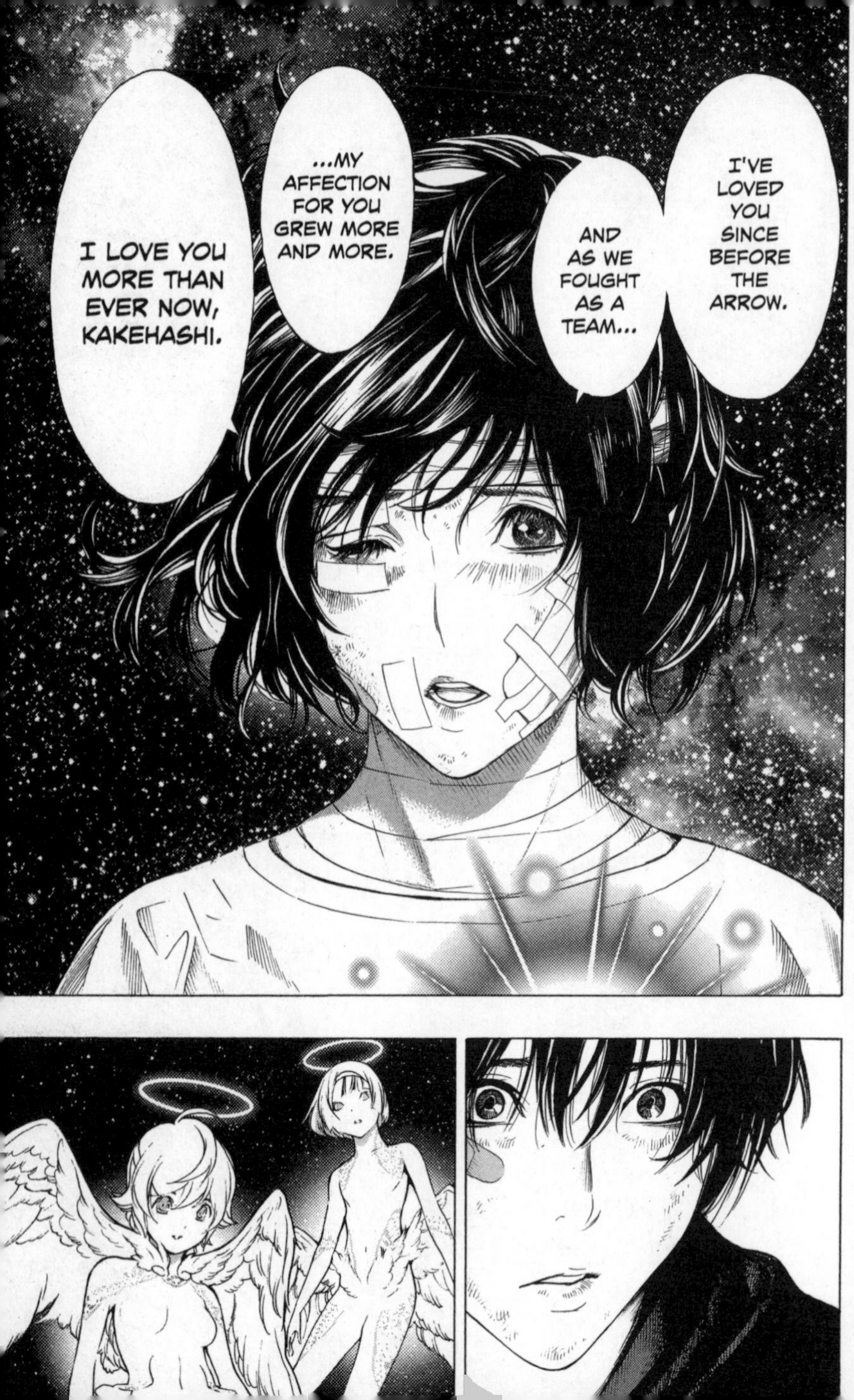
I'VE LOVED YOU SINCE BEFORE THE ARROW.
AND AS WE FOUGHT AS A TEAM...
...MY AFFECTION FOR YOU GREW MORE AND MORE.
I LOVE YOU MORE THAN EVER NOW, KAKEHASHI.

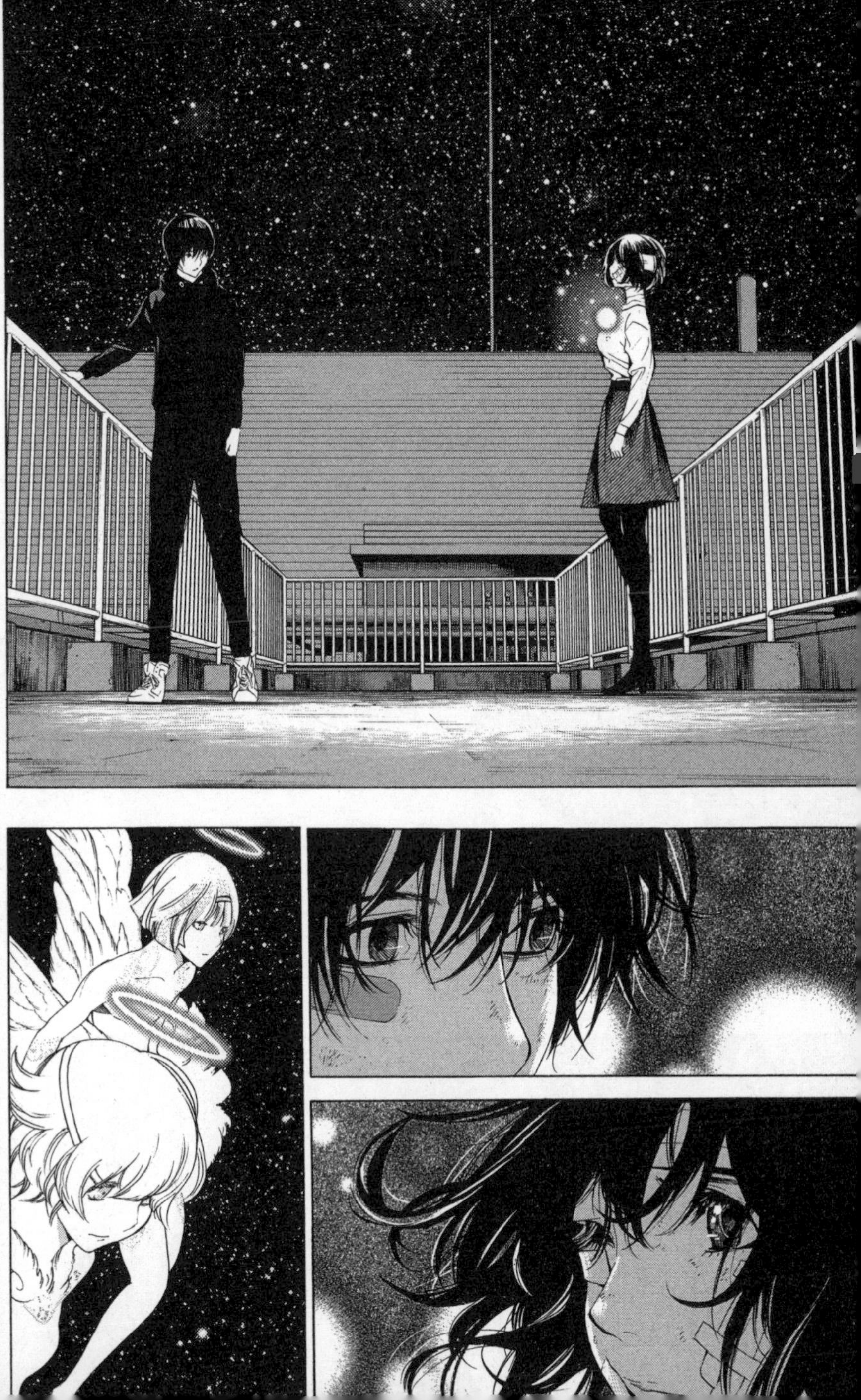

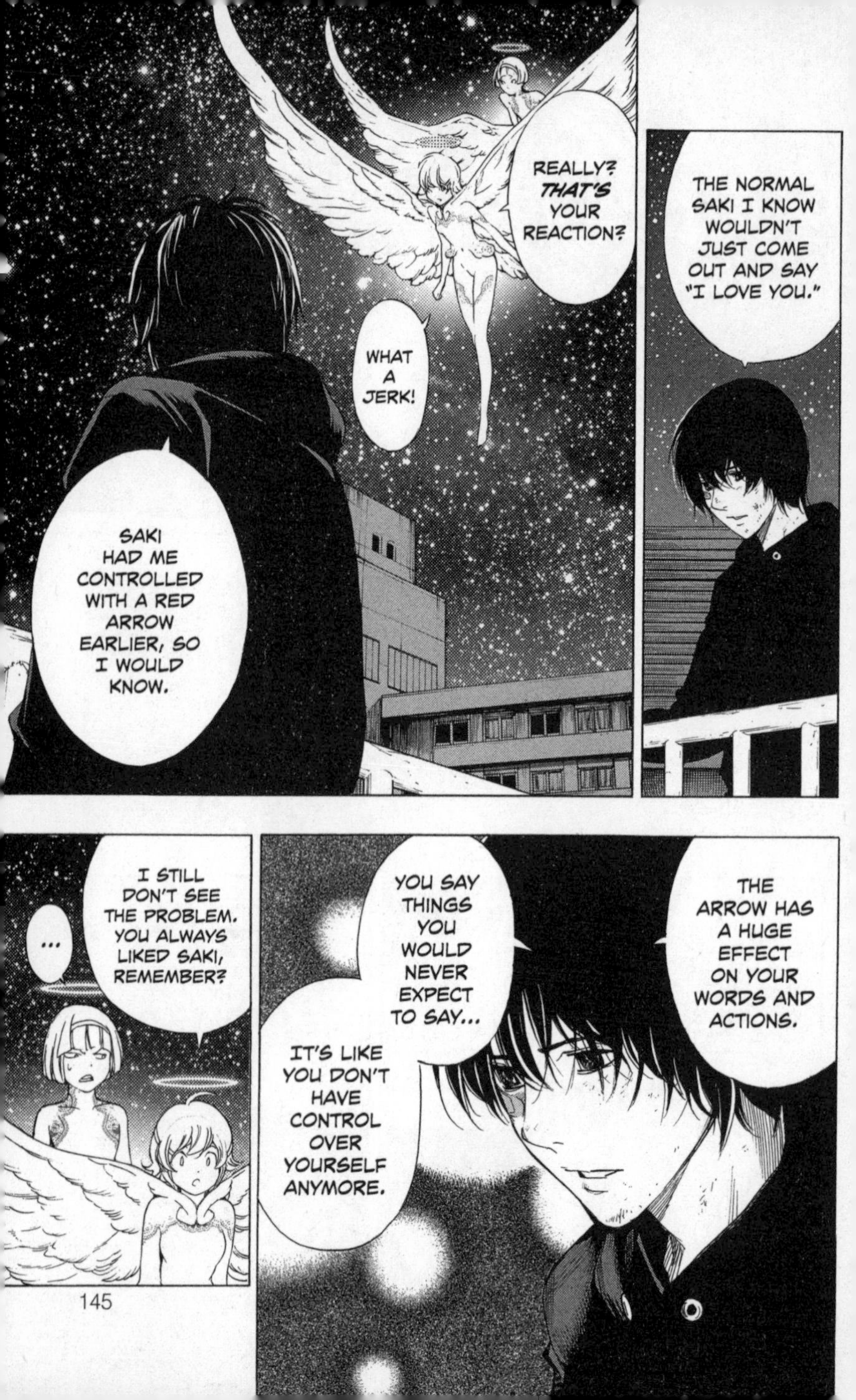
THE NORMAL SAKI I KNOW WOULDN'T JUST COME OUT AND SAY "I LOVE YOU."
REALLY? *THAT'S* YOUR REACTION?
WHAT A JERK!
SAKI HAD ME CONTROLLED WITH A RED ARROW EARLIER, SO I WOULD KNOW.
THE ARROW HAS A HUGE EFFECT ON YOUR WORDS AND ACTIONS.
YOU SAY THINGS YOU WOULD NEVER EXPECT TO SAY...
IT'S LIKE YOU DON'T HAVE CONTROL OVER YOURSELF ANYMORE.
I STILL DON'T SEE THE PROBLEM. YOU ALWAYS LIKED SAKI, REMEMBER?
...

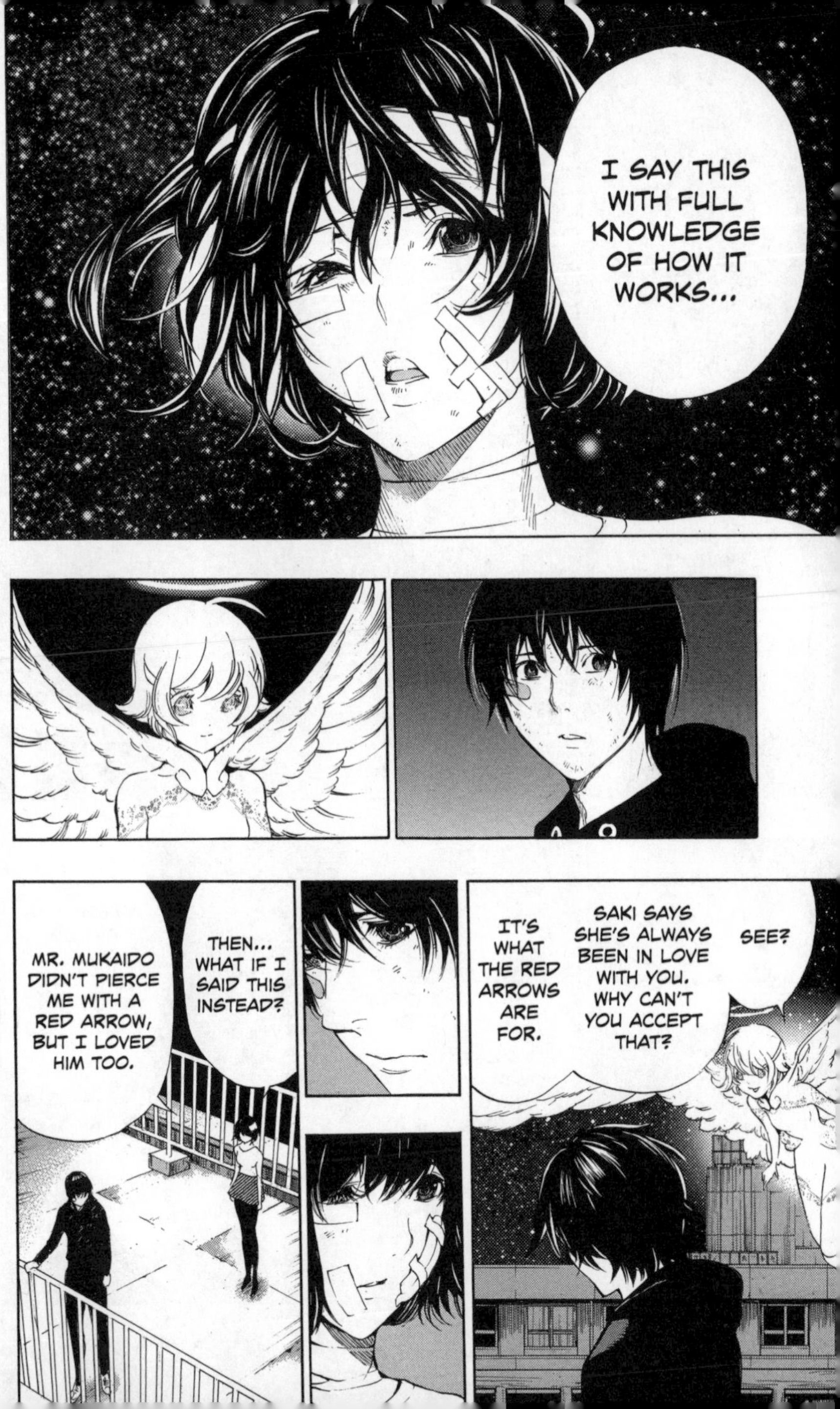
I SAY THIS WITH FULL KNOWLEDGE OF HOW IT WORKS...
SEE?
SAKI SAYS SHE'S ALWAYS BEEN IN LOVE WITH YOU. WHY CAN'T YOU ACCEPT THAT?
IT'S WHAT THE RED ARROWS ARE FOR.
THEN... WHAT IF I SAID THIS INSTEAD?
MR. MUKAIDO DIDN'T PIERCE ME WITH A RED ARROW, BUT I LOVED HIM TOO.

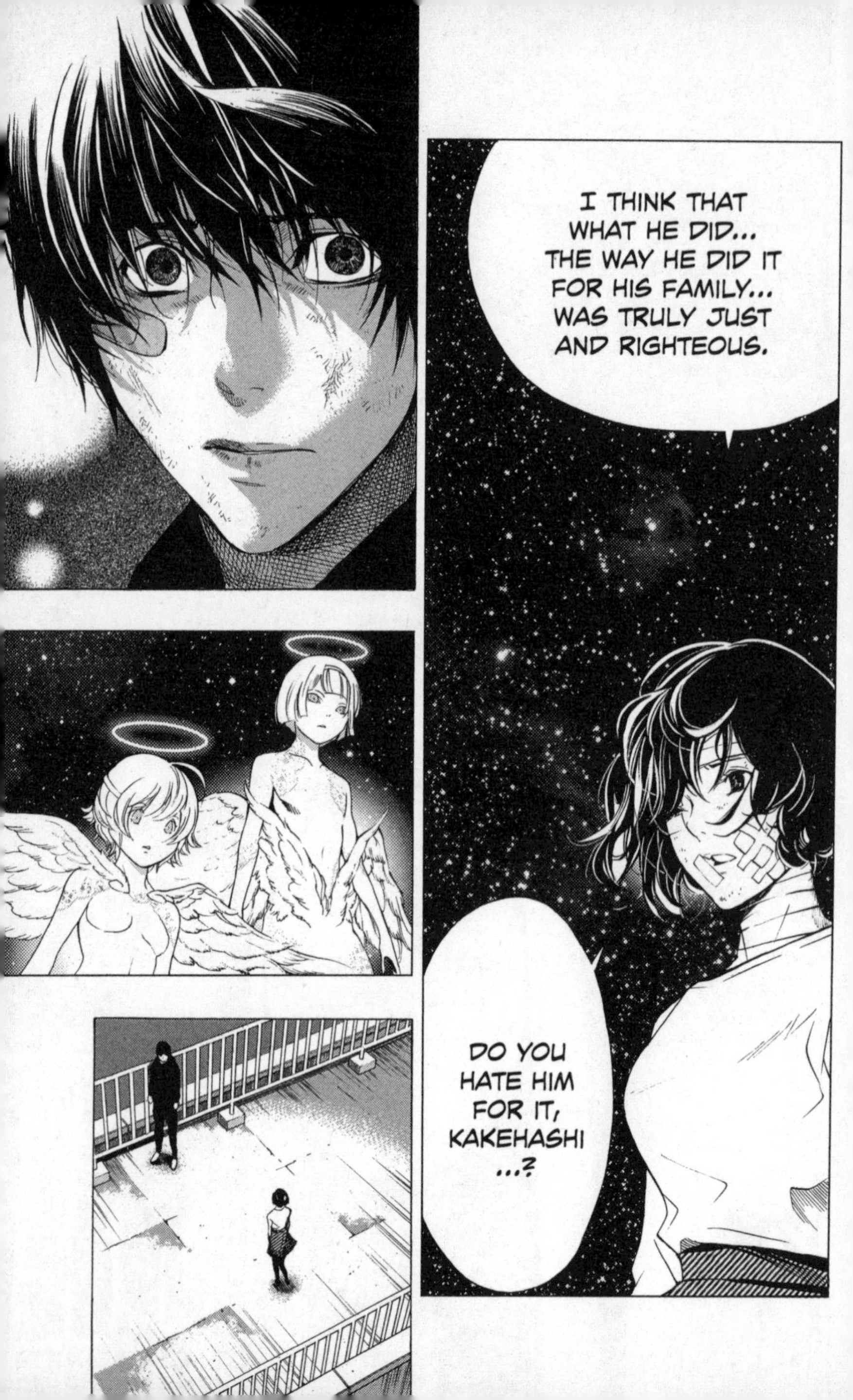
I THINK THAT WHAT HE DID... THE WAY HE DID IT FOR HIS FAMILY... WAS TRULY JUST AND RIGHTEOUS.
DO YOU HATE HIM FOR IT, KAKEHASHI ...?

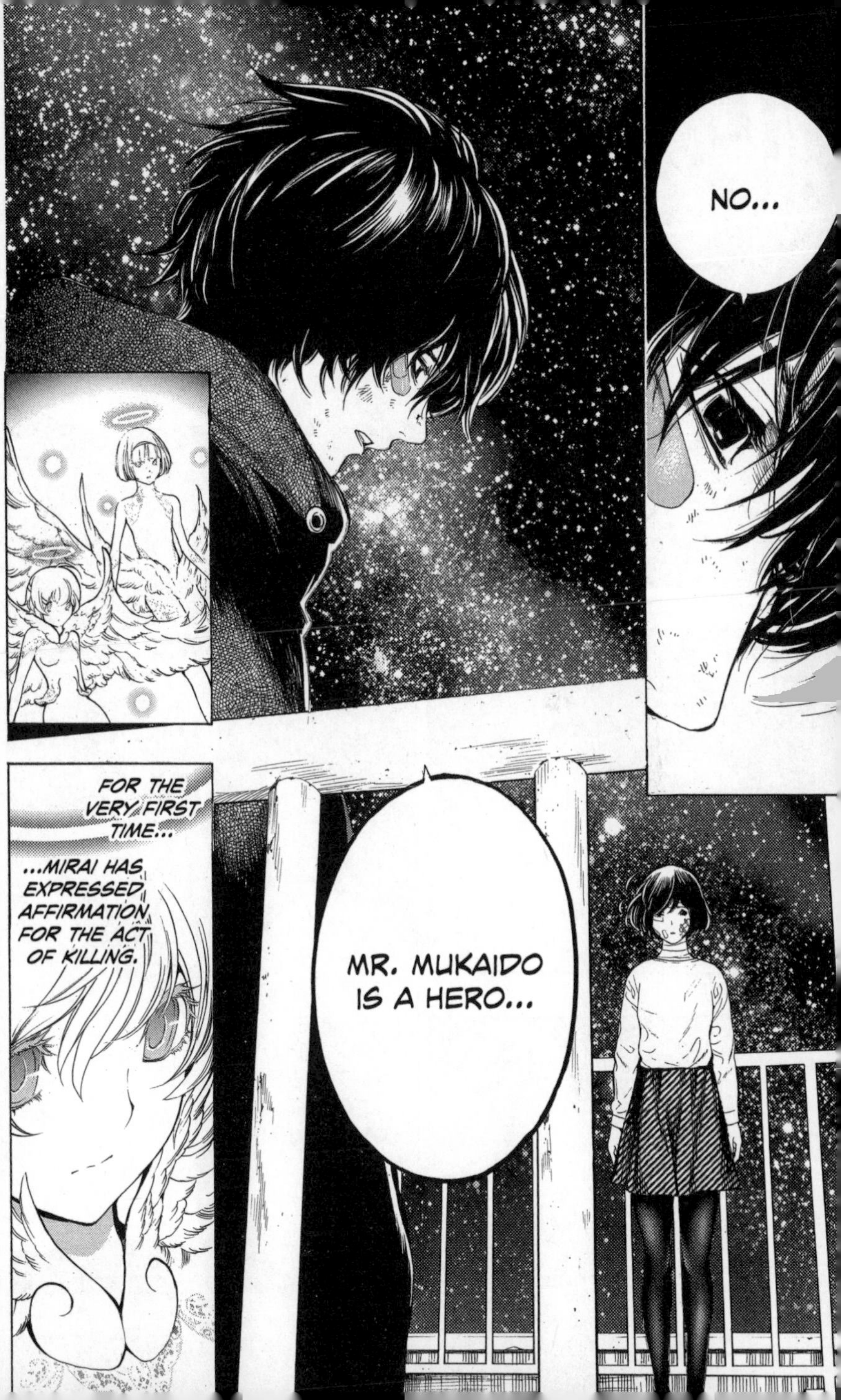
NO...
MR. MUKAIDO IS A HERO...
FOR THE VERY FIRST TIME...
...MIRAI HAS EXPRESSED AFFIRMATION FOR THE ACT OF KILLING.

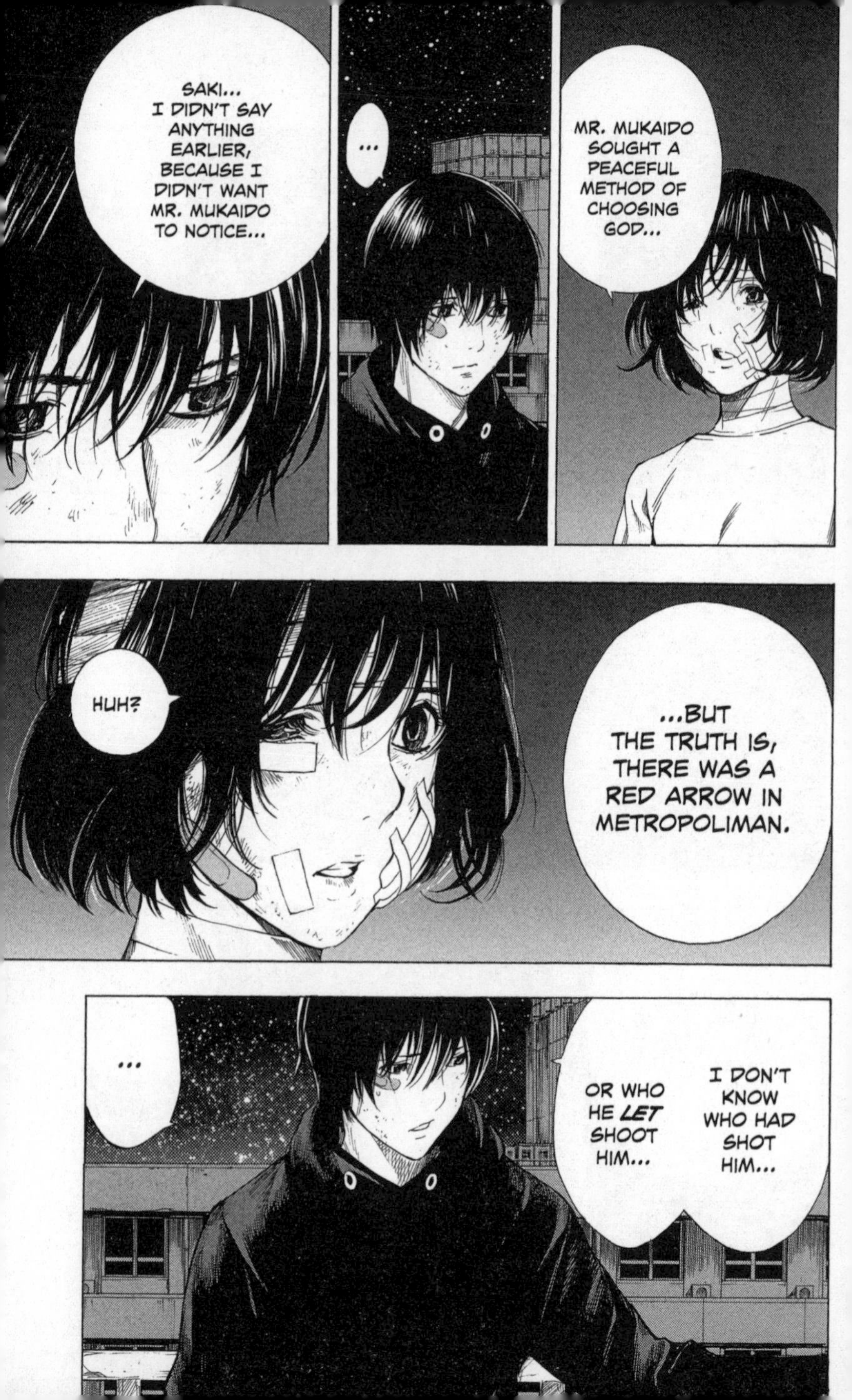
MR. MUKAIDO SOUGHT A PEACEFUL METHOD OF CHOOSING GOD...
...
SAKI... I DIDN'T SAY ANYTHING EARLIER, BECAUSE I DIDN'T WANT MR. MUKAIDO TO NOTICE...
...BUT THE TRUTH IS, THERE WAS A RED ARROW IN METROPOLIMAN.
HUH?
I DON'T KNOW WHO HAD SHOT HIM...
OR WHO HE *LET* SHOOT HIM...
...

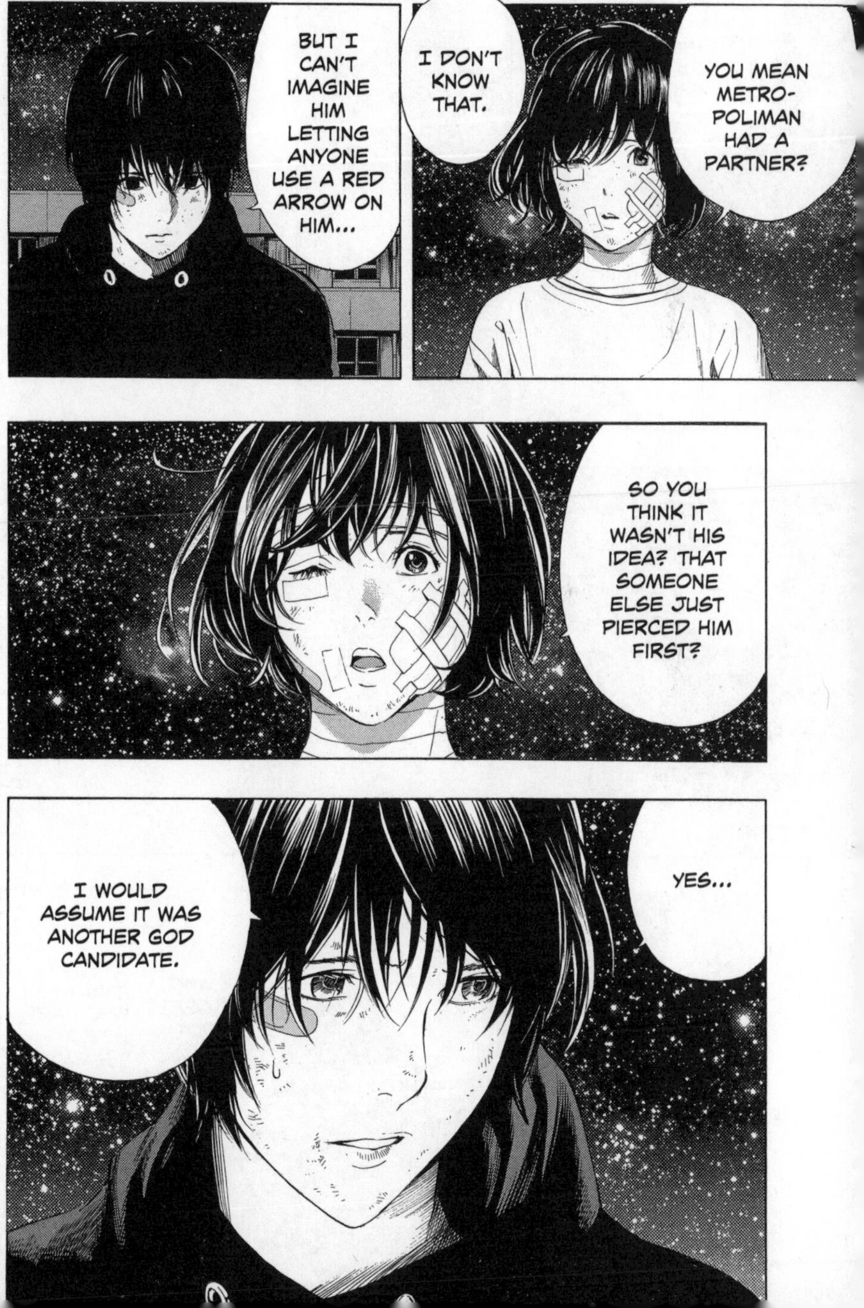
YOU MEAN METRO-POLIMAN HAD A PARTNER?
I DON'T KNOW THAT.
BUT I CAN'T IMAGINE HIM LETTING ANYONE USE A RED ARROW ON HIM...
SO YOU THINK IT WASN'T HIS IDEA? THAT SOMEONE ELSE JUST PIERCED HIM FIRST?
YES...
I WOULD ASSUME IT WAS ANOTHER GOD CANDIDATE.

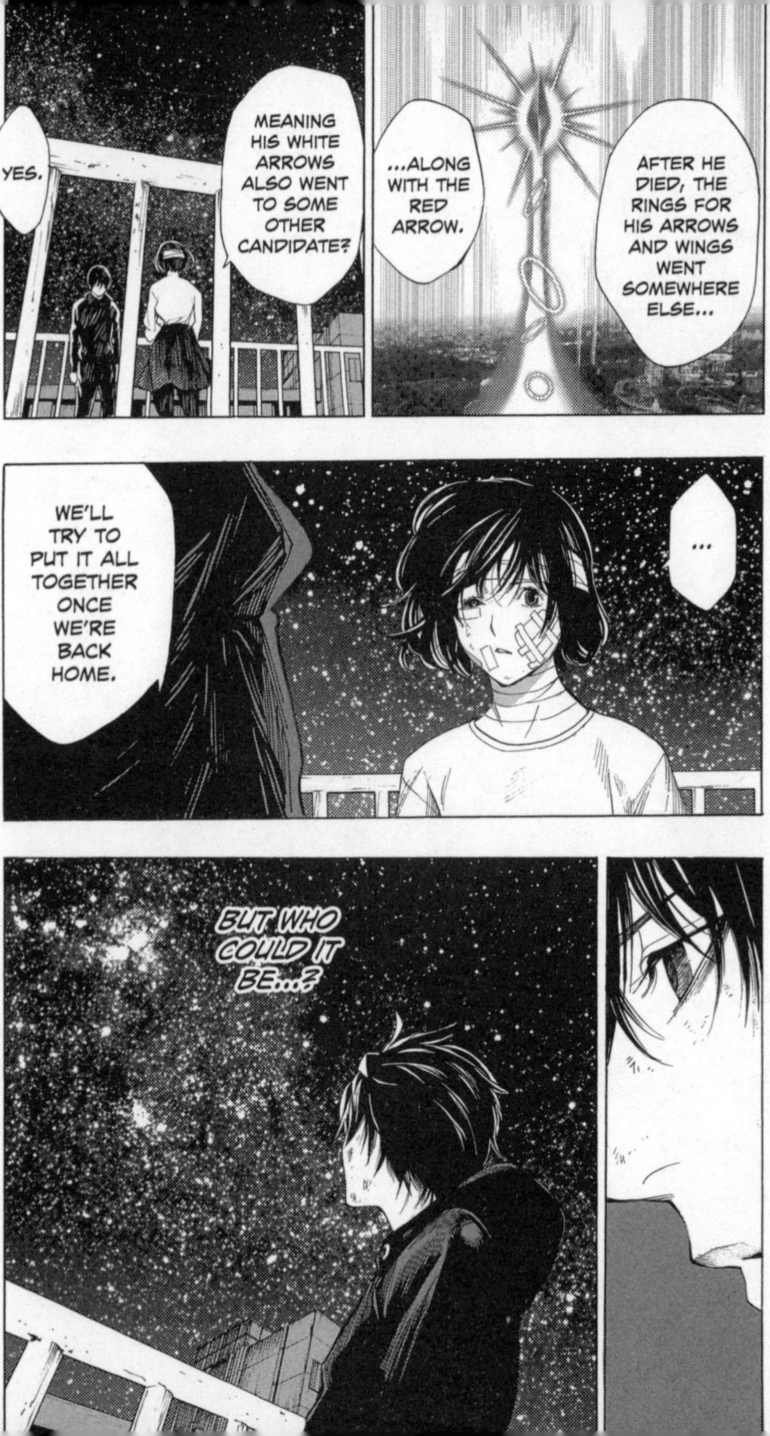
AFTER HE DIED, THE RINGS FOR HIS ARROWS AND WINGS WENT SOMEWHERE ELSE...
...ALONG WITH THE RED ARROW.
MEANING HIS WHITE ARROWS ALSO WENT TO SOME OTHER CANDIDATE?
YES.
...
WE'LL TRY TO PUT IT ALL TOGETHER ONCE WE'RE BACK HOME.
BUT WHO COULD IT BE...?

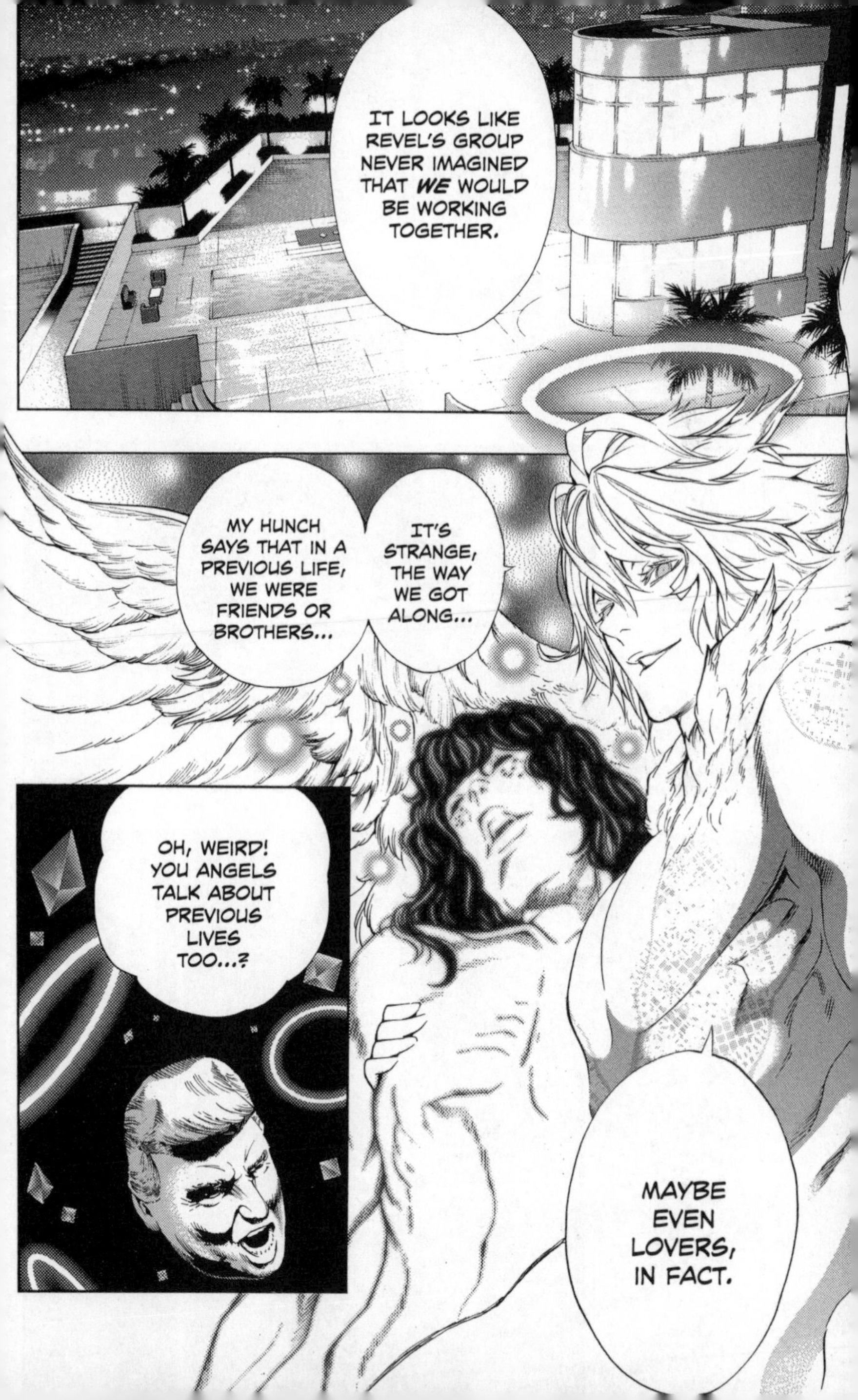
IT LOOKS LIKE REVEL'S GROUP NEVER IMAGINED THAT *WE* WOULD BE WORKING TOGETHER.
IT'S STRANGE, THE WAY WE GOT ALONG...
MY HUNCH SAYS THAT IN A PREVIOUS LIFE, WE WERE FRIENDS OR BROTHERS...
MAYBE EVEN LOVERS, IN FACT.
OH, WEIRD! YOU ANGELS TALK ABOUT PREVIOUS LIVES TOO...?

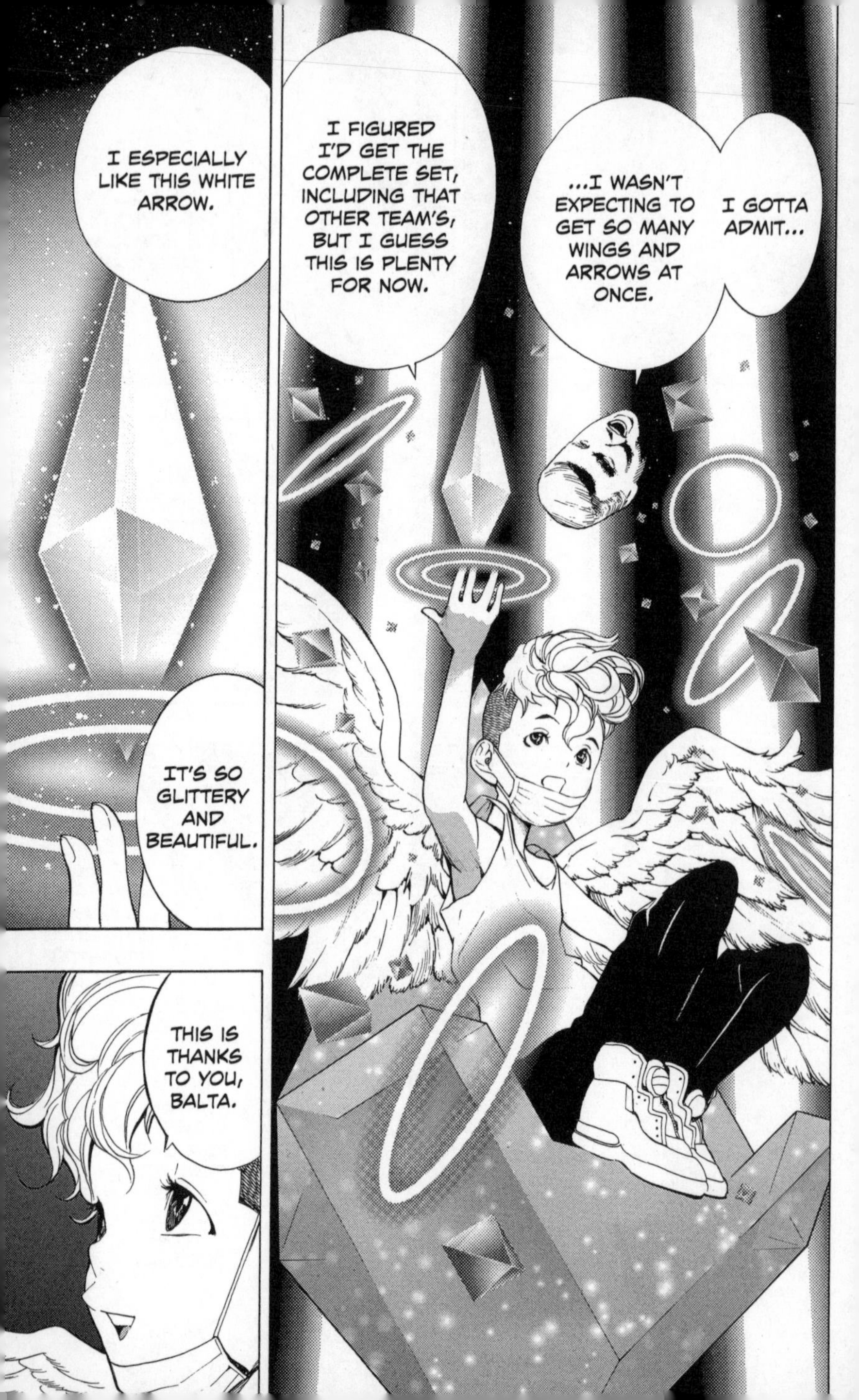
I GOTTA ADMIT...
...I WASN'T EXPECTING TO GET SO MANY WINGS AND ARROWS AT ONCE.
I FIGURED I'D GET THE COMPLETE SET, INCLUDING THAT OTHER TEAM'S, BUT I GUESS THIS IS PLENTY FOR NOW.
I ESPECIALLY LIKE THIS WHITE ARROW.
IT'S SO GLITTERY AND BEAUTIFUL.
THIS IS THANKS TO YOU, BALTA.

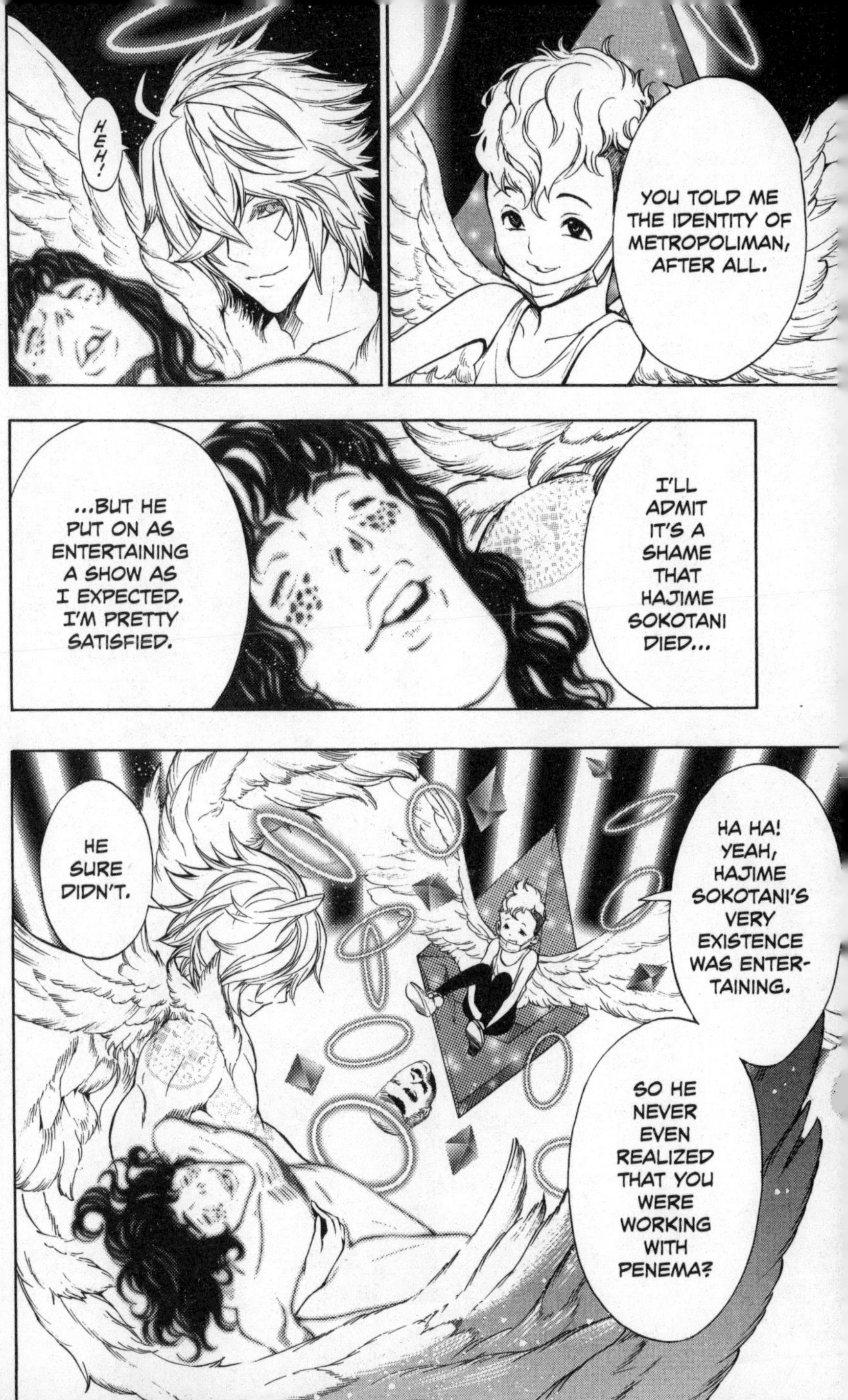
YOU TOLD ME THE IDENTITY OF METROPOLIMAN, AFTER ALL.
HEH!
I'LL ADMIT IT'S A SHAME THAT HAJIME SOKOTANI DIED...
...BUT HE PUT ON AS ENTERTAINING A SHOW AS I EXPECTED. I'M PRETTY SATISFIED.
HA HA! YEAH, HAJIME SOKOTANI'S VERY EXISTENCE WAS ENTER-TAINING.
SO HE NEVER EVEN REALIZED THAT YOU WERE WORKING WITH PENEMA?
HE SURE DIDN'T.

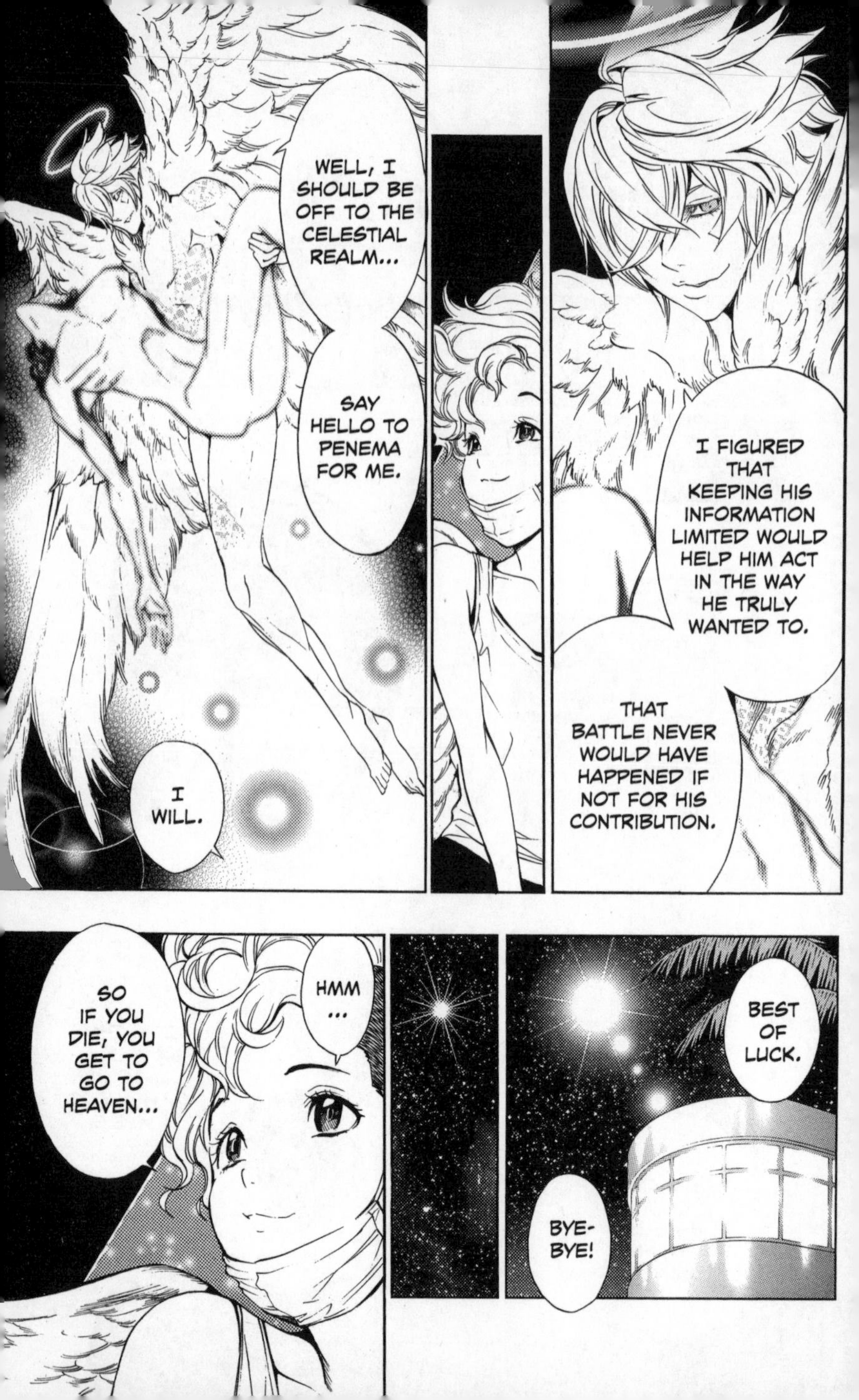
I FIGURED THAT KEEPING HIS INFORMATION LIMITED WOULD HELP HIM ACT IN THE WAY HE TRULY WANTED TO.
THAT BATTLE NEVER WOULD HAVE HAPPENED IF NOT FOR HIS CONTRIBUTION.
WELL, I SHOULD BE OFF TO THE CELESTIAL REALM...
SAY HELLO TO PENEMA FOR ME.
I WILL.
BEST OF LUCK.
BYE-BYE!
HMM ...
SO IF YOU DIE, YOU GET TO GO TO HEAVEN...

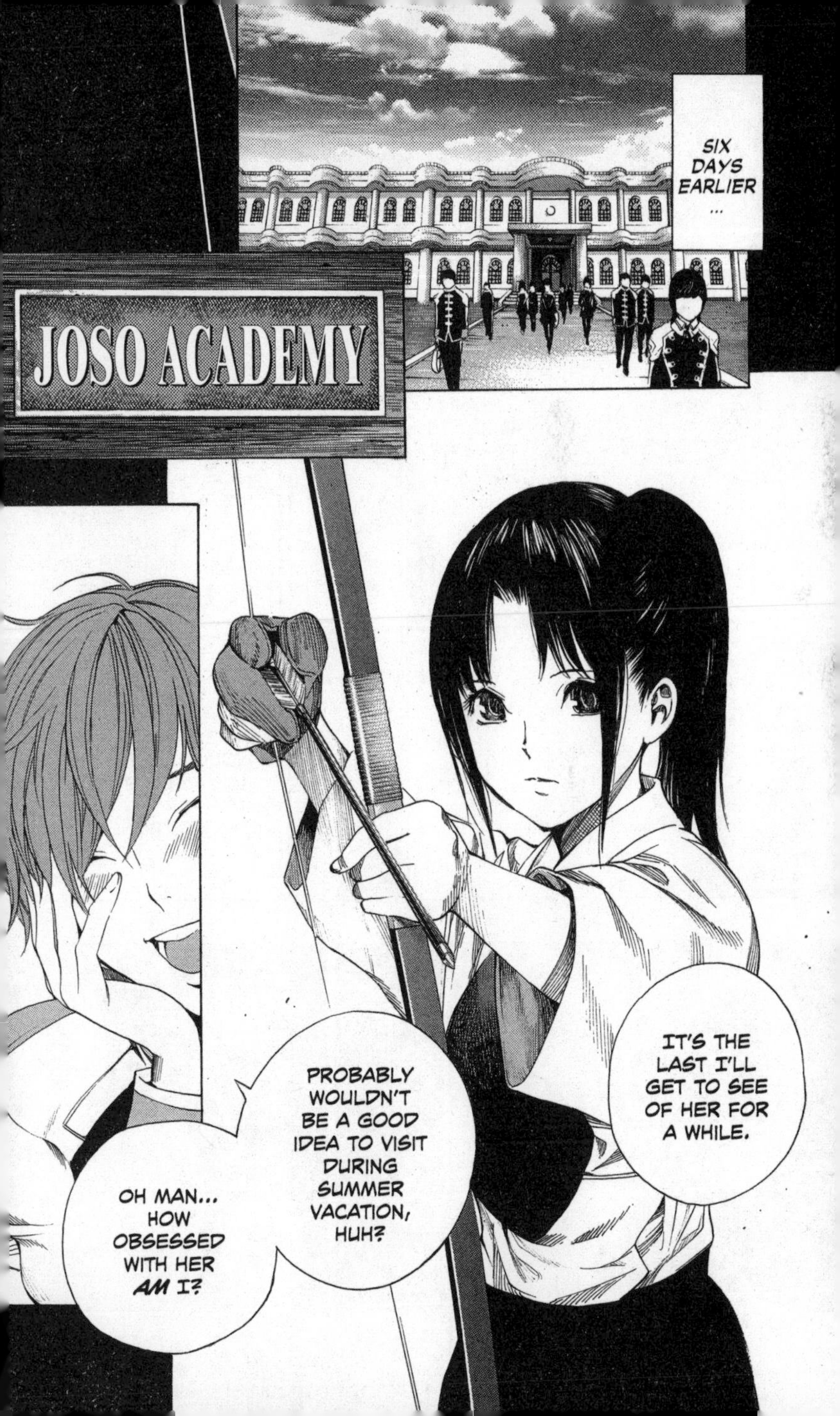
SIX DAYS EARLIER ...
JOSO ACADEMY
IT'S THE LAST I'LL GET TO SEE OF HER FOR A WHILE.
PROBABLY WOULDN'T BE A GOOD IDEA TO VISIT DURING SUMMER VACATION, HUH?
OH MAN... HOW OBSESSED WITH HER *AM* I?

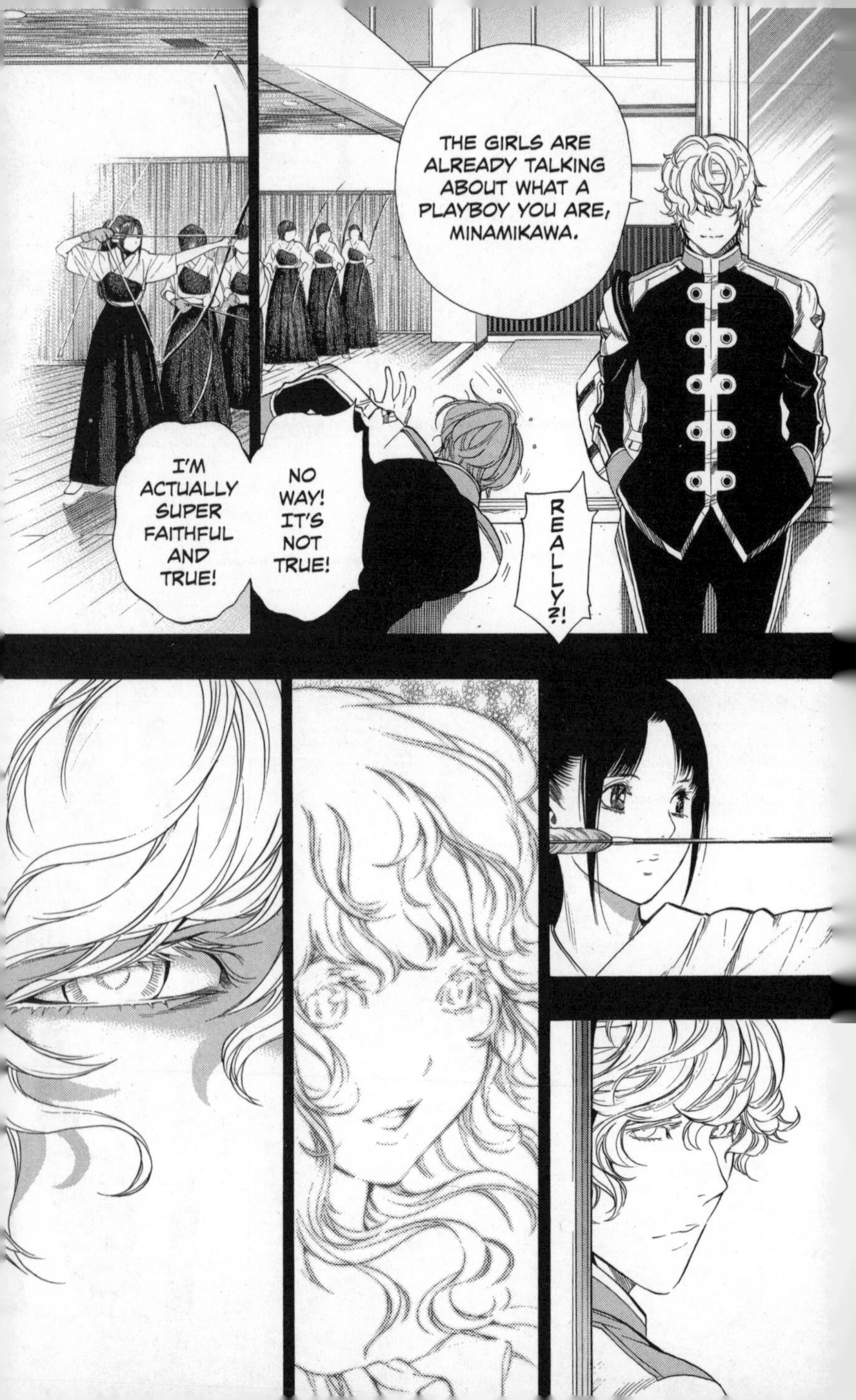
THE GIRLS ARE ALREADY TALKING ABOUT WHAT A PLAYBOY YOU ARE, MINAMIKAWA.
REALLY?!
NO WAY! IT'S NOT TRUE!
I'M ACTUALLY SUPER FAITHFUL AND TRUE!

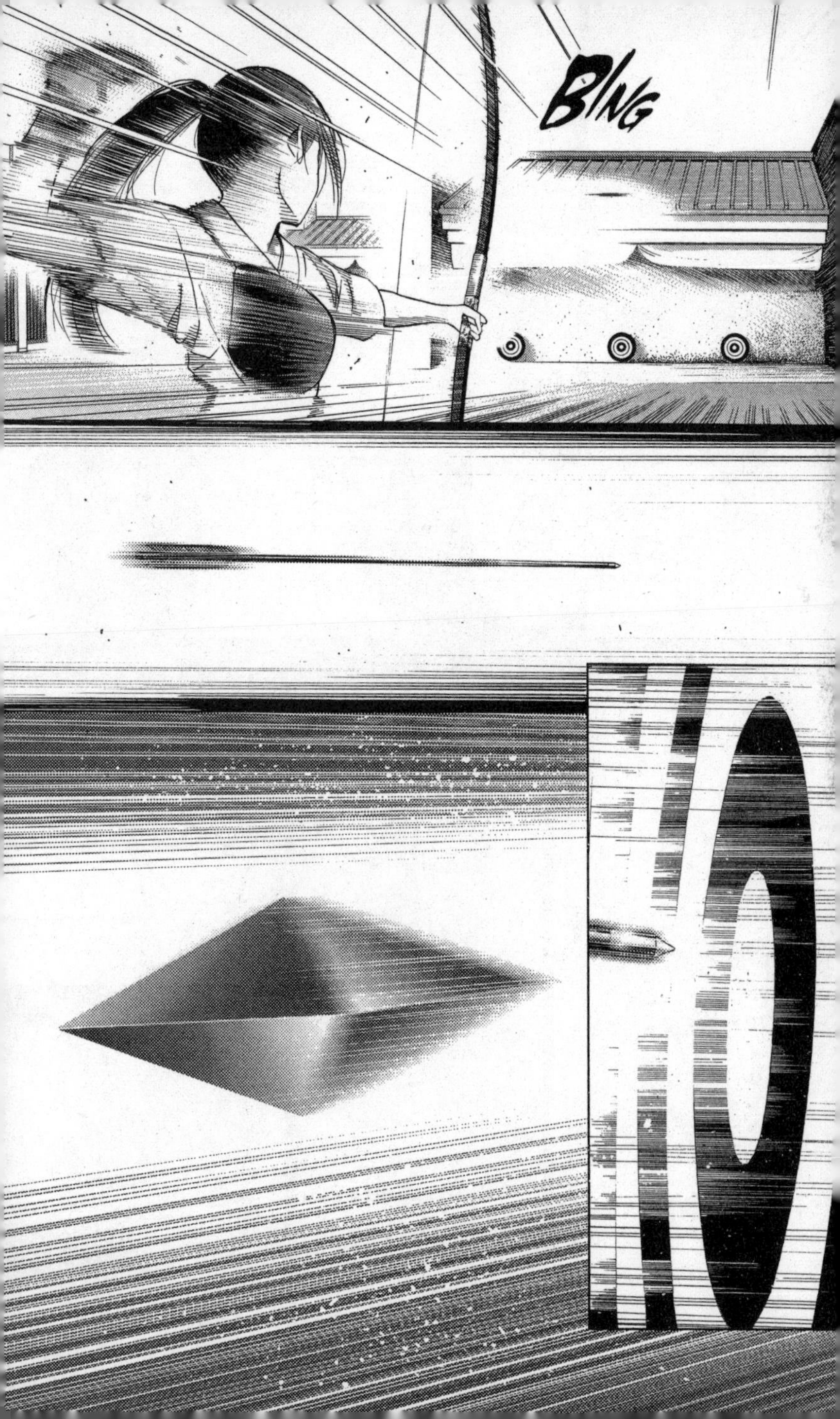
BING

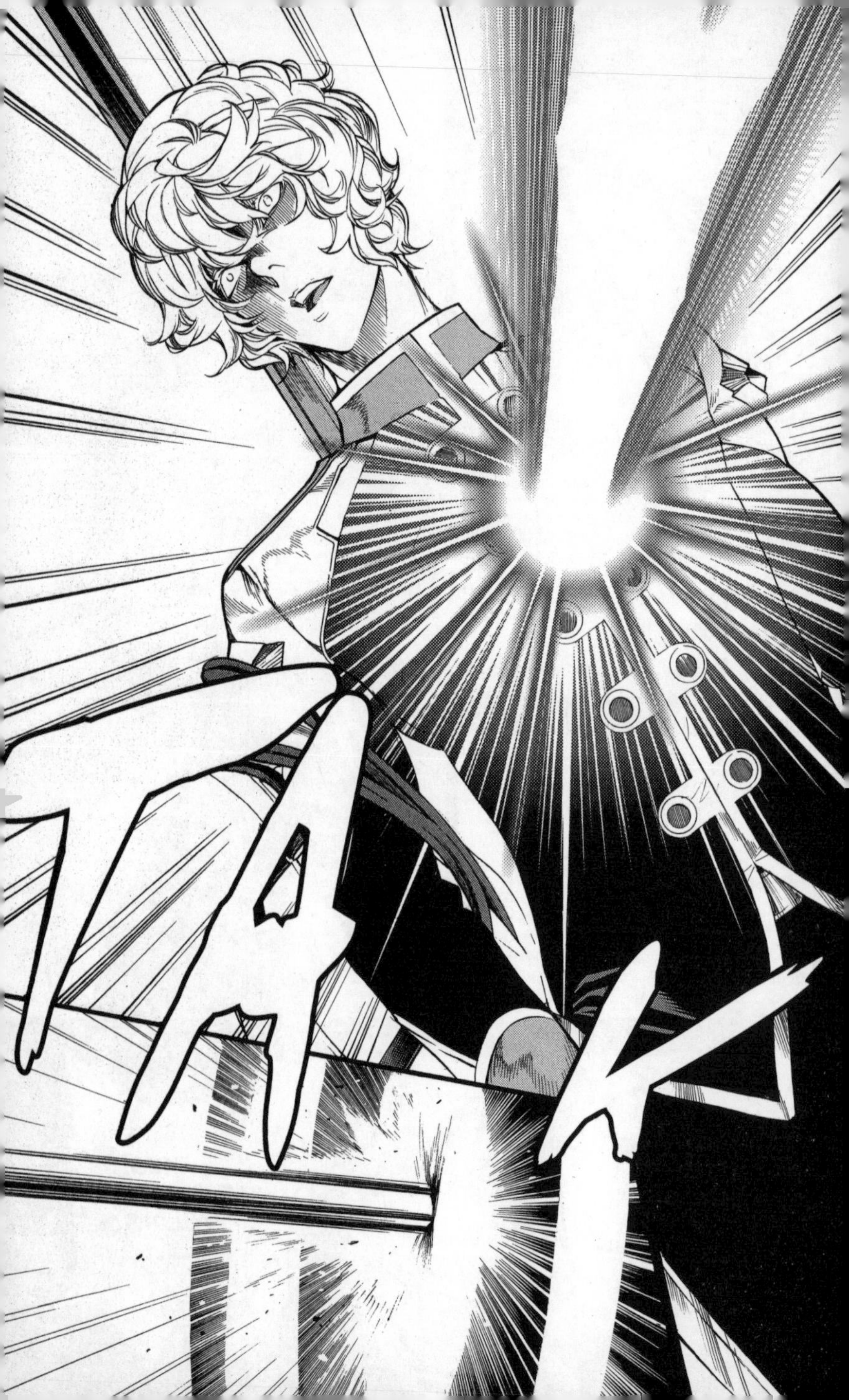

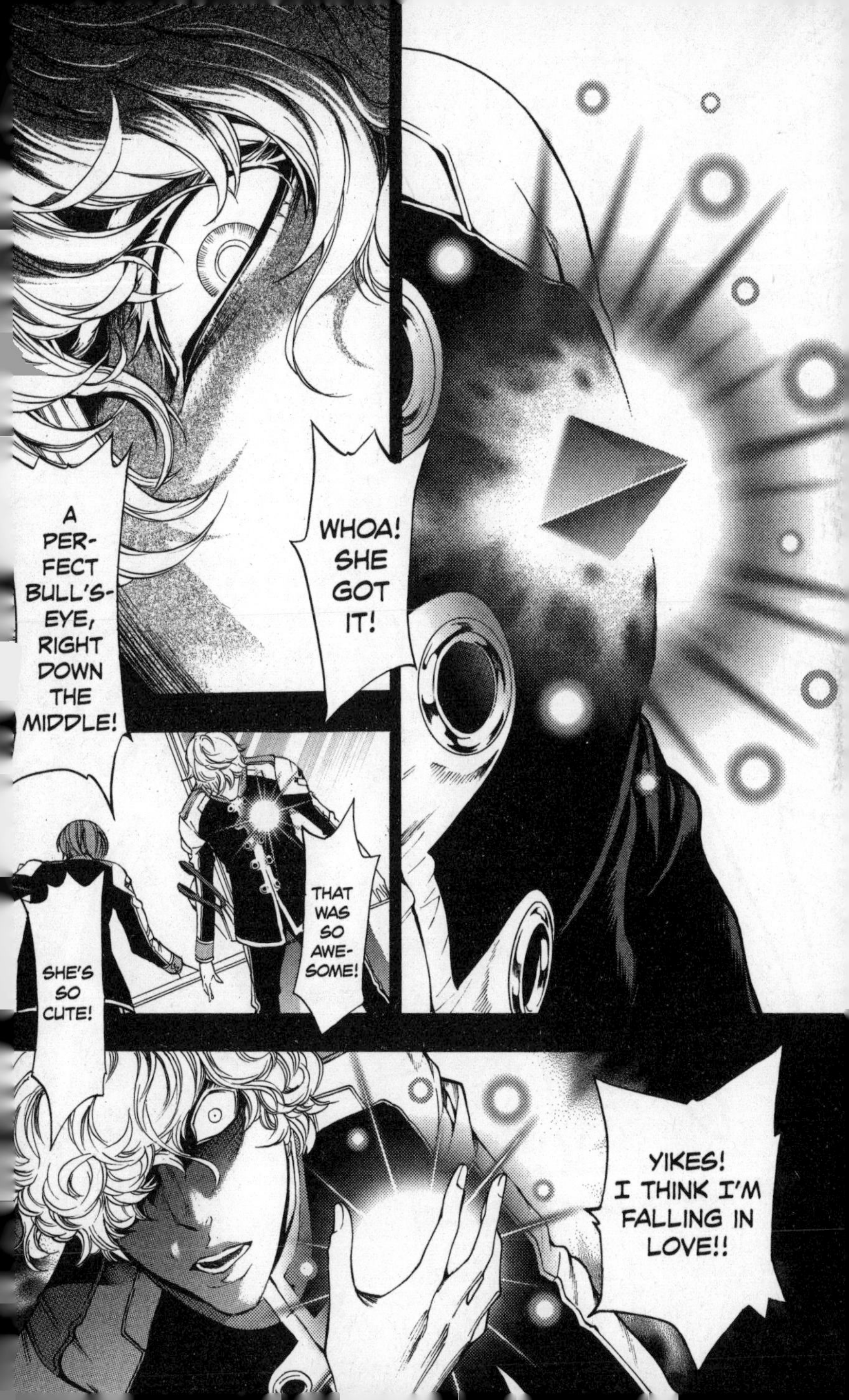
WHOA! SHE GOT IT!
A PERFECT BULL'S-EYE, RIGHT DOWN THE MIDDLE!
THAT WAS SO AWESOME!
SHE'S SO CUTE!
YIKES! I THINK I'M FALLING IN LOVE!!

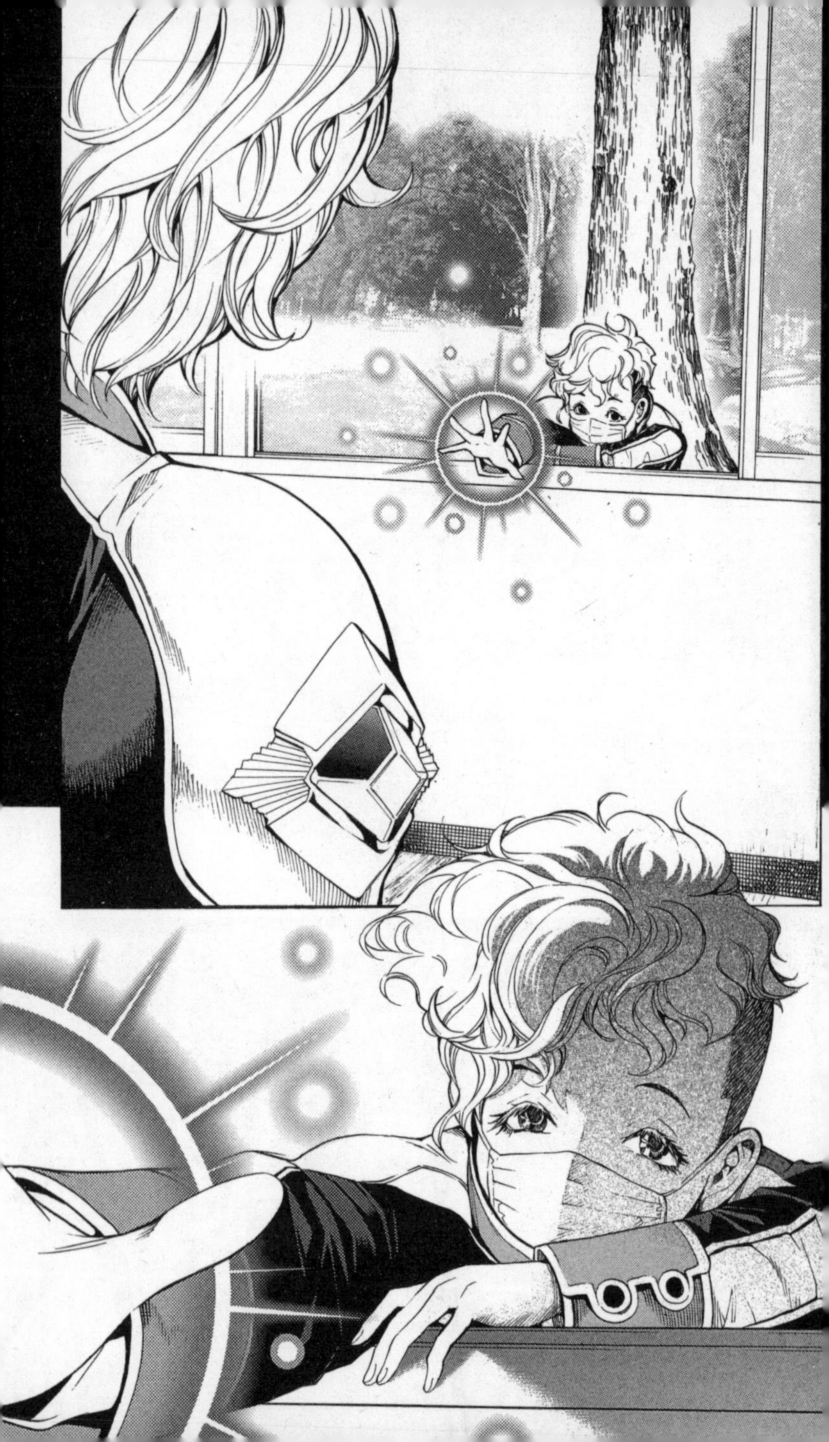

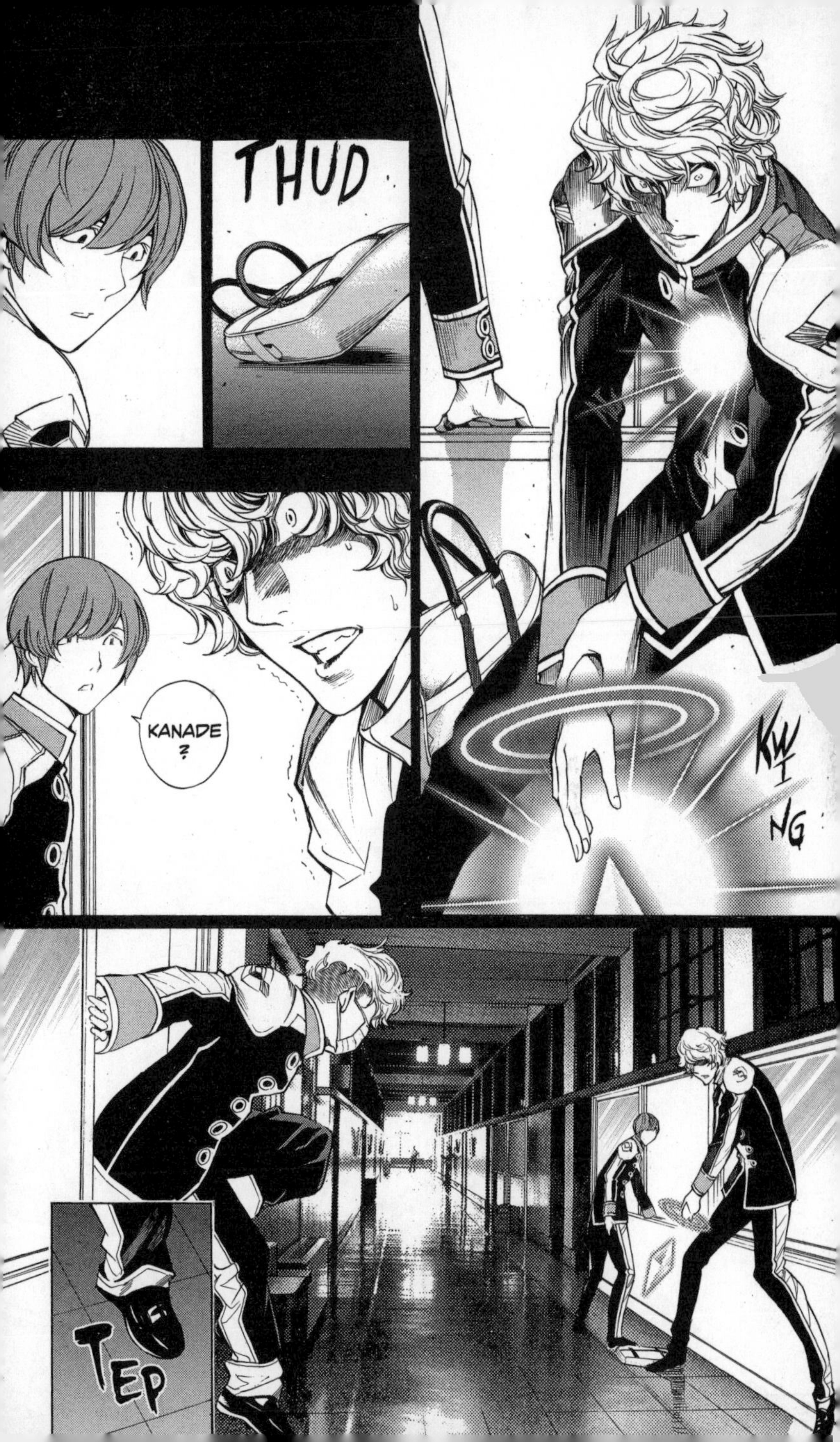
KWING
THUD
KANADE?
TEP

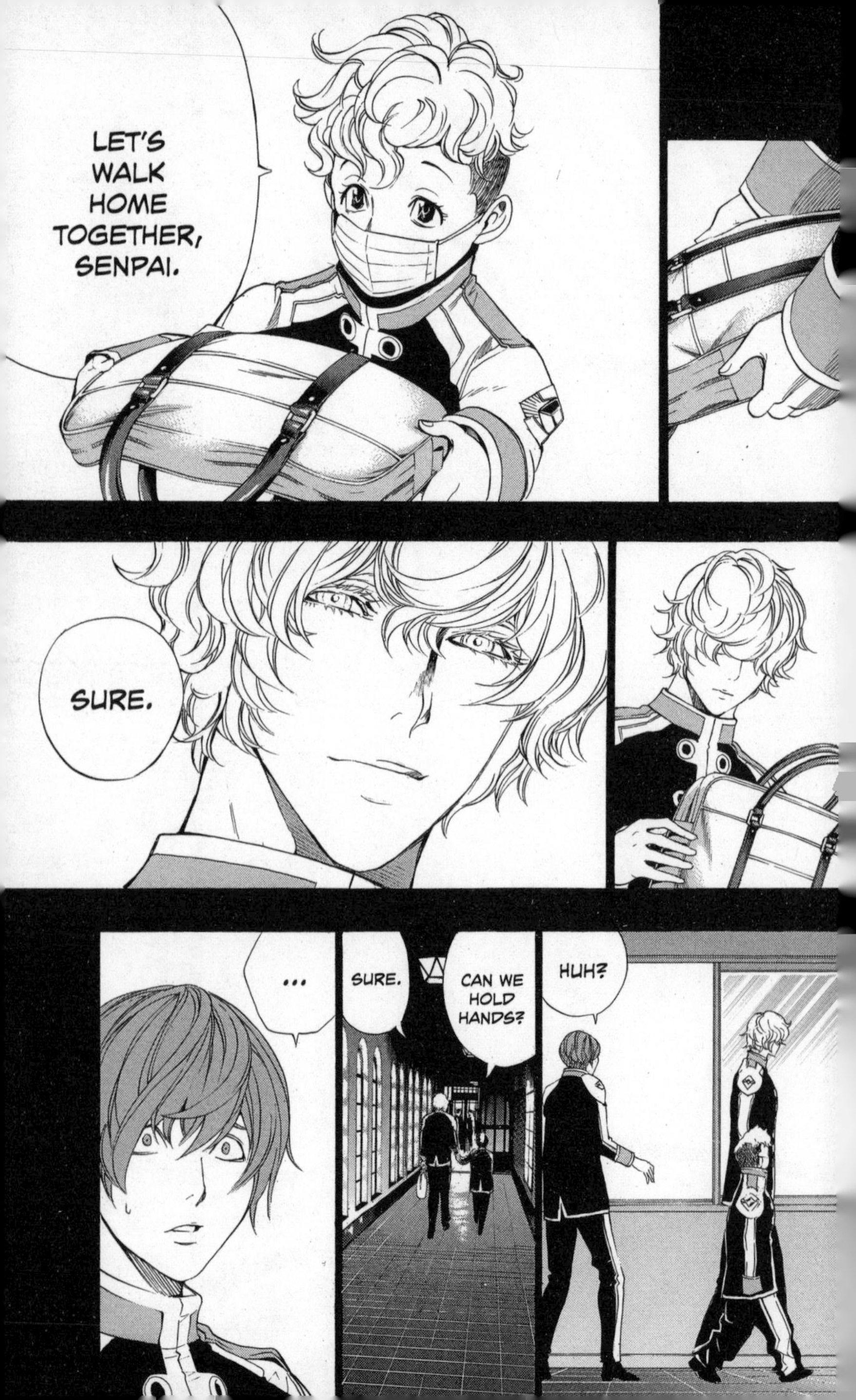
LET'S WALK HOME TOGETHER, SENPAI.
SURE.
HUH?
CAN WE HOLD HANDS?
SURE.
...

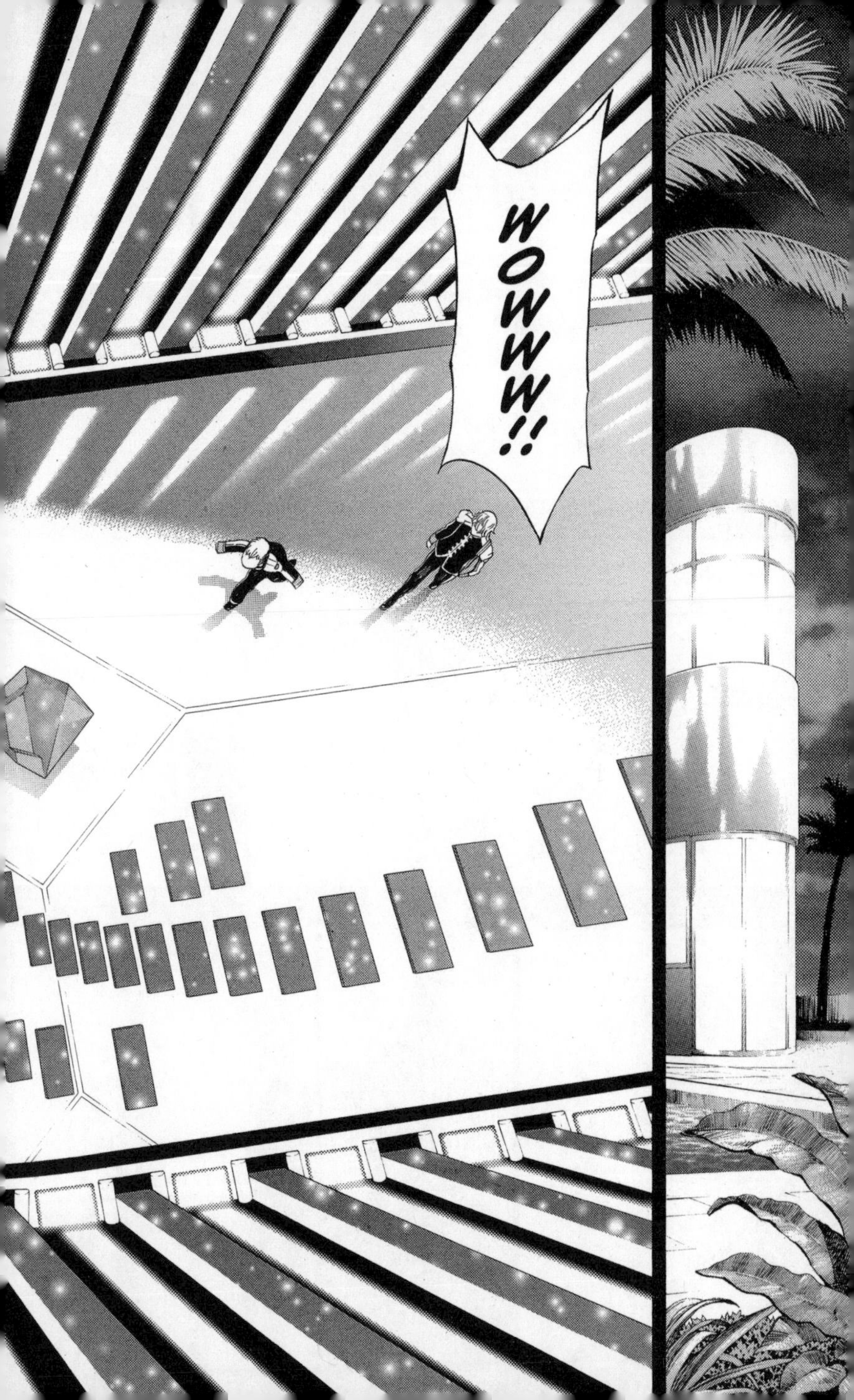
WOWWW!!

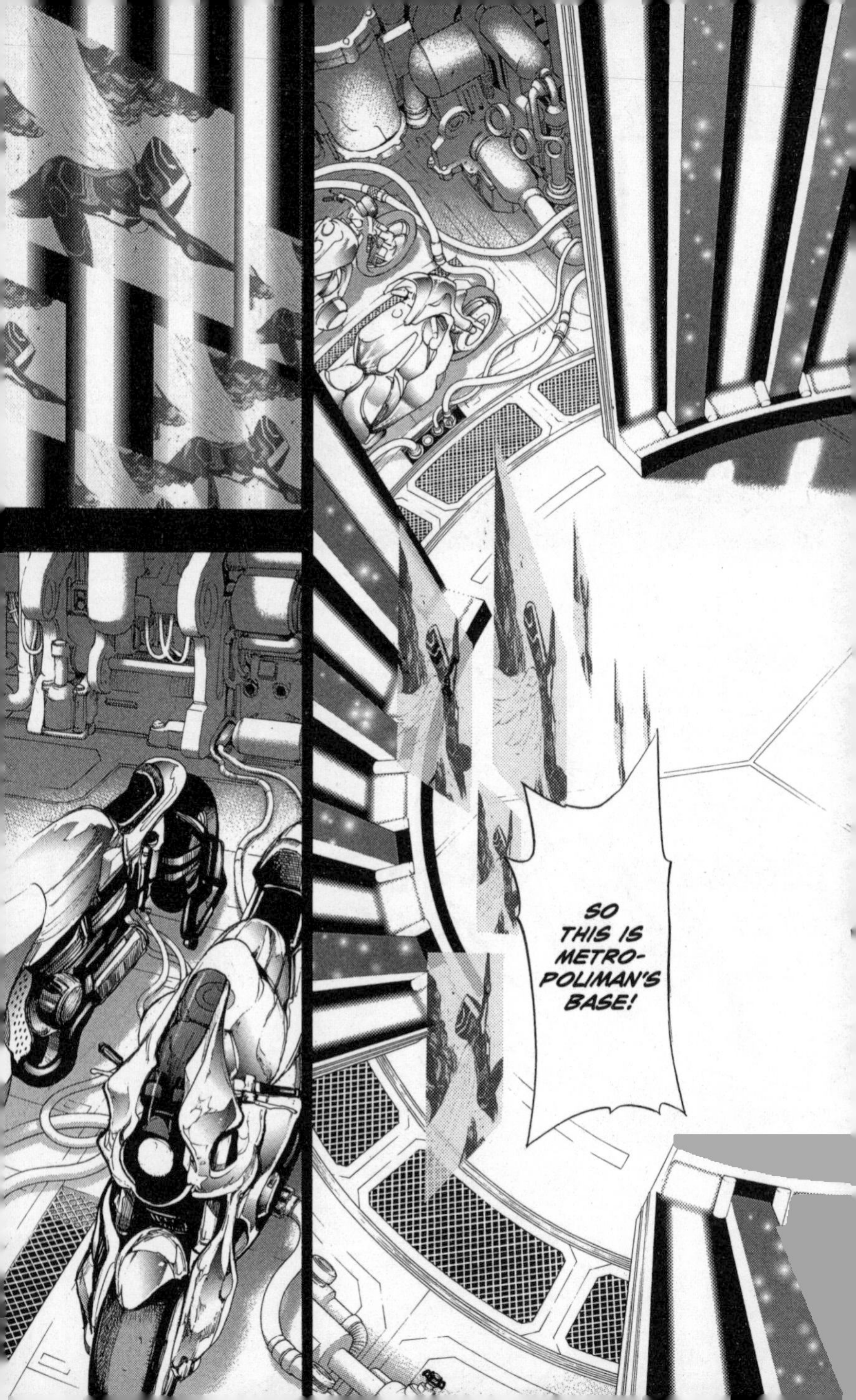
SO THIS IS METRO-POLIMAN'S BASE!

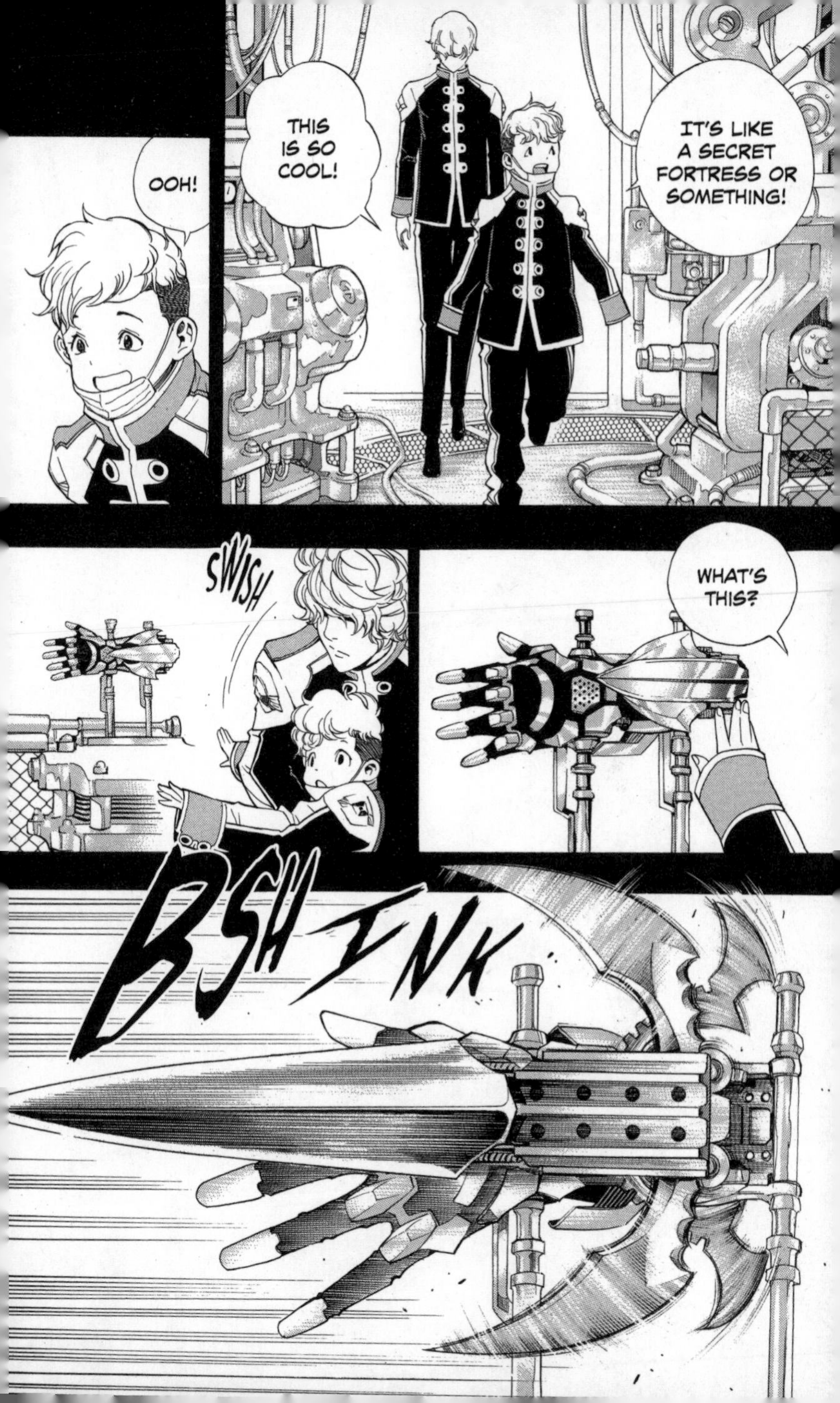
IT'S LIKE A SECRET FORTRESS OR SOMETHING!
THIS IS SO COOL!
OOH!
WHAT'S THIS?
SWISH
BSHINK

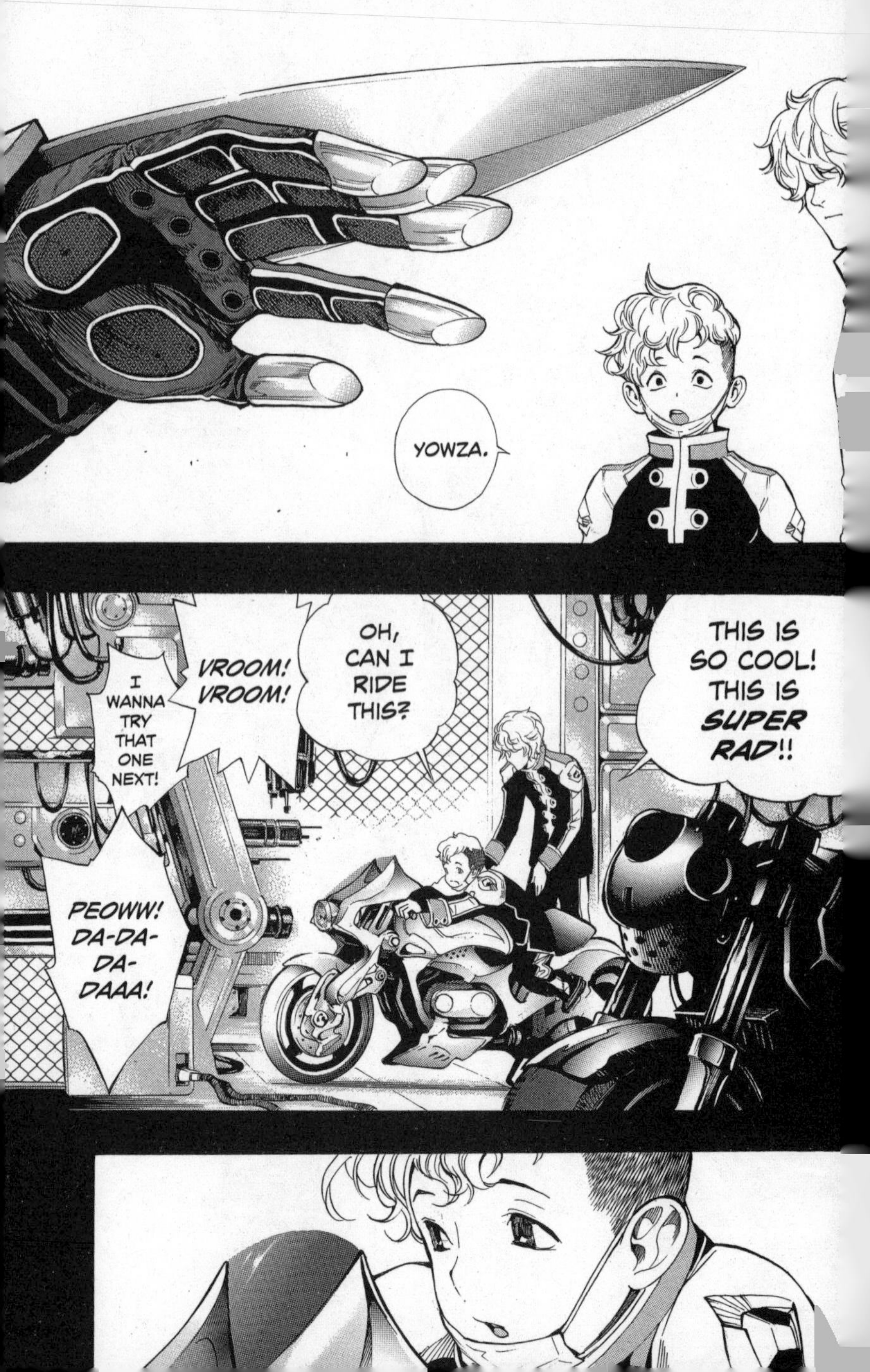
YOWZA.
THIS IS SO COOL! THIS IS SUPER RAD!!
OH, CAN I RIDE THIS?
VROOM! VROOM!
I WANNA TRY THAT ONE NEXT!
PEOWW! DA-DA-DA-DAAA!

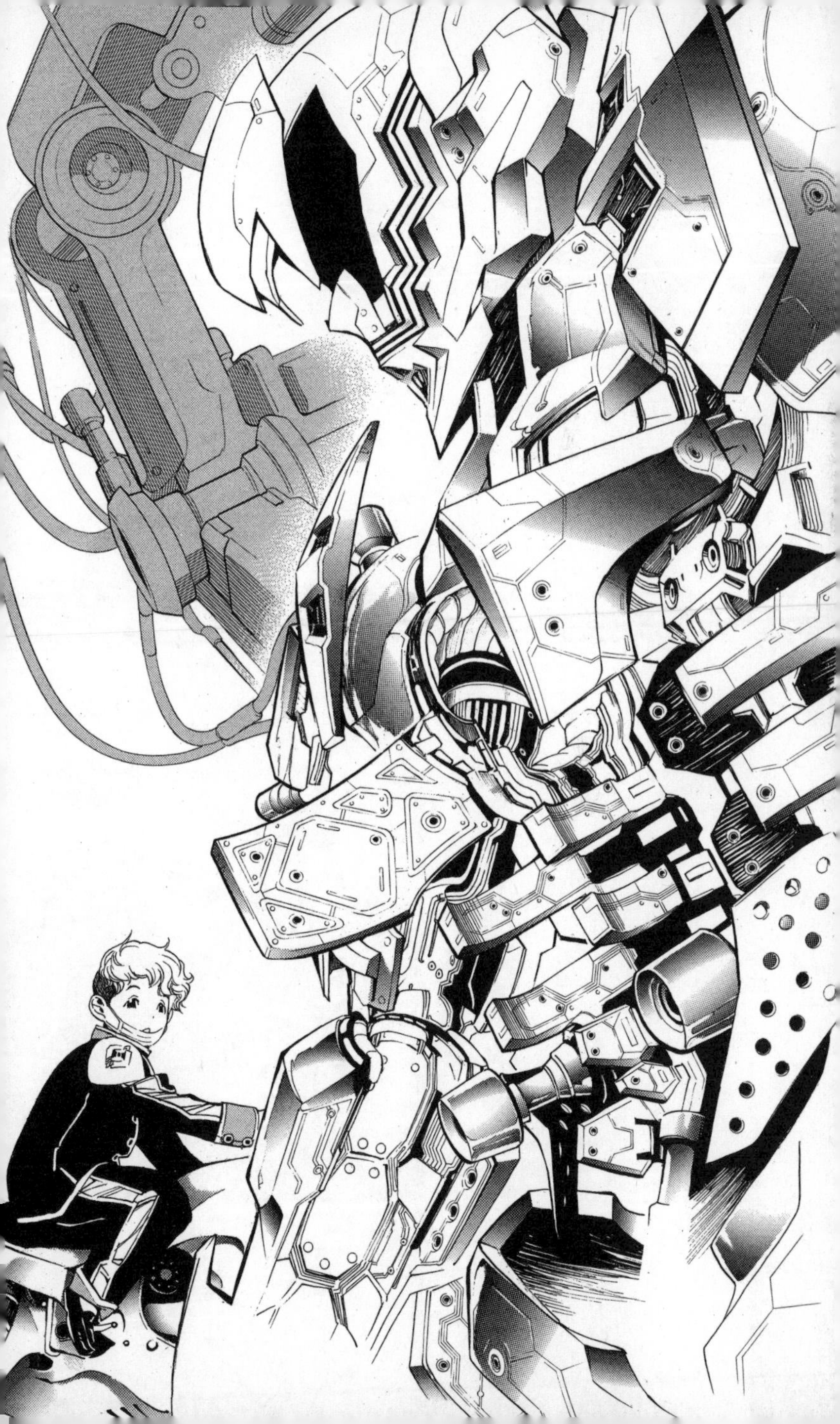

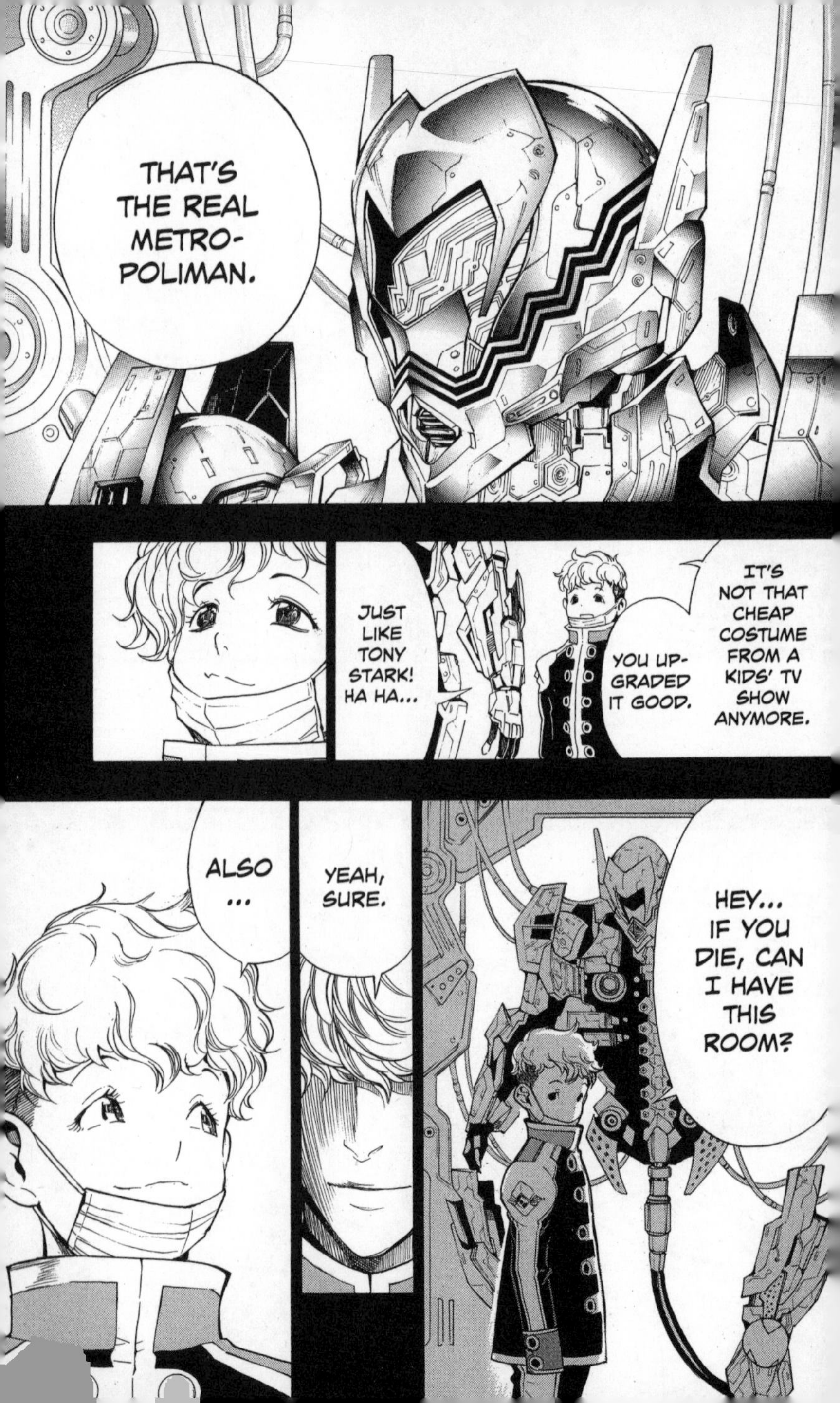
THAT'S THE REAL METRO-POLIMAN.
IT'S NOT THAT CHEAP COSTUME FROM A KIDS' TV SHOW ANYMORE.
YOU UP-GRADED IT GOOD.
JUST LIKE TONY STARK! HA HA...
HEY... IF YOU DIE, CAN I HAVE THIS ROOM?
YEAH, SURE.
ALSO...

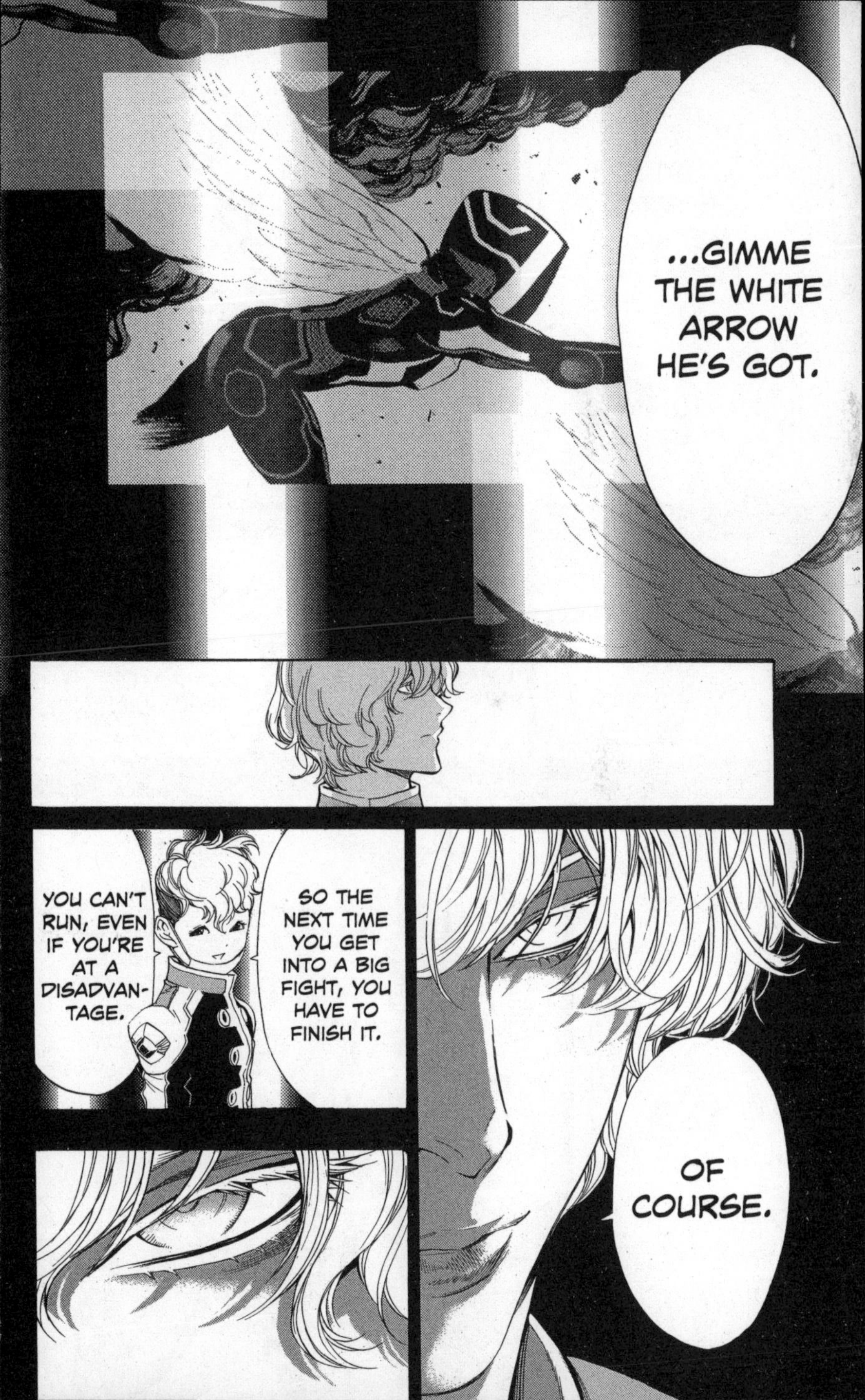
...GIMME THE WHITE ARROW HE'S GOT.
OF COURSE.
SO THE NEXT TIME YOU GET INTO A BIG FIGHT, YOU HAVE TO FINISH IT.
YOU CAN'T RUN, EVEN IF YOU'RE AT A DISADVAN-TAGE.

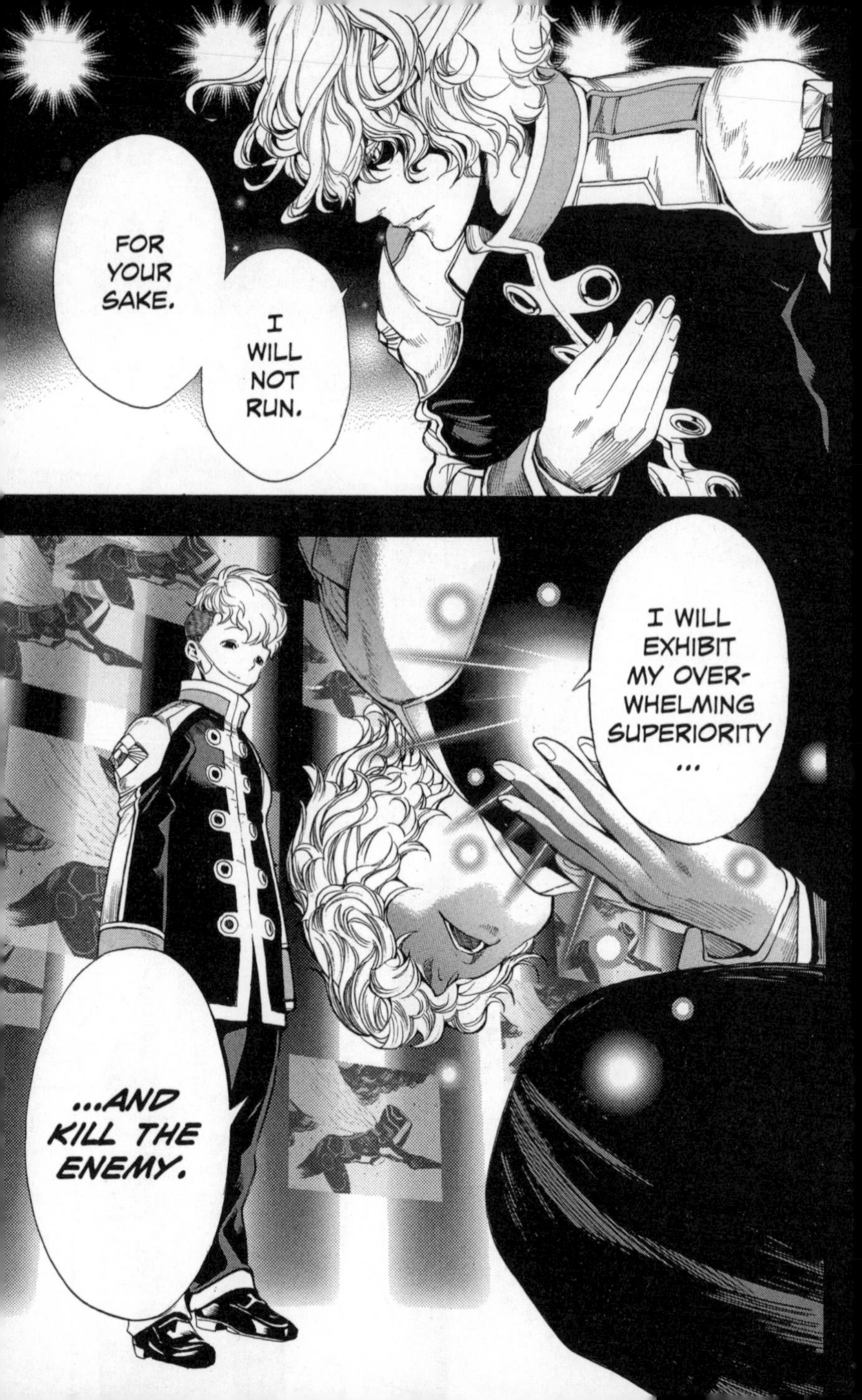
I WILL NOT RUN.
FOR YOUR SAKE.
I WILL EXHIBIT MY OVER-WHELMING SUPERIORITY ...
...AND KILL THE ENEMY.

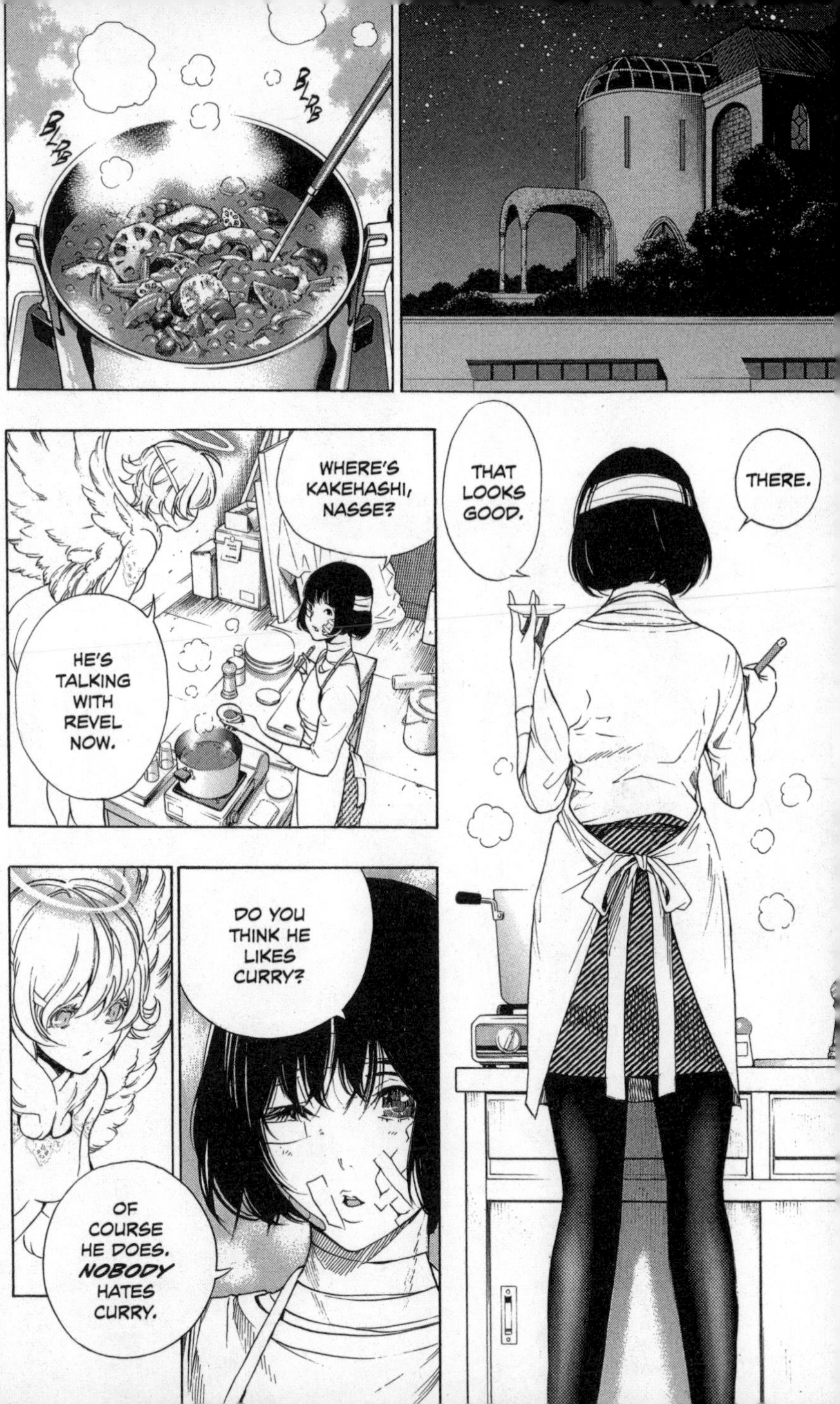
BLRB
BLRB
THERE.
THAT LOOKS GOOD.
WHERE'S KAKEHASHI, NASSE?
HE'S TALKING WITH REVEL NOW.
DO YOU THINK HE LIKES CURRY?
OF COURSE HE DOES. *NOBODY* HATES CURRY.

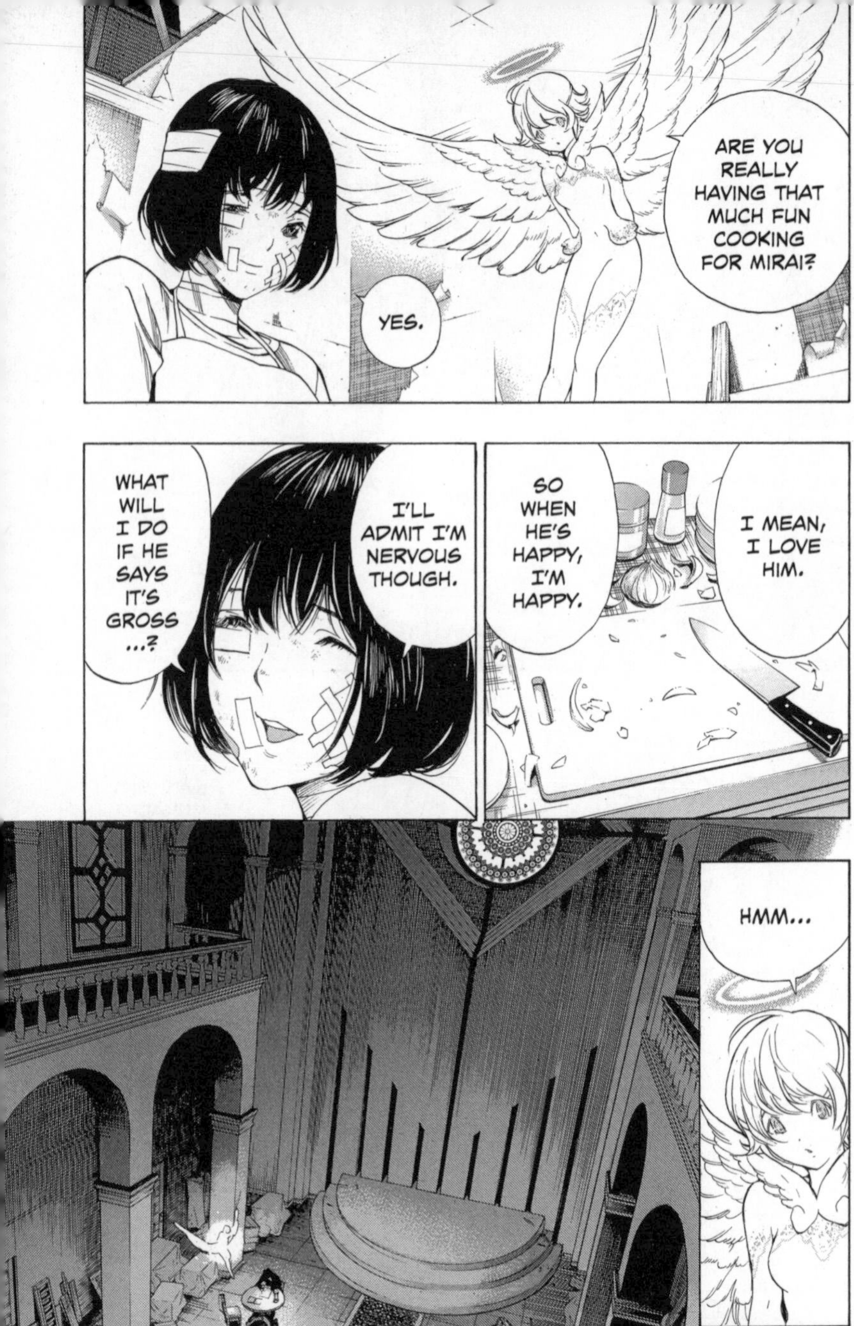
ARE YOU REALLY HAVING THAT MUCH FUN COOKING FOR MIRAI?
YES.
I MEAN, I LOVE HIM.
SO WHEN HE'S HAPPY, I'M HAPPY.
I'LL ADMIT I'M NERVOUS THOUGH.
WHAT WILL I DO IF HE SAYS IT'S GROSS ...?
HMM...

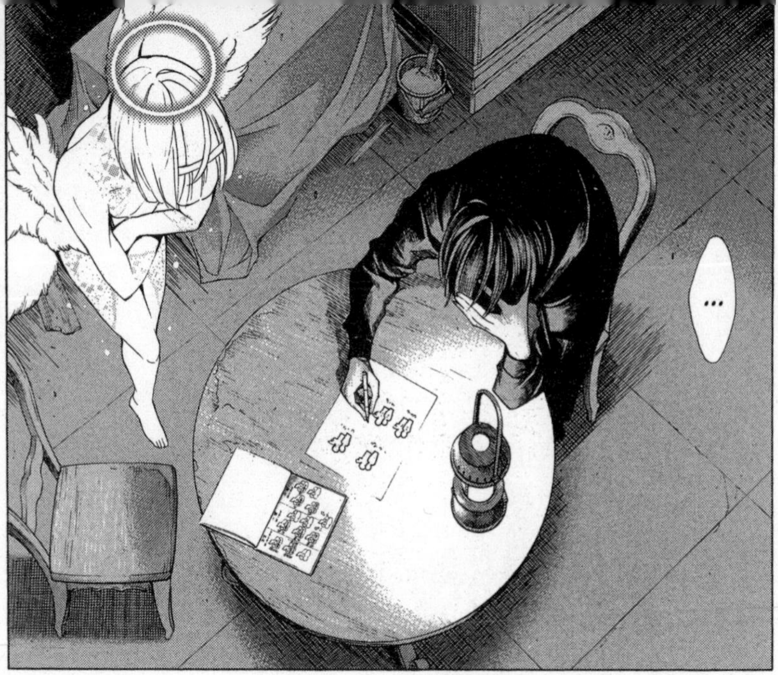
...
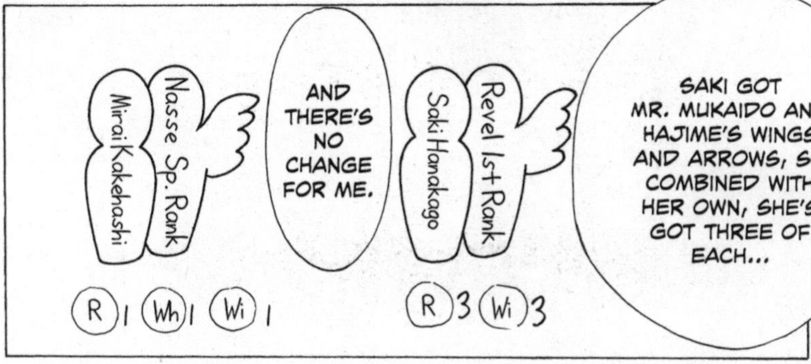
SAKI GOT MR. MUKAIDO AND HAJIME'S WINGS AND ARROWS, SO COMBINED WITH HER OWN, SHE'S GOT THREE OF EACH...
Revel 1st Rank
Saki Hanakago
R 3 Wi 3
AND THERE'S NO CHANGE FOR ME.
Nasse Sp. Rank
Mirai Kakehashi
R 1 Wh 1 Wi 1
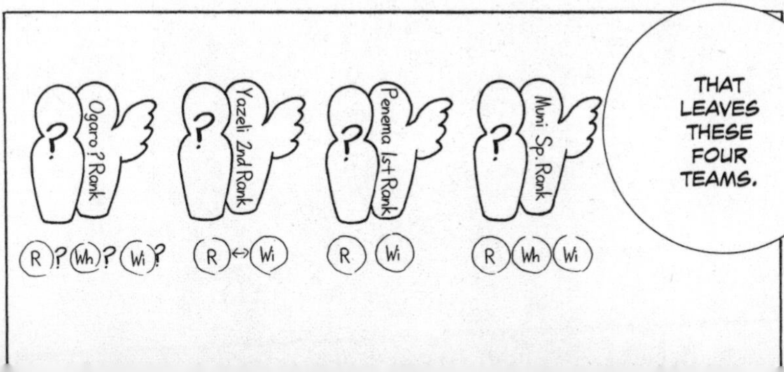
THAT LEAVES THESE FOUR TEAMS.
Muni Sp. Rank
R Wh Wi
Penema 1st Rank
R Wi
Yazeli 2nd Rank
R ↔ Wi
Ogaro ? Rank
R ? Wh ? Wi ?

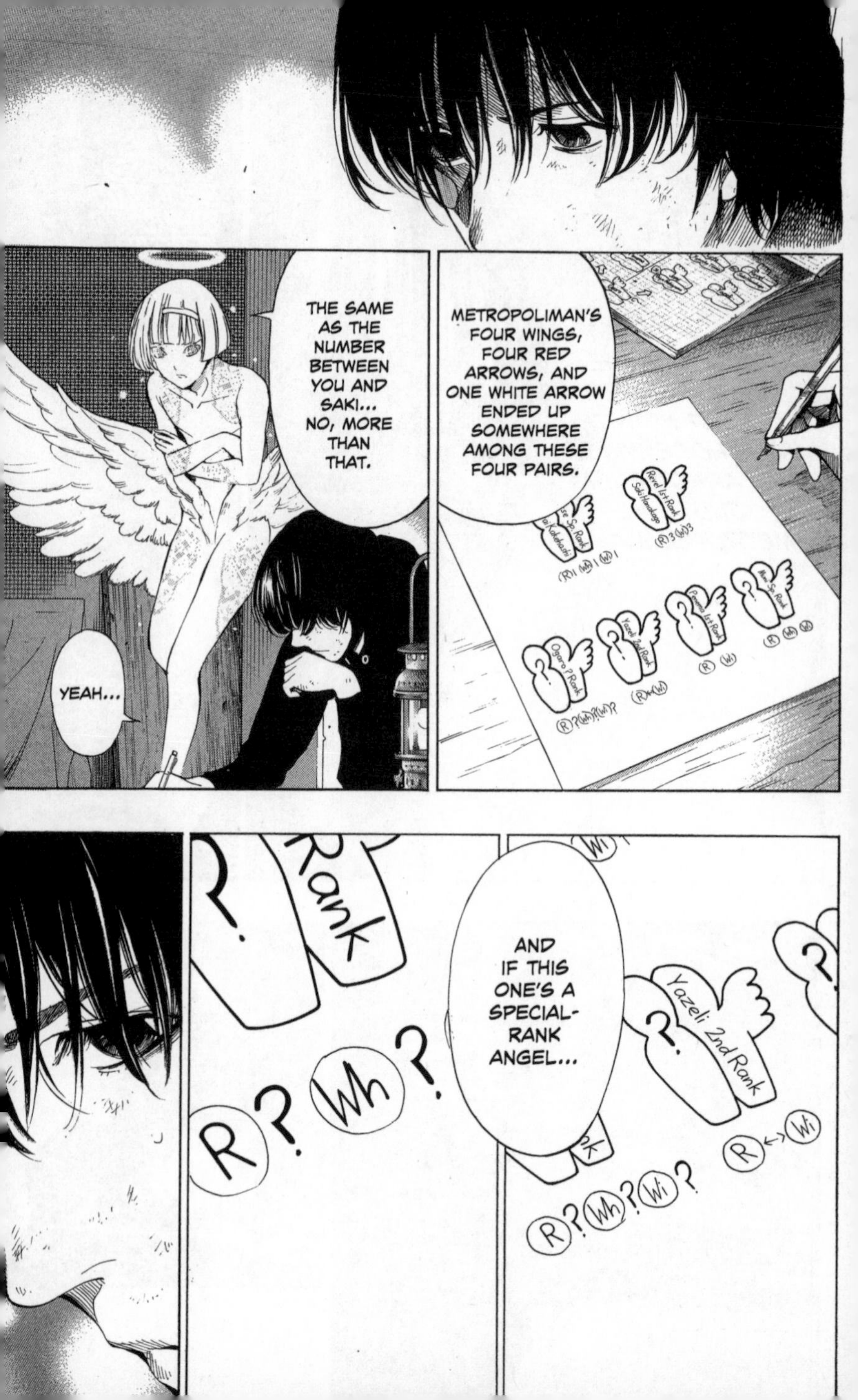
METROPOLIMAN'S FOUR WINGS, FOUR RED ARROWS, AND ONE WHITE ARROW ENDED UP SOMEWHERE AMONG THESE FOUR PAIRS.
Revel 1st Rank
Saki Hanakago
Yazeli 2nd Rank
Ogaro ? Rank
THE SAME AS THE NUMBER BETWEEN YOU AND SAKI... NO, MORE THAN THAT.
YEAH...
AND IF THIS ONE'S A SPECIAL-RANK ANGEL...
Yazeli 2nd Rank
R ↔ Wi
R ? Wh ? Wi ?
Rank
R ? Wh ?

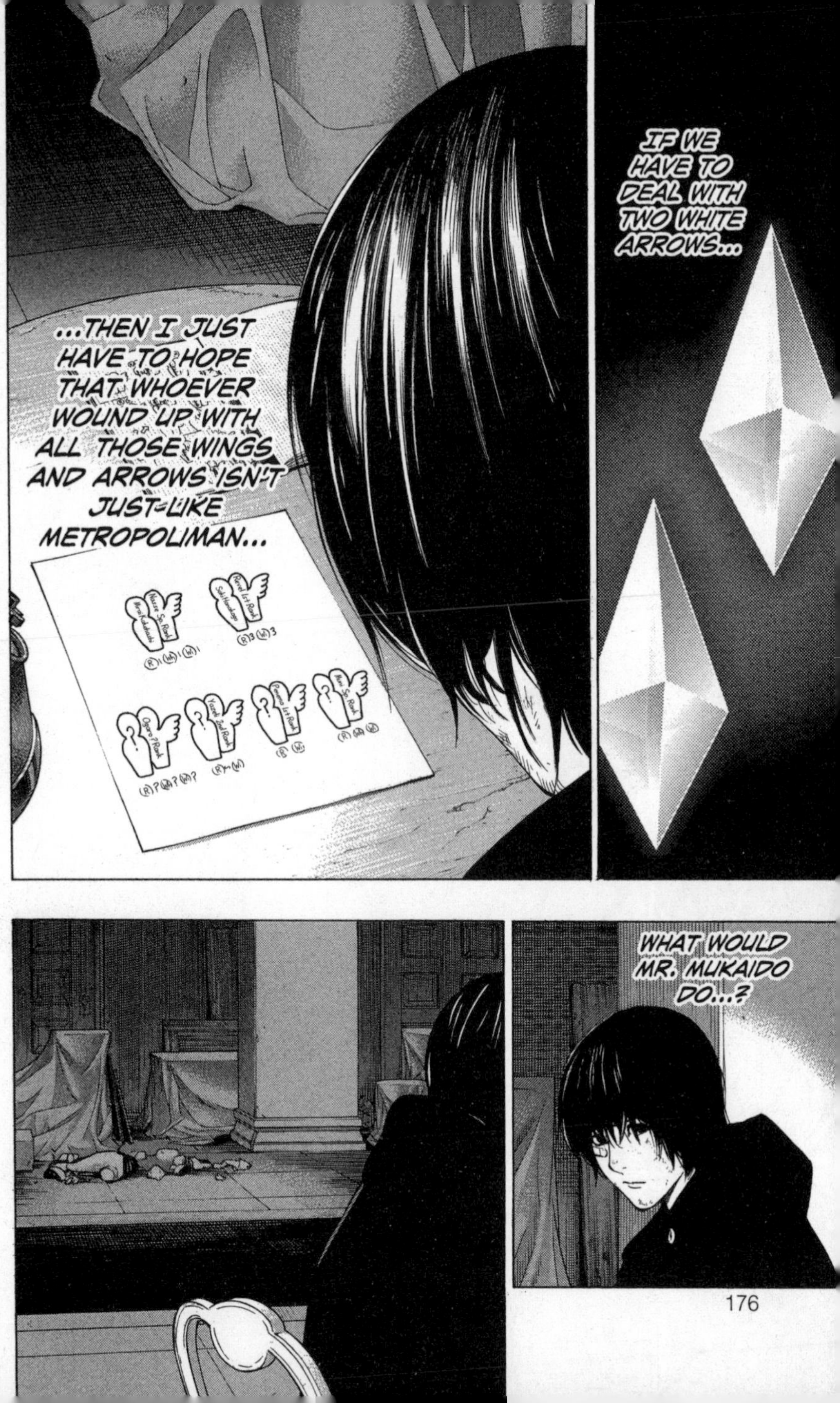
IF WE HAVE TO DEAL WITH TWO WHITE ARROWS...
...THEN I JUST HAVE TO HOPE THAT WHOEVER WOUND UP WITH ALL THOSE WINGS AND ARROWS ISN'T JUST LIKE METROPOLIMAN...
WHAT WOULD MR. MUKAIDO DO...?

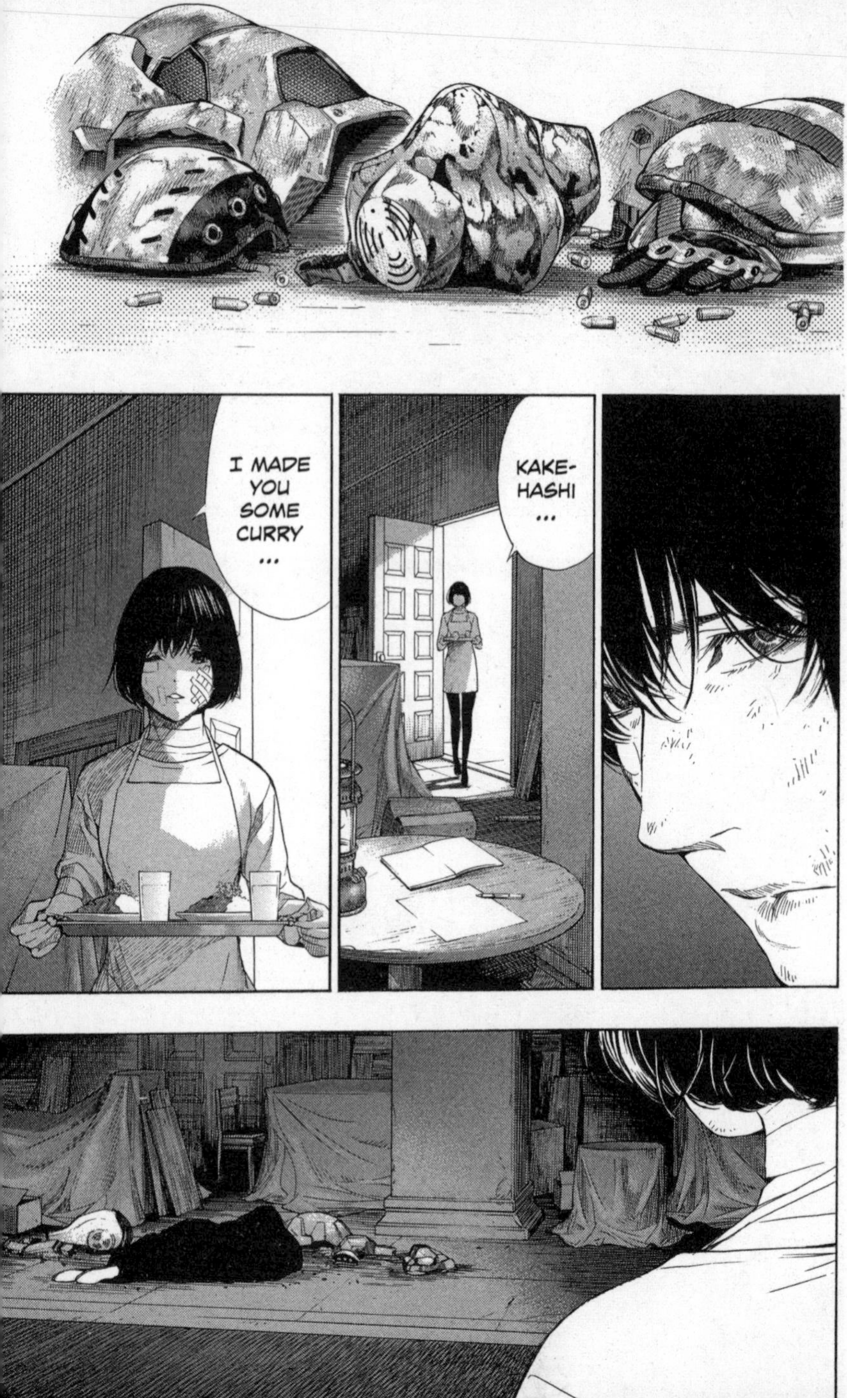
KAKE-HASHI ...
I MADE YOU SOME CURRY ...

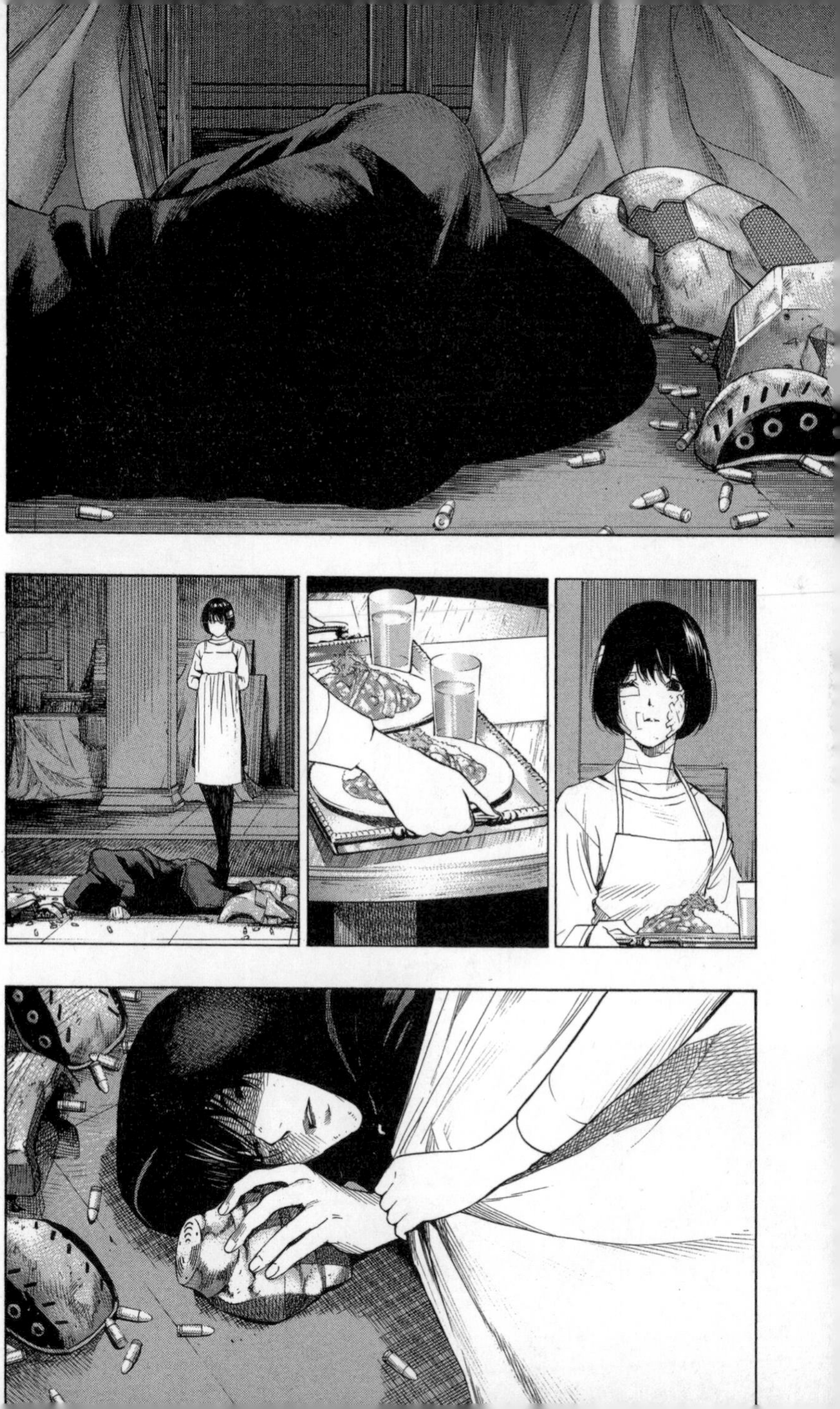

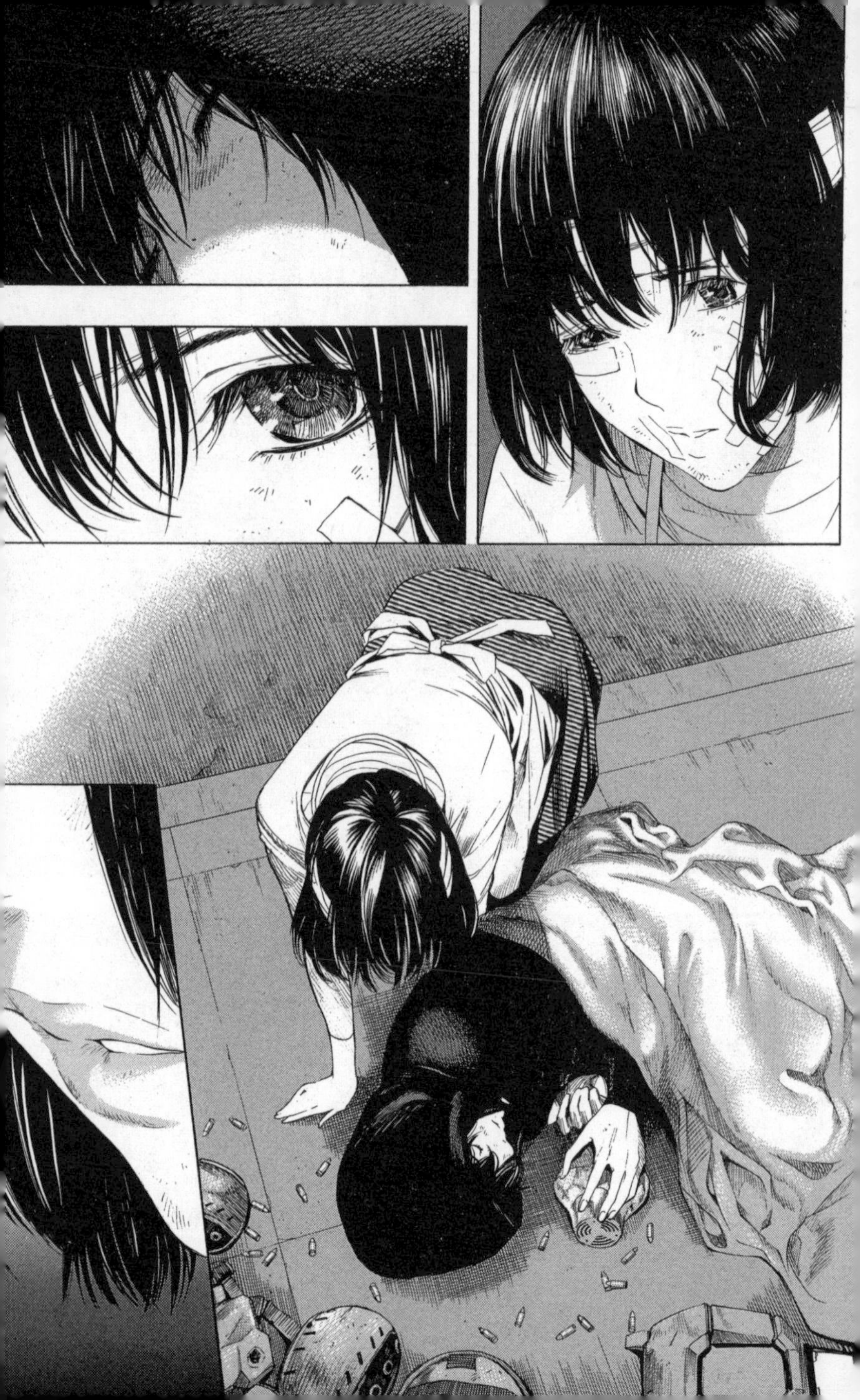

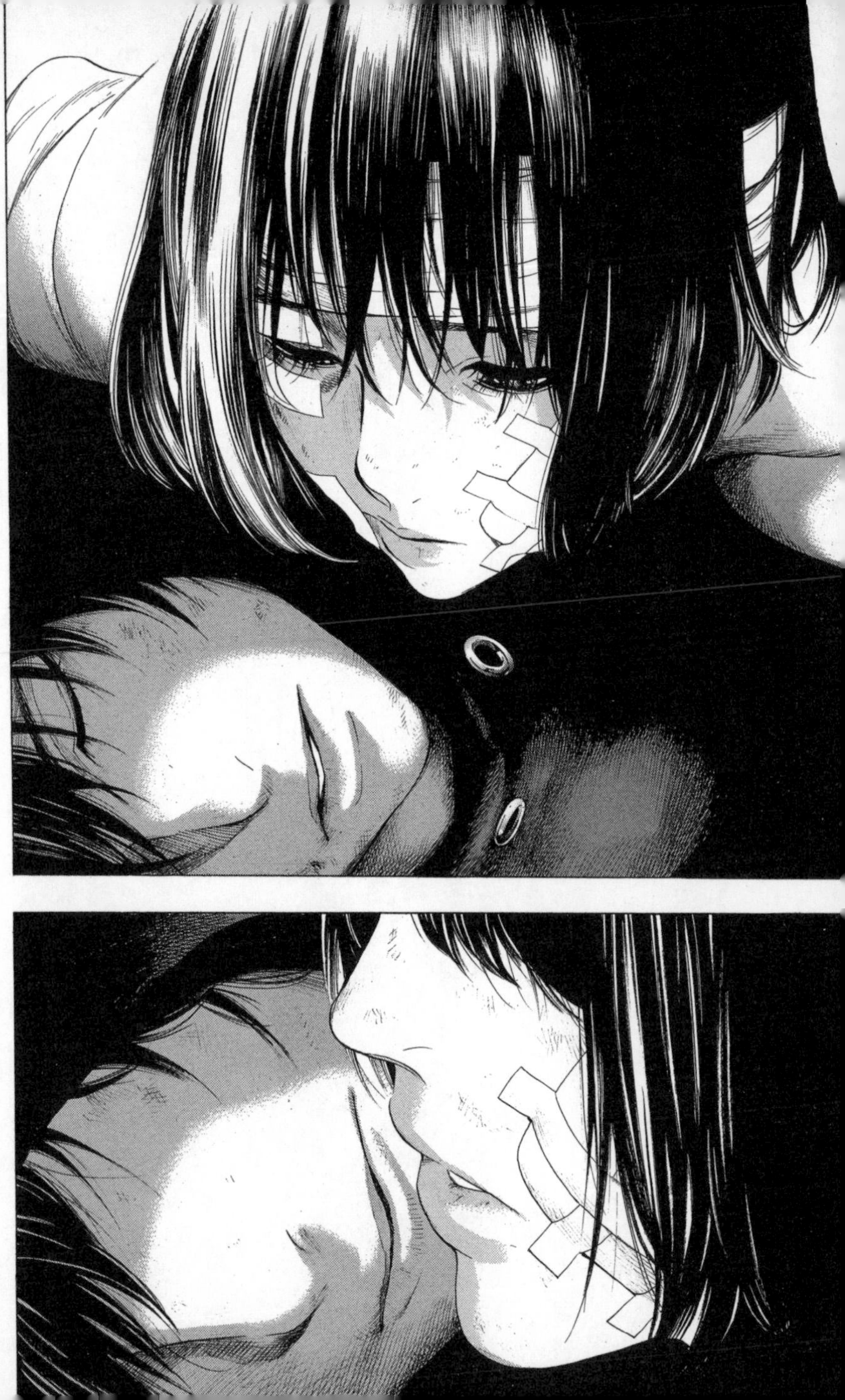

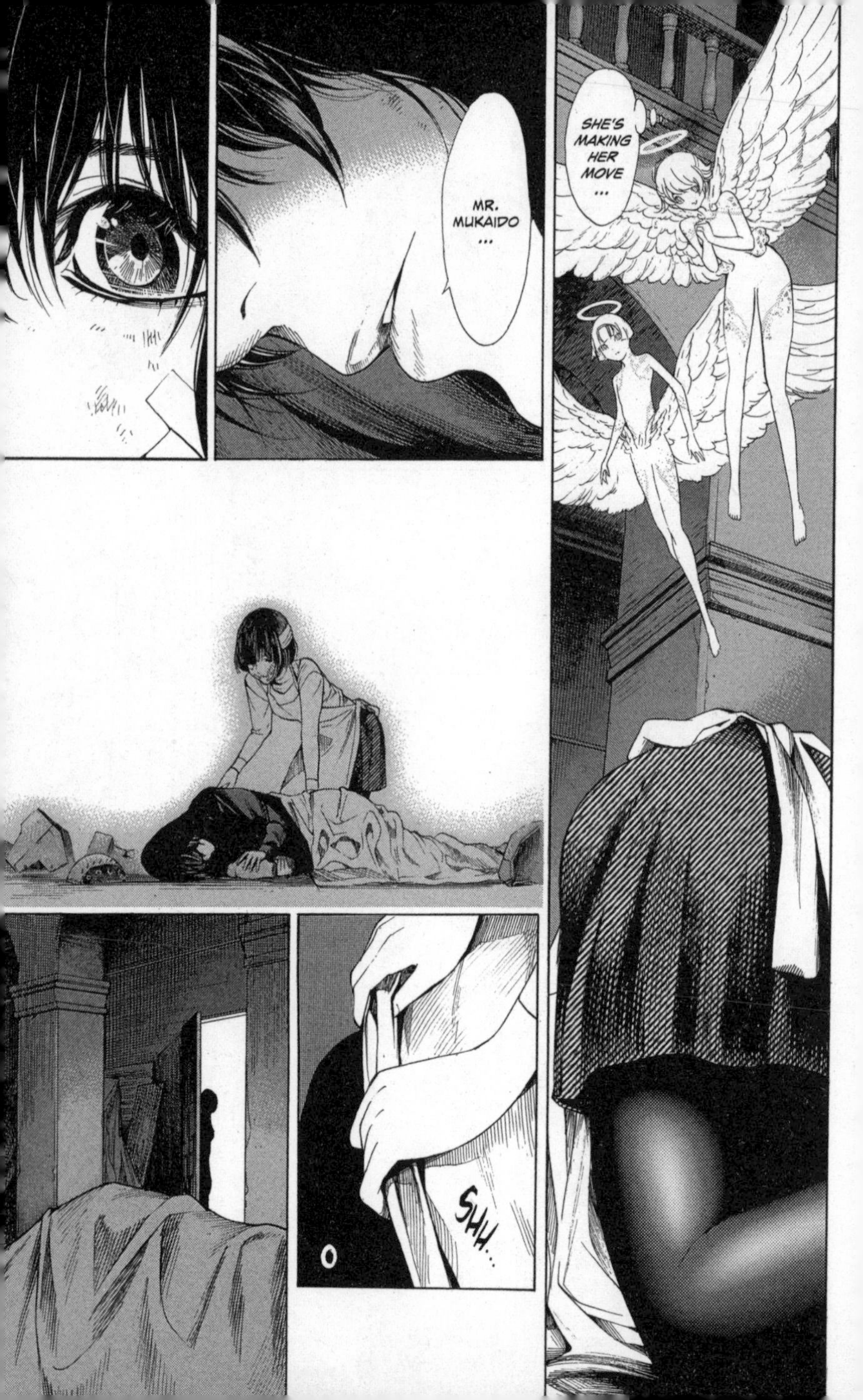
SHE'S MAKING HER MOVE ...
MR. MUKAIDO ...
SHH...

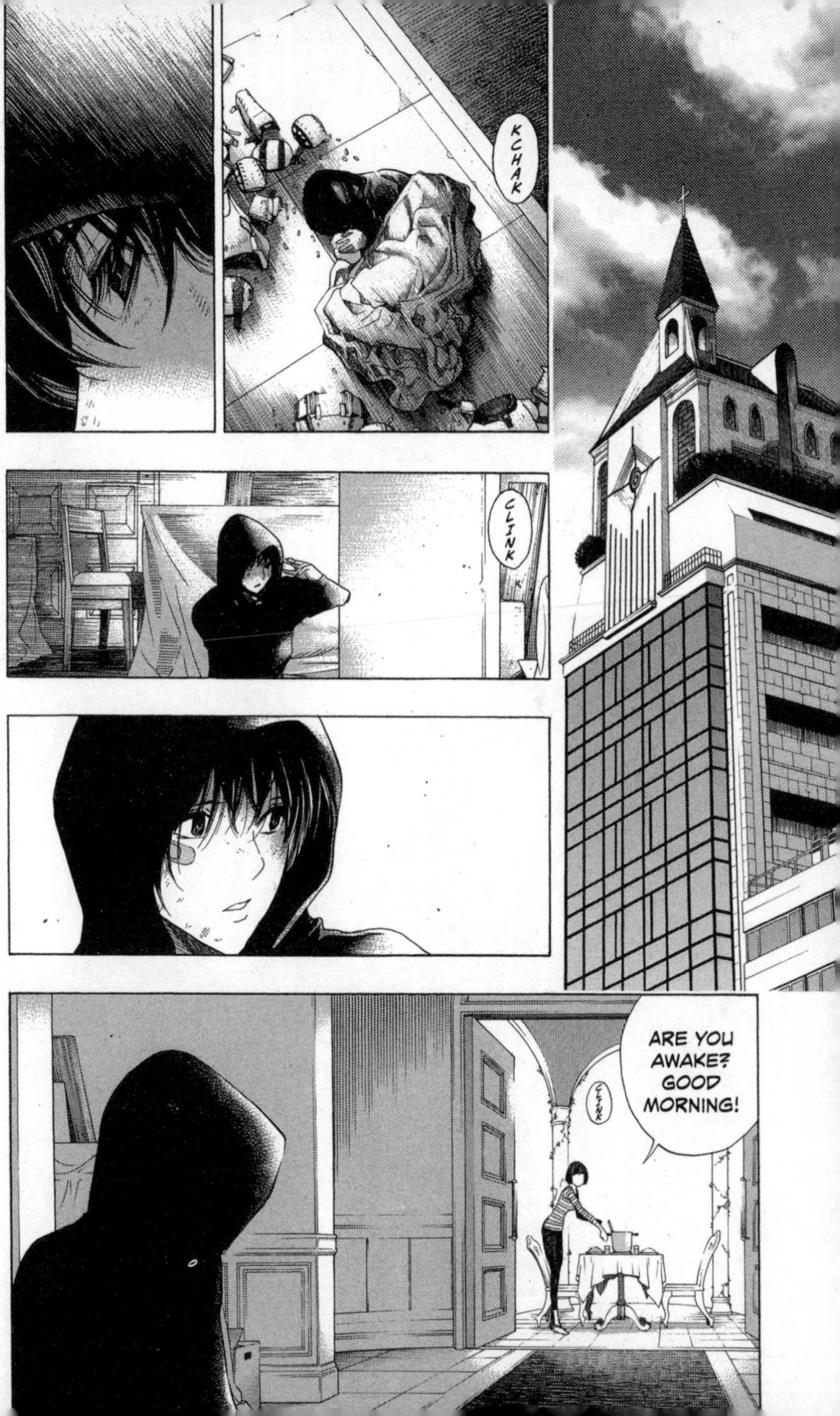
KCHAK
CLINK
ARE YOU AWAKE? GOOD MORNING!
CLINK

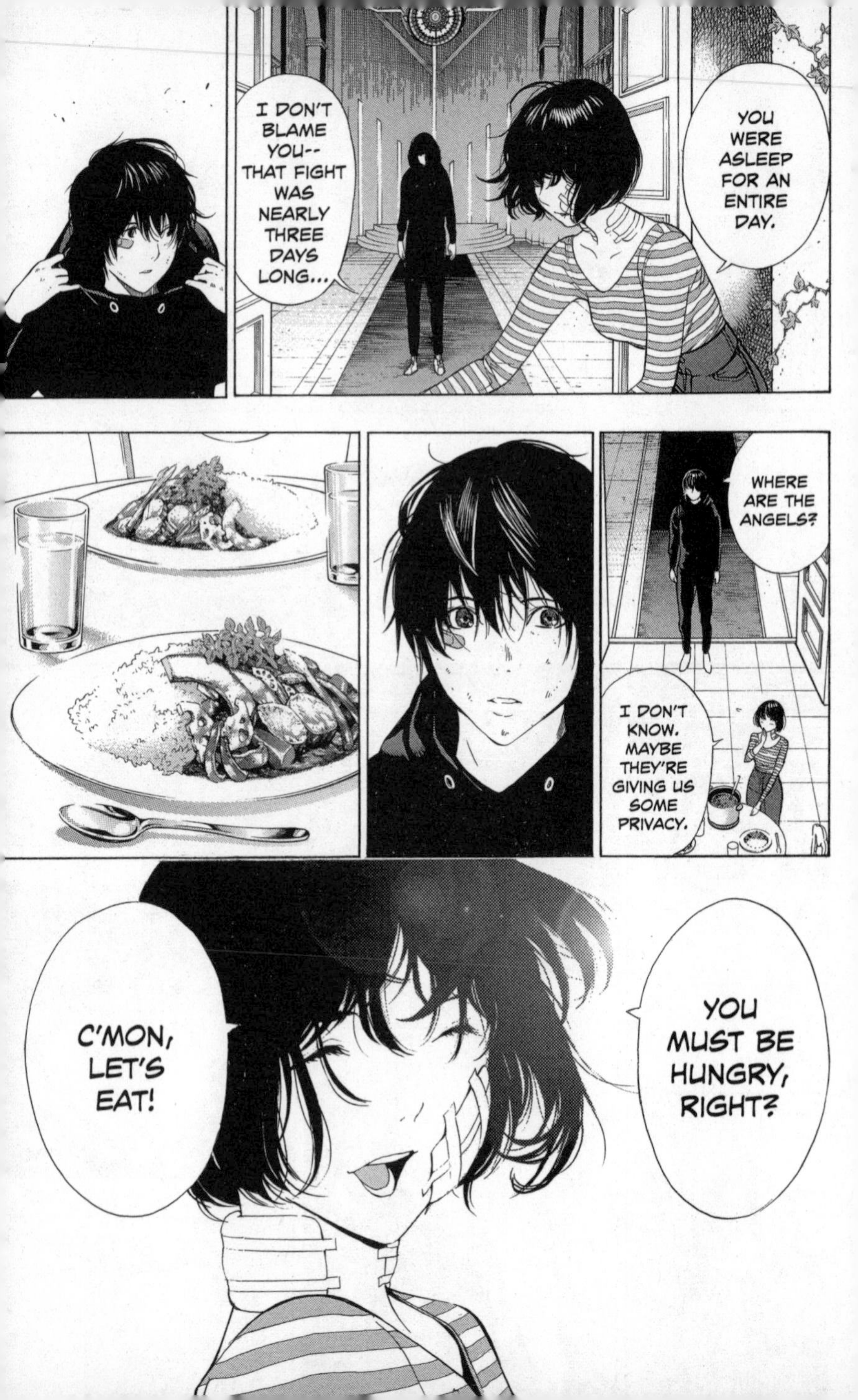

YOU WERE ASLEEP FOR AN ENTIRE DAY.
I DON'T BLAME YOU-- THAT FIGHT WAS NEARLY THREE DAYS LONG...
WHERE ARE THE ANGELS?
I DON'T KNOW. MAYBE THEY'RE GIVING US SOME PRIVACY.
YOU MUST BE HUNGRY, RIGHT?
C'MON, LET'S EAT!

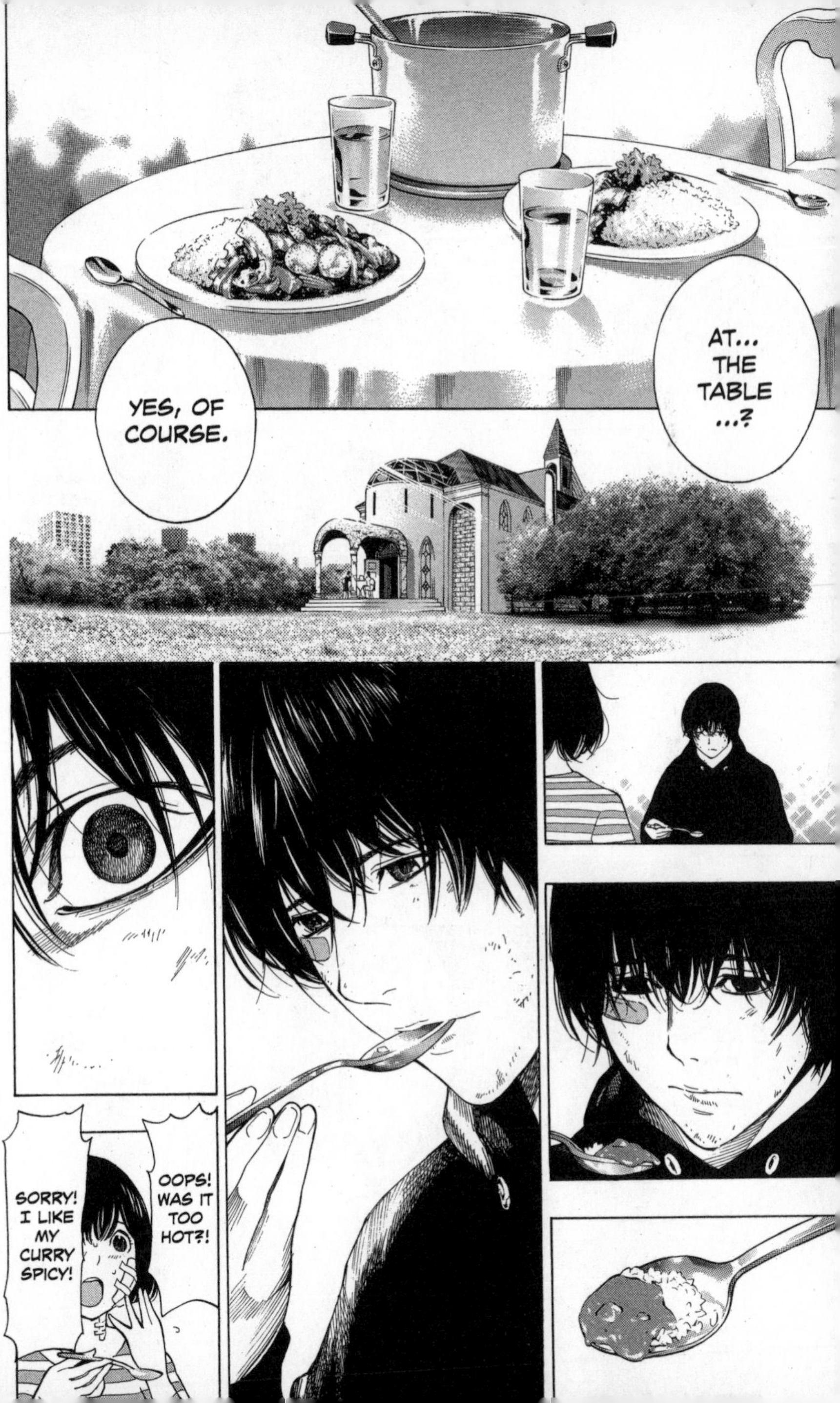
AT... THE TABLE ...?
YES, OF COURSE.
OOPS! WAS IT TOO HOT?!
SORRY! I LIKE MY CURRY SPICY!

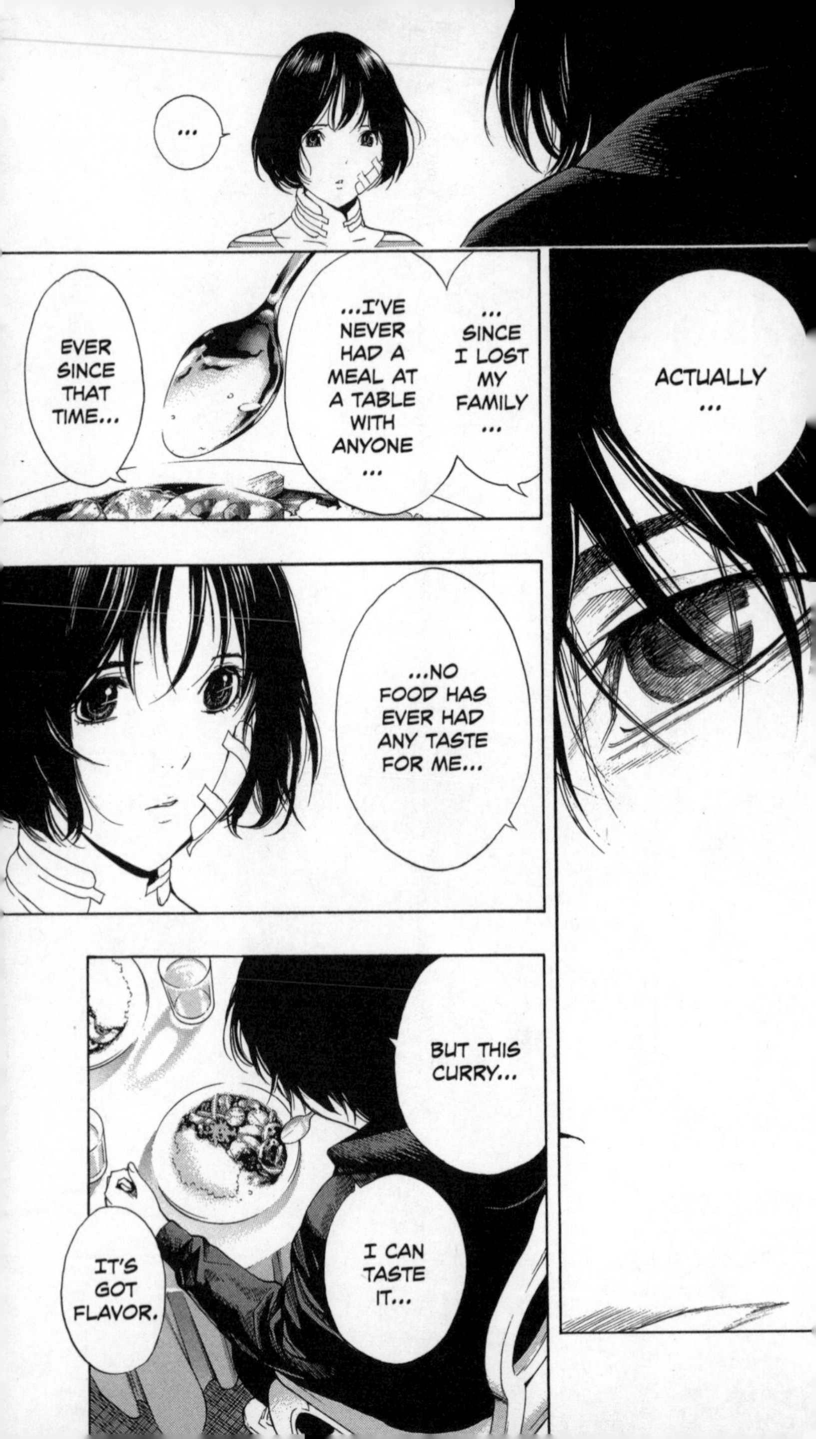
...
ACTUALLY...
... SINCE I LOST MY FAMILY ...
...I'VE NEVER HAD A MEAL AT A TABLE WITH ANYONE ...
EVER SINCE THAT TIME...
...NO FOOD HAS EVER HAD ANY TASTE FOR ME...
BUT THIS CURRY...
I CAN TASTE IT...
IT'S GOT FLAVOR.

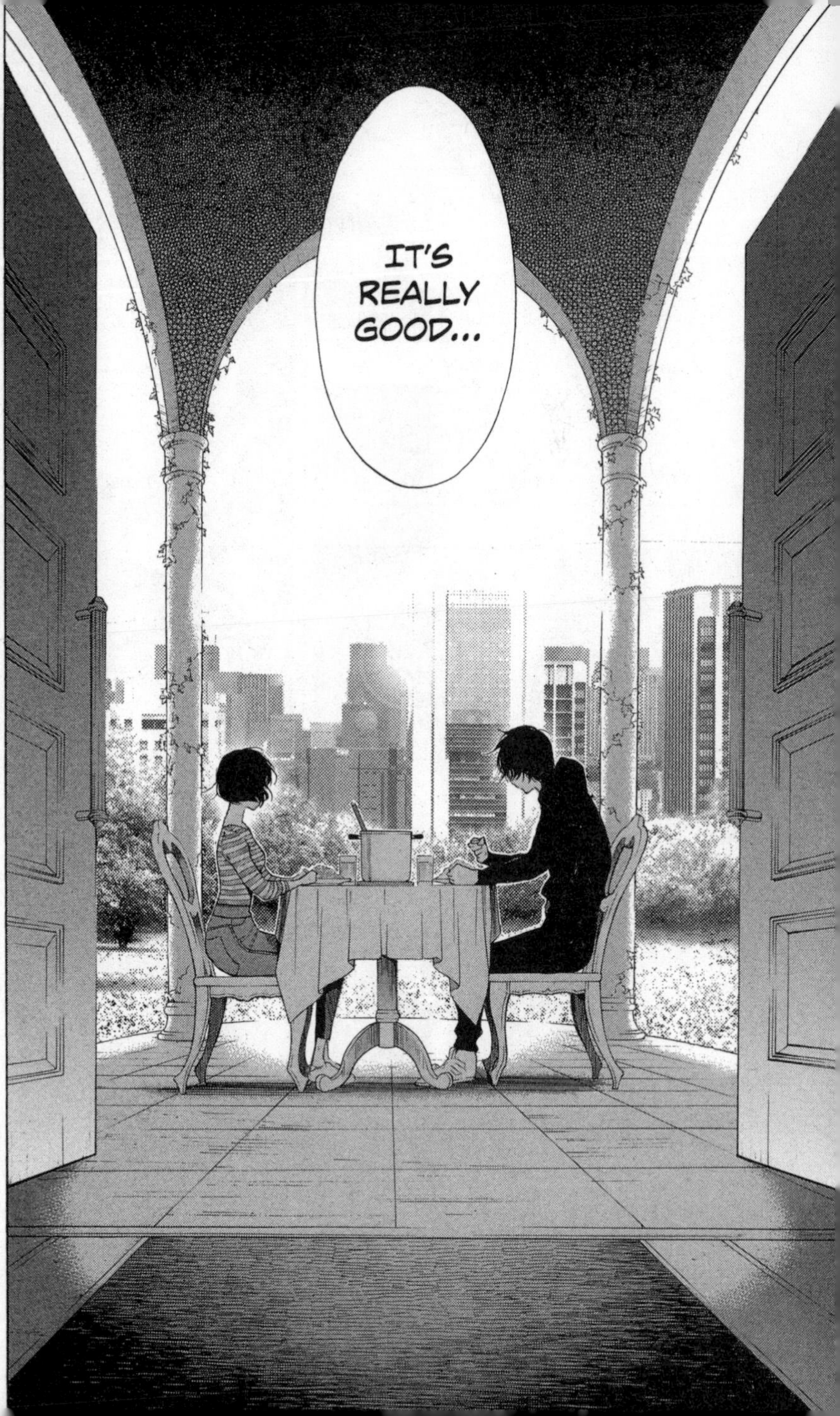
IT'S REALLY GOOD...

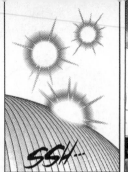

SSH...

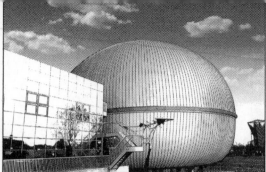

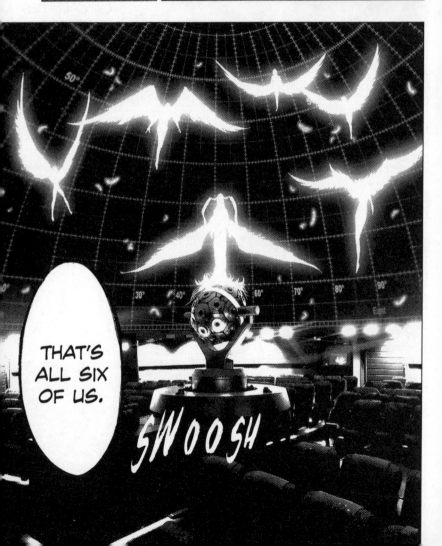

THAT'S ALL SIX OF US.

SWOOSH...

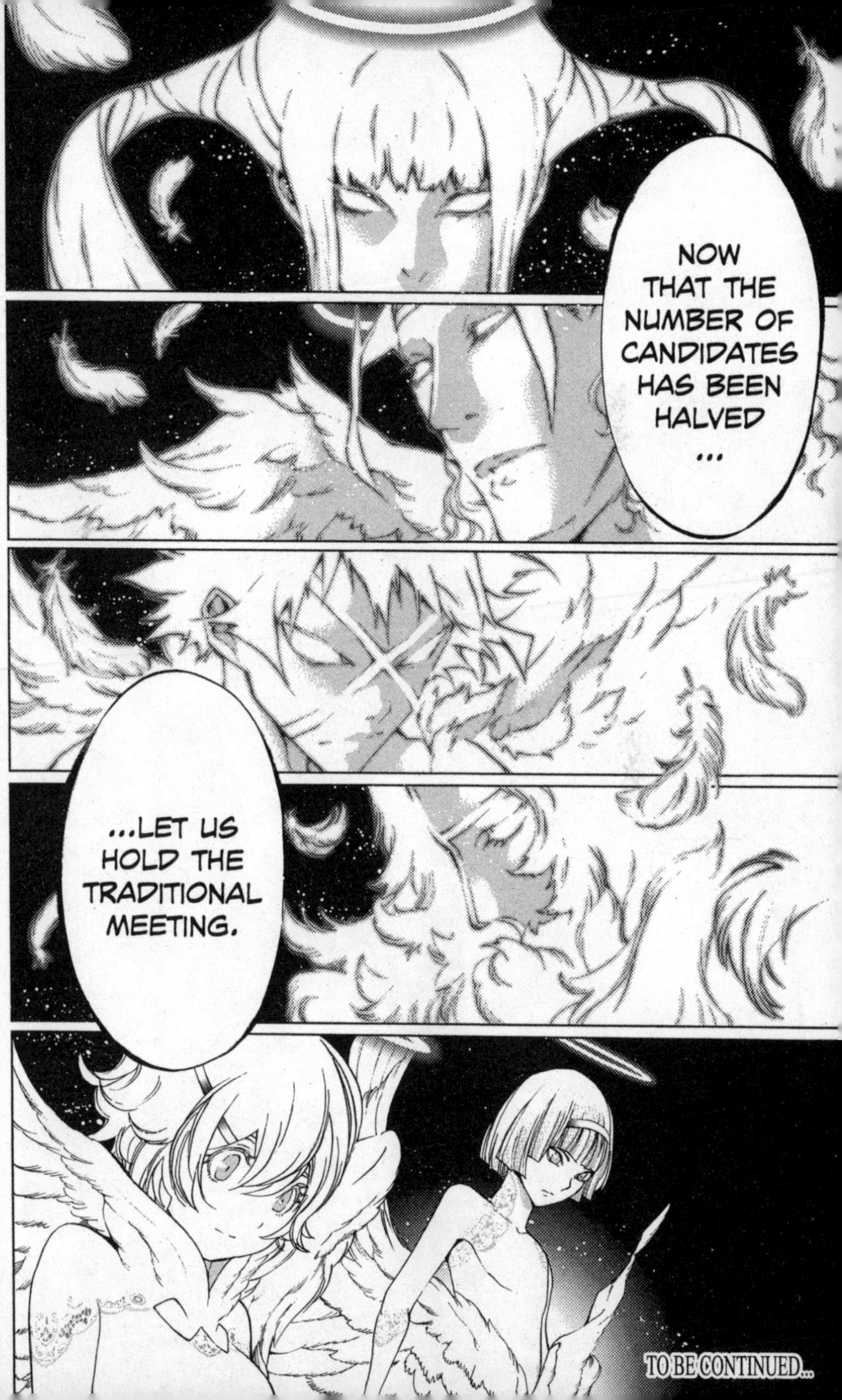
NOW THAT THE NUMBER OF CANDIDATES HAS BEEN HALVED ...
...LET US HOLD THE TRADITIONAL MEETING.
TO BE CONTINUED...

T sugu mi **Oh** b **a**

Born in Tokyo, Tsugumi Ohba is the author
of the hit series *Death Note* and *Bakuman*.

Ta **k** e sh i Oba **ta**

Takeshi Obata was born in 1969 in Niigata,
Japan, and first achieved international
recognition as the artist of the wildly popular
Shonen Jump title *Hikaru no Go*, which won the
2003 Tezuka Osamu Cultural Prize: Shinsei
"New Hope" Award and the 2000 Shogakukan
Manga Award. He went on to illustrate the smash
hit *Death Note* as well as the hugely successful
manga *Bakuman*. and *All You Need Is Kill*.

PLATINVM END

VOLUME 8
SHONEN JUMP Manga Edition

o

STORY Tsugumi Ohba
ART Takeshi Obata

o

TRANSLATION Stephen Paul
TOUCH-UP ART & LETTERING James Gaubatz
DESIGN Shawn Carrico
EDITOR Alexis Kirsch

o

ORIGINAL COVER DESIGN Narumi Noriko

o

o

o

Printed in the U.S.A.

Published by VIZ Media, LLC
P.O. Box 77010
San Francisco, CA 94107

o

10 9 8 7 6 5 4 3 2 1
First printing, April 2019

VIZ MEDIA
viz.com

SHONEN JUMP
shonenjump.com

ratings.viz.com
RATED M MATURE

PARENTAL ADVISORY
PLATINUM END is rated M for Mature and is recommended for mature readers. This volume contains suggestive themes.

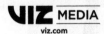

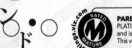

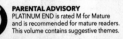

YOU'RE READING THE **WRONG WAY!**

PLATINUM END reads from right to left, starting in the upper-right corner. Japanese is read from right to left, meaning that action, sound effects and word-balloon order are completely reversed from English order.

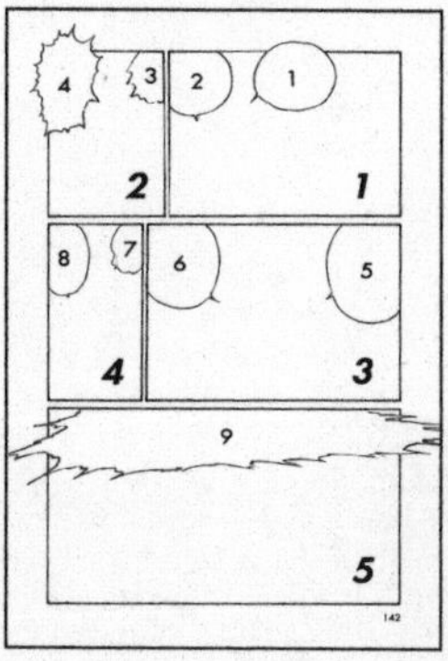

1
2
3
4
1
2
5
6
7
8
3
4
9
5
142

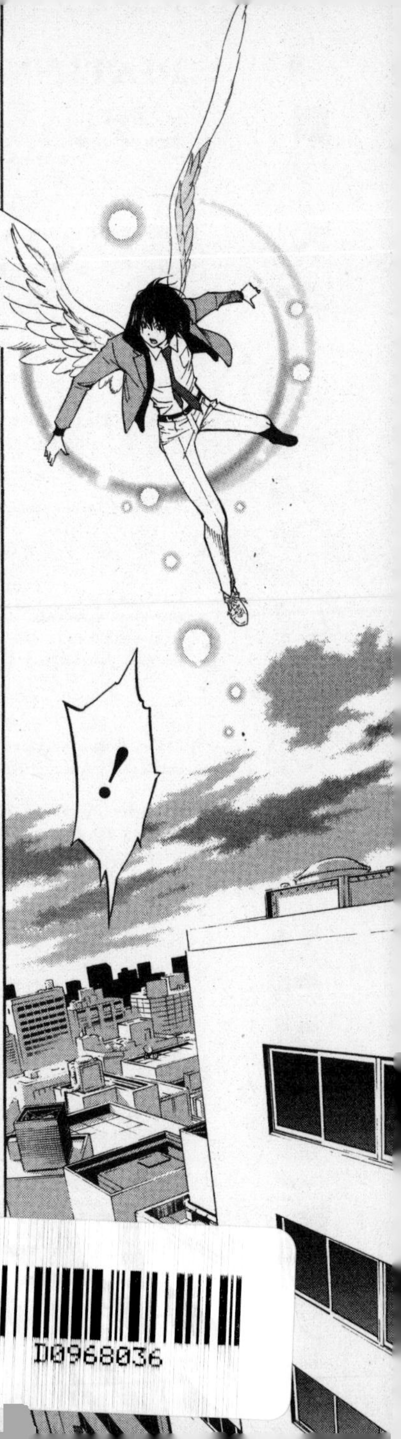

!